# REPUTATION AND
# INTERNATIONAL COOPERATION

# REPUTATION AND INTERNATIONAL COOPERATION

SOVEREIGN DEBT ACROSS

THREE CENTURIES

*Michael Tomz*

PRINCETON UNIVERSITY PRESS    PRINCETON AND OXFORD

Published by Princeton University Press, 41 William Street,
Princeton, New Jersey 08540
In the United Kingdom: Princeton University Press, 3 Market Place,
Woodstock, Oxfordshire OX20 1SY

Library of Congress Cataloging-in-Publication Data

Tomz, Michael.
Reputation and international cooperation : sovereign debt
across three centuries / Michael Tomz.
p. cm.
Includes bibliographical references and index.

ISBN-13: 978-0-691-12930-3 (cloth : alk. paper)
ISBN-13: 978-0-691-12469-7 (pbk : alk. paper)

1. Debts, External—History. 2. Debtor and creditor—History. I. Title.

HG3891.5.T66 2007
336.3'43509——dc22          2007005573

British Library Cataloging-in-Publication Data is available

This book has been composed in Sabon

Printed on acid-free paper. ∞

press.princeton.edu

Printed in the United States of America

10  9  8  7  6  5  4  3  2  1

To Julie, Emily, Anna, and David

# Contents

# Tables

# Figures

# Preface ————————————————————————

MY INTEREST in reputation and international cooperation began years ago, at Oxford, where I was studying for a master's degree in political philosophy. There, on the idyllic grounds of Magdalen College, I read Thomas Hobbes's *Leviathan* cover-to-cover for the first time. In a passage I found particularly intriguing, Hobbes argues that it is rational to keep promises even when there is no external enforcement. The argument unfolds in response to a character called the Fool, who challenges Hobbes to explain why one could not benefit by violating agreements in the state of nature, where no common power exists.

Hobbes's answer to the Fool emphasizes the reputational consequences of reneging. According to Hobbes, no one can "defend himself from destruction without the help of confederates." A person who breaks covenants, he warns, can "expect no other means of safety than what can be had from his own single power. He . . . cannot be received into any society that unite themselves for peace and defense but by the error of them that receive him; nor when he is received, be retained in it without seeing the danger of their error."

Hobbes's reply to the Fool stimulated me to reflect on many fascinating questions about reputation. How, exactly, do people form beliefs about the reliability of others, and under what conditions can people violate agreements at little or no reputational cost? Do concerns about reputation really sustain cooperation in the absence of a Leviathan? If so, need anarchy imply a "solitary, poor, nasty, brutish, and short" existence, as suggested by Hobbes in the most famous line of the book? How does the logic of reputation, which Hobbes applied to individuals in the state of nature, influence behavior in another anarchical setting, international relations? And what practical lessons can one draw to increase the likelihood of international cooperation?

In the years since I first encountered *Leviathan*, many other great books—and great scholars—have shaped my thinking about reputation and international cooperation. Two early and important influences were Robert Axelrod's *Evolution of Cooperation* and Robert Keohane's *After Hegemony*. Axelrod's book taught me how repeated interaction could contribute to cooperation under anarchy; Keohane's research demonstrated how much one can learn about international relations by focusing on problems of incomplete information. My theory of reputation, which involves ongoing interaction with informational asymmetries, builds upon the fundamental insights of these scholars and the vast literatures they spawned.

Jeff Frieden inspired me to study the issue of international debt, and to view it as a vehicle for understanding cooperation more generally. Through seminars and discussions when I was a Ph.D. student at Harvard, Jeff introduced me to the puzzle of international lending under anarchy. He exposed me to classic and cutting-edge research about debt by economists, historians, and political scientists. His own work, his enthusiasm for international finance, and his faith in the potential for scientific discovery were inspirations for this book.

The book is organized in nine chapters. In chapter 1, I lay out the core puzzle: without a global Leviathan to enforce contracts, why do private investors ever lend money abroad, and why do foreign governments ever repay? Chapter 2 then proposes a solution, a reputational theory of cooperation between sovereign debtors and foreign creditors. I test my theory and the leading alternatives in chapters 3–8, using newly collected data that cover all sovereign debtors over the last three centuries. Having found strong support for the reputational theory, I conclude in chapter 9 by summarizing the findings and discussing their implications, not only for debt, but also for the wider problem of cooperation under anarchy.

As I researched the subject of international debt, I incurred many international debts of my own. Data for this book came from archives and libraries in nine countries on three continents. It is my pleasure to acknowledge the many colleagues around the world who helped make this book possible. If I have failed to mention anyone who deserves thanks, I hope he or she will recognize the oversight as unintentional and not give me a reputation as an ungrateful type!

In Argentina, special thanks go to Mariano Tommasi for hosting me at the Universidad de San Andrés; to Marta Gutierrez for helping me at Biblioteca Tornquist; to Wenceslao Bunge for sharing his home; and to Luis Lavagna, Roberto Lavagna, and Gisela Sin for their advice and friendship. Robert Barros, Alejandro Catterberg, Isidoro Cheresky, Roberto Cortés Conde, Gerardo della Paolera, Carlos Fara, Roy Hora, and other academics in Argentina contributed their keen insights to this project. I met Alan Taylor during one of my research trips to Buenos Aires and have learned much from him over the years.

Many professionals in the United Kingdom assisted my research. I am especially grateful to Henry Gillett at the Bank of England Archives, and to the staff at Guildhall Library for providing access to the records of the Corporation of Foreign Bondholders. Specialists at the British Newspaper Library in Colindale, the National Archive in Kew, and the University of Glasgow were indispensable for my research. Finally, warm gratitude goes to Graham Ingham for arranging accommodations during one of my visits and—when the archives were closed—joining me on the tennis courts.

In Belgium, I could not have asked for a more generous colleague than Frans Buelens at the StudieCentrum voor Onderneming en Beurs, Universiteit Antwerpen. Frans pointed me to all the essential sources, and he shared unpublished data about foreign bonds on the Brussels stock exchange. Many Belgian librarians kindly and efficiently assisted with my research, especially Rudi De Groot at Katholieke Universiteit Leuven, Anke Jacobs at Universiteit Antwerpen, and Anne Lefèvre at Université Libre de Bruxelles.

For insight into French foreign investments, I owe the most to Marc Flandreau at the Institut d'Études Politiques de Paris. Marc shared his working papers and data, and he indicated where to find key pieces of information. I thank Robin Kraft and Leï Lacoste for their persistence in tracking down a complete collection of the *Cours authentique* at the Archive historique de la Bourse de Paris auprès de Euronext de Paris, and for sending the digital images I needed to construct an inventory of sovereign bonds on the Paris stock exchange.

Data from Germany were obtained through the good graces of numerous archivists, including Frank Berger at the Historisches Museum Frankfurt a.M.; Susanne Brockfeld at the Geheimes Staatsarchiv Preußischer Kulturbesitz in Berlin; Iris Erdmann at the Universitätsbibliothek Gießen; and Sylvia Goldhammer and Sigrid Kämpfer at the Institut für Stadtgeschichte Frankfurt a.M. Using the Stanford Overseas Studies Center in Germany as a base, Adele Faure and Danielle Lostaunau made many trips on my behalf to the Staatsbibliothek zu Berlin and the Zentral- und Landesbibliothek Berlin. I thank them all for their assistance in documenting the role Germany played in international finance before World War I.

Immense gratitude goes to Joost Jonker and Nico van Horn of Utrecht University in the Netherlands. Joost and Nico scoured the Dutch archives to compile the inventory of eighteenth-century loans analyzed in chapter 3. Guy Monod de Froideville sent stacks of stock market price sheets from the library of the Universiteit van Amsterdam. Additional data about Dutch finance came from a seemingly unlikely source, Spain. I thank José María Burrieza Mateos at the Archivo General de Simancas for his help with Spanish diplomatic reports about Dutch finance in the eighteenth century.

The analysis in chapter 6 would not have been possible without the help of many archivists in Switzerland. There, as in Germany, data were scattered across many financial centers. For their help in assembling a relatively complete picture of Swiss lending before World War I, I thank Blandine Blukacz-Louisfert at the Bibliothèque de l'Office des Nations Unies in Geneva; Ulrike Brill at the Bibliothek für Betriebswirtschaft /

Zentrale für Wirtschaftsdokumentation, Universität Zürich; Barbara Plaschy at the Schweizerische Landesbibliothek in Bern; Alexis Rivier at the Bibliothèque de Genève; and Matthias Wiesmann at the Schweizerisches Wirtschaftsarchiv, Universität Basel. Halfway around the globe, in New Zealand, Lyndon Moore at Victoria University of Wellington introduced me to the *Zürich Kursblatt* and provided digital samples from his private collection.

This book also draws extensively on archival and library collections from the United States. Although I cannot list all who helped, I want to single out Joe Puccio and Ronald Roaché at the Library of Congress for putting hundreds of books on advance reserve for my research trips to Washington, DC. I am equally grateful to John Petty and Richard Dine for granting access to the manuscripts of the Foreign Bondholders Protective Council. At the time, the trove was stored in an unheated, barely-lit warehouse in Flatbush, New York. Stanford Library curator Tony Angiletta took pity and relocated the files to Palo Alto. Today, the manuscripts reside in the special collections at Stanford, where they are available to any scholar with a passion for international economic history.

Other librarians at Stanford went above and beyond the call of duty to make this project possible. Stanford, founded only in 1891, did not have all the books and journals I needed for a project about sovereign debt since the 1700s. Interlibrary borrowing specialist Mary Munill solved my problem. Mary efficiently filled hundreds of requests for texts from around the globe. For my most audacious interlibrary needs, such as complete runs of *Der Aktionär*, the *Frankfurter Zeitung*, *L'Economiste français*, and *Saling's Börsen-Jahrbuch*, I turned to Rose Harrington, who always found ways to bring the material to Stanford.

The Stanford library generously purchased historical material for this project. Sarah Sussman acquired copies of key texts from Bibliothèque nationale de France, and Tony Angiletta added to the Stanford collection a microfilm edition of the Newspaper Cuttings Files of the Corporation of Foreign Bondholders. Tony also purchased the Corporation's annual reports from a used bookseller in London, stripped the bindings, and digitized the pages, making them full-text searchable on the Internet for me and other scholars.

For their unmatched skill in locating foreign documents, and for accommodating my numerous requests, I thank Stanford librarians Chuck Eckman, Eric Heath, and Joan Loftus. I am also grateful for the assistance of Assunta Pisani and Ben Stone at Stanford's Green Library, Steven Mandeville-Gamble in Special Collections, and Peter Latusek and Paul Reist in the library at the Graduate School of Business. I maintain a digital archive of all documents—primary and secondary—related to my research. The material cited in this book is, therefore, available to me at the click of a mouse. For advice about how to build this research archive, I am especially grateful to Steve Chapman, Preservation Librarian for Digital Initiatives at Harvard, and Stu Snydman, Manager of Digital Production Services at the Stanford Libraries.

Several scholars graciously shared data from their own research projects. Peter Lindert sent computer and paper records from his seminal work with Peter Morton; Barry Eichengreen supplied unpublished appendices from his articles with Richard Portes; Nathan Sussman and Yishay Yafeh granted permission to use their dataset of Japanese bond yields; and William Goetzmann and K. Geert Rouwenhorst made available electronic copies of the *Investor's Monthly Manual*. Scott Bennett unearthed a box of notecards containing bibliographic citations for the Correlates of War Militarized Interstate Disputes. The citations were an essential starting point for the research in chapter 6. Mario Boone and Jerry Raymond kindly provided digital images of historical government bonds, some of which appear on the cover of the book. Finally, Richard Gregg sent a full-size color photocopy of the infamous Poyaisian bond of 1822. Issued by Scottish con-man Gregor MacGregor on behalf of the fictitious Latin American country of Poyais, the bond hangs on my office wall as a testament to the lemons problem in nineteenth-century international finance.

An extraordinary group of Stanford Ph.D. students contributed to data collection and analysis for this project. I thank Catherine Duggan for working with me to compile a database of loans, debt defaults, and settlements between 1820 and 1914. Catherine reconciled seemingly contradictory pieces of evidence and helped me see important patterns in the data. This project owes much to her intelligence, diligence, and efficiency. My research on Germany would not have been possible without the aid of Carlos Starmanns and Thomas Brambor, who located and analyzed key German sources, many in Gothic script. Kimuli Kasara, Jeongah Kim, Moonhawk Kim, Maggie Peters, Julia Tobias, and Jessica Weeks made significant contributions as well.

I also want to acknowledge the talented Stanford undergraduates who logged countless hours exploring the topics of reputation and debt with me. Over three summers, a team of researchers read and hand-coded more than 96,000 pages from the Newspaper Cuttings Files of the Corporation of Foreign Bondholders. Participants in this prodigious effort included Kasey Alderete, Parilee Edison, Adele Faure, Emily Fenner, Victoria Gevlin, Eugenie Kim, John Kryzwicki, Jeff Lee, Brendan Marten, Milessa Muchmore, Carly Schuster, Sok Tea, and Lauren Young. For superb assistance with other aspects of this project, I thank Nicole Bonoff, Mallory Bounds, Jason Chen, Chris Couvelier, Jozefina Cutura, Summer Jackson, Gaby Kohan, Michelle Leeds, Christopher Lin, Jennifer Martínez, Julia Martínez, Oriana Mastro, Justin Mates, Theo Milonopoulos, Allison Reid, and Christina Riechers.

Finally, I acknowledge the highly competent and professional department administrators who have helped with this project: Hilary Anderson, Sarah Holmes, Angelita Mireles, Marie Toney, Eliana Vásquez, and my good friend Jackie Sargent.

Many mentors, colleagues, and friends commented on early drafts of the manuscript. This project began at Harvard, where I could not have asked for a better set of doctoral advisors. Jeff Frieden challenged and encouraged me at every step in the research process. His analytical rigor and encyclopedic knowledge contributed greatly to my analysis. Jorge Domínguez provided incisive criticisms and offered professional and personal advice when I needed it most. Gary King taught me much of what I know about political methodology and showed me how scientific research should be done. Lisa Martin constantly compelled me to deepen and clarify my ideas, especially about strategic interaction in world politics.

Colleagues in the Department of Political Science at Stanford generously donated their time and talent to this project. Nearly all assisted in some way. I especially want to thank Jim Fearon, Steve Haber, Simon Jackman, Steve Krasner, David Laitin, Isabela Mares, Scott Sagan, Ken Schultz, Jonathan Wand, and Barry Weingast. Judy Goldstein has been a fabulous mentor and collaborator throughout my time at Stanford. Finally, Paul Sniderman has set an unparalleled standard for collegiality. Although working in a different field of political science, Paul commented on many chapters and provided wise counsel during the review and publication process. I count him among my closest colleagues, and I view his career of scientific discovery as worthy of emulation.

I have also learned a great deal from faculty in other parts of the university. Current and former members of the Department of Economics and the Graduate School of Business helped me think about the theoretical and empirical issues raised in this book. Above all, I thank Mark Wright for numerous conversations about sovereign debt. By providing astute comments at a moment's notice, sharing insights from his own research, and collaborating with me on related projects, Mark greatly influenced this book. I am also grateful to Stanford economists Jeremy Bulow, Avner Greif, Peter Henry, Nick Hope, Jon Levin, Ron McKinnon, Steve Tadelis, and Gavin Wright, and to Stanford historian Zephyr Frank. I had the good fortune of meeting Ken Kletzer when he was a visiting professor at Stanford, and I appreciate all he taught me during his time in residence.

I am a bit awed by the number of people beyond Stanford who discussed this research with me or took the time to answer my email queries. I sincerely thank, among others, Jeremy Adelman, Vinnie Aggarwal, Leslie Elliot Armijo, Christina Arellano, Andrew Bailey, Michael Bailey, David Bearce, Bill Bernhard, Luis Bértola, Michael Bordo, Ted Brader, Lee Buchheit, Josh Busby, Marc Busch, Forrest Capie, Luis Catão, Kanchan

Chandra, Bill Clark, John Coatsworth, Christina Davis, Sarah Dix, Jorge Domínguez, Jonathan Eaton, Barry Eichengreen, Drew Erdmann, Rui Esteves, Carolyn Evans, Niall Ferguson, Martha Finnemore, Marc Flandreau, Caroline Fohlin, Page Fortna, John Freeman, Jeff Frieden, Márcio Garcia, Kristian Gleditsch, Jeff Glueck, Erica Gould, Joanne Gowa, Richard Grossman, Andrew Guzman, Galina Hale, Jude Hayes, Mike Hiscox, Mala Htun, Jacques Hymans, Nate Jensen, Bob Jervis, Joost Jonker, Miles Kahler, Devesh Kapur, Trish Kelly, Barbara Keys, Gary King, Ken Kletzer, Peter Koudijs, Pedro Lains, David Lake, David Leblang, Peter Lindert, Charles Lipson, Aaron Lobel, Carlos Marichal, Lisa Martin, Noel Mauer, Paolo Mauro, Sylvia Maxfield, Chris Meissner, Jon Mercer, Helen Milner, Diego Miranda, Ron Mitchell, Kris Mitchener, Ashoka Mody, Andy Moravcsik, Layna Mosley, Aldo Musacchio, Mark Nagel, Larry Neal, Vikram Nehru, John Oneal, Kathleen O'Neill, Barry O'Neill, Ken Oye, Şule Özler, Manuel Pastor, Lou Pauly, Pablo Pinto, Alejandro Poire, Daryl Press, Dennis Quinn, Eric Rasmusen, Rose Razaghian, Eric Reinhardt, James Riley, Albrecht Ritschl, Hugh Rockoff, Ron Rogowski, Andrew Rose, Peter Rosendorff, Bruce Russett, Sebastian Saiegh, Dick Salvucci, Javier Santiso, Anne Sartori, Shanker Satyanath, Ken Scheve, Gene Sessions, Beth Simmons, Alastair Smith, Duncan Snidal, Jack Snyder, David Stasavage, Randy Stone, Bill Summerhill, Nathan Sussman, Richard Sylla, Alan Taylor, Dan Treisman, Josh Tucker, Rob Van Houweling, Catalina Vizcarra, Jim Vreeland, Jessica Seddon Wallack, John Wallis, Barbara Walter, Marc Weidenmier, Tom Willett, Jason Wittenberg, Yishay Yafeh, and Jeromin Zettelmeyer. For detailed and helpful comments on the penultimate draft of the book, I am grateful to Tim Büthe, Lawrence Broz, and Bob Keohane. Bob also suggested the title of the book.

Parts of this book were presented at seminars and conventions across the country, and at the Stanford conference on Sovereign Debt and Latin America, funded through the generosity of Steve Haber and the Social Science History Institute. Paolo Mauro invited me to convey the key findings in a seminar at the International Monetary Fund, and then sponsored me as a visitor in the IMF Research Department. Mark Wright hosted me at the Federal Reserve Bank of Minneapolis, where I discussed my work with many fine economists. I am grateful for the comments I received from audience members at all these forums.

As this project was coming to a conclusion in fall 2006, several students at Stanford read and commented on the entire manuscript. I am especially grateful to Jessica Weeks for reviewing multiple drafts. Her brilliant analytical and writing skills improved every page of the book. Just when I thought the manuscript was done, Maggie Peters's comments led me to rewrite chapter 2, and Bethany Lacina's advice led me to remake several tables and figures. Ed Bruera, Luke Condra, Adele Faure, Laurel Harbridge, Brendan Marten, and Lauren Young also scrutinized the manuscript and assisted with the revisions. It is humbling and rewarding to learn so much from one's own students, even at the seemingly final stages of a research project.

Many institutions invested in my research. For financial support as a Ph.D. student at Harvard, I thank the David Rockefeller Center for Latin American Studies; the Harvard Business School; the MacArthur Foundation; the Mellon Foundation; the National Science Foundation; the Institute for the Study of World Politics; the Social Science Research Council; the Tinker Foundation; and the Weatherhead Center for International Affairs. As an assistant professor at Stanford, I received generous grants from the Freeman Spogli Institute for International Studies; the National Science Foundation (CAREER Grant SES-0548285); the Office of Technology Licensing; the Social Science History Institute; the Stanford Center for International Development; the Stanford Center for Latin American Studies; the Stanford Institute for the Quantitative Study of Society; and the Vice Provost for Undergraduate Education.

This book was completed during the 2006–7 academic year, when I was a Fellow at the Center for Advanced Study in the Behavioral Sciences. For funding that stimulating and productive year, I thank not only CASBS but also the Freeman Spogli Institute for International Studies, the Howard Foundation, and the Stanford Institute for Research in the Social Sciences. All these organizations helped bring this book to fruition.

It has been a pleasure to work with Chuck Myers and his colleagues at Princeton University Press. Chuck's suggestions greatly improved the manuscript, and his enthusiasm propelled the project to completion. Richard Isomaki copyedited the book, Tobiah Waldron helped prepare the index, and Mark Bellis and Meera Vaidyanathan professionally superintended the production process.

I am grateful to my parents, Robert and Jane Tomz, for supporting my interest in international affairs. They encouraged me to participate in high school debate and foreign extemporaneous speaking, through which I first learned about world politics and gained research skills that serve me today. At family gatherings, they often asked about my work, leading me to search for ways to communicate my hypotheses and findings to nonspecialists. They have my heartfelt thanks for so much encouragement and love.

This book is dedicated to my wife and our three young children. Julie has been by my side throughout the project, which required many late nights and trips away from home. I am eternally grateful for her patience, support, good humor, and love. Emily, Anna, and David became part of our family during this project, and they have brought excitement and joy to our lives every day. I hope they will grow to appreciate research and discovery as much as I do. And I hope someday, when they are old enough to read the book, they will think it has contributed to a better understanding of cooperation in our world.

# REPUTATION AND
# INTERNATIONAL COOPERATION

## Part I

### THEORY

# Chapter 1 _____

## The Puzzle of Cooperation
## in International Debt


EVERY DAY, LEADERS make promises to foreign governments and nonstate actors. They pledge to repay debts, supply foreign aid, curtail pollution, and limit their military arsenals. Leaders vow to lower barriers to international trade and capital, respect human rights at home, and promote democracy abroad. In principle, these commitments—some formal, some not—regulate how governments behave in world affairs.

Without a world government to enforce commitments, though, why should anyone take foreign leaders at their word? The answer is far from obvious. Some international agreements so clearly serve the interests of participants that defection would be unthinkable. Often, however, cheating would give the transgressor an immediate economic windfall, a military advantage, or a firmer grip on power at home. Moreover, the anarchical nature of world politics makes third-party enforcement of commitments unlikely. In this context, neither scholars nor political leaders can take international promise-keeping for granted.

This book examines one of the oldest and most pervasive types of international promises: debt contracts between sovereign governments and private foreign lenders. For centuries, bondholders and banks have lent money to foreign governments for a variety of objectives, including economic development, military procurement, and domestic consumption. The practice continues to this day. Private bondholders and banks now advance more than $100 billion per year to foreign governments around the world.[1]

International debt contracts raise serious problems of credibility. When a government borrows money on world capital markets, it pledges to repay the principal plus interest and fees according to a schedule in the loan agreement. After creditors disburse the funds, though, the government may be tempted to break its promise by refusing to make full and punctual installments. The government can suspend interest payments, slow the rate of amortization, or—even worse—repudiate the debt, thereby denouncing the obligation as illegitimate.

---

[1] According to the World Bank (2006, 2:3), disbursements by bondholders and banks to public borrowers in developing countries totaled US$101 billion in the year 2004 and $124 billion in 2005.

History abounds with examples of default on international loans. In January 2002 the Argentine administration stopped servicing roughly $100 billion in foreign bonds, triggering the largest default of all time. Its decision, though unprecedented in magnitude, represents only one entry in a litany of defaults by governments over the past few centuries. In a typical year, approximately 10 percent of governments fail to meet contractual obligations to foreign bondholders and commercial banks, and during systemic crises such as the Great Depression, nearly half the countries in the world have been in arrears on their international debts.[2]

Considering the inherent problem of credibility in world affairs, and given numerous cases of default throughout history, what gives bondholders and banks the confidence to lend money to foreign governments? Furthermore, why do governments ever repay their debts to private lenders in distant countries? There is, of course, a deep puzzle here—arguably one of the deepest in the study of politics: how does cooperation emerge in a condition of anarchy? The remainder of the book addresses this question in the context of international debt.

## The Puzzle

The literature on international relations offers two major perspectives about how credibility and cooperation can be sustained in an anarchical world. The first is *repeat play*, in which leaders cooperate today to ensure good relations in the future. The second is *issue linkage*, the process of connecting behavior in one area to the threat of sanctions in another. Both provide substantial insights into world politics, but neither—without amendment—adequately accounts for historical patterns of behavior in international finance. After noting the strengths and weaknesses of these approaches as applied to international debt, I propose a reputational theory that builds on models of repeat play but modifies them by conjoining two key features: incomplete information and political change. I then show, using three centuries of data from international capital markets, that this reputational theory offers new insight into relations between debtors and creditors.

### Repeat Play

One of the most fertile lines of research in international relations concerns the effects of repeat play. Using game theory, political scientists and economists have demonstrated that cooperation can arise from the threat of

---

[2] Suter 1990, 1992; Standard & Poor's 2004.

retaliation in ongoing relationships.[3] If two parties interact repeatedly with one another, each could retaliate tomorrow in response to uncooperative behavior today. The most severe retaliatory strategy is the grim trigger: "Cross me once and I will never cooperate with you again." A more forgiving strategy, tit-for-tat, requires players to mimic their opponents by matching each act of cooperation with cooperation and punishing each instance of defection by striking back once. Many other strategies could achieve the same objective of punishing cheaters in the future.

When the threat of retaliation is sufficiently plausible and severe, it can support cooperation even in the absence of third-party enforcement. As Robert Axelrod explains, the future can "cast a shadow back upon the present and thereby affect the current strategic situation."[4] Leaders who care enough about the future will calculate that the costs of forgoing cooperation tomorrow outweigh the immediate gains from behaving selfishly today.

It is easy to see how this logic could motivate governments to repay and give investors the confidence to lend. Most countries need to borrow not once but repeatedly to meet ongoing demands for economic development, national defense, and domestic consumption. Investors could, therefore, adopt a history-contingent strategy: penalize countries that default by barring them from new loans or by charging higher interest rates in subsequent years. Faced with this retributive strategy, credit-hungry governments would have powerful incentives to honor their debts, and investors could advance money with reasonable assurance of being repaid.[5]

Does existing research support the repeat-play theory? Surprisingly, the answer appears to be no. In their study of sovereign debt since the 1850s, Peter Lindert and Peter Morton conclude that "investors seem to pay little attention to the past repayment record of the borrowing governments. . . . [T]hey do not punish governments with a prior default history, undercutting the belief in a penalty that compels faithful repayment."[6] Other scholars, focusing on different time periods, have reached similar conclusions. Cardoso and Dornbusch, Eichengreen and Portes, and Jorgensen and Sachs note, for example, that countries that fell into arrears during the Great Depression did not subsequently receive worse terms of credit than countries that had paid in full.[7] One major study by Özler finds

---

[3] Early studies of cooperation in repeated games include Friedman 1971 and Taylor 1976. In the 1980s many researchers, including Axelrod (1981, 1984); Keohane (1984); Lipson (1984); Oye (1986); and Snidal (1985) began to apply these arguments to international relations.

[4] Axelrod 1984, 12.

[5] Authors have formalized this argument in various ways. The seminal formal model is Eaton and Gersovitz 1981.

[6] Lindert and Morton 1989, 40.

[7] Cardoso and Dornbusch 1989; Eichengreen and Portes 1989; Jorgensen and Sachs 1989.

that countries with histories of repayment difficulties were charged higher interest rates during the period 1968–81, but even then the default premiums were remarkably small.[8] The prevailing interpretation of history, it seems, is that international creditors ignore history!

How have scholars explained investors' apparent inattention to history? Some cite ignorance. Vinod Aggarwal opens his massive study of debt rescheduling by contending that "almost without exception, modern bankers have made mistakes as a result of their unfamiliarity with the turbulent history of international lending. Few lenders in the 1970s, for example, knew that sovereign countries had frequently defaulted on their debt payments in the past."[9] Others blame irrational exuberance: investors have been drawn into speculative manias and, without systematically weighing the consequences, have lent even to countries with records of default.[10] Whatever the reason, the received wisdom casts serious doubt on the use of history-contingent strategies to enforce debt contracts.

The repeat-play argument seems problematic not only in practice but also in theory. To bar a defaulter from capital markets or force it to pay higher interest rates, an aggrieved creditor would need the cooperation of most—if not all—current and future lenders around the world. Why, though, would profit-seeking bondholders and banks collaborate in punishing a government for defaulting on someone else's loans? The notion of retribution seems especially problematic because, for most of financial history, loans came from tens of thousands of scattered investors who probably could not have coalesced into a punishment cartel. Without extensive cooperation among creditors, the threat of punishment may not be credible. Ironically, the repeat-play argument may solve one credibility problem by creating another.[11]

We are, therefore, left with a puzzle. If existing research is correct in concluding that creditors ignore history, and if even retribution-minded creditors would face severe problems in organizing collective punishment, why do sovereign governments ever repay their debts? Perhaps even more

---

[8] Özler 1993. In a recent study of the period 1880–1913, Flandreau and Zumer (2004, 39) find that past defaults increased yields on government bonds, but the effects were "too small to act as a systematic deterrent."

[9] Aggarwal 1996, 15.

[10] See, e.g., Chancellor 1999; Marichal 1989.

[11] See, e.g., Eaton 1990; Eaton, Gersovitz, and Stiglitz 1986; Glick 1986; Greif, Milgrom, and Weingast 1994; Hellwig 1986; Kletzer 1988; Schultz and Weingast 1998, 2003; and Weingast 1997. Bulow and Rogoff (1989b) advance a related critique: if countries borrow to smooth their consumption, they can default against one creditor and use the proceeds from the loan to purchase a consumption-insurance contract from another lender (the insurer). For responses to the Bulow-Rogoff critique, including discussions of how creditors could tacitly collude to punish defaulters, see Amador 2002; Kletzer and Wright 2000; and Wright 2002.

troublesome, what inspires investors to lend billions of dollars to governments each year, if not the ability to withhold credit in an ongoing lending
relationship? A second possibility is issue linkage.

## Issue Linkage

In a complex and interdependent world, countries and nonstate actors can
enforce agreements by linking issues, that is, by threatening to retaliate in
one area of world affairs if foreigners behave selfishly in another.[12] Actors
might, for example, sever economic relations with countries that violate
arms control agreements or apply military pressure against parties that
fail to respect human rights. Provided the links between issues are credible, leaders will think twice before crossing foreigners, since the gain from
cheating on one issue may be outweighed by the loss of cooperation on
another.

This insight, so central to international relations theory, may explain
how debt contracts have been enforced for centuries. On their own or
with help from their home government, banks and bondholders could
impose nonfinancial penalties on countries that default. Charles Lipson
usefully refers to this kind of retaliation as an "extrinsic" sanction because it involves punishment on an issue distinct from the one that
sparked the dispute.[13] In contrast, the repeat-play strategy of withholding
access to capital is an "intrinsic" sanction because creditors strike back
in the same issue area in which the borrower cheated in the first place.

Creditors could impose various extrinsic sanctions on defaulters. One
option is military intervention. The idea of using arms to extract repayment may seem odd today, but many scholars believe this mode of enforcement prevailed until the early twentieth century. Martha Finnemore,
for example, writes that militarized debt collection was "accepted practice" in the nineteenth century and fell from favor only after the Second
Hague Peace Conference in 1907.[14] Some academics judge that military
pressure was commonly used to collect debts.[15] Others think creditors
applied police powers selectively, sending gunboats to compel debtors in
only a few colorful cases.[16] Ultimately, though, the prospect of military

---

[12] The concept of issue linkage has a long intellectual history. See, e.g., Keohane and
Nye 1977; Tollison and Willett 1979; Haas 1980; Stein 1980; Keohane 1984; Axelrod and
Keohane 1985; Oye 1985; Snidal 1985; McGinnis 1986; Martin 1992; Keohane and Martin
1995; Lohmann 1997; Aggarwal 1998; and Davis 2003, 2004.

[13] Lipson 1981, 630.

[14] Finnemore 2003, 24.

[15] See, e.g., Mitchener and Weidenmier 2005b, 2.

[16] See, e.g., Mauro, Sussman, and Yafeh 2006, chap. 7; Mosley 2003, 268–71.

force should have mattered more than the frequency. According to economists Paul De Grauwe and Michele Fratianni, the *mere threat* of gunboats influenced the behavior of nineteenth-century borrowers.[17]

References to gunboat diplomacy appear not only in scholarly writings, but also in the modern financial press. During the debt crisis of the 1980s, for example, the *Wall Street Journal* ran the following front-page headline: "Theodore Roosevelt Knew How to Collect on Defaulted Loans— He Would Send in the Marines to Protect U.S. Bankers from Deadbeat Nations." The *Journal* contrasted the modern era of peaceful debt renegotiation with a previous age, in which "governments employed soldiers rather than accountants and lawyers to resolve international financial problems."[18] To the extent that this characterization is accurate, military force kept debtors honest for at least part of world history.

A second type of extrinsic sanction involves commerce rather than military cruisers. In many models of sovereign debt, lenders motivate the borrower to repay by establishing a tactical link between finance and trade.[19] If a government defaults, private creditors retaliate not by denying access to future loans but by disrupting commercial relations. Creditors seize goods that belong to the debtor, withhold short-term credit for imports and exports, or (with the help of their home government) impose an embargo on commercial relations with the defaulting state. Confronted with cross-issue retribution of this type, governments may find it worthwhile to repay.

As Philip Lane points out, "The imposition of trade sanctions on the offending country" is "the classic punishment . . . in the sovereign debt literature."[20] It is easy to see why. Countries gain significantly from international trade, due to the principle of comparative advantage. The prospect of losing trade could, therefore, dissuade debtors from cheating on loans. Moreover, the age of gunboat diplomacy may have passed, but trade sanctions remain a potential weapon in the arsenal of creditors. Linkages between debt and trade could, therefore, explain repayment not only before World War I, but also in more modern times.

Empirical research on the topic has just begun, however, and the available evidence is contradictory. In two recent studies, Andrew Rose shows

[17] De Grauwe and Fratianni 1984, 158.

[18] *Wall Street Journal*, January 12, 1984, 1.

[19] This argument appears in the seminal work of Gersovitz (1983) and Bulow and Rogoff (1989a) and in more recent papers by Aizenman (1989, 1991); Boot and Kanatas (1995); Diwan (1990); Egli (1997); Fafchamps (1996); Fernández and Özler (1989); Gibson and Sundaresan (2005); Klimenko (2002); Marin and Schnitzer (2003); Rose (2005); and Rose and Spiegel (2004), among many others.

[20] Lane 2004, 2.

that trade declines after countries reschedule their debts at the expense of creditors, and that countries receive more loans from large trading partners than from small ones.[21] Both findings are broadly consistent with the trade sanctions hypothesis. On the other hand, Martinez and Sandleris and Mitchener and Weidenmier find no evidence that debtor-creditor trade falls in response to default, and William English demonstrates that many U.S. states repaid their foreign debts during the nineteenth century, even though they were immune to trade sanctions from Britain.[22]

The trade sanctions hypothesis also suffers from the same theoretical weakness as the repeat-play argument. To exclude a defaulter from international trade, each lender would need help from many foreign actors. Countries and firms that trade with the defaulter—and ones that potentially could do so—would need to collude, even if they were not party to the original loan. Without collusion, the defaulter could minimize its punishment by increasing ties with other buyers and sellers, or by transshipping its products through other states. Trade sanctions, like credit embargoes, raise daunting problems of collective action.

Once again, we are left with a puzzle. Military coercion may have contributed to debt repayment during the 1800s (a theme I reexamine later in the book), but it cannot explain lending and repayment today. The trade sanctions hypothesis, in contrast, has greater explanatory potential across countries and over time and is "widely accepted" among economic theorists.[23] Nevertheless, it is not obvious that traders worldwide would unite against a defaulter, and evidence about the hypothesized link between debt and trade remains limited and mixed. At this point, we cannot confidently say why countries repay their foreign debts or what gives private investors the assurance to lend.

## Toward a Reputation-Based Solution

This book argues that we can make progress toward understanding the behavior of debtors and creditors by developing a dynamic theory of reputation—one that combines repeat play with uncertainty and political change. Building on classical theories of repeated interaction, I relax the

---

[21] Rose 2005; Rose and Spiegel 2004. See also Weidenmier 2005 on trade sanctions and Southern Confederacy debt.

[22] Martinez and Sandleris 2006; Mitchener and Weidenmier 2005b; English 1996. See also Wright 2004b for a discussion of the strengths and limitations of the evidence in Rose and Spiegel 2004.

[23] Rose 2005, 190.

standard assumption of complete information about the preferences of foreign governments and allow preferences to change over time. These two innovations transform the standard repeat-play theory into a dynamic model of reputation in which investors continually update their beliefs about the type of government they are confronting. The evolving beliefs of investors, which constitute the borrower's reputation in foreign eyes, are fundamental to both lending and repayment. I discuss incomplete information and political change below, incorporate them into a theory of reputation in chapter 2, and test the theory's explanatory power in the remainder of the book.

Models of repeat play in international debt typically involve complete information about the preferences of players. In their seminal paper, Jonathan Eaton and Mark Gersovitz assume that lenders "know all relevant characteristics of individual borrowers," including the fact that governments "are inherently dishonest."[24] When dealing with governments in a complete-information setting, investors enforce cooperation by threatening to apply the grim trigger: a country that defaults will experience a permanent financial boycott. Many other modelers adopt the same assumption that investors fully understand the preferences of the borrower.[25]

These complete-information models contain a reputational element; creditors condition their lending decisions on whether the borrower repaid in the past. However, the concept of reputation in these models is limited in ways that have important theoretical and empirical implications. Under conditions of complete information, creditors already know the type of debtor they are confronting. There is no opportunity to develop beliefs—and therefore no opportunity to learn—about resolve, competence, and other attributes that could be relevant to repayment. I define the reputation of an actor as the impression others hold about its preferences and abilities. Complete-information models leave no room for changes in impressions, and therefore remove the possibility of updating or learning.

[24] Eaton and Gersovitz 1981, 290.

[25] Some repeat-play models allow the income of the sovereign to fluctuate randomly in response to exogenous shocks, such as natural disasters and changes in commodity prices. Neither investors nor politicians know exactly when disaster will strike, nor can they anticipate when the sovereign will face better conditions.

Nevertheless, actors are presumed to know in advance the probability and magnitude of all shocks that could affect the sovereign. Consequently, investors have nothing to learn about the sovereign's vulnerability to external shocks, much less its resolve and competence in the face of circumstances beyond its control. Reputation-based approaches are distinctive, since they allow investors to update their beliefs about determination, competence, and other features of the debtor that could influence the likelihood of repayment.

Researchers justify the complete-information assumption in three ways. Some say it "accurately reflects reality" because creditors know with high precision the preferences and abilities of debtors they face.[26] For these researchers, the notion of incomplete information about the debtor is fairly "implausible."[27] Others contend that models of incomplete information are "not necessary" to account for relations between debtors and creditors.[28] In the interest of parsimony they delete what they judge superfluous. Still others believe the use of incomplete information is "unlikely to yield empirically testable models," whereas complete-information approaches can be evaluated with evidence.[29]

Vinod Aggarwal advances many of these arguments in *Debt Games*, the leading study in political science of international debt rescheduling. Aggarwal develops a "situational theory of bargaining" that identifies domestic and international constraints actors face in the wake of a default. His theory assumes that "each player knows both players' payoffs and the rules of the game." According to Aggarwal, this "assumption of complete information not only provides a more tractable model, but also more accurately reflects reality." Models of incomplete information, in contrast, would be "unwieldy" for empirical work.[30]

The concerns are understandable but, I believe, misplaced. As we will see, the assumption of incomplete information is not only plausible but also useful to explain defaults, settlements, risk premiums, seasoning effects, and other patterns in international debt markets through the centuries. Moreover, the battery of empirical tests in this book demonstrates that researchers can in fact use evidence to evaluate reputational theories with incomplete information. We have learned much from models of repeat play with complete information. Now we can deepen our understanding of debtor-creditor relations and broaden the range of predictable phenomena by placing incomplete information at the center of the analysis.

My reputational theory leaves room not only for incomplete information but also for political change. The workhorse models in economics and political science, such as the iterated prisoner's dilemma, treat preferences as static. Players have identical incentives (they repeat a game with unchanging payoffs) round after round. The assumption of constant preferences is appropriate for some kinds of actors. In the realm of international debt, for example, it makes sense to characterize private creditors

[26] Aggarwal 1996, 544.
[27] Buiter 1988, 613.
[28] Kletzer and Wright 2000, 635.
[29] Kletzer 1988, 602.
[30] Aggarwal 1996, 55, 70, 544.

as having consistent preferences for profit. But it is less realistic and, I argue, less useful to view government preferences as immutable.

The Argentine default of January 2002 provides a case in point. Analysis reveals that the Argentine default occurred in response to *changing* domestic preferences about the value of compliance.[31] Notwithstanding the complexities of international finance, most Argentine citizens had strong opinions about whether the debt should be repaid and let those opinions guide their votes. In 1999 a majority opposed default and turned against presidential candidate Eduardo Duhalde when he called for a suspension of debt payments. The eventual winner of the 1999 presidential election, Fernando de la Rúa, had campaigned on a platform of honoring the debt. By 2001, however, the policy of repayment became increasingly unpopular. When mass opinion tipped in favor of default, citizens handed de la Rúa a devastating defeat in congressional elections, drove him to resign the presidency, and replaced him with a new leader who declared a moratorium on debt payments as his first public act. By ruling out such swings in public opinion and government ideology, static-preference models of reputation fail to explain the largest default in financial history.

The more general lesson is that political change, either at the highest levels of government or within the populace, can cause government preferences about debt to shift. Diverse domestic opinions make these changes possible. Political leaders, parties, and citizens are not uniformly in favor of debt servicing, nor are they uniformly opposed. Opinion tends to be divided, especially in developing countries during times of crisis, because debt repayment creates economic winners and losers.[32] Recent research shows that elites and masses understand the distributional effects of debt repayment and use them as a basis for policy preferences.[33] Domestic changes—revolutions, coups d'état, institutional reforms, elections, and shifts in the prodebt and antidebt coalitions—could, therefore, alter government preferences about repayment. These insights can be usefully integrated into theories of reputation.

In the remainder of this book, I develop and test a theory of reputation in international relations, with particular application to financial relations between sovereign borrowers and foreign lenders. The theory, which incorporates both incomplete information and political change, explains why investors lend and governments repay. Beyond that, it generates a wide range of testable implications about the *dynamics* of debtor-creditor relations. The theory predicts how investors treat first-time borrowers, and how risk premiums evolve as borrowers become more seasoned. It

---

[31] Tomz 2005a.
[32] Frieden 1988, 1989b, 1991.
[33] Tomz 2005b.

explains how debtors ascend or descend the reputational ladder due to the interaction between their behavior and the historical context, and then clarifies how changes in reputation affect access to capital. A theory of reputation that includes uncertainty and political change helps explain why countries with favorable reputations sometimes default, and why nations with histories of noncompliance suddenly settle with foreign creditors. Still more fundamentally, the theory contributes to a deeper understanding of cooperation under anarchy.

# Chapter 2 _____

## A Theory of Cooperation through Reputation

THIS CHAPTER presents a reputational theory of cooperation between sovereign governments and foreign investors. I introduce the theory in four steps. First, I explain how reputations form under conditions of incomplete information. In my theory, the preferences of governments vary: some governments find it more costly than others to maintain good relations with foreign creditors. Investors cannot directly observe the preferences of foreign governments, but they do have beliefs about each government's type. These beliefs, which constitute the government's reputation, evolve as investors interpret behavior in context. Did the government repay its debts, investors ask, and were economic conditions good or bad? I argue that reputations shift when a government acts contrary to its perceived type.

I then extend the theory to allow for domestic political change. Political preferences can fluctuate over time; a country governed by a prodebt coalition at one moment may come under the influence of antidebt lobbies in the next. Just as investors cannot observe preferences directly, they cannot know for certain that preferences have changed. They can, however, infer whether political shifts have taken place by monitoring the behavior of successive governments. The possibility of political change makes reputations fragile and helps account for the termination and resumption of international cooperation.

Third, I explain how reputations—formed under conditions of incomplete information and political instability—affect incentives to cooperate. In my theory, concerns about reputation motivate countries to repay and inspire investors to lend. The theory not only suggests a plausible mechanism for debtor-creditor cooperation but also generates many testable implications. The theory predicts which countries can borrow, the terms of loans that are offered, and how relations between debtors and creditors evolve with economic and political circumstances.

Fourth, I distinguish my theory from alternative perspectives on reputation and cooperation. In particular, I consider psychological theories of reputation, which hold that participants in international relations interpret history in systematically biased ways. I also discuss rationalist theories in which actors place little weight on history, and therefore consider reputation irrelevant. Finally, I consider theories of issue linkage or direct sanctions, which suggest nonreputational sources of cooperation between debtors and creditors. In subsequent chapters I test the predictions of these theories against evidence since the 1700s.

## Reputations under Incomplete Information

Before making a loan, foreign investors would like to know the probability of default and the value they could recover in the event of a contractual breach. Such calculations are difficult, particularly under the conditions of incomplete information that prevail in international relations, but they are essential for assessing loans. Some bondholders and banks use mathematical models. Others rely on judgment, qualitative techniques, or third-party advice. Nearly all, though, find some way to learn about risks and potential returns.

### The Problem of Incomplete Information

Investors naturally seek knowledge of the borrower's economic resources. Does the foreign government have the funds to pay interest on schedule, and will it be able to reimburse the principal when the loan comes due? Some measures of economic capacity, such as earnings from international trade and the level of outstanding debt, have been available to investors for centuries. Other indicators, like gross domestic product, have been collected systematically for a large sample of countries only since the 1950s. These variables shed valuable light on the economic resources of borrowers.

Economic variables do not provide a complete picture of risks and potential returns, though, because the fate of an international loan ultimately depends on the borrower's *willingness* to pay. With no global Leviathan to prohibit breaches of contract, even governments with ample funds can choose to default. In debt, as in other spheres of international relations, governments uphold their commitments when the benefits of compliance outweigh the costs of reneging. Investors therefore require information about the political preferences of foreign governments.

Political factors are especially important because they determine how leaders balance debt repayment against other priorities. Governments can, if they choose, make sacrifices to meet at least part of their foreign obligations. They can cut public spending, increase taxes on citizens, sell state-owned assets, and commandeer foreign exchange from private exporters. When a government pleads poverty in negotiations with international creditors, this almost never implies that the government is penniless. Rather, it signals a lack of political will to elevate the foreign debt over other concerns.

Unfortunately for investors, the preferences of foreign governments are not directly observable. Preferences, unlike economic statistics, exist in the hearts and minds of foreign leaders. This fact puts investors in a difficult position; they must make loans with only partial information about a key variable in the investment equation. Below, I develop a theory to explain how investors address this problem.

### Reputations as Beliefs about Types

Investors know that adverse economic shocks can affect a government's ability to repay. Most countries are small players in global markets, and therefore have little influence over the international interest rate and the price of tradable goods. Countries are also powerless to prevent droughts, floods, hurricanes, and earthquakes from destroying crops and manufacturing facilities. When international interest rates rise, the value of exports falls, or natural disasters strike, governments struggle to raise revenue and foreign exchange for debt service.[1]

But investors also know that governments respond to negative shocks in different ways. Some governments tighten their belts; they impose austerity at home to meet commitments abroad. Other governments appear more fickle; they remain faithful during auspicious years but default when external conditions deteriorate. Still other governments deliberately snub creditors in good times as well as bad.

Why do governments respond differently to similar economic conditions? The answer, I suggest, is heterogeneous preferences. In the reputational theory developed here, governments protect and enhance their access to capital by paying existing obligations on schedule. The reward for honesty comes at a cost, however. To keep payments flowing, governments may need to raise taxes or cut spending, which could upset domestic constituents. Debt repayments pose economic and political dilemmas, especially during hard times.

Many factors could affect how governments balance the costs and benefits of debt repayment. The political strength of incumbents, the willingness of citizens to tolerate austerity, and the power of contending interest groups could all come into play. So, too, could the time horizons of leaders—their patience for reputational rewards that might not materialize for months or years. Even morals could enter the calculation, since some

---

[1] Some have argued that debt contracts implicitly take these kinds of contingencies into account. See, e.g., Alesina 1988; Calvo 1989; Carlson, Husain, and Zimmerman 1997; Grossman and Van Huyck 1988; and Obstfeld and Rogoff 1996, 360–61. Others have called for more explicit contingencies in loan contracts, e.g., Borensztein and Mauro (2004).

leaders oppose defaulting on ethical grounds, whereas others avoid letting personal principles shape government policy.

The exact sources of heterogeneity are interesting in their own right, but are not the focus of this book. For the reputational argument to succeed, we need only accept that preferences are diverse. The combination of heterogeneous preferences and incomplete information makes reputations possible.

My theory of reputation involves three types of debtors, which I call *stalwarts*, *fair-weathers*, and *lemons*.[2] Each type has distinct preferences that contribute to different patterns of behavior. Stalwarts have the strongest preference for debt repayment. For stalwarts, the value of foreign capital is high, time horizons are long, and the antipayment coalition is weak, so the reputational benefits of debt service almost always outweigh the costs. Countries with stalwart preferences tend to pay during good times and bad. Fair-weathers, in contrast, have intermediate preferences. The value they attach to future loans is sufficient to motivate repayment in good times, but not during bad ones. Finally, lemons receive the least utility from paying their debts. Governments with lemonlike preferences regularly default in bad times and sometimes break faith in good times, as well.

Bondholders and banks cannot fully know the type of government they are confronting, but they do have beliefs about whether they are dealing with a stalwart, a fair-weather, or a lemon. Those beliefs constitute the reputation of the borrower in the eyes of international investors. As with all beliefs, assessments about the preferences of a foreign government may be erroneous. The reputations in this model nonetheless represent the best guesses investors can make about the debtor, given the information at their disposal.

### Learning from Behavior in Context

What information do investors use to learn about political preferences? I contend that investors form beliefs by observing behavior in context: they consider the debtor's record of repayment and the economic circumstances it faced. Repayment records, carefully recorded by individuals and institutions, provide clues about political preferences that are difficult to measure directly. Data about economic circumstances, when available, add further perspective by helping investors see how governments re-

---

[2] The term "lemon" is inspired by Akerlof 1970. I also draw inspiration from, and build upon, the work of Cole, Dow, and English (1995) and Eaton (1996), who propose models in which some sovereign debtors are more far-sighted or sensitive to the costs of default than others.

spond to tests of varying degrees of difficulty. The interplay of these two types of information, actual payments and economic shocks, gives investors the raw materials to discern the borrower's type.

I assume that investors use information in rational ways: they update their beliefs about a government in response to new facts.[3] At each stage in the learning process, investors strike a compromise between their prior views and fresh data. If incoming news corroborates investors' preconceptions, beliefs remain the same.[4] If, on the other hand, the latest data challenge existing views, investors adjust by taking a weighted average of old and new evidence. The greater the reliability of new evidence relative to old, the more investors discount their prior beliefs and assign heavy weight to breaking news.

My argument does not require that all people possess identical cognitive abilities or learn rationally in all spheres of life. After all, psychologists have identified a conservative bias in human learning: once people form a first impression, they often downplay dissonant evidence and give undue weight to their initial views.[5] The proper question is not whether people learn rationally in all circumstances, but under what conditions their learning approximates the rational ideal.

For two reasons, the behavior of international investors should be fairly rational. First, private investors—and the institutions that advise them—have a strong profit motive to update their beliefs instead of clinging to outmoded views that could lead to financial ruin. Second, although investors might respond defensively to data that challenged their personal beliefs, such as religious convictions or moral values, they generally do not have a strong stake in defending views about the creditworthiness of foreign governments.

### How Reputations Change

If investors make rational use of information about behavior and context, then reputations should change when governments act contrary to their perceived type, given the circumstances. Suppose a government is widely (though perhaps erroneously) perceived as a fair-weather. If the government defies expectations by servicing its debts under austere conditions, it will improve its standing in the eyes of investors. By the same logic, a

---

[3] The process is essentially Bayesian. For an introduction to Bayesian inference, see Gelman et al. 2004.

[4] The confirmatory data mainly give investors more confidence in their prior estimates.

[5] Nisbett and Ross 1980, chap. 8. Most psychologists rely on laboratory experiments with undergraduates, but Tetlock (1999, 2005) has found a similar conservative bias in studies of experts. The most wide-ranging and important analysis of perceptual errors by decision makers in international relations is Jervis 1976.

| | Reputed Stalwart | | Reputed Fair-Weather | | Reputed Lemon | |
|---|---|---|---|---|---|---|
| | Favorable conditions | Adverse conditions | Favorable conditions | Adverse conditions | Favorable conditions | Adverse conditions |
| Repay | X | X | X | ⬆ | ⬆ | ⬆ |
| Default | ⬇ | ⬇ | ⬇ | X | X | X |

FIGURE 2.1: REPUTATIONS CHANGE WHEN GOVERNMENTS ACT CONTRARY TO THEIR PERCEIVED TYPE
Arrows indicate the direction of change in reputation. X's indicate no change.

decision to default under favorable circumstances will cause the government's reputation to sink. But a putative fair-weather that meets expectations by defaulting under duress and paying when the yoke is light will experience little change in reputation. In these cases, behavior conveys little new information about the government's preferences. Thus, governments that are perceived as fair-weathers should not suffer much reputational loss by defaulting during external crises such as world wars and global economic contractions.

Parallel predictions apply to other perceived types. Consider a reputed stalwart. Any default by this government would lead investors to assign lower credit ratings, reflecting news that the government is not always willing to service its international debts. Given its preeminent reputation, an alleged stalwart must pay under all circumstances if it hopes retain a class-A rating. At the opposite extreme, governments with lemonlike ratings have many opportunities to enhance their reputations. By offering an adequate settlement on defaulted debt and servicing any loans it manages to receive, a reputed lemon can elevate its standing and gain greater access to capital markets. In all these examples the lesson is the same: investors change their beliefs when governments act in surprising ways. Figure 2.1 summarizes these predictions.

The argument has an important corollary: reputations can improve even when external conditions are *favorable*.[6] The existence of lemons makes this improvement possible. Investors know that stalwarts and fair-weathers tend to honor their debts under auspicious conditions, whereas lemons sometimes default under those same circumstances. A government that pays during good times can, therefore, distinguish itself from a lemon. Whether this behavior has any effect on reputation depends on prior beliefs about the government. If investors already knew with certainty that the government was not a lemon, such behavior would confirm

---

[6] Diamond (1989) develops a similar argument about the dynamics of reputation in domestic debt markets, but his model does not allow for exogenous shocks, and it presumes that lenders can foreclose on the assets of defaulters, which is unlikely in an international setting.

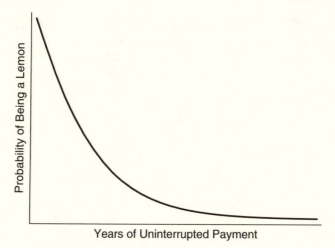

FIGURE 2.2: EVEN IN GOOD TIMES, REPUTATION IMPROVES AS THE DEBTOR BECOMES A SEASONED PAYER

expectations and cause no change in reputation. If, on the other hand, investors admitted some chance that the government was a lemon, payment would count as contrary evidence and cause a reputational gain. The process will exhibit diminishing marginal returns, with each additional payment enhancing reputation by a smaller amount. At some point, when investors become highly certain that the government is not a lemon, paying under favorable conditions will only preserve—not improve—the government's reputation. Figure 2.2 displays the expected pattern.

The argument can be expressed as a general claim about the way reputations change in world affairs. Leaders and citizens regularly form beliefs about the preferences of foreign governments. A government alters those beliefs (its reputation) by defying expectations: acting contrary to its perceived type, given the circumstances. Likewise, a government preserves its reputation by behaving as anticipated, thereby validating beliefs observers hold about the government's characteristics.

## Reputations and Political Change

Existing theories of reputation almost always treat the preferences of players as fixed.[7] External circumstances are allowed to fluctuate, but internal attributes are not. This simplification, though useful for many kinds of

---

[7] For a review, see Mailath and Samuelson 2006. A small literature has begun to explore the consequences of allowing types to change. See Cole, Dow, and English 1995; Mailath and Samuelson 2001; and Phelan 2006.

relationships, misses a fundamental feature of politics. Perhaps individuals never change their stripes, but governments surely do.

I therefore extend my theory by considering how reputations develop when government preferences (or types) can change. Investors cannot directly observe shifts in preferences, but by analyzing the borrower's behavior they can begin to infer whether a domestic transformation has taken place. Incorporating unstable preferences into models of reputation has two effects: it creates slack for reputations to change, and it provides a mechanism for the initiation and termination of cooperation. I discuss these effects in order.

### Reputational Destruction and Recovery

In models of reputation with perpetual types, an interesting paradox arises. If types never change, then the body of accumulated data about the government's preferences will eventually become large enough to overwhelm any new observations. At that point, the process of reputation-formation will grind to a halt, and governments with sterling reputations will be able to default without harming their image. Good reputations, once built, will become nearly impossible to destroy.[8]

This paradox follows directly from rational rules of learning. For a rational learner, each piece of evidence that confirms prior beliefs only makes those priors stronger. Eventually the priors become so firmly established (in Bayesian terms, the priors become so precise) that new information, whether consonant or dissonant, hardly budges them one way or the other. The logic is analogous to computing the mean of a sample: when the number of observations is large, adding one more case will have only a small effect on the overall average.

A similar logic applies to learning about debtors. Consider a nation that has paid faithfully for decades through good times and bad. Investors confidently classify the debtor as a stalwart. In fact, so much evidence about the nation's stalwart credentials has accumulated that, in the estimation of investors, there is practically no chance the government could be any other type. What was once a mere hunch about the country's willingness to pay has now hardened into a taken-for-granted fact.

But suppose one day the country confounds expectations by defaulting. In a model where types never change, the default would seem highly anomalous. Investors might downgrade the debtor slightly, but with so much evidence in the debtor's favor, this one misstep would have little effect. Given the debtor's long history of good behavior, it may take de-

---

[8] Cripps, Mailath, and Samuelson 2004.

cades of sustained and blatant default to overturn the prior belief that the borrower deserved a high credit rating.

Adding a dose of political instability to theories of reputation solves this problem. Now investors need not regard the default as an inexplicable event. Instead, they can view the default as a signal of shifting preferences—a notice that the country, once run by stalwarts, has fallen under the control of fair-weathers or lemons. It is often said that reputations are hard to build and easy to destroy. Models that allow for political change can reproduce this intuition; standard theories of reputation with persistent types cannot.

The Russian default of 1917 illustrates the need to relax the conventional assumption that types never change. In the century before the Russian Revolution, the czarist governments regularly serviced their debts, and Russian bonds were seen as safe investments. After the Revolution, the new Soviet leaders not only suspended payments but actually repudiated their foreign debts by denouncing them as illegitimate contracts. In a model with constant types, this single act of defiance would have little effect. But in a theory where types can change over time, investors who observed the repudiation would conclude that preferences had shifted. By repudiating the debt, the Soviet leaders squandered their reputational patrimony.

Political instability creates room not only for reputational destruction, but also for reputational recovery. To see how this process works, consider a government that enters office carrying the reputational baggage of its predecessors, who were widely regarded as lemons. By acknowledging the debts of previous administrations and settling any existing defaults, the new government displays higher resolve and competence than expected. After a probationary period, investors become convinced that a better rating would be appropriate and upgrade the government to fair-weather status. The assumption of political instability therefore makes it possible for countries to return to grace after long stretches of willful nonperformance. In offering a fair settlement for past defaults, debtors signal that they are no longer lemons and begin, however slowly, to climb the reputational ladder.[9]

Importantly, the theory in this book allows for political change, but it does not assume that investors are knowledgeable about domestic politics. Investors can, in fact, be ignorant of elections, coups, cabinet shakeups, and other political events in the borrowing state. My theory only requires that investors acknowledge the potential for political change. The mere possibility of shifting preferences makes reputations fragile, thereby contributing to reputational destruction and recovery.

[9] As discussed in part 2, financial institutions (bondholder councils, rating agencies, etc.) help investors judge whether settlements are fair, given the circumstances.

*Initiating and Terminating Cooperation*

Instability not only allows reputations to change but also generates variation in behavior. Research about repeat play and issue linkage has tended to emphasize the optimal equilibrium, in which strategies of conditional retaliation motivate players to cooperate indefinitely. But if the equilibrium is cooperation, why do relations ever break down, and how do relations get restored? One answer, already noted, involves exogenous shocks. Some countries stop cooperating during hard times and resume after the shocks have passed. This answer is powerful but incomplete; it cannot explain starts and stops when external conditions remain the same.

A theory with political instability can complete the picture. With static preferences, it is hard to say why a long-standing payer would begin defecting during good times, or why a previously intransigent defaulter would make great sacrifices to settle its debts. These patterns become intelligible in a model where preferences change. By including political instability in theories of reputation, then, we can better understand why reputations shift abruptly and why behavior changes even when external conditions do not.

## How Reputations Affect Incentives to Cooperate

In previous sections, I explained how reputations form under conditions of incomplete information and political instability. To complete the theory and derive testable implications, I now consider how reputations affect the incentives of investors and governments.

*Reputation and the Incentives of Investors*

Investors use the reputation of the borrower—their beliefs about the borrower's preferences—to inform their risk assessments and lending decisions. Other factors equal, countries with bad reputations are seen as less likely to repay. The risk of default does not necessarily deter investors from lending, however. Investors and borrowers can benefit from exchange, even when the borrower might not service debts on time and in full. As Vincent Crawford explains, it is "not optimal to structure a loan agreement so that default . . . will not occur under any foreseeable circumstance, because risk sharing is an important source of potential gain for both borrowers and lenders."[10] For this reason, investors will

[10] Crawford 1987, 2.

lend to governments that might default, provided the probability of default is not too high and the anticipated salvage value—the amount investors could recover after a breach of contract—would still make the loan profitable.

Nevertheless, the terms of loans to a foreign government should reflect beliefs about the government's type. I argue that the investors respond to the reputations of borrowers in three ways. First, they *charge* for risk: they increase the expected return to compensate for the danger of default. Investors raise interest rates, impose fees, and purchase loans at a discount (require the borrower to pay interest and amortization on more money than it actually receives). The compensation for uncertainty is called the risk premium, which analysts often measure as the difference between the interest rate on a risky loan and the rate on an otherwise similar asset that has little or no chance of default.

Risk premiums create their own problems, however. Raising interest rates by some fixed percentage generally will not improve expected returns by a commensurate amount, because higher rates have two opposing effects: they increase the contractual obligation, but they also exacerbate the probability of default. At some point, increasing the interest rate will perversely reduce the expected return, as the heightened probability of default overwhelms the gains from charging a steeper price. Interest premiums can provide some indemnification against risk, but investors cannot raise rates without limit to compensate for the possibility of default.

Investors respond to reputation not only by charging for risk but also by *controlling* it. Often, they design contracts to reduce the probability of default and stabilize the projected cash flow. Over the centuries, investors have required governments to offer collateral and, in some cases, put pledged assets under the direct supervision of foreign banks or bondholder committees. These remedies are of somewhat limited use in international relations, however. As discussed in part 2 of this book, it has been extremely difficult—and, for most of history, illegal—to seize the assets of a foreign sovereign, and few debtors have consented to foreign control of their customshouses. More promising strategies include shortening maturities, requiring sinking funds, and asking third parties—ones with good reputations—to guarantee loans. Through these and other devices, investors attempt to limit the level of risk.[11]

Finally, when the reputation of the borrower is especially bad, investors *avoid* risk by refusing to lend. They prefer this "credit rationing" strategy when a government seems so risky that no interest rate can compensate

---

[11] Investors might also control the level of risk by focusing their loans on easily monitored projects, such as railroads and infrastructure. See Bordo, Eichengreen, and Irwin 1999, 29–30.

for the possibility of default and no contractual provisions can keep uncertainty within reasonable bounds. In this case, investors anticipate that
they would lose money (or incur an unattractive combination of risk and
return) by offering credit to the government. They would do better by
seeking alternative borrowers or refraining from lending altogether.[12]

Investors choose the optimal combination of risk premiums, contractual protections, and credit rationing, given their beliefs about the government's type. Other variables being equal, putative stalwarts receive easier
credit than reputed fair-weathers, which, in turn, enjoy better access to
international capital markets than governments classified as lemons. Any
borrower perceived as willing to pay during good times and bad can attract large loans at nearly risk-free rates, without having to offer collateral
or other legal enhancements. Investors rely more heavily on risk premiums and contractual protections when dealing with apparent fair-weathers, since those governments are expected to default when external conditions deteriorate. Finally, investors avoid lending to proven lemons and
governments that have not settled existing defaults. Lemons pose such
enormous risks that credit rationing is the optimal course of action.

I have argued that all investors learn in approximately the same way
and have similar options for coping with the risks of international lending.
I now refine the predictions by suggesting that bondholders and banks
convert beliefs into actions in slightly different ways. Bondholders have
overwhelming incentives to allocate credit based on their beliefs about
the government's type. Commercial banks, in contrast, have conflicting
priorities.

Most importantly, commercial banks have incentives to offer "defensive loans" to governments that have already defaulted. In the short term,
new loans could help the government pay interest on previous debts,
thereby sparing the banks from having to declare defaults and record
losses on their balance sheets. Over the longer term, new loans could
help the debtor revitalize its economy and increase the chance of eventual
repayment. Banks are large enough to engage in defensive lending, either
by themselves or in concert with others.

Private bondholders, on the other hand, lack the motive and the means
to engage in defensive lending. No individual bondholder has enough resources to offer defensive loans unilaterally, and it would be nearly impossible for thousands of bondholders to cooperate in extending such credit.
An investment house could float an emergency bond, but it would have

---

[12] This "credit rationing" phenomenon means that markets may not clear because the
supply of international loans does not meet the demands of extremely risky borrowers.

trouble finding a market for the new security.[13] Without some means of coercing the mass of atomized bondholders into providing new credit, the emergency issue would be doomed.

The incentives of bondholders and banks differ for a second reason: commercial banks, unlike bondholders, deal with foreign governments on many dimensions. They maintain branches in foreign countries, provide trade credit, and manage the foreign reserves of central banks. These activities provide commercial banks with a steady flow of income. Banks may, therefore, offer "loss-leader" loans to promote good relations with foreign politicians and businessmen, to stimulate the economy of the borrowing state, and to advance other lines of business. Bondholders, again, have neither the means nor the motive to offer loss-leader loans. In light of these differences, the relationship between the reputation of the borrower and the terms of loans should be stronger for bondholders than for commercial banks.

I close by emphasizing two important points about how investors use reputation. First, investors in my theory are entirely forward-looking. They raise interest rates, shorten maturities, and withhold credit to guard against future risk, not to retaliate against past cheating. The history of compliance with loan contracts is relevant as a source of data for making forecasts, not as a trigger for retribution. Retaliatory strategies, such as the grim trigger or tit-for-tat, play no role in my reputational theory.

Second, my theory requires no collective action on the part of creditors. Investors need not collude, or even know each other, to respond in similar ways. If a government defaults without adequate justification, it acquires a lemonlike reputation not only in the eyes of current investors, but also in the estimation of other individuals and institutions around the world. These parties have no incentive to extend new credit, because each independently knows that lending to a lemon would be a money-losing proposition. Thus, my theory provides a convenient solution to the problems of credibility and collective action that were discussed in chapter 1.

## Reputation and the Incentives of Governments

I now complete the theory by explaining how reputations affect the incentives of governments. Governments understand that investors are watching, and that investors update their beliefs as a function of behavior and context. An administration that defaults when external conditions

---

[13] In theory, each bondholder could gain from a defensive loan, which might increase the government's ability and willingness to service existing debts, but no single bondholder has an incentive to purchase the emergency bond.

do not justify a lapse of payments will signal (correctly or not) that it is a lemon. Likewise, a government with a history of consistent payments will earn the reputation of a stalwart, and a government that adjusts its payments to external conditions will be classified as a fair-weather. Governments know that investors and rating agencies use these simple rules, among others, to screen debtors. They also anticipate that investors will avoid lending to apparent lemons and will offer high-cost credit to reputed fair-weathers.

Given their understanding of investors, how will governments behave? A genuine stalwart could default, but it knows that any interruption of payments would damage its reputation. For stalwarts, who have relatively weak antidebt coalitions and strong preferences for future credit, the cost of breaking faith typically outweighs the benefits. To a genuine fair-weather, the domestic political costs of mimicking a stalwart generally outweigh the benefits of easier access to capital, while the fear of being miscategorized as a lemon deters the fair-weather from behaving opportunistically during favorable times. Finally, genuine lemons know they could improve their access to foreign money by making sacrifices. Nevertheless, lemons place such little value on access to future loans and face such high political costs of repayment that emulating a higher-rated government typically will not be worth the price. On average, sincere behavior is the best response to the updating rules investors use.[14]

## Testable Implications

My theory not only suggests a reputational rationale for international cooperation, but also generates many concrete predictions about the dynamics of debtor-creditor relations. In particular, investors should charge new borrowers an uncertainty premium, to compensate for the risk that the newcomer could be a lemon. If the country services its debts punctually over a number of years, thereby demonstrating its reliability, its terms of credit should gradually improve. This seasoning process will exhibit diminishing marginal returns, with each additional act of repayment enhancing access to credit by an ever-smaller amount. Over time, the interest

[14] The theory developed here does not rule out the possibility of mimicking, in which lemons and fair-weathers emulate more reputable types to boost their reputations, and stalwarts default in order to reap an immediate windfall. Given the preference profile of stalwarts, fair-weathers, and lemons, though, the costs of emulation will typically outweigh the benefits. The theory is also consistent with mixed strategies, provided that stalwarts repay with a higher probability than fair-weathers, who in turn meet their commitments more often than lemons.

rates of a consistent payer will approach the baseline rate that investors offer to low-risk borrowers.

In contrast, governments that default will lose access to capital markets. Investors will not risk another loan until the borrower settles its arrears, thereby distinguishing itself from a lemon. After all, defaulters that refuse to settle during bad times can earn no more than a fair-weather rating. Rational investors will not lend to such countries until economic conditions improve. Once good times return, though, governments that remain in default will be classified as lemons and consequently fail to attract new loans. Thus, in both bad and good times, the settlement of existing defaults should be a precondition for getting new loans from private investors.

More generally, investors will alter the terms of credit when a government acts contrary to its perceived type. They will grant easier access to a government that exceeds expectations, but tighten credit when politicians display less resolve and competence than previously anticipated. Thus, putative fair-weathers that surprise the markets by repaying during hard times will experience a reputational surge and win easier access to capital. Likewise, putative stalwarts that default will suffer a reputational loss and cease to attract loans at favorable rates.

Investors, credit analysts, and government officials should not only behave according to this reputational logic, but also express it in writings and speeches. The effects of reputation should be evident across countries and over time, rather than being limited to one historical moment or one corner of the globe. To the extent that uncertainty premiums, seasoning effects, credit rationing, settlement payments, and adjustments to surprise appear in the historical data, we should gain confidence in the reputational theory.

## Alternative Theories

The theory of reputation I develop in this book not only implies that history matters, but also explains *how* actors use history to infer the preferences of foreign governments. Reputations, I argue, reflect both behavior and context. In the area of international debt, investors rationally analyze whether the borrower repaid and the economic circumstances it faced at the time. These pieces of information—the decisions of the government and the difficulty of the test—provide important insight about the borrower's preferences and ultimately shape patterns of cooperation and conflict.

I now contrast my theory with two alternative views about reputation. The first says that actors in international relations interpret history in biased ways; the second maintains that international actors view history as relatively uninformative. I also consider a nonreputational theory, issue linkage, which holds that countries repay their debts to avoid punishment in other areas of international relations.

## Biased Learning and Reputation

I have claimed that reputations emerge from the impartial analysis of history. Undoubtedly there will be exceptions—no social scientific theory can explain all variation in human behavior—but when the stakes are high (as in global finance), people will tend to interpret history rationally.

Others have proposed a different logic, in which psychological biases distort how people learn from history, and therefore skew their conclusions about the characteristics of foreign governments. Jonathan Mercer pioneered this psychological approach to reputation.[15] In an influential book, Mercer contends that reputations change when governments act in undesirable, rather than unexpected, ways. People update their beliefs about a foreign government, he argues, only when the government acts against observers' interests. His desire-based theory of reputation represents an important alternative to my more rationalist account.

Mercer's desire-based theory of reputation rests on four assumptions. First, when explaining the behavior of a government, observers judge how much responsibility rests with the external situation and how much is due to the actor's internal characteristics or disposition. In other words, observers decide whether to make a situational attribution or a dispositional one. Second, a reputation is a judgment about someone else's character or disposition. Together, these first two assumptions imply that "a dispositional (or character-based) attribution is necessary to generate a reputation."[16]

Third, "people interpret behavior in either situational or dispositional terms depending on the desirability of that behavior. [They] use dispositional attributions to explain an out-group's undesirable behavior, and situational attributions to explain an out-group's desirable behavior."[17] In psychological studies, the term *out-group* refers to people that are seen as outsiders. Finally, Mercer assumes that all foreign governments are members of the out-group.

From these four assumptions, it logically follows that in international relations, "only undesirable behavior can generate a reputation."[18] When people see undesirable behavior by a foreign government, they assume

[15] Mercer 1996.
[16] Mercer 1996, 45.
[17] Mercer 1996, 9.
[18] Mercer 1996, 46.

the unwanted action stems from disposition and update their beliefs about the government's type. But when people see a foreign government acting in desirable ways, they credit the situation instead of the government's entrenched characteristics.

The predictions of desire-based theory differ sharply from my own. I have hypothesized that, by repaying debts, governments can improve their reputations in the eyes of foreign investors. Desire-based theory leads to different predictions: repayment does not improve one's reputation, and reputations deteriorate over time. If investors, who dislike default, follow the logic of desire-based theory, they will make dispositional attributions when a government defaults but cite the situation when the government repays. Consequently a sovereign cannot earn a reputation for honesty or reliability in relations with foreign investors, and its standing before lenders can never improve. As Mercer notes, the sovereign "cannot win."

The two theories also make different predictions about the effect of contextual variables. In my theory, investors use data about context to refine their inferences. Repayment during an economic depression, for example, counts as a stronger signal of resolve than repayment during good times. But in desire-based theory, contextual variables play no independent explanatory role. When deciding whether to make a situational attribution, desire-based observers ironically ignore data about the situation and focus instead on whether the government behaved desirably. If the behavior seems desirable, observers seize upon real or imagined circumstances to rationalize what the government did, but if the behavior seems undesirable, they overlook potentially exculpatory data about the economic, political, or social context.

One can, therefore, test my theory against the desire-based alternative. If desire-based theory is correct, countries that repay should not receive progressively higher credit ratings and lower interest rates. Moreover, the consequences of default and repayment should not depend on actual economic circumstances. Finally, in books and articles about investment, experts should not make dispositional attributions when governments repay. I predict the opposite patterns.

### Current Calculations without Reputation

My theory and the desire-based alternative should be tested not only against each other, but also against the null hypothesis that decision makers tend to ignore history. Perhaps international actors—both public officials and private citizens such as investors—focus on the "here and now." They judge the credibility of foreign governments by studying fresh intelligence, not by reviewing the annals of international relations. A government's history of compliance with international commitments would, therefore, have little effect on beliefs about the government today.

Why would decision makers pay little attention to past actions? Daryl Press provides a plausible rationale.[19] His "current calculus" theory does not portray leaders as ignorant or dim-witted. Rather, it envisages leaders as careful thinkers who use history only in low-pressure situations. Historical analogies are, according to current calculus theory, "quick-and-dirty heuristics," mental shortcuts that simplify inferences. These heuristics serve people well for mundane calculations such as "the odds that our friend will show up at the movies," but they are reckless to invoke in more serious situations. As the stakes increase, people "abandon simple heuristics in favor of more careful 'systematic' reasoning."[20]

Current calculus theory makes two important assumptions that differ from my own. First, current calculus theory presumes that decision makers can, if they choose, measure the preferences and abilities of foreign governments directly and in real time. Second, current calculus theory says that the predictive power of current intelligence significantly exceeds the predictive power of history. For this reason, leaders in high-stakes situations expend extra effort "to gather more data and to model the situation more thoroughly," rather than drawing lessons from the past.[21]

In contrast, I assume that history contains unique and valuable information. As any participant or scholar of international relations knows, it is difficult to measure what foreign leaders want and what price they would pay to get it.[22] One can make educated guesses based on current information about political actors and institutions. But such information is likely to be incomplete, and the interpretation will depend on assumptions about how politics in each country works. Without disputing the value of current intelligence, I suggest that history has something to add. By observing past behavior in a variety of circumstances, one can gain additional insight into the preferences of foreign governments. Moreover, even if one could learn everything about foreign politics by direct observation, rather than historical inference, it is not obvious that people would make the investment. After all, current calculations are costly; they require extensive study of politics in foreign countries. Past actions, in contrast, provide insight on the cheap.

Both views of decision making are, of course, plausible. The best way to judge my theory against current calculus theory is not to debate the assumptions, but to investigate whether actors refer to past behavior

---

[19] Press 2005.

[20] Press 2005, 6.

[21] Press 2005, 23.

[22] On the challenges associated with knowing the motivations of countries and their leaders, see Frieden 1999.

when judging the credibility of foreign governments. If current calculus theory is correct in the area of sovereign debt, investors should not cite the repayment record of the government as an important indicator of creditworthiness. Instead, they should emphasize direct, real-time measures of political and economic conditions. Moreover, we should not expect past defaults or repayments to influence interest rates and access to capital, after controlling for information investors had at the time.

It is harder to say what current calculus theory predicts about the behavior of debtors. If investors focus entirely on the here and now, foreign governments should not expect default to have reputational consequences. They should recognize that credibility depends on current conditions and not obsess about their repayment records. It might seem, therefore, that one could test current calculus theory against my own not only by scrutinizing the behavior of lenders, but also by studying the behavior of borrowers.

Press insists that current calculus theory makes no such prediction, however. The theory says that leaders reject past actions as a basis for judging the credibility of other states, including foreign borrowers. But those same leaders could, without contradicting Press's theory, mistakenly assume that everyone else—prospective lenders included—draws inferences from the past. In fact, Press's own reading of history suggests that leaders invest heavily in their own reputations while ignoring everyone else's. Why would leaders behave this way? Press acknowledges that his "rationalist story seems to have a nonrationalist underpinning."[23]

In part 2, I test current calculus theory by investigating whether lenders ignore the past. I also explore the possibility that *both* lenders and borrowers disregard history. This stronger version of current calculus theory would eliminate any reputational incentive to repay and force us to consider other sources of debtor-creditor cooperation.

## Issue Linkage and Cooperation

Many scholars argue that cooperation between debtors and creditors stems from issue linkage, rather than reputation. The key idea was introduced in chapter 1. Either by themselves or with help from their governments, creditors establish a tactical link between financial and nonfinancial relations. They threaten to retaliate against defaulters by sending gunboats or disrupting trade. These "direct sanctions," as they are called in the economics literature, can create powerful incentives to repay.

---

[23] Press 2005, 158.

Reputational and linkage theories are not mutually exclusive, but they are logically distinct. To understand why investors lend and governments repay, it is important to establish the empirical prevalence of these two mechanisms. Across countries and over the centuries, have lending and repayment been sustained mainly by concerns about reputation, or by threats of cannon fire and commercial interference? Having already derived many testable implications of my reputational theory, I conclude by describing an empirical strategy for detecting the presence of issue linkage.

Linkage models make specific predictions about the behavior of debtors and creditors. For instance, countries that are highly vulnerable to military and commercial retaliation should service their debts more scrupulously than countries that can better withstand retaliation. By extension, investors should withhold loans from militarily and commercially invulnerable countries, while offering the lowest interest rates to governments than can be punished most easily. Moreover, if a debtor decides to default selectively by repaying some debts but reneging on others, it should minimize the cost of noncompliance by giving priority to the strongest creditors—those most capable of imposing sanctions—while relegating relatively weaker creditors to the bottom of the repayment queue. Finally, investment analysts and credit rating agencies, which are paid to offer accurate and useful advice, should emphasize the threat of direct sanctions as a key criterion in lending decisions. These patterns, and others derived later in the book, are not implied by my theory of reputation.

## Plan for Subsequent Chapters

The reputational theory in this book provides a general explanation for compliance with debt contracts and other international commitments. In a condition of anarchy, governments uphold their international commitments to avoid being classified as unreliable types and excluded from potentially beneficial agreements. The theory not only accounts for cooperation under anarchy, but also generates a wide range of predictions about the dynamics of debtor-creditor relations.

Part 2 tests the predictions of my theory and the leading alternatives. For each theory I identify many observable implications: patterns of behavior we would expect to find if the theory epitomized debtor-creditor relations. I then measure how extensively the expected patterns appear in data from international capital markets. My strategy involves putting each theory at risk as many times as possible by scrutinizing a large number of observable implications over the past three hundred years.

Chapters 3 through 5 test key predictions of my reputational theory. In chapter 3, I examine how investors treated new and seasoned borrowers during the 1700s and 1800s. Those two centuries are particularly interesting because many new countries emerged and tapped capital markets for the first time. Statistical and qualitative data indicate that investors demanded a significant premium from new borrowers, precisely because they lacked information about the type of government they were confronting. Without the reassurance of a long and unblemished credit history, investors prudently decided to cover their risks. As the chapter shows, countries that repaid their early debts were able to reborrow at lower interest rates, which converged asymptotically to the levels of well-seasoned debtors. In contrast, countries that defaulted on their first loans were branded as unreliable. Until those countries settled their defaults, thereby signaling a commitment to repayment, investors refrained from offering new credit.

Chapter 4 considers a different source of evidence. Over the centuries, an industry has emerged to advise investors about lending money to foreign governments. Bankers, financial analysts, and rating agencies have commented in countless books and articles on which sovereigns were most creditworthy and for what reasons. In the competitive world of investment analysis, these authors have strong pecuniary incentives to offer accurate and useful advice. Through a systematic analysis of expert opinion, we can gauge the importance of reputation and issue linkage. The data, drawn from a representative sample of investment texts published in the United States and Britain during the 1920s, strongly support the reputational theory. The vast majority of authors identified reputation as a top consideration when investing in foreign securities, and their comments revealed a logic of reputation that closely matched my theory. In contrast, I found very little discussion of direct sanctions. Other data, including the content of bond advertisements, rating manuals, and securities regulations, as well as remarks from bankers and fund managers during the late 1990s, corroborate these findings.

Chapter 5 reinforces the analysis by examining how reputations formed in good times and bad. During the boom period of the 1920s, as in the most prosperous phases of the eighteenth and nineteenth centuries, investors charged higher rates to new borrowers. Moreover, they steered clear of apparent lemons that defaulted when external conditions did not justify a lapse. The Great Depression made it difficult for investors to distinguish lemons from fair-weathers, but it provided new opportunities to identify the stalwarts. Under my theory, a putative fair-weather that pays during hard times will climb the reputational ladder, and investors will extend easier credit that reflects new beliefs about the debtor. I test this proposition against data from the Great Depression, when a few hard-hit debtors exceeded expectations by meeting their obligations in full. Detailed case studies show that these surprising payers were able to refinance their debts at lower interest rates. Moreover, both archival data and investment commentary attribute the outcome to the reputation those countries gained by paying under adversity.

The evidence in chapters 3–5 not only supports my theory, but also casts doubt on alternative models of reputation in international relations. Contrary to desire-based theory, investors make dispositional attributions even when the borrower behaves in desirable ways, and they take situational data (such as the Great Depression) into account when interpreting the behavior of foreign governments. Against current calculus theory, investors regularly use past actions to predict future behavior. There is, therefore, a strong correlation between credit histories and access to capital, even after controlling for other indicators available to investors. Finally, the desire of leaders to protect and enhance their reputations follows naturally from my theory, but is perplexing if not inexplicable in current calculus and desire-based models.

Chapters 6 through 8 test the predictions of nonreputational theories, in which investors use issue linkage and other retaliatory strategies to enforce cooperation. Chapter 6 focuses on the gunboat hypothesis. Many scholars have argued that, before World War I, creditor countries used their militaries to deter governments from defaulting and to collect debts from deadbeats. I show that the apparent correlation between default and military intervention is spurious. Debt default and military intervention coincided, not because the great powers sent forces to assist bondholders, but because they were responding to civil wars, territorial conflicts, and tort claims that happened to arise while debtors were in default. Moreover, creditors generally did not threaten foreign borrowers with military retaliation, and patterns of lending and repayment do not fit the military linkage hypothesis. Thus, contrary to popular wisdom, there is surprisingly little evidence of a systematic connection between military power and debt repayment.

Chapter 7 studies the hypothesized linkage between debt and trade. After dismissing the prospect of punishment via asset seizure and trade credits, the chapter focuses on the ultimate commercial sanction: a trade embargo imposed on behalf of creditors by their home government. The chapter presents a detailed study of Argentine debt policy in the 1930s, which scholars often cite to illustrate the plausibility of trade sanctions. Contrary to the conventional wisdom, I show that Argentina repaid its debts to signal its resolve and enhance its reputation, not to avert a trade war with Britain. I then check the generality of this conclusion by conducting a cross-country investigation of debtor behavior during the 1930s, the decade when linkage between debt and trade supposedly reached its height. My statistical analysis shows that governments did not service debts in proportion to their dependence on trade with creditors, nor did they offer preferential treatment to the lenders that were most capable of imposing a trade embargo.

Chapter 8 considers a final measure of retaliatory power: the cohesion of the creditor cartel. At least in theory, a rock-solid cartel could impose penalties that are beyond the reach of atomized lenders. I show that commercial banks are far stronger and better organized than private bondholders. Nevertheless, investors over the centuries have tended to lend directly, in the form of bonds, rather than maximizing their punishment power by lending through banks and other organized intermediaries. I then consider a unique moment in history, the late twentieth century, when both bondholders and banks played key roles in sovereign lending. During that period, borrowers did not treat organized creditors (banks) better than disorganized ones (bondholders). Moreover, organized creditors did not charge lower rates than disorganized ones. In short, the cohesion of creditors—so important in theories of sanctioning—appears to have little impact on the actual behavior of borrowers and lenders.

The empirical evidence in this book points overwhelmingly in one direction. Across three centuries of international finance, reputations have formed in consistent ways and profoundly influenced the flow of international capital. Direct sanctions, by comparison, have played a surprisingly minor role in debtor-creditor relations. Chapter 9 concludes the book by discussing the policy implications of these findings, and how my theory of reputation could apply to other areas of international relations.

# Part II

## EVIDENCE

# Chapter 3 ————————————————————————————

## Reputations of New and Seasoned Borrowers

THIS CHAPTER BEGINS the empirical analysis by testing three implications of the reputational theory. First, investors will offer worse credit to an unproven government than to better-known entities, as compensation for the risk that the new borrower is a lemon. The compensation will take the form of an "uncertainty premium": an extra interest charge, above and beyond the baseline rate a seasoned borrower would pay for access to foreign capital. Furthermore, when information is so poor that credit histories offer the primary—if not the only—basis for assessing risk, the premium should be roughly the same for all new borrowers in the same cohort.

Second, if the new borrower services its debts punctually over a number of years, thereby distinguishing itself from a lemon, its access to credit will improve. The improvement will occur even when the borrower pays during good times, but should be especially pronounced if it honors the debt when external conditions warrant a default. This seasoning process will exhibit diminishing marginal returns, with each additional payment enhancing reputation by a smaller amount. At some point, when investors become highly certain that the government is not a lemon, paying during a good situation will only preserve—not improve—the government's reputation. Thus, the risk premiums of seasoned borrowers should converge asymptotically to a baseline rate.

Third, the theory predicts that impenitent defaulters will not be able to raise new capital on international markets. If a borrower defaults and refuses to offer adequate compensation, rational investors will shy away from extending new loans for fear of throwing good money after bad. The exclusion will continue, even across changes in government, until an administration offers what investors regard as a fair settlement. By signaling that the country is no longer under the control of a bad type, debt settlements make investors more willing to commit new funds.

I test these hypotheses against a unique collection of data from the eighteenth and nineteenth centuries. Specifically, I identify key moments when new borrowers emerged on the scene, and I ask how credit markets treated those newcomers, relative to more established borrowers. I also investigate the dynamics of reputation by testing whether the uncertainty premium declined over time, conditional on a healthy record of repayment. Finally, I follow the history of countries that defaulted to see whether they could raise new capital without first offering a settlement to creditors. The empirical analysis, based on primary sources compiled here for the first time, strongly supports all three hypotheses about how reputations form in capital markets.

## The Amsterdam Market in the Eighteenth Century

During the eighteenth century, many sovereign governments borrowed money on international markets. With few exceptions, they turned to the Dutch province of Holland, a region of unrivaled wealth and commercial supremacy, and one with surplus capital that could be channeled abroad.[1] The leading governments of the world and a number of minor principalities floated bonds on the Amsterdam market during the 1700s.[2] Lending expanded steadily throughout the century, reaching a peak just before the Napoleonic Wars that brought the system to a halt. By investigating how Dutch investors treated new borrowers, as distinguished from seasoned ones, we can gain a clearer sense of how reputations formed during this important period.

Dutch investors of the 1700s did not possess detailed information about the socioeconomic health of foreign borrowers. According to historian James Riley, "Neither the political nor the commercial news available in Dutch periodicals was sufficient to evaluate creditworthiness among debtor states. Nor were government revenue and expenditure accounts often published elsewhere."[3] Without reliable information about political and economic fundamentals that affected the propensity to default, the Dutch probably relied on the credit histories of governments to guide their lending decisions.

To see whether investors demanded higher yields from new borrowers, I first needed information about when each country began raising money in Amsterdam. I therefore built an inventory of foreign government loans that were launched on the Amsterdam market between 1695 and the Napoleonic Wars. The data, gathered in collaboration with Joost Jonker and Nico van Horn at Utrecht University, came from the Nederlandsch Economisch-Historisch Archief, the Gemeentearchief, and other repositories of manuscripts and published texts.[4] Our final list contained 577

[1] Other financial centers included Geneva, Hamburg, Genoa, Frankfurt, Vienna, and London, but Amsterdam dominated the market for foreign government loans.

[2] Riley 1980; Vries and Woude 1997, 139–47.

[3] Riley 1980, 39.

[4] The sources are listed in the bibliography at the end of the book. I thank Joost Jonker and Nico van Horn for their work in the Dutch archives. The sample begins with 1695. There were earlier Dutch loans, the first taking place in 1616, when 248,000 guilders were

bonds, the first issued in 1695, when Deutz & Soon underwrote a 1.55-million-guilder loan to the government of Austria with an interest rate of 5 percent and a maturity of 12 years. This new inventory of Dutch loans is the most comprehensive and detailed in existence. It reveals when countries borrowed in Amsterdam during the eighteenth century, as well as the nominal interest rates and sizes of most loans.[5]

I also gathered data on bond yields in order to compare the perceived riskiness of borrowers. In finance, the yield measures the annual income of a bond as a percentage of its market price. As argued in chapter 2, investors respond to risk—up to a point—by charging higher interest rates and paying lower prices. Consequently, the yield of a bond, computed as the nominal interest rate divided by the current price, should increase with the perceived riskiness of the borrower.

The earliest surviving interest rate and price quotations appear in a handwritten report from Vizconde de la Herrería, Spanish ambassador at The Hague, to his foreign minister, the Marqués de Grimaldi. De la Herrería's report, on deposit at the General Archive of Simancas in Spain, contains interest rates and prices for several government loans that were traded in Amsterdam during July 1771.[6] I used the data in the report to compute current yields for sovereign borrowers in 1771.[7]

Table 3.1 reports the bond yields, along with the years in which the countries first borrowed. In this table and throughout the chapter, I define a new borrower as a country with a credit history of less than 10 years. According to the table, the average yield on loans to new borrowers was

---

advanced to the elector of Brandenburg. But most Dutch capital flows during the seventeenth century were foreign *direct* investments, rather than international loans.

[5] Although the inventory is extensive, we cannot be sure we found every eighteenth-century foreign loan. Omissions would bias the analysis against my reputational theory, however. If the inventory is incomplete, some seasoned borrowers may be misclassified as new ones. This would tend to reduce average yields in the new-borrower category, and therefore narrow the observed gap between new and seasoned borrowers.

[6] Vizconde de la Herrería to Marqués de Grimaldi, November 19, 1772, Sección de Estado, Legajo 6364, Archivo General de Simancas.

[7] For each country, I identified the lowest nominal interest rate on bonds that were not guaranteed by a foreign power, and then calculated yields based on the average of the minimum and the maximum quoted price for bonds at that interest rate. The report also contains interest rates and price quotations for loans to plantation communities in the West Indies, including Essequibo/Demerara, the Danish Islands, Grenada, and Surinam. As these were not sovereign, and thus not comparable with countries like Denmark and Sweden, I excluded them from the analysis. De la Herrería did not list prices for two seasoned borrowers, England and France. In 1771 France issued a 4 percent bond, which I used to approximate the yield. Yields on English bonds were at least as low, so adding England to table 3.1 would only accentuate the difference between seasoned and new borrowers. Herrería did not include an entry for one new borrower, Prussia, which floated its first bond in 1769 at 5 percent, the level typically charged to new borrowers.

TABLE 3.1
Bond Yields of Seasoned and New Borrowers, Amsterdam, 1771

|                      | Earliest Loan | Yield in 1771 |
|----------------------|---------------|---------------|
| Seasoned borrowers   |               |               |
| Austria              | 1695          | 3.8           |
| France               | 1720          | 4.0           |
| Saxony               | 1730          | 4.0           |
| Danzig               | 1734          | 4.9           |
| Denmark              | 1757          | 4.0           |
| Average              |               | 4.1           |
| New borrowers        |               |               |
| Leipzig              | 1764          | 4.2           |
| Brunswick Luneburg   | 1765          | 5.1           |
| Mecklenburg          | 1765          | 5.0           |
| Sweden               | 1767          | 5.0           |
| Russia               | 1768          | 5.1           |
| Spain                | 1769          | 6.1           |
| Average              |               | 5.1           |

Source: Yields were computed by the author from the report of Vizconde de la Herrería, November 19, 1772. The yield for France was ap-
proximated from the 4 percent bond it launched in 1771. Loan dates were
obtained from the database of new issues described in the text.
Note: The earliest loan is defined as the first known loan in Amsterdam
since 1695.

a full percentage point higher than yields for more seasoned debtors. In
relative terms this represents a substantial difference: new borrowers
were charged approximately 25 percent more than established participants in capital markets. Moreover, this estimate does not include the
outsized commissions that underwriters demanded from new borrowers
to cover the extra risk and labor costs of marketing the bonds of unproven states.

The considerable disparity in yields almost certainly did not arise by
chance. A $t$-test for equality of means indicates a probability of less than
.01 of observing a difference this large if investors truly did not discriminate according to the length of the credit history.[8] This finding is robust
to the elimination of any country in the list and to changes in the "cut-

[8] The difference in means is 0.95 percentage points, with a standard error of 0.30 and a
$t$-statistic of 3.2 with 8.9 degrees of freedom. The probability of observing a difference this
large in repeated draws from populations with equal means is .01. The 95 percent confidence interval around the difference in means runs from 0.27 to 1.63.

date" that separates new from seasoned borrowers.[9] Moreover, even within the class of new borrowers, yields fell with experience. Leipzig, the most proven of the new entrants (with approximately seven years of faithful repayment), boasted a yield only slightly higher than the average of its fully seasoned counterparts. Spain, in contrast, was the newest and riskiest borrower in the set. Thus, investors demanded a premium from countries that lacked a substantial credit history.[10]

The gap in table 3.1 gradually narrowed as the new borrowers repaid their debts, demonstrating that they, too, could be trusted. By the 1780s the average risk differential in table 3.1 had almost completely disappeared. Having distinguished themselves from lemons through more than a decade of punctual repayment, countries like Russia and Sweden could borrow in the 1780s at the same low rates as Austria and Denmark. At precisely that moment, however, Poland and the United States approached the Dutch market for the first time. Investors charged those new borrowers a premium, perhaps to guard against the risk of lemons.

Evidence of these patterns comes from a second unique document, a "price courant" of bonds that were traded in Amsterdam on October 6, 1783. Based on the nominal interest rates and prices in the document, I computed current yields for the same foreign borrowers Herrería had considered more than a decade earlier.[11] The results appear in table 3.2. The top portion of the table contains the most seasoned borrowers, all of which had issued debt on the Dutch market before the 1760s. The middle cluster is composed of sovereigns that launched their first bonds in Amsterdam during the years 1764–69, and the bottom section reports the

---

[9] For instance, reclassifying Leipzig as a seasoned borrower only strengthens the result; shifting Denmark to the set of new borrowers weakens the finding only slightly; and dropping Sweden, which experienced political upheaval in 1771, has no effect.

[10] The evidence in table 3.1 is strong but not unassailable. If the economies of seasoned borrowers were significantly healthier than the economies of new borrowers, current calculus theory predicts that investors would have charged seasoned borrowers less, not because of their unblemished record, but instead because of their economic fundamentals. As noted earlier, though, Dutch investors had little information about the economic conditions of borrowers (Riley 1980, 39). Economic statistics did not become widely available to foreign investors until the late nineteenth century. Statistical analysis for that time period, presented later in this chapter, confirms that even after controlling for such variables, investors required significantly higher yields from new borrowers than from seasoned ones.

[11] Oudermeulen 1791, vol. 2, part 2, 263–68. As with the Herrería data, I identified (for each borrower) the lowest nominal interest rate on bonds that were not guaranteed by a foreign power, and then calculated yields based on the average of the minimum and the maximum quoted price for bonds at that interest rate. In the case of Poland this was not possible, since the only entry pertained to a 5 percent bond guaranteed by Russia, which must have improved the marketability of the issue. Thus, the yield for Poland in table 3.2 probably represents a lower bound.

TABLE 3.2
Bond Yields of Seasoned and New Borrowers, Amsterdam, 1783

|  | Earliest Loan | Yield in 1783 |
|---|---|---|
| **Long-established borrowers** | | |
| Austria | 1695 | 3.5 |
| France | 1720 | 3.9 |
| Saxony | 1730 | 4.9 |
| Danzig | 1734 | 5.0 |
| Denmark | 1757 | 4.0 |
| Average | | 4.3 |
| **Recently seasoned borrowers** | | |
| Leipzig | 1764 | 3.5 |
| Brunswick Luneburg | 1765 | 4.9 |
| Mecklenburg | 1765 | 4.0 |
| Sweden | 1767 | 4.1 |
| Russia | 1768 | 4.2 |
| Spain | 1769 | 5.4 |
| Average | | 4.3 |
| **New (unseasoned) borrowers** | | |
| Poland | 1776 | 5.0 |
| United States | 1778 | 5.1 |
| Average | | 5.0 |

Source: Yields were computed by the author from Oudermeulen 1791, which gives interest rates and prices for October 6, 1783. Loan dates were obtained from the database of new issues described in the text.
Note: The earliest loan is defined as the first known loan in Amsterdam since 1695.

yields of two new states, Poland and the United States, which did not approach the Dutch market until 1776 or later.

A comparison of the yields across these three clusters supports the theory of reputation in chapter 2. On average, bonds of highly seasoned borrowers in the top panel carried a yield of 4.3 percent. Those countries had long ago demonstrated their commitment to pay, causing investors to waive the uncertainty premium. Additional years of borrowing and repayment conveyed relatively little new information about the creditworthiness of the borrower, which helps explain why the yields in the top panel were no lower than what investors had demanded in 1771.[12] By

---

[12] The average yield for long-established borrowers was actually a bit higher in 1783 than in 1771, but we cannot reject the hypothesis that difference arose purely by chance (p-value = .55). Moreover, Oudermeulen (1791) did not provide price data for Saxony's 3.5 percent bond, which probably carried a lower yield than the one reported in table 3.2.

continuing to borrow and repay during the late eighteenth century, countries in the top panel confirmed what investors already knew.

Remarkably, countries in the middle panel also boasted yields of 4.3 percent on average, down from 5.1 percent a decade earlier. By 1783 investors had monitored the repayment patterns of newcomers like Russia and Sweden for more than a decade and had been satisfied with the punctual record of repayment. Consequently, the yields of every country in the middle panel fell, and most managed to join the 4 percent club. Based on the data in table 3.2, it is statistically impossible to distinguish the yields of long-established borrowers with those in the intermediate group.[13] Apparently, the new borrowers of 1765–70 had become proven veterans by the 1780s.

The finding holds, albeit less strongly, if we eliminate small principalities and focus on major powers: Austria, France, and Denmark in the top panel, and Russia, Sweden, and Spain in the middle. Using that subset of data, the mean for well-established debtors is approximately 3.8 percent, while the average for more recently seasoned borrowers is 0.75 percentage points higher. Though substantial, a gap of that size represents a marked improvement over the 1.4-percentage-point differential that separated the seasoned and new powers a decade earlier. This difference continued to narrow over the next few years. Figure 3.1 traces the evolution of bonds for Spain, whose relatively high yield in 1783 raised the average for the intermediate group. The figure shows that, by the late 1780s, Spanish yields had converged asymptotically with the other seasoned borrowers. At that point, all six powers could borrow in Amsterdam at the same low rate of around 4 percent.

Table 3.2 further demonstrates that, as in 1771, investors in 1783 treated new borrowers differently from seasoned ones. The bottom panel displays the yields for Poland and the United States, whose bonds appeared on the Dutch market for the first time in the late 1770s. Investors demanded a new-country rate of 5 percent from both states, repeating the pattern from 1771. The United States, in particular, had trouble raising money in Amsterdam, and John Adams decried the high interest rates and commissions his government was required to pay.[14] Although the United States did not always maintain punctual service on those early loans, Hamilton's funding plan of 1790 helped establish the credit of the United States, which eventually proved its creditworthiness and joined the ranks of low-risk borrowers.

---

[13] The difference between the average yields of the two groups is only 0.08 percentage points, with a 95 percent confidence interval that runs from −1.00 to 0.83.

[14] Winter 1977.

FIGURE 3.1: YIELDS OF SPANISH BONDS ON THE AMSTERDAM MARKET, 1783–93
*Source*: Author's calculations from Oudermeulen 1791 and the *Maandelijksche Nederlandsche Mercurius*.

Finally, the yields in tables 3.1 and 3.2 clustered around two levels, 4 and 5 percent. This bimodal distribution is intelligible given the information-poor environment of the eighteenth century. Investors distinguished seasoned borrowers from unseasoned ones, but within each category it proved difficult to differentiate, since indicators of wealth, government revenues, and foreign trade were not available on a timely and consistent basis. Although reputational theory does not explain all the variation in yields, credit records played a central role in investment decisions.

In summary, Dutch investors of the 1700s applied a simple rule when lending to foreign governments: charge higher rates to unseasoned borrowers than to ones with a history of repayment. Through a policy of regular annuity payments and punctual amortization, governments signaled their creditworthiness and obtained lower interest rates, but diminishing returns eventually set in. In Amsterdam the yields of proven borrowers asymptotically approached 3.5–4 percent, the baseline rate for seasoned sovereigns.[15] Empirically, the process of convergence took any-

[15] Riley (1980, 55, 94) provides qualitative confirmation of these results: "Numerous sources indicate that investors judged borrowers chiefly by the regularity of annuity payments and the punctuality of reimbursements. Those satisfied, Dutch rentiers were confident in the integrity of their investment and . . . willing to reinvest in prolongations or take up

where from 10 to 20 years. Overall, data from the 1700s provide strong evidence of uncertainty premiums and seasoning effects, both of which were predicted by the reputational theory in chapter 2.

Dutch lending reached its peak in the 1770s–1790s, only to be interrupted by the Napoleonic Wars. When French troops occupied Amsterdam in 1795, the underwriting of new loans virtually ground to a halt. The crisis naturally led to a pandemic of defaults across Europe, but all the major borrowers settled their arrears and resumed payment after the hostilities ceased. Russia, for instance, defaulted in 1812 in response to the Napoleonic invasion but restarted payments soon after Waterloo. According to historian Marten Buist, the quick resumption of payment after an excusable default "earned Russia a reputation for creditworthiness and solidity . . . from which she was to profit until the collapse of the czarist régime in 1917."[16] In the aftermath of the war, though, a new financial center had emerged, located not in Holland but across the North Sea in England.

## The London Market in the Early Nineteenth Century

The British lending boom began in 1817, when Baring Brothers collaborated with the Dutch house of Hope & Co. to underwrite a loan for France. A year later N. M. Rothschild arranged the first postwar foreign loan denominated in sterling: a five-million-pound credit for the Kingdom of Prussia. By the mid-1820s most European governments had raised debt on the London market, as had the newly independent Latin American states. For the next century, London served as the center of international finance.[17]

Did British investors demand higher yields from new borrowers, as did the Dutch in the 1700s? To find out, I built a comprehensive inventory of foreign government bonds that were issued and traded in London during

---

fresh loans." In Amsterdam, "the operative principle" was that repayers "would be able to reduce credit costs in later loans."

[16] Buist 1974, 274.

[17] Many studies contributed to my understanding of nineteenth-century lending. See especially Aggarwal 1996; Bordo and Rockoff 1996; Clarke 1878; Clemens and Williamson 2004; Dawson 1990; Edelstein 1982; Feis 1930; Ferguson 1998, 1999, 2005b, 2006; Ferguson and Schularick 2006; Fishlow 1985; Flandreau 2003; Flandreau and Zumer 2004; Jenks 1927; Kelly 1998; Kindleberger 1993, chap. 12; Lindert and Morton 1989; Mauro, Sussman, and Yafeh 2006; Mitchener and Weidenmier 2005b; Mosley 2003, chap. 7; Obstfeld and Taylor 2003, 2004; O'Rourke and Williamson 1999, chaps. 11–12; Rippy 1959; Suter 1990, 1992; and Taylor 2006. For statistics on British capital exports in this period, see Stone 1999. The best historical analysis of Latin American debt and default over the long run remains Marichal 1989.

the years 1817–1913. Specialized yearbooks such as *Fortune's Epitome of the Stocks and Public Funds* and *Fenn's Compendium of the English and Foreign Funds* proved invaluable, because they listed every foreign bond and summarized the borrower's record of repayment.[18] I then identified the two periods in which the greatest number of new borrowers emerged: the 1820s and the 1870s. Both periods offer new opportunities to test for uncertainty premiums, seasoning effects, and other implications of the reputational theory. I examine the 1820s first, and consider the 1870s later in the chapter.

During the early 1820s, British investors not only purchased the bonds of established borrowers, but also lent to new countries that were borrowing abroad for the first time. Table 3.3 documents the coexistence of seasoned and new borrowers on the London Stock Exchange. The upper half of the table lists seasoned borrowers that had proven their mettle on the Amsterdam exchange, thereby demonstrating a propensity to repay foreign debts. In contrast, the bottom half lists the new states of Latin America and Europe that emerged after the Napoleonic Wars and issued their first foreign bonds during the years 1822–24.

Like their Dutch predecessors, British investors of the 1820s lent to these states under conditions of poor information. "The financial press was virtually non-existent," so investors could not turn to specialized financial newspapers and journals for information about the creditworthiness of foreign states.[19] In fact, the *Bankers' Magazine* and the *Economist*, two of the earliest investment periodicals, began publication only in the 1840s. Before then, investors learned about foreign countries through popular travel accounts, an occasional investment manual, and a money-market column that first appeared in the London *Times* and other newspapers around 1822. British papers did not station correspondents in Latin America and other distant regions, but instead relied upon merchant reports and foreign newspapers that arrived via mail packet. In this low-information environment, the credit history of borrowers should have had a substantial impact on investment decisions.

I tested for uncertainty premiums by analyzing the yields of new and seasoned borrowers in July 1824 and July 1825. The dates were chosen to maximize the number of countries in the sample. As table 3.3 shows, the young states did not raise debt simultaneously, but instead floated loans in a staggered fashion. Colombia, Chile, and Peru borrowed in 1822; Argentina, Brazil, Mexico, and Greece waited until 1824. Moreover, although Austria and Portugal had amassed records on the Amsterdam market, they

---

[18] The bibliography contains a complete list of investment manuals that I consulted to build the inventory.

[19] Dawson 1990, 17.

TABLE 3.3
Bond Yields of Seasoned and New Borrowers, London, 1824–25

| | Earliest Loan | Yield in 1824 | Yield in 1825 |
|---|---|---|---|
| **Seasoned borrowers** | | | |
| Austria | 1695 | 5.3 | 5.1 |
| Denmark | 1757 | 5.1 | 5.0 |
| France | 1720 | 5.0 | 4.9 |
| Naples | 1807 | 5.7 | 5.4 |
| Portugal | 1802 | 5.7 | 5.7 |
| Prussia | 1769 | 5.1 | 4.9 |
| Russia | 1768 | 5.3 | 5.2 |
| Average | | 5.3 | 5.1 |
| **New borrowers** | | | |
| Argentina | 1824 | 7.0 | 6.5 |
| Brazil | 1824 | [a] | 6.1 |
| Chile | 1822 | 8.0 | 7.4 |
| Colombia[b] | 1822 | 7.4 | 6.9 |
| Greece | 1824 | 10.7 | 11.8 |
| Mexico | 1824 | 9.2 | 6.6 |
| Peru | 1822 | 10.1 | 8.0 |
| Average | | 8.7 | 7.6 |
| Difference in yield | | 3.4 | 2.5 |
| Standard error | | 0.6 | 0.7 |

*Source*: Yields were computed by the author from *Course of the Exchange*, July 1824 and July 1825. Loan dates were obtained from the database of new issues described in the text.

*Note*: The earliest loan is defined as the first known loan in either Amsterdam or London since 1695. The yeilds are monthly averages.

[a] Data were not available for Brazil in July 1824, since it did not borrow until October of that year.

[b] Refers to the territory of Gran Colombia, which comprised the future nations of Colombia, Ecuador, and Venezuela.

did not borrow in London until late 1823, so quotations were not available for these states during the earliest phase of British lending. By 1824–25, price data were available for all the countries in the table.

The dates were also chosen to avoid biasing the estimates by including defaulters in the sample. For many investors the lending boom of the 1820s ended with a discouraging bust, in which the new borrowers in table 3.3 (except Brazil) suspended payment on their foreign debts. Several Latin American countries defaulted in 1826, and investors correctly anticipated that others would follow suit. The hypothesis under investigation—that investors require high interest rates from unproven borrowers—assumes that the borrower has not revealed its type. Once the borrower defaults, thereby demonstrating its unreliability, yields should soar. Had I extended the sample period past 1825, the enormous yields of defaulters would have artificially inflated the average difference between seasoned and new borrowers.

The focus on 1824–25 does exclude a few countries, but their absence should not noticeably affect the results. In the category of new borrowers, the first omitted entry is Poyais, a fictitious state that nonetheless borrowed on the London market in 1822! Poyais does not appear in table 3.3 because investors discovered the fraud in 1823 and ceased to trade the worthless paper. The second excluded newcomer is the United Provinces of Central America, a confederation that included Costa Rica, El Salvador, Guatemala, Honduras, and Nicaragua. These Central American states floated their first bond in November 1825, after the sample period ended. Including them would not have changed the conclusions, however. Through the beginning of 1826 the yield on Central American bonds fluctuated between 9.0 and 10.9 percent, roughly in line with other new borrowers at the time and considerably higher than more seasoned states. The sample period also excludes one seasoned borrower, Spain, which defaulted in May 1824.

Table 3.3 summarizes the yields of seasoned and new borrowers in 1824 and 1825. In both years, British investors required an uncertainty premium from new borrowers. The mean yield for newcomers always exceeded the mean for seasoned ones, sometimes by a considerable margin. For instance, in July 1825 bonds of the seasoned states were trading at 5.1 percent, on average, while the bonds of new entrants yielded 7.6 percent, leaving a gap of 2.5 percentage points. Moreover, in both years the *minimum* yield among the new borrowers always exceeded the *maximum* yield of a seasoned state, suggesting that the averages do not mask a high degree of variance. To verify this, the final row of the table reports the standard error around each difference in yield. The differences are at least three times larger than their standard errors, satisfying any reasonable test of statistical significance. Even with such a small sample, the probability that the observed differences arose purely by chance is less than 1 in 100.[20]

These patterns are consistent with more qualitative statements from the period. For instance, the London *Times* emphasized to investors that these were "new states" and that anyone who bought South American bonds was doing so "at his own risk."[21] In 1828, after nearly all the new states had defaulted, bondholders convened to see what assistance they could

---

[20] The 95 percent confidence intervals around the differences are 1.9 to 5.0 for 1824 and 0.6 to 4.3 for 1825.

[21] *Times* (London), August 27, 1825, 2.

obtain from British authorities. During the meeting, Alexander Baring, MP, reminded the participants that since investors had demanded "very high interest" rates from those new states, "it must have been pretty generally understood" that there was a "proportionate risk" of the loans going sour.[22]

Particularly during the early years of the lending boom, investors found it difficult to distinguish among Latin American states. Evidently credit history was a critical piece of information. Though there were some notable exceptions such as Brazil, states without a record looked roughly the same and their debt was sold at low levels, reflecting the risk of dealing with a potential lemon.

The loan to the fictitious Central American country of Poyais confirms lenders' inability to distinguish among new Latin American borrowers. Poyais managed to borrow on the same terms as the legitimate states of Chile, Colombia, and Peru. Figure 3.2 depicts the yields on Poyaisian bonds (the dots), compared with a thin solid line that traces the average yields for the three genuine Latin American states that had borrowed around the same time. When investors discovered the fraud and certified Poyais as the sourest of lemons, yields soared above 120 percent and trade in the worthless paper ceased. The story of Poyais is worth recounting because it illustrates how investors lumped unfamiliar borrowers into a single, undifferentiated category and charged them an identical uncertainty premium, just as the reputational theory predicts.

The Poyaisian fraud was devised by Gregor MacGregor, a Scottish adventurer, during a trip to the Mosquito Coast, a 200-mile stretch along the Caribbean shore of modern-day Honduras and Nicaragua.[23] When MacGregor landed on the swampy littoral in 1820 he found several wandering tribes of Mosquito Indians that had once allied with Britain in wars against Spain. MacGregor befriended the Mosquito king, who—allegedly after many glasses of whiskey—granted the Scotsman a concession of 8 million acres along the Río Tinto. The adventurer quickly returned to London and attempted to raise money for his imaginary country, which derived its name from the Poyer Indian tribe.

To excite interest in the new land, a book entitled *Sketch of the Mosquito Shore, including the Territory of Poyais* was published in Edinburgh in 1822.[24] The author, Thomas Strangeways, styled himself as "Captain of the First Native Poyer Regiment and Aide-de-Camp to His Highness Gregor, Cazique of Poyais" and offered a dazzling portrait of a fertile and hospitable land that was ripe for colonization. The sketch was a fabrica-

---

[22] *Morning Chronicle* (London), May 2, 1828, 3; *Times* (London), May 2, 1828, 3.
[23] For a recent account, see Sinclair 2003.
[24] Strangeways 1822.

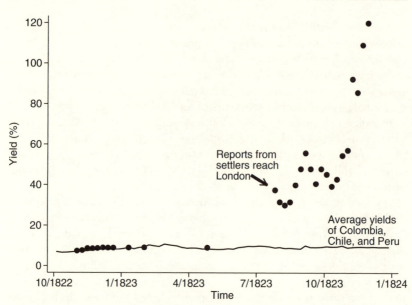

FIGURE 3.2: YIELDS OF POYAISIAN BONDS COMPARED WITH YIELDS OF
COLOMBIA, CHILE, AND PERU, LONDON MARKET, 1822–24
*Source*: Author's calculations from end-of-week prices in the *Course of the Exchange*.

tion, and many passages had been cribbed from descriptions of Jamaica
and the West Indies. Far from the paradise that Strangeways described,
Poyais was "a paltry town of huts and long houses."[25]

It took more than a year for news of the fiction to spread among British
investors. In the meantime, MacGregor managed to raise £200,000 on
the London market at 6 percent interest.[26] His "Poyais Bond" was offered
in October 1822 on an installment plan at 80 percent of par value (implying a yield of approximately 7.5 percent), with £15 down and the balance due in January and February 1823. As figure 3.2 shows, the yields
on Poyaisian bonds closely paralleled those of legitimate Latin American
states for at least six months. Evidently, investors treated Poyais like any
other New World country.

The fraud was exposed in August 1823, when reports from the first
Poyaisian settlers reached London. In addition to issuing bonds, Mac-
Gregor had sold land grants to Scottish Highlanders who dreamed of a
new life in this "free and independent state, under the government of its
own Cazique."[27] The first group of 70 would-be colonists sailed in Janu-

---

[25] Hasbrouck 1927, 443–45.

[26] *Times* (London), October 28, 1822, 2.

[27] The quote is from an advertisement in the *Sentinel* (Glasgow), July 24, 1822, 333.

ary 1823 on the *Honduras Packet*, and another 170 followed a month later. Before departing, most surrendered their English and Scottish pound notes to agents of MacGregor in exchange for Poyaisian currency, which had been specially engraved for this purpose. When the settlers arrived, they found not the paradise described in advertisements, but four shacks and a hostile Indian tribe. Most contracted tropical diseases and began to die from fever or starvation.[28]

When news of the scandal eventually reached Great Britain, prices of Poyaisian bonds plummeted. The *Times* decried the Poyais fraud, saying that the adventurer had "gulled" investors into buying a "sham security."[29] Exposed in Britain, MacGregor next fled to France, where he applied for a loan of ten thousand francs in 1824. By then, "the credit of the Cazique had fallen on the Paris as well as on the London Exchange," and the request for funds was denied. According to the *Times*, "every reader who can read" knew about the swindles perpetrated by His Highness Gregor I.[30]

The Poyaisian episode illustrates a classic market for lemons.[31] Under conditions of incomplete information, investors could not distinguish between genuine and imaginary countries, which were all charged a similarly high rate of interest. The account also reveals how bondholders updated their beliefs in response to disastrous news from settlers and futile attempts to redeem their interest coupons for cash. By August 1823, investors had obtained enough information to distinguish the bonds of Poyais from those of legitimate countries.

The theory in chapter 2 not only predicts uncertainty premiums for unproven borrowers, but also implies that rational investors withhold loans from countries in default. Events unfolded as expected. Figure 3.3 shows that countries that defaulted could not borrow anew until they had offered creditors an acceptable settlement. Each dot in the figure represents a new loan that the country contracted on the London market between 1820 and 1870. The horizontal lines, in contrast, mark the years in which the country was in default on its foreign debts. The lines end only when bondholders accepted the settlement. The striking lesson from this figure is that countries could not float new bonds until they settled their previous defaults.[32] This finding stands in stark contrast with the

---

[28] Gregg 1999.

[29] *Times* (London), September 1, 1823, 2; August 25, 1823, 3; August 26, 1823, 2–3.

[30] *Times* (London), October 14, 1824, 2.

[31] Akerlof 1970.

[32] In a few cases, countries issued new loans in the same year that they settled their past defaults. The new loans were part of the settlement package.

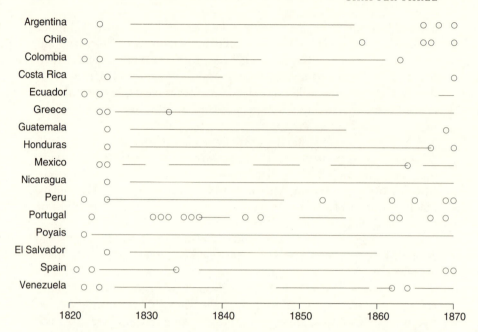

FIGURE 3.3: NEW LOANS AND DEFAULT EPISODES, LONDON MARKET, 1820–70
The dots represent new loans on the London market from 1820 to 1870, and
the horizontal lines mark the episodes of default. Only one state, Greece (1833),
borrowed while in default.
Source: Dates of new loans come from Corporation of Foreign Bondholders, *Annual
Report 5* (1878); Clarke 1878; and bond yearbooks listed in the bibliography.
Default intervals are from Suter 1900 and 1992.

notion that creditors ignore history. On the contrary, they mind history
in the way chapter 2 predicts.

Only one country, Greece, presents a challenge to this pattern. Greece
borrowed for the first time on the London market in 1824 and issued a
second bond one year later. The last payment on these loans took place
in January 1826, after which the government entered a phase of default
that lasted for more than a half century. During this protracted period of
nonpayment, Greece raised an additional sixty million francs on the London market. The loan of 1833, which appears prominently in the middle
of the Greek default line in figure 3.3, appears puzzling until one considers
the special circumstances that enabled the loan to transpire.

In 1827 England, France, and Russia intervened to assist Greece in its
struggle for independence from Turkey. Having secured the autonomy of
this new state, the protecting powers chose Prince Otto of Bavaria as the
first king of modern Greece. By the terms on which Otto accepted the

throne, the three powers agreed to guarantee a loan.[33] Investors accepted the loan—which was not even quoted on the London Stock Exchange—not because they had developed a renewed faith in the creditworthiness of Greece, but because the loan came with the backing of three seasoned borrowers, all of whom had upheld their domestic and foreign obligations during the 1820s.

The loan prospectus not only mentioned the tri-power guarantee, but also pledged "all the revenues of Greece" as security for the new debt. This feature of the contract sparked angry protests from existing bondholders, since those same revenues had been hypothecated for payment of the bonds that were now in default. Holders of the 1824 and 1825 bonds voiced their complaints to Lord Palmerston, the British secretary of state for foreign affairs, who sympathized with the injustice but argued that the establishment of a regular government in Greece would benefit all bondholders. Aggrieved creditors also appealed to the House of Lords, all to no avail. The foreign policy interests of Britain had trumped the interests of bondholders, and the great-power guarantee allowed Greece to float a loan that would not have occurred under normal market conditions.[34]

Data from the early nineteenth century also support the seasoning hypothesis. By keeping their promises, the seasoned borrowers in the top section of table 3.3 confirmed their reputation for creditworthiness. Thomas Fortune wrote in the 1833 edition of his *Epitome of the Public Funds*, the leading investment handbook of the day, that Danish loans had "always enjoyed great favor with the public" on account of the "punctuality and straightforwardness which the government . . . has hitherto observed in all its financial dealings." He expressed a similar view of the debts of Austria, France, Naples, Prussia, and Russia.[35] For all these countries, the policy of consistent repayment during the 1820s reinforced what investors knew. Consequently, the risk premiums on seasoned borrowers declined only slightly from their levels in the 1820s.

In contrast, the risk premium associated with Brazilian debt dropped dramatically over the next 30 years. Among the new borrowers that paid uncertainty premiums in the early 1820s, only Brazil honored its debts to the last shilling. This behavior distinguished Brazil from the lemons, causing its risk premium to converge asymptotically toward the baseline rate

[33] Levandis 1944.

[34] *Times* (London), August 24, 1832, 3. The loan of 1833 proved to be a costly commitment, not for the bondholders who extended the money, but for the guarantors that were incessantly called to make good on their pledge. Greece offered a few token payments, but in general it neglected not only the bonds of 1824 and 1825, but also the tri-power loan of 1833. Finally, in exasperation, the great powers repaid the principal in 1871.

[35] Fortune, *Fortune's Epitome* (1883), 116, 118, 122, 129, 145.

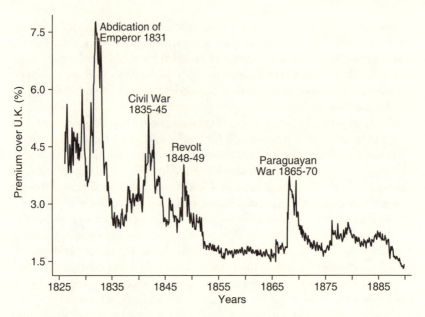

FIGURE 3.4: RISK PREMIUM ON BRAZILIAN BONDS, LONDON MARKET, 1825–90
*Source*: Author's calculations from Taylor 2001.

for seasoned borrowers. Figure 3.4 displays the premium, defined as the spread over U.K. consolidated debt, from 1825 through 1890. The figure shows a consistent downward curve that bottomed out at about 1.5 percentage points by the early 1850s. A few sharp spikes interrupted the progression, but they arose from easily identifiable events such as the abdication of the Portuguese emperor in 1831, the civil wars that raged from 1835 until 1845,[36] the Revolt of the Confederation of the Equator in 1848–49, and the war with Paraguay from 1865 through 1870. Notwithstanding the spikes, figure 3.4 shows the kind of asymptotic trajectory we would expect from the dynamic theory of reputation.

Moreover, market analysts of the nineteenth century attributed the fall in yields to a consistent policy of debt repayment. As early as 1833, the leading investment manual remarked that "there seems to be an anxiety" on the part of Brazilian leaders "to stand well with their creditors" in England.[37] By 1841 the London *Times* concluded that Brazilian debt "rated . . . as one of the first foreign stocks in the market," precisely be-

[36] Civil wars raged in Santa Catarina, Rio Grande do Sul, Pará, Maranhao, Minas Gerais and São Paulo, among others. The bloodiest conflict, the Cabanagem rebellion in northern Brazil, left 30,000 dead.
[37] Fortune, *Fortune's Epitome* (1833), 132.

cause of "the punctuality which has hitherto been observed" in the payment of interest and principal.[38]

When the risk premium touched bottom in the 1850s, Brazilian debt traded at approximately the same rates as Belgian, French, and Russian securities. In his *Epitome of the Public Funds*, Fortune offered a convincing explanation: "Throughout all its difficulties and embarrassments—and they were many and great—the Government punctually and honorably provided for the dividends as they became due, and at no period have its foreign creditors suffered in the smallest degree." Fortune added that "the punctuality of the payment of the dividends" and "the disposition evinced to preserve the credit of the country" gave Brazilian debt a first-rate standing.[39] The other leading bond manual, *Fenn's Compendium of the English and Foreign Funds*, concurred: "The credit of the empire of Brazil has always been well maintained" and is now "inferior to no country in the London Money Market."[40] Thus, the leading investment analysts joined the popular press in saluting Brazil's impressive record, and they attributed its low yields to a punctilious habit of repayment.

In summary, evidence from the early nineteenth century coheres with the theory of reputation advanced in this book. Just as in Amsterdam, new borrowers on the London market paid higher interest rates than more established debtors. Moreover, with a few exceptions, new entrants—whether real or fictitious—paid roughly similar uncertainty premiums, at least during the first few years of lending. The within-group variation eventually increased as additional news arrived from South America, but the higher variance did not obscure a stark difference in means across the two kinds of borrowers. In time, the newcomers that honored their obligations experienced a significant reduction in rates, which occurred because they distinguished themselves from lemons. By contrast, the countries that suspended payments could not reborrow until they settled their defaults. Thus, reputations formed in a consistent way both in Amsterdam and in London, and they exerted powerful effects on the ability of states to borrow.

## The London Market in the Late Nineteenth Century

The next opportunity for an empirical test comes in the 1870s, when many longtime defaulters resumed payments and returned to the market and when several new states raised capital for the first time. To check for

---

[38] *Times* (London), October 1, 1841, 5.
[39] Fortune, *Fortune's Epitome* (1850), 170; (1856), 237.
[40] Fenn, *Fenn's Compendium* (1855), 141; (1860), 210.

uncertainty premiums and seasoning effects, I calculated the yields of all sovereign bond issues that were quoted in London in January 1872. As in the preceding section, this date was chosen to maximize the number of borrowers in the sample. Countries entered the market through the beginning of 1872, so shifting the sample even one year earlier would have excluded newcomers like Bolivia, Liberia, and Paraguay. Moving the date any later would have contaminated the sample with defaults, which began in January 1873 when Honduras and Santo Domingo suspended payments. The choice of January 1872 struck an appropriate balance, since it incorporated all new borrowers and minimized the incidence of actual defaults.

For this analysis, I sorted the debtors into four groups. The first group included the seasoned payers, which had been borrowing for decades and had never defaulted on debts to English creditors. Some of these countries had also proven themselves on the Amsterdam market. The second group contained countries that had settled their defaults from the 1820s and then issued new debt, a pattern that was depicted in figure 3.3. The third category was reserved for new borrowers, those that tapped global capital markets for the first time in the decade prior to 1872. Finally, I identified the lemons: countries that defaulted in the 1860s or even earlier, when external conditions did not warrant a lapse of payment, and refused to make amends with creditors. In total the sample contained 30 countries, most classified as seasoned, settled, or new.

Yield data for all four groups appear in table 3.4.[41] As expected, there was a progressive increase in yields from seasoned borrowers (5.5 percent on average) to settlers (8.0 percent) and new borrowers (8.6 percent). Investors apparently had written off the lemons, which occupied the bottom of the list. The average yield of nearly 27 percent implied that, in the minds of British bondholders, the probability of repayment was extremely small.

Do the differences in table 3.4 pass a statistical test of significance? The difference in means between seasoned and new borrowers was 3.1 percentage points. The 95 percent confidence interval around this estimate stretched from 1.8 to 4.4 points, well to the right of zero, so we can be sure that the difference was not an artifact of this sample. Likewise, rates were substantially lower for seasoned payers than for states that had settled past defaults. The gap in yields was 2.5 percentage points, on average, with a 95 percent confidence range from 0.7 to 4.4 percentage points. Based on the information in table 3.4, it is somewhat more difficult

---

[41] Values in the table represent yields for a representative bond of each country. Bonds with foreign guarantees and exceptional collateral were eliminated from consideration, since the yields did not reflect the true creditworthiness of the borrower.

TABLE 3.4
Bond Yields of Four Types of Borrowers, London, 1872

|  | *Earliest Loan* | *Yield in 1872* |
|---|---|---|
| Seasoned payers |  |  |
| Belgium | 1832 | 4.4 |
| Brazil | 1824 | 5.2 |
| Denmark | 1757 | 4.7 |
| France | 1720 | 6.1 |
| Italy | 1805 | 5.3 |
| Netherlands | 1814 | 4.4 |
| Russia | 1769 | 5.4 |
| Sweden | 1767 | 4.9 |
| Turkey | 1852 | 8.8 |
|    Average |  | 5.5 |
| Settled and reborrowed |  |  |
| Argentina | 1824 | 6.3 |
| Chile | 1822 | 5.9 |
| Colombia | 1822[a] | 8.3 |
| Costa Rica | 1826[b] | 7.9 |
| Guatemala | 1826[b] | 8.7 |
| Honduras | 1826[b] | 12.7 |
| Peru | 1822 | 5.2 |
| Portugal | 1802 | 7.8 |
| Spain | 1770 | 9.4 |
|    Average |  | 8.0 |
| New borrowers |  |  |
| Bolivia | 1872 | 9.0 |
| Egypt | 1862 | 7.4 |
| Japan | 1870 | 8.0 |
| Liberia | 1871 | 8.2 |
| Paraguay | 1871 | 9.6 |
| Romania | 1864 | 7.8 |
| Santo Domingo | 1869 | 10.7 |
| Uruguay | 1864 | 8.0 |
|    Average |  | 8.6 |

TABLE 3.4 (*cont.*)
Bond Yields of Four Types of Borrowers, London, 1872

|  | Earliest Loan | Yield in 1872 |
|---|---|---|
| Proven lemons |  |  |
| Ecuador | 1822[a] | 12.5 |
| Greece | 1824 | 40.0 |
| Mexico | 1824 | 20.0 |
| Venezuela | 1822[b] | 35.3 |
| Average |  | 26.9 |

*Source*: Yields were computed by the author from the *Economist*, January 1872.

*Note*: The earliest loan is defined as the first known foreign loan in Amsterdam or London since 1695. Among the lemons, Ecuador had been in default since 1868, Greece since 1827, Mexico since 1866, and Venezuela since 1864.

[a] Borrowed in 1822 as part of Gran Colombia.

[b] Borrowed in 1826 as part of the United Provinces of Central America.

to distinguish the settlers from new borrowers: although newcomers were charged higher rates, the half-point gap could have arisen by chance alone. Lemons stood in a class by themselves, both substantively and statistically.

However, the foregoing analysis does not control for economic variables that might affect the bond yield and covary with the four categories. In the analyses of the Amsterdam market and of the London market in the early nineteenth century, it would not have been possible or even appropriate to include economic controls, because such data did not exist for investors in the 1700s or the 1820s. The situation began to change in the mid–nineteenth century, when bond manuals began summarizing the economic conditions of major borrowers. An early attempt by Fenn (1860) provides the population, revenue, debt, and trade statistics for the principal states and colonies, all converted into British pounds. "No such return, that can at all be relied upon" existed prior to 1860, he claimed, and Fenn hoped his novel compilation would serve investors well.[42] It is conceivable that investors incorporated such information into their portfolio decisions during the 1860s and 1870s.[43]

Which variables, if omitted, could bias the analysis? One candidate is the stock of external debt, either by itself or—more likely—relative to the exports that were necessary to raise foreign exchange for repayment. Other factors equal, a larger debt-to-export ratio (hereafter called the

---

[42] Fenn, *Fenn's Compendium* (1860), vii–viii.

[43] For analyses of the effects of economic variables (debt-sustainability indicators) on creditworthiness in the late nineteenth century, see Flandreau, Le Cacheux, and Zumer 1998 and Flandreau 2003.

debt ratio) should increase the probability of default and result in higher yields. Furthermore, the debt ratio could be correlated with seasoning: established borrowers presumably had larger debts than new entrants, and therefore larger debt ratios on average. If nineteenth-century investors factored this variable into their decisions, as modern securities traders do, its omission from the statistical analysis would bias the results. Fortunately, the bias would be conservative, since the rising stock of debt would counterbalance the seasoning effects. Thus, omitting the debt ratio might lead to *understating* the effect of seasoning on the bond yield. Controlling for the debt ratio should widen, not narrow, the gap between seasoned and new borrowers.

The second potential spoiler is wealth. A cursory look at table 3.4 suggests that seasoned borrowers were probably wealthier, on average, than other countries in the sample, and therefore more capable of servicing their foreign debts. Some underdeveloped economies, including Brazil, Russia, and Turkey, appear on the list of proven borrowers, but they sit alongside the world's wealthiest states, such as Belgium, Denmark, France, and the Netherlands. The average wealth of new borrowers was undoubtedly lower. To some extent, this discrepancy in wealth may have arisen through seasoning. Due to their prompt repayment, countries at the top of the list enjoyed privileged access to international capital flows necessary for economic growth. If wealth is endogenous in this way, controlling for it could lead me to underestimate the true impact of seasoning on yields.[44] Nevertheless, a certain component of wealth is exogenous and correlated with the four categories of borrowers. In the regression analysis that follows, I treat all wealth as exogenous, even though this approach stacks the deck against the seasoning hypothesis.

Unfortunately for investors, direct measurements of wealth did not exist during the 1870s. Even now, after more than a century of archival research, scholars have managed to develop retrospective estimates of wealth and income for only a handful of European and Latin American countries. In the statistical analysis below, I adopt the same proxy variables investors probably used in the late nineteenth century: the value of exports per capita. According to the leading investment manual of the time, "There is, perhaps, no better available test of a nation's wealth than its foreign trade; for, as a rule, countries which are rich have those things which other nations covet, and countries which are poor have not."[45] The manual proceeded to compare countries according to the value of exports, standardized by population. Modern scholarship confirms the utility of

---

[44] As a general rule, one should not control for the *consequence* of the key explanatory variable of interest.

[45] Fenn, *Fenn's Compendium* (1883), xviii.

this yardstick. For instance, Victor Bulmer-Thomas has shown that a single variable, exports per head, explained more than 80 percent of the variation in real GDP per capita among Latin American states on the eve of World War I.[46] Thus, the quantitative intuitions of investors in the 1800s were demonstrably accurate.

Data for the two economic variables were culled from statistical compilations by Charles Fenn (1873) and Robert Baxter (1871). In a few cases it was impossible to find economic variables, so the missing data were multiply imputed.[47] As suspected, exports per capita covaried strongly across the groups. The average for seasoned borrowers was £4.2, much higher than for settlers (£2.5), new borrowers (£1.7), or proven lemons (£1). The debt ratio also varied across groups, though not exactly as anticipated. The highest debt ratio belonged to the settlers (£7.6), compared with £4.8 for seasoned borrowers and £4.7 for lemons. New borrowers, which had not yet accumulated large debts, brought up the rear with a ratio of £2.5.

I regressed the natural logarithm of the yields in table 3.4 on the level of exports per person, the ratio of debt to exports, and dummy variables for settler, new borrower, and lemon (the omitted category is seasoned borrower, whose effect is impounded in the constant term).[48] The equation appears below, where the subscript $i$ indexes the country.

$$\ln(\text{yield}_i) = \beta_1 + \beta_2 \text{Settled}_i + \beta_3 \text{New}_i + \beta_4 \text{Lemon}_i + \beta_5 \frac{\text{Exports}_i}{\text{Population}_i} + \beta_6 \frac{\text{Debt}_i}{\text{Exports}_i} + \varepsilon_i$$

Regression results appear in table 3.5. The first column pertains to the full sample of 30 countries, and the second is a restricted sample that excludes the four lemons. In both samples, economic variables exerted the expected effect on the dependent variable. Other things equal, yields declined with wealth (as proxied by exports per person) and increased with the debt ratio.[49] The coefficients on both variables were estimated

---

[46] Bulmer-Thomas 1994, 153.

[47] Trade data were missing for three of the thirty countries, making it impossible to construct ratios of exports/population and debt/exports. I imputed the ratios via the EMis algorithm (expectation-maximization with importance sampling) developed by King et al. (2001) and implemented in software by Honaker et al. (2001). I imputed five datasets, which were identical for all observed data and differed only in the imputations of economic variables for the three countries that did not report trade statistics.

[48] The four categories (seasoned, settled, new debtor, and lemon) were mutually exclusive and exhaustive. The log transformation improved the fit of the regression, but analysis of untransformed bond yields led to the same fundamental conclusions.

[49] For ease of presentation, both economic variables were recalibrated in *hundreds* of pounds per person, such that averages for the full sample were 0.026 and 0.050, respectively.

TABLE 3.5
Regression Analysis of Bond Yields, London, 1872

| Variable | Full Sample | | | Sample without Lemons | | |
|---|---|---|---|---|---|---|
| | Estimated Coefficient | Standard Error | t-statistic | Estimated Coefficient | Standard Error | t-statistic |
| Settled | 0.29 | 0.10 | 2.9 | 0.29 | 0.10 | 2.9 |
| New debtor | 0.48 | 0.07 | 6.8 | 0.48 | 0.07 | 6.8 |
| Lemon | 1.48 | 0.27 | 5.4 | | | |
| Exports per person | −1.27 | 0.76 | 1.7 | −1.56 | 0.71 | 2.2 |
| Debt ratio | 2.06 | 0.87 | 2.4 | 2.16 | 0.84 | 2.6 |
| Constant | 1.63 | 0.07 | 23.0 | 1.64 | 0.07 | 23.3 |

*Note*: Multiple-imputation estimates from ordinary least squares (OLS) regression with robust standard errors. The dependent variable in both models is the natural log of the yield. Debt ratio is debt divided by exports. $N = 30$ in the full sample, $N = 26$ in the sample without lemons.

with reasonably high precision, with *t*-statistics ranging from 1.7 to 2.6, so it is safe to conclude that investors incorporated these variables into their portfolio decisions. The potency of economic variables increased when lemons were dropped from the sample, perhaps because standard ratios are less relevant for countries that repeatedly refuse to pay.

The most important conclusion from table 3.5, however, is that seasoning effects persisted despite the introduction of control variables. The coefficients on the dummy variables climbed in stepwise fashion from seasoned debtors to settlers, new entrants, and lemons. Moreover, the standard errors were small for a sample of this size, increasing confidence in the conclusions given less formally in table 3.4.

The dependent variable was measured in the natural log metric, which can be difficult to interpret. For additional insight I converted the estimates from table 3.5 into a more comprehensible scale.[50] Specifically, I set the two economic control variables equal to their sample means, and then used stochastic simulation to approximate the sampling distribution of the expected yield for each type of debtor. All interpretations were based on the regression that excludes lemons, thereby giving the maximum possible weight to the control variables.

Figure 3.5 summarizes the results. The central dot in each boxplot gives the estimated yield for seasoned, settled, and new borrowers, after stripping out the effect of economic variables. The central squares define the interquartile ranges (twenty-fifth through seventy-fifth percentiles), and

[50] The procedure is described by King, Tomz, and Wittenberg (2000) and was implemented with the *Clarify* software developed by Tomz, Wittenberg, and King (2003).

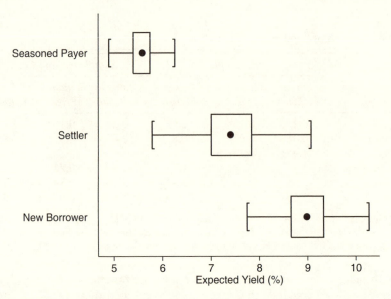

FIGURE 3.5: EXPECTED YIELDS OF SEASONED PAYERS, SETTLERS, AND NEW
BORROWERS, LONDON MARKET, 1872
*Source*: Regression estimates from the sample without lemons in table 3.5.

the wingspans mark the 95 percent confidence intervals. The figure shows,
with tremendous confidence, a difference between seasoned and new borrowers. The point estimates for these two categories are 5.6 versus 9.0
percent, and the sampling distributions do not overlap. It is a bit harder
to distinguish the states that settled from either the seasoned borrowers
or the newcomers. Although the point estimate for the settler's yield falls
smartly in the middle, at 7.4 percent, the confidence intervals stretch far
in both directions, reflecting considerable diversity in this class of borrowers. Some, which had settled and repaid for a long time, began to look
like seasoned borrowers, while others, which had only recently settled and
launched new bonds, more closely resembled the newcomers. Overall, the
results are consistent with the theory in chapter 2.

We can gain further insight by probing more deeply into the various
subcategories of table 3.4. Consider the seasoned borrowers. We have
already seen how Brazil lowered its yield through a consistent record of
repayment. Table 3.4 places the yield on Brazilian bonds in the middle of
the pack, higher than long-standing borrowers like Denmark and Sweden
but lower than Italy or Russia. The position of Brazil is striking, given
that its income per capita at that moment was lower than settlers like
Argentina, Portugal, and Spain, and on par with countries like Japan (a

new borrower) and Mexico (a lemon).[51] Brazil earned its position as a first-rate borrower through a consistent pattern of repayment, from which it never deviated until the mid-1890s.

Two countries in the seasoned category, Turkey and France, had above-average yields. Though seasoned by the coding criteria, Turkey had been borrowing only since 1854 and was the newest of the proven borrowers. Moreover, as many bond manuals and newspaper reports acknowledged, the country was experiencing severe financial trouble due to a bloated foreign debt and a debt-export ratio of more than £13, one of the highest in the sample and 2.8 times the seasoned-country average. In an age when economic information was increasingly available to investors, news of financial trouble elevated the yields on Turkish bonds, thereby introducing variation into the category of seasoned borrowers.

The French yield in table 3.4 is also high, but one should put it in proper context. During the early 1870s France suffered a humiliating defeat in the Franco-Prussian War, and it was beset by domestic turmoil that eventually led to the imposition of martial law. Given such an inauspicious backdrop, it is remarkable that French bonds yielded only 6 percent and that the government raised several new loans on the London market. One such issue was the "National Defense" loan, a ten-million-pound credit underwritten by J. S. Morgan & Co. in October 1870. In an interview with George Smalley, London correspondent of the *New York Tribune*, Junius Morgan explained why he took the loan. The rationale is worth quoting at length, because it shows why bankers and investors placed their faith in seasoned borrowers.

> When it first occurred to me that something might be done, I looked up the financial history of France. I found that since 1789 there had been a dozen separate governments—Monarchy, First Republic, Directory, Consulate, Empire, the Bourbons again, then the Orleanists, then the Second Republic, followed by the Second (or third) Empire, and so on. Between these successive governments there were enmities of many kinds; dynastic, personal, political. Each successor, with one exception, hated its predecessor. It was one long civil war. But I found this also. Not one of these governments had ever repudiated or questioned the validity of any financial obligation contracted by any other. The continuing financial solidarity of France was unbroken. It was plainly a policy rooted in the minds of the people and of the governing forces of France. I saw no reason why it should be broken in this case more than in any other; less, perhaps, than in many others since this money was wanted for the defense

---

[51] These conclusions are based on retrospective calculations of GDP per capita at purchasing power parity in 1870, as reported in Maddison 1995.

TABLE 3.6
Regression Analysis of Bond Yields of Settlers, London, 1872

| Variable | Estimated Coefficient | Standard Error | t-statistic |
|---|---|---|---|
| Years since settlement | −0.11 | 0.04 | 2.6 |
| Years without default on new bonds | −0.19 | 0.04 | 5.5 |
| Constant | 11.34 | 1.31 | 8.6 |

*Note*: Estimates from ordinary least squares (OLS) regression with robust standard errors. The dependent variable is the bond yield. $N = 9$, $R^2 = .71$, and the standard error of the regression is 1.37.

of the country. That was good enough for me. There was no gamble. I thought it a safe operation, as it turned out.[52]

Next consider the subcategory of settlers. Members of that group not only made amends with creditors, but also issued new debt and serviced it regularly over a number of years, thereby separating themselves from lemons. Within this class of borrowers, countries that settled relatively quickly should have commanded lower rates than those that remained in default from the 1820s through the late 1860s. Moreover, countries with the longest record of uninterrupted payment on postsettlement bonds should have gotten preferential treatment as they approached the ideal of a seasoned borrower. To test these hypotheses, I regressed the yield on two explanatory variables: the number of years since settlement, and the number of years without default on postsettlement bonds.

The results appear in table 3.6. For ease of interpretation I expressed the dependent variable in percentage points, even though estimates on the log metric would have had slightly higher *t*-statistics. The table shows that, other factors equal, the cost of delaying a settlement by 10 years was about 1.1 percentage points, while an additional decade of full payment on postsettlement bonds reduced the yield by about 1.9 points, a rapid rate of convergence. As before, standard errors around these estimates were miniscule, and therefore give confidence in the predictions of the dynamic reputational theory. Moreover, the two key variables in table 3.6 explained more than 71 percent of the variation in yield, once more showing that investors attached overriding importance to the credit history of the borrower.

Finally consider the category of new borrowers. Throughout this chapter I have coded new borrowers as countries with a credit history of less than 10 years. If the seasoning hypothesis is correct, though, the most experienced borrowers *within* this group should have boasted lower

[52] Morgan, quoted in Smalley 1912, 216–17.

TABLE 3.7
Regression Analysis of Bond Yields of New Borrowers, London, 1872

| Variable | Estimated Coefficient | Standard Error | t-statistic |
|---|---|---|---|
| Years of experience | −0.16 | 0.05 | 3.2 |
| Constant | 9.24 | 0.53 | 17.4 |

*Note*: Estimates from ordinary least squares (OLS) regression with robust standard errors. The dependent variable is the bond yield. $N = 8$, $R^2 = .32$, and the standard error of the regression is 0.99.

yields than the true novices. To investigate this possibility I regressed the yields of new borrowers on their years of experience. Even with a sample of only eight borrowers, the results in table 3.7 fit the theory. Each additional year of experience cut the yield by 0.16 percentage points, on average. The regression estimate was more than three times its standard error. Clearly, investors discriminated even within the category of new borrowers based on the length of uninterrupted debt service.

Investment commentary from the 1870s supports these quantitative results. In 1872, the *Economist* published a set of basic guidelines for all investors in foreign bonds. The important rule to bear in mind, the magazine argued, was "a caution against borrowers for the first time." It was far safer to extend credit to "recognized Governments which have a standing in the market than to States which are not known, however promising they may be."[53] In a similar spirit, one London securities dealer argued that France or Russia "are old customers, and can be trusted as such." To the same category belonged "the names of other states which have honorably fulfilled their obligations." In contrast, he singled out as highest risks the states that were "making practically their first application to the money market. They are . . . new customers and should be treated precisely as such."[54]

Among the new borrowers, only Japan maintained full payment throughout the 1870s. Santo Domingo was the first to fall, in January 1873. Liberia and Paraguay suspended payments a year later, Bolivia stopped servicing its debts in 1875, and Egypt, Romania, and Uruguay defaulted in 1876. How did markets treat the only newcomer that kept faith with creditors? I conclude this section by investigating the experience of Japan, which—like Brazil a half century earlier—amassed a perfect credit record and eventually joined the ranks of seasoned borrowers.

In the early seventeenth century the central administration of Japan introduced a policy of seclusion (*sakoku*). The Shogun decreed that any

[53] *Economist*, April 27, 1872, 512–13.
[54] George Webbe Medley in United Kingdom, House of Commons, Select Committee on Loans to Foreign States 1875, 279.

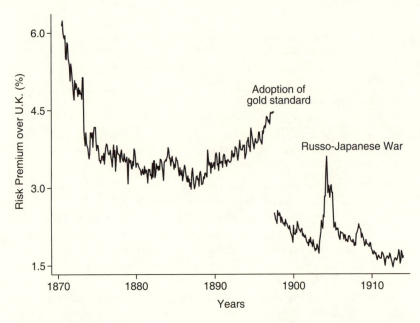

FIGURE 3.6: RISK PREMIUM ON JAPANESE BONDS, LONDON MARKET, 1870–1914
*Source*: Data provided by Nathan Sussman. The discontinuity in 1897 is due to a change in the benchmark bond.

person who left the country would be executed, and he prohibited foreigners from visiting Japanese ports. Exceptions to this rule were limited to a few Chinese junks coming to Nagasaki and to a Dutch trading post on the island of Dejima. Dutch merchants traveled within Japan under escort and only for approved purposes. Not surprisingly, Japan did not borrow on international markets during this period. The policy of extreme isolation lasted until the mid–nineteenth century, when Commodore Perry began to pry open the Japanese market.

The major turning point came in 1868, with the fall of the House of Tokugawa and the restoration of the emperor. The new leaders chose the name Meiji, meaning enlightened rule, and began to pursue contact with the West. Two years later Japan floated its first loan on the London market: a one-million-pound credit, to be redeemed gradually over 13 years. With a nominal interest rate of 9 percent and an issue price of 98 percent, the yield at launch was nearly 9.2 percent, quite high compared with seasoned borrowers of the time.

Investors demanded this enormous yield because Japan had not yet proven its creditworthiness through years of faithful repayment. The *Economist* provided the rationale: "Do we know what all the various bodies and persons having power in that polity may think of paying money to foreigners? . . . Are we sure that this new nation can be trusted with the greatest of pecuniary temptations—that of borrowing from persons they have never seen?" The magazine professed "ignorance of the people and Government, and of their political character" and noted that "we could only learn by the experience of years whether . . . their civilization is advanced enough and their political character trustworthy enough to permit of our lending to them safely."[55]

Over time Japan did satisfy its critics, and the risk premium fell. Figure 3.6 plots the yield on Japanese bonds, minus the risk-free U.K. consol rate, from 1870 until the beginning of World War I. The parabolic downward trend is unmistakable. From a high of more than 9 percent at the onset of the regime, the spread fell to around 3 percent in 1890. After a temporary rise in the 1890s (spurred in part by military insecurity and the Sino-Japanese War), it plunged with the adoption of the gold standard, which some scholars have called a "good housekeeping seal of approval."[56] This kind of reputational spillover, in which behavior on one issue affects reputation in another, deserves further investigation. Overall, though, a scrupulous policy of repayment allowed Japan to lower its yields when other countries in its borrowing cohort, having defaulted on their debts, were shut out of capital markets. As in the eighteenth and early nineteenth centuries, the evidence from this period accords with my theory of reputation.

## Conclusion

In this chapter, I have shown how reputations formed across two centuries of international financial history. Consistent with the logic in chapter 2, new borrowers were charged an uncertainty premium, which declined asymptotically toward a baseline rate in response to a policy of faithful repayment. Governments that defaulted, on the other hand, could not raise additional capital on international markets until they offered an acceptable settlement. Support for these propositions comes not only from quantitative data, but also from commentary in the popular press and leading investment manuals of the time. Thus, the evidence aligns closely with the theory of reputation developed in this book.

[55] *Economist*, April 30, 1870, 530; January 18, 1873, 61.
[56] Bordo and Rockoff 1996; Sussman and Yafeh 2000. The benchmark bond changed at approximately the same time, however, making it difficult to know how much of the drop in Japanese bond yields was caused by Japan's move to the gold standard. For a skeptical view of the gold standard's effect on bond yields in the nineteenth century, see Flandreau and Zumer 2004.

# Chapter 4

## Reputation in Expert Opinion

THE PREVIOUS CHAPTER tested three predictions of my reputational theory: investors charge premiums to new borrowers, offer progressively better terms to consistent payers, and withhold loans from defaulters that do not settle their arrears. Data from the eighteenth and nineteenth centuries strongly supported all three predictions.

This chapter considers another implication of my theory: experts who disseminate advice about foreign investment will make recommendations that reflect the theory's logic. Rating agencies, bankers, and financial commentators regularly publish views on which sovereigns are most creditworthy and for what reasons. They face powerful incentives to get recommendations right. In the field of investment analysis, participants who offer sound advice gain fame and fortune, whereas those who emphasize the wrong criteria lose readers and go out of business.

If the reputational theory in this book is correct, the writings of investment advisors should display two patterns. First, advisors should emphasize the credit histories of governments. They may mention other factors, as well, but reputation should be a primary criterion. Second, advisors should evaluate behavior in economic and political context, as hypothesized in chapter 2. If investment advisors only rarely mention credit histories, or if they seem insensitive to context, such patterns would call my reputational theory into question.

Although this chapter focuses primarily on reputation, the evidence herein pertains to issue linkage, as well. According to linkage theory, countries repay their debts to avoid punishment in other areas of international relations. If investment experts perceive this mechanism as important, their analyses should refer to extrinsic sanctions such as military retaliation or trade embargoes.

Of course, reputation and linkage theories are not mutually exclusive; advisors could urge investors to weigh both considerations. Nevertheless, our faith in each theoretical perspective should be proportional to the number and the quality of pertinent references. If the writings of investment advisors abound with discussion of reputation but contain relatively few comments about the borrower's vulnerability to extrinsic sanctions, such a discovery would underscore the explanatory power of reputation relative to more punitive means of achieving cooperation between debtors and creditors.

I begin the chapter by systematically analyzing the writings of experts during an important period for international lending. My content analysis of a representative sample of texts confirms the importance of reputation, not only in absolute terms but also relative to issue linkage. I then show that advisors take context into account as entailed by my theory of reputation.

## A Systematic Study of the Investment Literature, 1919–29

My analysis of investment commentary focuses on U.S. and British texts between 1919 and 1929. The period was chosen for two reasons. First, those years witnessed an incredible outpouring of advice about foreign lending, due mainly to the rise of the United States as an international lender. On the eve of World War I the United States owed the rest of the world nearly $3.7 billion. War reversed the situation, leaving the country with more than $12.5 billion in net foreign assets. Intergovernmental war debts accounted for three-quarters of this total, but the United States also began to establish itself as a leading supplier of portfolio and direct investment.[1] The trend intensified during the 1920s, when U.S. citizens lent billions of dollars to governments and corporations around the world. This lending boom created an intense demand for investment advice, which firms and individual authors willingly supplied. Hundreds of books and articles appeared in the United States. At the same time, the British continued to publish their own advice manuals, creating the potential for systematic analysis of a large body of literature from both sides of the Atlantic.

Second, the opportunity to obtain a representative sample was especially available for the interwar years. I wanted to approach the literature scientifically, not by picking texts that favored models of reputation but by examining publications that represented the breadth of available literature. Consequently, I needed extensive and objective lists of texts from which I could draw a random sample. I found such lists for the interwar period.

My sample is based on four specialized interwar bibliographies.[2] The first, *Sources of Investment Information* (1930), was commissioned by the Investment Bankers Association of America and compiled by a team

[1] Lewis 1938, 447.

[2] Special Libraries Association Exhibit Committee 1930; Cavanaugh 1929; Badger 1928; and U.S. Securities and Exchange Commission Library 1937. All four bibliographies were published in the United States, but they contained many citations to British experts, as well as American ones.

of experts from the Special Libraries Association. The book was written for banking houses and private citizens, and it directed attention "to a suitable and practicable number of sources" that were "readily accessible" at the time.

The second bibliography, *Some Sources of Information on Stocks and Bonds* (1929), was prepared by the chief librarian of Standard Statistics Company, a rating agency that eventually merged with Poor's Publishing to establish Standard & Poor's. This bibliography, like the previous one, contained items that bankers, rating agencies, and investors used to make decisions.

The third source of citations, Badger's *Investment Principles and Practices* (1928), contained the most extensive bibliography of any investment textbook from the period. Written by a professor of economics at Brown University, the book had a remarkable publication record that suggests how seriously students and investors regarded the scholarship. Originally published in 1928, the text went through six printings by 1935. A second edition appeared one year later and itself ran through five printings. The author issued a third edition in 1941 and six printings later released a fourth edition. The bibliography from the first edition was extremely thorough and of immense use in identifying texts people might have used.

The final list of citations was compiled by the U.S. Securities and Exchange Commission Library. Congress established the S.E.C. in 1934 to protect the interests of investors, and the commission compiled a list of publications it could consult to achieve its goals. The *List of References on Securities which are of General Interest to the S.E.C.* (1937) was nearly 600 pages long and contained more than 11,000 citations on various investment topics.

I detected no effort by the bibliographers to advance a specific argument or defend a parochial point of view. All four apparently had a common aim: to list a wide range of investment texts that were available at the time. Their efforts allowed me, more than 70 years later, to obtain a representative sample of expert opinion about lending to foreign governments.

From each bibliography I recorded citations to books published in the United States or Britain between 1919 and 1929. A more encompassing study might have included journal articles, but I focused on books because they offered more thorough discussions of the criteria for sovereign lending. To qualify for inclusion, a book had to appear under one of the following bibliographic headings: "government bonds," "foreign securities," or "foreign investments." I also admitted all books in the generic category of "investments," since many general advice manuals contained a chapter about foreign loans.

I recorded all pertinent citations from the first three bibliographies and took a systematic sample from the fourth. The need for sampling arose because the S.E.C. bibliography contained 465 entries under the general heading of investments. I took every twelfth entry, resulting in a sample of around forty texts, comparable to the other bibliographies. Citations from these four sources constituted my initial list of texts.

I next eliminated any repeat appearances by authors. Some individuals and firms published several books or even multiple editions of the same book. Their views presumably did not change much from one text to the next. Including multiple entries from the same author would have been tantamount to interviewing the same individual time and again, and treating each interview as if it were a wholly new and statistically independent observation. This would have biased the analysis by giving undue weight to the views of repeat publishers. When an author or firm appeared more than once in the list of citations, I chose the item that was published nearest to 1925, the midpoint of the interwar lending boom.

Two other criteria narrowed the list. First, I discarded any book that, according to its title, focused on a single country. Potentially unique conclusions about a single country would not have contributed to general inferences about investment. Second, I dropped any book that, judging from its title, covered intergovernmental war debts as distinct from loans by private bondholders and commercial banks.

The final list contained 44 books. A thorough search of libraries in the United States and abroad uncovered every book on the list. For each book, I noted what criteria the author advocated to evaluate the creditworthiness of a foreign government. The books mentioned many criteria and emphasized some more heavily than others. I focused on three that were relevant to the theories addressed in this book: the reputation of the borrower, the threat of military intervention, and the prospect of commercial retaliation. Each criterion received a score on a six-point scale:

1. The most important factor
2. Among the top three factors
3. One of many considerations
4. Conceivably relevant, but unlikely to play a role
5. Not mentioned
6. Importance is expressly denied

Approximately 39 percent of the books (17 of 44) did not contain any hints or general principles for lending to foreign governments. This result was not too surprising. I had cast the net widely by including books not only under narrow headings such as "foreign government bonds," but also under the catchall category of "investments." The broad sweep picked up general treatises with chapters on foreign lending, but also included books that dealt exclusively with domestic stock markets or contained only a couple of sentences about foreign securities. The remaining 27 books contained a rich enough discussion to code the importance of reputation, military sanctions, and trade sanctions as criteria for investments.[3]

The 27 books in my sample were written by a wide range of investment experts. Some authors worked for bond-rating agencies including Moody's and Fitch, and for top financial institutions such as Brown Brothers & Co.; Lee, Higginson & Co.; Paine, Webber & Co.; and Bank of America. The list also included an accountant from Lybrand, Ross & Co., a financial consultant, the president of a British investment trust, and the vice president of the American Academy of Political and Social Science. Editors of the *Economist* and the *New Statesman* also made the final cut, as did an attorney, an agent from the U.S. Commerce Department, and several financial publicists. Finally, the list included a how-to manual by the American Bankers Association and standard texts by professors from Columbia, Harvard, Michigan, New York University, Northwestern, and other leading universities. If such a diverse and distinguished group could agree on the importance of credit histories, this would constitute strong evidence for reputational theory.

Table 4.1 gives the percentage of analysts (out of a total sample of 27) that expressed each perspective. The consensus about reputation was striking. Thirty percent of authors explicitly identified reputation as the most important factor to keep in mind when lending money to a foreign government. Other authors listed considerations without singling out one as the most important. In particular, 44 percent felt that reputation deserved to be among the top three but did not provide rankings within that set. A further 22 percent advised investors to weigh many factors, including the credit history of the government. Only one author in the sample (4 percent of the total) failed to mention reputation at all. That author emphasized current economic variables such as per capita levels of debt and wealth.[4] Thus, evidence from an unbiased sample of investment commentary overwhelmingly supports reputation-based theory.

Why did analysts pay such close attention to the credit histories of governments? They understood that it was nearly impossible to coerce gov-

---

[3] The 27 books were American Institute of Banking 1924; Atkins 1926; Badger 1928; Bonner 1925; Chamberlain and Edwards 1927; Clay 1920; Davies 1927; Edwards 1926; Hallinan 1927; Herschel 1925; Jones 1919; Jordan 1929; Kimber 1919; Kirshman 1924; Lagerquist 1921; Lincoln 1926; Lyon 1926; Madden and Nadler 1929; Montgomery 1925; Moody 1925; Morris 1928; Patterson 1928; Raymond 1925; Rollins 1926; Sakolski 1925; Taylor 1924; and Withers 1926.

[4] Clay 1920, 63–66.

TABLE 4.1
References to Reputation, Military Intervention, and Trade
Sanctions in Expert Texts, 1919–29

| Importance | Reputation | Military | Trade |
|---|---|---|---|
| The most important | 30% | 0% | 0% |
| Among the top three | **44** | 0 | 0 |
| One of many factors | 22 | 22 | 4 |
| Conceivable but unlikely | 0 | 11 | 0 |
| Not mentioned | 4 | **48** | **96** |
| Expressly denied | 0 | 19 | 0 |
| Total | 100 | 100 | 100 |

Source: Author's analysis of American Institute of Banking 1924; Atkins 1926; Badger 1928; Bonner 1925; Chamberlain and Edwards 1927; Clay 1920; Davies 1927; Edwards 1926; Hallinan 1927; Herschel 1925; Jones 1919; Jordan 1929; Kimber 1919; Kirshman 1924; Lagerquist 1921; Lincoln 1926; Lyon 1926; Madden and Nadler 1929; Montgomery 1925; Moody 1925; Morris 1928; Patterson 1928; Raymond 1925; Rollins 1926; Sakolski 1925; Taylor 1924; and Withers 1926.

Note: The table presents the percentage of analysts who expressed each perspective. Modal response appears in bold. The sample size is 27.

ernments into honoring foreign debts, and therefore emphasized that repayment depended on the "good faith" or "character" of leaders and citizens. Dwight Morrow, senior partner at J. P. Morgan during the 1920s, provided the logic:

> Loans are made to foreign governments in reliance primarily upon the good faith of those governments. . . . In international loans there is no ultimate effective sanction analogous to the domestic sheriff. But there remains our reliance upon good faith. . . . The credit of governments is not easily built up. It may easily be shattered. And it must never be forgotten that there are rules of conduct accepted by the silent approval of civilized men, the breach of which hurts the one committing the breach much more than the one against whom it is committed. . . . If good faith cannot be relied upon it is better that the loan not be made.[5]

Analysts of the 1920s did not always define "good faith" or "character," but it is clear from dozens of texts that the phrases referred to the debtor's sense of morality, its competence in economic management, and its willingness to accept austerity to avert a default. The authors noted that character could evolve or even shift abruptly, especially during periods of revolution and domestic turmoil, but generally maintained that

[5] Morrow, April 1926 public address, as quoted in Jordan 1934, 231–32.

"character in the case of a nation as in an individual is rather a constant force and changes but slowly. Hence the investor and dealer in securities does well to scan the history of a borrowing state to uncover its conduct in the past."[6] Analysts also acknowledged that they could not measure character directly; they used credit histories to make inferences about this intangible but important variable. "The only way in which this character factor can be evaluated," wrote a top consultant to New York banks, "is by a study of the history of the country to see how it has conducted itself in the past."[7]

Although analysts peered into the past for information about the borrower, they used the historical data to make forecasts about the future. "Bankers almost universally recognize an unimpeachable record for financial uprightness as one of the most important considerations" in lending to a foreign government, wrote one analyst, because "past performances throw a flood of light on the probable future of a security issue."[8] If countries could not be forced to pay, investors had no choice but to look carefully before leaping. Analysts helped in this regard by studying the credit history of the borrower and using it to project the likelihood of repayment.

Given these comments, it is not surprising that analysts devoted far less attention to the prospect of military sanctions. Only 22 percent of analysts discussed military retaliation as if it were a possible method of enforcing contracts, and in most cases it was hard to tell whether they were presenting a straw man. Consider the following ambiguous passage:

> The citizen of a foreign nation . . . can only make requests for payment. If the payment is not forthcoming, he may succeed in persuading his own government to continue the requests on his behalf in the form of diplomatic correspondence. On the failure of these methods, there remains only the gunboat possibility. . . . Good faith, then, it appears, forms an even more important element of public than of private credit. The reputation of a government for a long period of prompt fulfillment of its promise to pay the interest (and principal insofar as it has made any promises to repay principal) of its debt indicates a conscious knowledge on the part of the debtor of the importance of good faith as an element of government credit. The lender feels that he can rely on the continuing intention of the government to fulfill its promises. . . . But if a debtor government, although possessing ample resources, refuses to pay, the creditor is helpless.[9]

[6] Edwards 1926, 127.
[7] Atkins 1927, 24.
[8] Kirshman 1924, 286–87.
[9] Lyon 1926, 82.

I placed this reference and others like it in the "one of many" category, since the text mentioned the possibility of gunboats. Other interpretations may be equally defensible, however. The author concludes that creditors are "helpless" against governments that refuse to pay and can only protect themselves by screening carefully in advance, using the credit histories of borrowers as a guide to intentions. This suggests that the author did not regard military retaliation as a serious possibility, after all. Even so, I erred in favor of sanctions by counting this passage and others like it as evidence of belief in enforcement by gunboats.

Even with coding rules that were especially charitable to sanctioning, the typical investment commentator—represented by the mode of the distribution in table 4.1—did not mention the prospect of military retaliation, and nearly a fifth explicitly advised against incorporating it into investment decisions. Moreover, of those authors who did mention the military, not one placed it ahead of reputation. The notion of military enforcement deserves further analysis, given that half the authors discussed it in some capacity (see chapter 6). Table 4.1 shows, however, that professional analysts of the 1920s placed far more stock in reputation than in military retaliation.

The gap between linkage theory and reality was even starker for commercial retaliation. In all the investment texts of the period, I found only one mention of trade sanctions as a means of enforcing debt contracts. The author, Albert Kimber of Fitch Rating Service, alleged that Ecuador resumed payment on its foreign debts in 1919 "due to an intimation received from Washington that unless the Ecuadorian Government should make some effort to fulfill its obligations, imports of cocoa from that country into the United States might be prohibited."[10]

Two facts suggest that Kimber attached relatively little importance to this claim. First, he placed it in a section on the history of Ecuador and never extrapolated it to a general point about the causes of creditworthiness. Second, the book contained an entirely separate chapter, called "National Credit Factors," that told investors how to evaluate the bankability of sovereigns. The chapter emphasized credit history, political stability, and wealth but never mentioned the prospect of trade sanctions or offered it as a criterion for investment. Nevertheless, I again erred on the side of sanctions by counting the reference to Ecuador as evidence that, according to Kimber, investors should incorporate the threat of trade sanctions into their investment decisions.

As table 4.1 shows, no other analysts mentioned the possibility of a trade embargo or other forms of commercial retaliation. The silence on

[10] Kimber 1919, 198.

this issue is striking, since many modern theorists insist that only the prospect of trade sanctions can lead governments to repay and afford investors the confidence to lend. At least during the interwar period, a systematic analysis of investment commentary did not support this proposition. In a world where individuals and firms were paid for accurate advice about foreign investments, the failure to mention trade sanctions counts as powerful evidence against that theory. As chapter 7 shows, the actual behavior of debtors and creditors does not support the theory, either.

## Three Additional Pieces of Evidence

The previous analysis of investment commentary identified reputation as one of the most important factors in the minds of international lenders. Experts believed that the past record of a government exposed its willingness to repay, and therefore provided valuable evidence about creditworthiness. Before examining whether investors were sensitive to context—whether they judged the credit record of a government conditional on the economic and political circumstances it faced—I consider three additional pieces of evidence about the importance experts assigned to reputation.

First, the credit history of the borrower appeared prominently not only in investment advice manuals, but also in advertising campaigns. When underwriters marketed a bond to the public, they developed advertisements or "circulars" that described the loans and explained why people should buy them. The book *Foreign Securities* summarized the typical contents of bond advertisements: "The past debt record of a borrower is of keen interest to a banker or investment security dealer, and if the obligor has never defaulted, or if the record is clear in recent years, this fact is usually given a prominent place in a bond circular or advertisement."[11] In contrast, my research did not uncover any circulars that promoted a bond by arguing that the borrower was vulnerable to commercial or military sanctions. The absence of such references again casts doubt on issue linkage theories, since banks had a financial incentive to advertise any factors that would have enhanced the attractiveness of securities they sold.

Second, the annual reports of rating firms contained extended discussions of the credit histories of borrowers, sometimes going back a hundred years or more. Raters apparently felt that such information would help investors screen borrowers. As the book *Testing before Investing* explained, "Some countries have had the unfortunate habit of repudiating their bonds when the burden of paying for them becomes heavy. This attitude depends considerably upon general customs and business ethics

[11] Madden and Nadler 1929, 91.

of the people, so that it is not likely to improve overnight. The records of such repudiations are given in the investment manuals to serve as a guide for the prospective investor."[12] The manuals contained no parallel discussions of vulnerability to commercial embargoes or military retaliation. Apparently, rating agencies did not assign much importance to extrinsic sanctions as a means of enforcing debt contracts.

Third, regulators required foreign governments to disclose their credit histories before listing bonds on the stock exchange. Governments with a record of defaults preferred to hide their checkered past, but regulators demanded disclosures to protect investors. In the 1920s, for example, the New York Stock Exchange (NYSE) refused to list a foreign bond until the borrower provided detailed information about its "past debt records," including its pattern of defaults on interest and principal. The president of the NYSE justified the rule in the following terms: "In this process of absorbing foreign investments, the American investing public should be afforded information sufficient to enable it to judge adequately concerning the values of the securities."[13] The NYSE believed that the credit histories of borrowers revealed essential information about the safety of investments. In contrast, regulators did not require statements about vulnerability to economic and military sanctions. If such information were pertinent to protect investors, U.S. regulators should have demanded it.

## The Importance of Context

The previous section showed the importance of reputation for analysts, bankers, and regulators of the 1920s. My theory further predicts that investors (and their advisors) do not evaluate credit histories in a vacuum. Instead, they consider the economic and political *context* that might lead governments to repay or default.

Indeed, my survey of expert opinion found that many analysts interpreted history in context. Two directors from the Institute of International Finance, which was founded by New York University and the Investment Bankers Association of America, wrote in 1929, "The past debt record, important as it is, cannot be taken alone without some further investigation of the facts, not only those attendant upon a default but also those which may be responsible for what otherwise appears to be a satisfactory

---

[12] Lincoln 1926, 61–62.

[13] *Foreign Securities Investor*, February 18, 1925, 8. The Securities and Exchange Commission broadened the rule. Under the Securities Act of 1933–34, any foreign government that wanted to float a new bond on the U.S. market, whether listed or not, was required to state any defaults it committed within the last 20 years.

debt history."[14] The vice president of Fitch Rating Service concurred: "Bad
records in government financing are numerous enough," but "it is not the
fact of repudiation that is in itself significant, but attendant circumstances
and the record of developments leading up to the default."[15]

The investment literature of the 1920s drew a "marked distinction . . .
between willful repudiation and unavoidable defalcations."[16] Certain
governments behaved like lemons by defaulting when external conditions
did not justify it, and thereby destroyed their reputations in international
markets. As the Fitch vice president noted, "Any nation that deliberately
defaults in the payment of its foreign debts finds its credit gone and its
national development blocked; its reputation for honesty is destroyed and
later borrowing impossible except upon ruinous terms. This is economic
suicide. Russia, at the present time, is an example of a nation in this
position."[17]

Many authors of the interwar period cited the Russian default as the
leading example of lemonlike behavior. Shortly after the revolution of
1917, the Soviet government annulled its foreign debts. Commentators
maintained that the repudiation was "purely political" and voluntary,
since it arose not from adverse external shocks but from a radical revolution that changed the government's type.[18] As one analyst put it, the credit
of Russia was good even as late as 1915, but the "wheel of political fortune" brought to power an extreme party that destroyed the country's
reputation.[19] Analysts invariably denounced the outcome as a "flagrant
case" of "voluntary repudiation" and singled out Russia as "the outstanding example of bad faith to foreign security holders."[20]

However, analysts understood that defaults could arise not only from
willful repudiation, as in the case of Russia, but also from unforeseen
disasters. In the words of one top financial consultant from the period,
"It is essential to distinguish the motive lying behind any default. In many
cases . . . the debtor would have been perfectly willing to pay the debt if
it lay within his power. Situations arise in the case of nations, as well as
for individuals, which are beyond the control of the contracting parties
and which render impossible the repayment of the loan."[21] According to
the literature, exogenous shocks that might cause a country to suspend
payments include wars, acts of God such as earthquakes and hurricanes,

[14] Madden and Nadler 1929, 91.
[15] Kimber 1919, 221.
[16] Lagerquist 1921, 604.
[17] Kimber 1919, 149.
[18] Kimber 1919, 204; Lagerquist 1921, 665.
[19] Herschel 1925, 131.
[20] Kirshman 1924, 685; Madden and Nadler 1929, 245; Montgomery 1933, 1118.
[21] Atkins 1927, 24.

and dramatic changes in international commodity prices. Any of these could excuse a default as having arisen from "uncontrollable causes."[22]

With these kinds of shocks in mind, analysts took pains to distinguish excusable defaults from voluntary repudiation. "Defaults that are the result of transactions or of circumstances over which the obligor has no control, such as a natural catastrophe, are not in the class of deliberate defaults and should be placed in a different category in making an analysis of the credit position of a country."[23] Consistent with the theory of reputation in chapter 2, then, interwar analysts used available data about external conditions to separate fair-weathers from lemons, tolerating defaults by the former while condemning opportunism by the latter.

Investment experts did not downplay how hard it was to discern whether defaults arose from exogenous shocks or willful intransigence. In his book *Tests of a Foreign Government Bond*, the vice president of the American Academy of Political and Social Science acknowledged that "it is not a simple matter to distinguish between defaults of interest or principal which result from bad faith and those which sometimes arise out of economic circumstances beyond the power of the borrower to control."[24] And yet analysts insisted that such distinctions were crucial.

To judge which defaults arose from unwillingness rather than inability to pay, investors throughout history established investigative committees. Sometimes called bondholders councils, these committees studied the circumstances that led to defaults and opined on the fairness of settlements. Such councils had no coercive power, no capacity to slap sanctions on the defaulting state. In fact, most councils lacked even the legal authorization to negotiate on behalf of bondholders. Instead, the councils appealed to the debtor's sense of reputation and morality and then waited for the sovereign to end the default. When the debtor advanced a proposal for settlement, the council judged whether the terms seemed fair given the situation. If satisfied, the council recommended the plan to bondholders, who could then decide whether to accept the recommendation or to withhold approval.

The most important council of the nineteenth and twentieth centuries was the Corporation of Foreign Bondholders (CFB), a British organization established in 1868 and eventually incorporated by an act of Parliament. From its beginnings, the CFB conceived of itself as a supplier of information, rather than a lobby for coercive measures. At the first meeting of the organization, for example, one bondholder urged the council to seek military support from the British government to collect foreign debts. The

[22] Royal Institute of International Affairs 1937, 286.
[23] Madden and Nadler 1929, 91–92.
[24] Patterson 1928, 26.

chairman firmly refused, and the *Economist* concurred that if bondholders were "to embroil the Government of any great country in the task of enforcing their claims, it would have been a thousand times better for the commerce of the world that they had never formed such an Association [of bondholders] at all. Let them consider that their true aim is . . . to bring the power of an informed public opinion, and that only, to bear on dishonest and defaulting governments."[25] This view set the future direction of CFB policy.[26]

Above all, the CFB helped investors distinguish between fair-weather payers and lemons. As one investment analyst of the 1920s wrote, the CFB

> separates the sheep from the goats of the defaulting governments on the basis of investigation and indicates those that it believes are in default because of unwillingness to pay and those which are in default because of real inability to pay. At the unwilling it points the finger of scorn. . . . To the unable it gives good financial advice. There is no doubt that the Council is a valuable agency. If it did nothing else, and it accomplishes much, it makes most important contributions to our fund of financial information.[27]

The CFB published annual reports and circulated them around the world, thereby providing investors with the data they needed to screen sovereign borrowers.[28] Each report contained what the council itself described as a "black list" of debtors that refused to offer an acceptable settlement to creditors.[29]

Other countries developed similar organizations as the need arose. For instance, the United States, a newcomer to the field of international lending, had no bondholder council on the eve of the Great Depression. When defaults began in the early 1930s, however, investors founded the Foreign Bondholders Protective Council (FBPC) with the help of the U.S. Department of State. Like its British counterpart, the FBPC possessed no coercive power and could not act authoritatively on behalf of bondholders, but it could collect data and determine whether governments were taking reasonable steps to honor their debts. The FBPC published its own annual reports, with evaluations of settlement plans and blacklists of countries that defaulted on dollar bonds. In this way, the FBPC gave investors yet another source of data to distinguish the lemons from more creditworthy types.

Even when bondholder councils determined that a default arose from inability rather than unwillingness to pay, advisors cautioned against re-

---

[25] *Economist*, November 14, 1868, 1301.
[26] Ronald 1935, 425.
[27] Lyon 1926, 97–98.
[28] U.S. Securities and Exchange Commission 1937.
[29] Corporation of Foreign Bondholders, *Annual Report* 33 (1907), 11.

suming lending until two additional conditions had been met. First, economic conditions needed to improve. According to the vice president of the American Academy, "If past defaults are to be attributed to a lack of economic capacity then bad faith need not be hurriedly charged, though the investor will assure himself that the economic causes of default have been rectified before hazarding his capital."[30] Second, the debtor needed to make amends with creditors. An "unavoidable" default would have "no bearing upon future state credit," provided the borrower "subsequently redeemed" its debts.[31]

In summary, analysts of the 1920s not only attached high importance to reputation, but also sensitized readers to contextual variables. A country that defaulted without a legitimate excuse sent ominous signals to the investment community, which branded the nation as a "willful defaulter" and recommended against new loans. In contrast, analysts did not blacklist nations that suspended payments due to uncontrollable circumstances, provided that the defaulters offered acceptable settlements after the temporary shocks had passed.

## The Opinions of Contemporary Bankers

The previous sections used investment literature from the 1920s to gauge the importance of reputation and understand how analysts measured it. These results corroborate the findings from the eighteenth and nineteenth centuries, when the importance of reputation manifested itself not only in bond yields and lending decisions, but also in commentary in bond manuals and newspaper reports. Before concluding, I briefly consider the opinions of experts who analyze foreign investments and manage portfolios today.

The data come from open-ended interviews with bankers and fund managers in 1999. My goal in these interviews was to gain background information about how sovereign debt works in the modern period, and to gauge views about the relative importance of reputation and issue linkage. The interviews were neither systematic nor comprehensive, and therefore should receive less weight than the textual analysis of the 1920s. Nevertheless, the statements of bankers and financial experts at the turn of the twenty-first century corroborate the evidence from earlier eras.

Tellingly, I did not meet or correspond with a single banker who believed that issue linkage was more powerful or important than reputation. In fact, bankers typically dismissed issue linkage as irrelevant or implausi-

---

[30] Patterson 1928, 27.
[31] Chamberlain and Edwards 1927, 161.

ble. The following three quotations fairly represent the general tone of the interviews. An official at the Institute of Export in London said, "I would strongly support your first possibility that default sends a negative signal to lenders. In the case of sovereign indebtedness, it is unlikely that any 'punishment' factor would feature."[32] Likewise, the head of finance at the U.S. Export-Import Bank in Washington insisted, "The punishment mechanism is by far the weaker mechanism. Debt problems do, however, signal to creditors that lending should become more conservative or pricey."[33] Finally, a managing director of JP Morgan and a former vice president of the World Bank explained, "If a government interrupts debt service payments its credit rating will decline, and spreads on outstanding debt will increase. Banks generally would not have a punitive intention to reduce their exposure. They would simply be reacting to the changed assessment of risk."[34]

Thus, available data from the late 1990s replicates the patterns from earlier periods. Across time, notions of reputation have been central to debtor-creditor relations, while sanctions have played little if any role.

## Conclusion

This chapter tested my theory of reputation by examining the recommendations of investment experts. It first considered the written advice of investment analysts during the 1920s. In a systematic and unbiased sample of texts, analysts overwhelmingly emphasized the reputation of the borrower as a key criterion for investment. They placed far less emphasis on military retaliation and, with only one exception, never mentioned trade sanctions as a potential enforcement tool. Thus, the evidence strongly supported reputation-based models of debt and, at the same time, cast doubt on the practical relevance of extrinsic sanctions.

This kind of textual analysis should be taken as reliable for two reasons. First, investment analysts have a pecuniary incentive to publish honest and accurate recommendations. Social scientists know that individuals do not always reveal their true beliefs or intentions. In personal interviews, published texts, and even private correspondence, actors sometimes misrepresent themselves, and scholars take that possibility into account. In the industry considered here, however, analysts have a financial motive to offer sincere recommendations. They are, for the most part, paid to tell the truth. We should, therefore, be especially willing to take their state-

[32] July 22, 1999.
[33] August 30, 1999.
[34] July 23, 1999.

ments at face value. Second, my sample was unbiased, since it came from specialized and objective bibliographies of the time.

The chapter presented several additional pieces of evidence, all of which reinforce the central conclusion. When banks market bonds to the public, they have every reason to highlight features that would make the security attractive. They emphasize the credit history of the borrower but do not mention vulnerability to extrinsic sanctions. Likewise, rating manuals chronicle the defaults and repayments of each country so investors can screen before making an investment. In contrast, they devote no space to the retaliatory power of creditors. Finally, regulators seek to protect investors by requiring disclosure, not about the nation's vulnerability to extrinsic sanctions, but about its record of defaults and repayments.

The chapter showed that analysts not only keep reputation foremost in their minds, but also think about reputation as hypothesized in chapter 2. In particular, analysts use contextual information to interpret credit histories. They shun governments that default without good cause, but also understand that defaults arise for reasons beyond the control of the borrower. In the next chapter I show that investors, like their advisors, take context into account; they interpret default records differently during good times and bad.

# Chapter 5

## Reputations during Good Times and Bad

CHAPTER 4 showed that investment experts—analysts, bankers, and regulators—attach high importance to reputation. They regard past performance as one of the first tests of a foreign government bond, and they study repayment records to learn about the borrower's type. The evidence also confirmed that experts use contextual information to interpret past performance. They consider, in particular, whether the borrower defaulted in good times or bad.

I now extend the analysis by investigating whether actual investment decisions reflect this kind of contextual reasoning. My empirical analysis focuses on the interwar period, which offers significant variation in both economic conditions and credit histories.[1] After growing rapidly for most of the 1920s, the world economy contracted sharply during the Great Depression. In these boom and bust phases, some countries repaid their debts, whereas others fell into arrears. The interwar period therefore offers an opportunity to test whether reputations—and investments—reflect the interaction of behavior and context. The chapter analyzes how reputations formed during the lending boom of the 1920s, and then considers how reputations changed during the depression that began in 1929.

### The Treatment of Lemons during Good Times

Most countries honored their debts during the roaring 1920s, but a few suspended payments without a valid excuse. In my theory, such acts of defiance send unambiguously negative signals about the borrower's type; they reveal the perpetrator as a lemon and dissuade investors from lending. I test this prediction by identifying defaults in the 1920s and documenting how investors responded.

Several countries failed to pay their debts during the 1920s, even though they had no obvious economic warrant. Russia headed the list

---

[1] Several fine studies have examined debtor-creditor relations during the interwar years; they provide a starting point for the analysis in this chapter. See especially Díaz Alejandro 1983; Eichengreen 1991, 1992; Eichengreen and Portes 1986, 1989; Fishlow 1985, 1989; Jorgensen and Sachs 1989; Kindleberger 1986; Lindert and Morton 1989; Marichal 1989; Obstfeld and Taylor 2003, 2004; Oye 1992; Simmons 1994; and Suter 1990, 1992.

of apparent lemons. Shortly after the revolution of 1917, Soviet leaders decreed that debts contracted by the czars were null and void. Observers viewed the Soviet repudiation as a political act, rather than a response to economic shocks. Notwithstanding several attempts by Western creditors to negotiate a solution, the country remained in complete default until the 1990s.

Mexico, too, had little economic excuse for its arrears. After borrowing abroad under Porfirio Díaz, the conservative general who governed Mexico for decades, Mexico stopped paying in 1914. Observers attributed the default to the revolution that brought liberals to power. According to Albert Kimber, the vice president of Fitch Rating Service, there was "no good reason why the debt charges should not be paid." As a result of their behavior, he wrote, "The Mexican people are discredited in the eyes of other nations and the Mexican Government cannot borrow a dollar in any money market of the world."[2]

Similarly, Ecuador defaulted and refused to compensate its creditors. Notorious for its stop-and-go record, the country offered in 1908 to settle its infractions once and for all. The plan collapsed two years later, when Ecuador reverted to its previous policy of nonpayment. Servicing resumed in 1911, but Ecuador again defaulted in 1914 and made no transfers to creditors for more than a decade. As the Corporation of Foreign Bondholders argued in report after report, the Ecuadorian default had arisen not from a lack of means, but from a lack of desire to pay foreign debts. Investors received a glimmer of hope in 1926 when Ecuador brought interest payments up to date, but by January 1927 the country defaulted once again. Thus, throughout the economic boom of the 1920s, Ecuador lived up to its reputation as a lemon. China, Honduras, Liberia, Paraguay, and Turkey rounded out the list of countries that remained in default for much of the 1920s.

As predicted, not one of these lemons raised a cent on international markets during the boom period. Table 5.1 shows the relationship between credit history and access to capital for sovereign countries with at least a half million people. The table distinguishes three groups of countries: those in default during the 1920s, those that serviced their international obligations completely from 1921 through the end of the decade, and those that lacked a foreign credit history. For each group, the table reports who borrowed in the 1920s and who did not.[3]

---

[2] Kimber 1919, 277, 291.

[3] To qualify as a borrower, the central government had to issue at least one foreign bond that was publicly traded on a stock exchange and did not carry the guarantee of another sovereign. This criterion helped ensure that each loan reflected the perceived creditworthiness of the borrower, rather than the reputation of the guarantor or the ulterior motives of a private corporation that held the entire debt. I did not, for example, count a loan to

TABLE 5.1
Relationship between Credit History and New Borrowing in the 1920s

| Credit History | Borrowed in the 1920s | Did Not Borrow in the 1920s |
|---|---|---|
| In default in the 1920s | | China, Ecuador, Honduras, Liberia, Mexico, Paraguay, Russia, Turkey |
| No default 1921–29 | Argentina, Australia, Belgium, Bolivia, Brazil, Bulgaria, Canada, Chile, Colombia, Costa Rica, Cuba, Denmark, Dominican Republic, El Salvador, France, Greece, Guatemala, Haiti, Italy, Japan, Netherlands, New Zealand, Norway, Panama, Peru, Portugal, Siam, South Africa, Sweden, Switzerland, Uruguay | Egypt, Nicaragua, Persia, Spain, Venezuela |
| No credit history | Austria, Czechoslovakia, Estonia, Finland, Germany, Hungary, Ireland, Poland, Romania, Yugoslavia | Afghanistan, Albania, Ethiopia, Latvia, Lithuania |

Source: Author's compilation from Moody's Investors Service, *Moody's Manual of Investments*; and Kimber, *Kimber's Record of Government Debts*.

The void in the upper left cell of table 5.1 demonstrates that countries could not reborrow while they remained in default. Russia, Mexico, Ecuador, and others may have saved money in the short run by refusing to service their debts, but they lost access to new credit as a consequence. Investors would not venture additional capital to countries that had "the resources and the ability to pay" but did "not regard obligations in the same light as the average Britisher or American does."[4] In contrast, investors lent to more than 30 experienced borrowers that were servicing their debts, and to an additional 10 countries with no credit history at all. Thus, investors of the 1920s practiced the same form of credit rationing that was evident in previous periods.

The lemons of the 1920s failed to borrow, not because they were targets of a retaliatory credit embargo, but because they frightened potential investors by signaling a low regard for foreign commitments. Commentators in the 1920s emphasized that bondholders could not coalesce to punish a defaulter. "It is more or less impracticable for the holders of a particular issue to get together for united action," one analyst explained,

---

Albania that included the full backing of the Italian Treasury, nor a loan to Latvia that was privately held by the Swedish Match Trust. In the latter case, the loan arose not from the inherent creditworthiness of Latvia, but from an agreement that gave the Swedish firm a monopoly on match production.

[4] Badger 1928, 700.

and for this reason repayment "depends mostly on the good faith of the obligor," whose "past record in such matters is more to be trusted than the wording of the contract."[5]

Five countries in table 5.1 did not issue new debt, even though they met their obligations in full. These cases seem puzzling for reputational theory. Why didn't investors lend to Egypt, Nicaragua, Persia, Spain, and Venezuela, all of which were in good standing? There are two possible answers. Either investors stayed away for purely economic reasons, or the repayers did not want new loans.

Both explanations have some plausibility. When economic data are available, investors base their decisions not only on credit histories but also on the borrower's capacity to repay. Moreover, developing countries sometimes choose to eschew international markets. In the late 1800s, for example, Spain launched a campaign to repatriate its foreign debt and replace external issues with internal ones. Venezuela, another seemingly puzzling case in table 5.1, adopted a similar policy during the interwar period: to commemorate the centenary of the death of Simón Bolívar, liberator of South America during the wars of independence from Spain, the government remitted double the amount required under contract until it retired the entire foreign debt in 1930.

Both explanations fall outside the scope of reputational theory. It is important to stress here, as before, that reputational theory does not account for all behavior by lenders and borrowers. Nonreputational factors affect both lending and repayment. Nevertheless, table 5.1 contains a notably small number of exceptional cases. Most of the variance in the table is consistent with the reputational theory developed in this book.

## The Treatment of New Borrowers during Good Times

The final row of table 5.1 lists countries that lacked credit histories. Afghanistan and Albania, although sovereign before World War I, had no history of foreign debt as of the 1920s. Czechoslovakia, Estonia, Finland, Ireland, Latvia, Lithuania, Poland, and Yugoslavia, on the other hand, had recently emerged as new countries. Following the investment literature of the period, I also included Romania as a new country, since it was "an aggregation of previously unrelated and politically hostile territories."[6] Finally, I added Germany and the rump states of the Austro-Hungarian Empire to the roster of new countries, since they had changed so

[5] Kirshman 1924, 291.
[6] Taylor 1924, 112.

radically during the war. The conclusions presented below do not depend on these coding decisions, however.

The existence of unseasoned borrowers allowed me to test, once again, the hypothesis that investors demanded higher yields from new borrowers than from established ones. As a first step, I computed yields for 266 sovereign bonds that were traded in London or New York during 1928.[7] By that year, all new borrowers had entered the market but investors had not yet anticipated the defaults of the Great Depression. I next sorted the sovereigns into four groups: seasoned borrowers, which had borrowed repeatedly but never defaulted; settlers, which had suspended payments at some point but were now honoring their debts in full; new borrowers, which had less than 10 years of experience; and lemons, which had defaulted without good cause and not yet settled their arrears. Yields increased in stepwise fashion across these groups. Seasoned borrowers had the lowest yields, with an unweighted average of 5.3 percent across the 77 bonds in that category. Settlers came next (5.9 percent, $N = 122$ bonds), followed by new entrants (7.0 percent, $N = 28$ bonds), and lemons (38.5 percent, $N = 39$ bonds).

To verify that these differences did not arise from chance or confounding influences, I regressed the natural log of the bond yield on dummy variables for each category of borrower, plus a battery of controls. As in chapter 3, lemons did not belong in the regression with other types of borrowers, because investors paid little attention to the economic statistics of countries that refused to pay regardless of their capacity. I therefore restricted the sample to seasoned borrowers, settlers, and new entrants. The final sample contained 227 bonds drawn from 41 sovereign countries.

The regression contained two economic control variables. The first was relative wealth, the per capita wealth of the borrower as a proportion of the U.S. level. As late as 1928, investors still did not have accurate and comprehensive statistics on national income. Bond manuals and textbooks of the 1920s instead recommended per capita wealth. Moody's Investors Service wrote in 1925 that "in spite of their crudeness," estimates of per capita wealth constituted "the best single index to the credit standing of nations."[8] In my sample, the wealth of seasoned payers such as Canada and Switzerland was more than 80 percent of the U.S. level, whereas most Latin American states had less than a fifth of U.S. wealth on a per capita basis. In the few cases where wealth was not reported, I imputed it from

[7] For each bond, I calculated a yield by dividing the nominal interest rate by the average of the bond's high and low prices for the year 1928. Interest rates and high-low prices came from Moody's Investors Service, *Moody's Manual of Investments*.

[8] Moody's Investors Service, *Moody's Manual of Investments* (1925), xxxiv.

data on motor vehicles per capita, which were highly correlated with wealth levels.[9]

The second economic control was the ratio of debt to wealth. Other factors equal, countries with larger debts should have higher yields. Analysts of the time pointed out, however, that wealthy countries could handle large debts more easily than poor countries, and therefore used the ratio of debt to wealth as an instructive measure of bankability. I included this variable, both because it accorded with investment commentary from the period, and because it was a precursor to more modern measures such as debt to gross domestic product.[10]

Finally, I included two dummy variables to capture variation in the characteristics of the bonds. One indicated the few cases in which foreign powers controlled customs revenues or other collateral on the bond. The other represented whether the bond was denominated in dollars or sterling, since the challenges of remitting foreign funds may not have been equal for the two currencies.

The statistical results appear in table 5.2. As expected, the coefficients on the settler and new borrower variables were positive and each was estimated with considerable precision.[11] Both types had significantly higher yields than seasoned borrowers, the reference category. Other explanatory variables exerted the anticipated effects, as well. Investors required lower yields from wealthier borrowers, and they demanded higher yields from nations with outsized debts in relation to wealth. Dollar bonds had slightly higher yields, perhaps due to exchange rate risks and other differences between the New York and London markets. Finally, both foreign control over the customshouse and the presence of an external guarantee reduced the risk of default, thereby lowering the yield on sovereign bonds.

The dependent variable in table 5.2 was measured in a log metric, making it difficult to interpret the magnitude of the coefficients. Holding other variables constant, what was the size of the uncertainty premium—the extra yield investors required from new borrowers, to cover the risk that the unproven entity could be an unreliable type? I used simulation to answer this question. Specifically, I imagined a bond that was issued by a

[9] Data on motor vehicles per capita were obtained from League of Nations 1931, 18–23, 186–88. In a bivariate regression of wealth on vehicles, $R^2 = .73$.

[10] Data on indebtedness were obtained from Moody's Investors Service, *Moody's Manual of Investments*; and Redmond & Co. 1928.

[11] Most countries issued several bonds, which were not statistically independent of each other. The presence of such dependent observations could deflate the standard errors and increase the *t*-statistics. To address this problem I corrected the standard errors for clustering. There were 227 observations but only 41 independent clusters. The corrected standard errors appear in table 5.2.

TABLE 5.2
Regression Analysis of Bond Yields in 1928

| Variable | Estimated Coefficient | Standard Error | t-statistic |
|---|---|---|---|
| Settler | 0.09 | 0.03 | 2.8 |
| New borrower | 0.20 | 0.04 | 4.4 |
| Relative wealth | −0.45 | 0.07 | 6.4 |
| Debt/wealth | 0.46 | 0.16 | 2.8 |
| Financial control | −0.20 | 0.04 | 4.7 |
| Dollar debt | 0.16 | 0.02 | 8.3 |
| Constant | 1.72 | 0.05 | 34.8 |

Source: Author's compilations from League of Nations 1931; Moody's Investors Service, Moody's Manual of Investments; and Redmond & Co. 1928.

Note: Estimates from ordinary least squares (OLS) regression with robust standard errors, clustered by country. The dependent variable is the natural log of yields. The omitted category is seasoned borrower, whose average bond yields are impounded in the constant term. The sample includes $N = 227$ bonds from 41 countries, and does not include guaranteed loans or the bonds of lemons. $R^2 = .60$, and the standard error of the regression is 0.12.

seasoned borrower of average wealth and debt as a share of wealth. I further supposed that the bond was denominated in dollars and did not involve collateral controlled by a foreign power. I calculated the expected yield for such a bond and compared it to anticipated yield on an identical bond issued by a new borrower. The difference between these two quantities represents the average uncertainty premium of the late 1920s.

The simulation shows that, even controlling for economic variables and the idiosyncrasies of particular bonds, new borrowers were at a substantial disadvantage. Compared with experienced borrowers, newcomers had to pay a premium of 1.3 percentage points. The 95 percent confidence interval around this estimate ranged from 0.7 to 1.9, indicating that investors treated these two classes of borrowers differently.

The results are robust to changes in coding. The territorial predecessors of Austria, Hungary, and Germany had borrowed during the nineteenth and early twentieth centuries, and had not always honored their debts in full. When I reclassified all three states as settlers rather than new borrowers, the results remained essentially the same: the expected uncertainty premium was 1.2 percentage points, with a confidence interval of 0.6 to 1.8. I also noticed that, among new borrowers, Ireland appeared to be an outlier. Dropping Ireland from the sample increased the new-borrower premium slightly, to 1.4 percentage points on average.

Why did investors demand such a premium from new borrowers? Analysts of the 1920s attributed it to uncertainty about the borrower's type. A top consultant to the banking industry wrote in 1927:

It is somewhat difficult to evaluate the "character" of the people of the "new" countries of Europe, such as Finland and Czechoslovakia, for example. Their history as independent nations is too recent to permit the same sureness of judgment as in the case of Denmark and Portugal, for instance. They need a period of "seasoning" before the same weight can be given to their records as to those of older countries.[12]

The dean of the business school at New York University gave a similar interpretation.

Political entities of recent birth, like Poland, Czechoslovakia, or the Kingdom of Serbs, Croats and Slovenes, have somewhat uncertain credit because they are new. It will take them some years to acquire title to the fullest confidence. Countries like Roumania, an aggregation of previously unrelated and politically hostile territories, are in the same credit position. Such new countries must put up ample collateral security when they borrow in foreign money markets, and even then must pay high rates of interest because of the element of risk in their obligations.[13]

Hartley Withers, editor of the *Economist* magazine, agreed. With countries like Argentina, "There is at least a record to work on," he noted, "but how can anyone make a guess concerning the probable performance of the frisky European three-year-olds who have lately made their appearance?" Withers himself preferred a "mature vintage," a country that had paid "for half a century or even for twenty years" and thus acquired a distinctive "aroma, like a bottle that is whiskered with honorable cobwebs."[14]

Perhaps the clearest and most succinct statement came from Thomas Lamont, senior partner at J. P. Morgan. An authority on international lending, Lamont had not only underwritten bonds for sovereigns around the world but had also chaired an international commission that negotiated with Mexico after the revolution. According to Lamont, "Investments in the government bonds of new or backward countries yield higher rates of return. They are less seasoned and investors, therefore, require a higher rate of interest."[15]

Evidence from the 1920s, therefore, reinforces the conclusions from earlier eras. Like their predecessors from the eighteenth and nineteenth centuries, investors of the interwar period demanded higher yields from new borrowers than from proven entities. Moreover, leading bankers, consultants, academics, and editors explained that the premium arose from uncertainty about the borrower's type. These findings increase confidence not only in the predictive power of reputational theory, but also in its causal logic.

[12] Atkins 1927, 24.
[13] Taylor 1924, 112.
[14] Withers 1926, 89–90.
[15] Lamont 1920, 122.

## What Happens during Bad Times?

By any measure, the Great Depression of the 1930s qualifies as one of the most severe crises in the history of international finance. Economic activity contracted sharply not only in core economies such as the United States and the United Kingdom but also in peripheral nations that had borrowed money on international markets. To repay their foreign debts, which were typically denominated in British pounds or U.S. dollars, governments needed foreign exchange. Prior to 1929 they met their needs through two sources. First, they issued new bonds in New York and London and used the proceeds to service preexisting debts, in a process known as rollover. Second, they exported primary products such as wheat, copper, tobacco, and beef to core nations, thereby earning the hard currency they needed to meet their obligations. The depression greatly limited both options.

Even before the crash of October 1929, the supply of international loans began to dry up. According to Barry Eichengreen and Richard Portes, "The mounting boom on Wall Street diverted American funds from foreign to domestic uses and, like a powerful suction pump, siphoned off liquidity from the rest of the world."[16] By the beginning of 1929, creditor countries such as the United States had reached the crossover point at which earnings from loans exceeded the value of new capital issues. Thus, developing regions experienced a net capital outflow. The situation eased temporarily in early 1930 when, due to more favorable market conditions, countries such as Argentina, Canada, and Germany floated several new bonds on the New York market. Thereafter, the global depression brought capital markets to a standstill. During 1931–32 U.S. investors extended almost no new loans, making it impossible for countries to roll over their debts.

The depression also made it increasingly difficult for countries to pursue an export-oriented strategy of repayment. Faced with an economic slowdown at home, manufacturers and consumers in core countries like the United States reduced their demand for imports, causing the price of primary commodities to tumble. Since capital markets were already extremely tight, the fall in prices meant that countries could service their debts only by exporting ever-greater quantities. In effect, the depression increased the real burden of debts, requiring countries to pay more (in terms of commodities or services) than they originally intended. Moreover, policymakers in the United States, Britain, and other countries responded to the depression by increasing protectionist barriers, which impeded international trade. Faced with the twin shocks of depression and

---

[16] Eichengreen and Portes 1989, 73.

protectionism, many debtors experienced steep reductions in the value of their exports, and thus had trouble earning foreign exchange to service their debts.

Defaults began in January 1931, when Bolivia suspended payment on its foreign bonds. Within only a few years, the debt crisis had spread throughout Latin America and Eastern Europe, leaving barely half of sovereign borrowers in full compliance with their debt contracts. To quantify the spread of the crisis, I calculated a compliance score for each country and year from 1929 until 1938. Compliance, in this context, was defined as the amount of interest the sovereign paid in foreign currency, divided by the value contractually required. A country that transferred $3 million in interest to creditors during a given year, even though it should have paid $5 million, would have earned a compliance score of .6 for that year.

I focused on interest rather than amortization for two reasons. First, I found no clear standard for comparing amortization rates across countries. Some bonds of the interwar period had sinking funds, which required the sovereign to retire the debt gradually over a number of years instead of repaying the entire loan in one lump sum at maturity. Other bonds had no such provisions. It seemed unwise to compare compliance rates along a dimension that appeared in some contracts but was absent from others. Second, creditors attached far greater importance to interest payments than to amortization. Even before the depression struck, analysts wrote that the suspension of amortization typically "causes little concern to creditors," since "the investor is not likely to be interested so much in the payment of principal or in the regularity of the amortization payments so long as the interest payments are made regularly."[17] During the depression, the financial press classified violations of the sinking fund clause as the "mildest" form of default, about which "no fair-minded bondholder should object."[18] In contrast, observers regarded the suspension of interest as a serious act of default.

To calculate compliance with interest obligations, I collected data on the performance of all sovereign bonds denominated in U.S. dollars or British pounds and traded on international markets during the 1930s. My database, compiled by hand from bond manuals by Fitch, Kimber, Moody's Investors Service, White, Weld & Co., and other publicists, included details on 388 bonds on an annual basis. From the amounts outstanding and the interest rate schedules, I calculated how much each sovereign should have transferred to creditors in any given year. My database also contained records of more than 10,000 separate cash payments that

[17] Madden and Nadler 1929, 270.
[18] *Bankers Magazine*, March 1934, 314; *Barron's*, May 25, 1931, 16; September 26, 1932, 23.

sovereigns made or missed during the period under study. By aggregating these payments, I determined how much the sovereign actually paid. The ratio of actual to ideal payments gave my measure of compliance.

Figure 5.1 plots compliance by country and year for 53 sovereigns. The horizontal axis of each subfigure marks time from 1929 through 1938, and the vertical axis gives compliance on a scale from 0 to 1. The figure shows considerable variation across debtors and over time. Consider the top three rows. Argentina, Australia, Belgium, and Canada met all interest obligations during this period. Austria came close, though it slipped slightly in 1938 after becoming part of the German Reich. At the opposite extreme, Bolivia defaulted in 1931 and made no payments for the remainder of the decade. Chile likewise defaulted at an early date, though it made gestures to creditors in the late 1930s. The remaining states—Brazil and Bulgaria—met part of their contractual obligations.

If creditors were truly sensitive to context, they should have acknowledged the external sources of default and not rushed to charge bad faith. Indeed, such logic pervades the financial literature of the 1930s. As Moody's Investors Service explained in 1934, the "sole basic reason" for defaults was that the typical debtor "has been unable to dispose of its produce to the rest of the world at a price sufficiently high to provide it with dollar funds required for dollar debt services." Given the circumstances, Moody's found it "scarcely surprising that many debtor countries were unable during this depression to stand the strain and were forced to suspend or modify external debt services." The rating agency concluded that nearly all defaults had been "occasioned not by intent to escape obligations but by inability to acquire the necessary foreign funds."[19]

Though no country went to the Russian extreme of repudiating its debts, a few probably paid less than investors expected, even given the difficult economic circumstances. In 1937 the Royal Institute of International Affairs reported some dissatisfaction with Greece, which had defaulted in 1932 and offered a relatively constant stream of partial payments for the remainder of the decade. According to the institute, "Many observers believe that the Greek Government is in a position to make better offers to its external creditors and that its default must, in some

---

[19] Moody's Investors Service, *Moody's Manual of Investments* (1934), A32–33. Bankers apparently agreed. Testifying before the Senate Finance Committee, Ray Morris of Brown Brothers attributed the defaults to "overpowering economic necessity," rather than "willful" intransigence by debtors. He cited the example of Chile, which relied on copper and nitrate exports to generate government revenues and foreign exchange. "With these now at a standstill, some interruption of service on her foreign debt became practically inevitable." But "these defaults will be made good as soon as economic conditions permit." Morris's testimony appears in U.S. Congress, Senate Committee on Finance 1931–32, 1576.

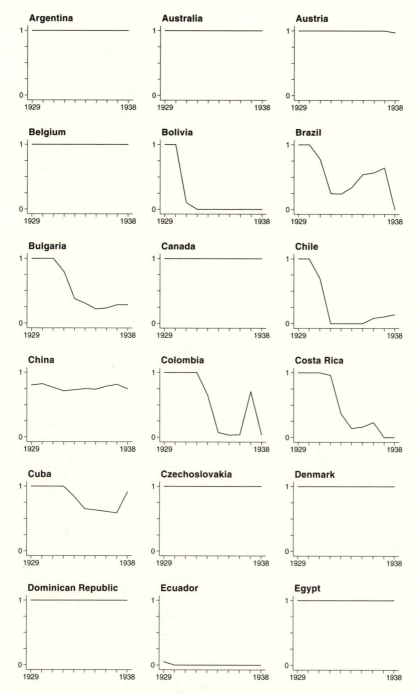

FIGURE 5.1: COMPLIANCE WITH FOREIGN DEBT CONTRACTS, 1929–38
Source: Compiled from Fitch, *The Fitch Bond Book*; Kimber, *Kimber's Record of Government Debts*; Moody's Investors Service, *Moody's Manual of Investments*; Iselin, *Foreign Bonds Issued in the United States*; and White, Weld & Co., *Foreign Dollar Bonds*.

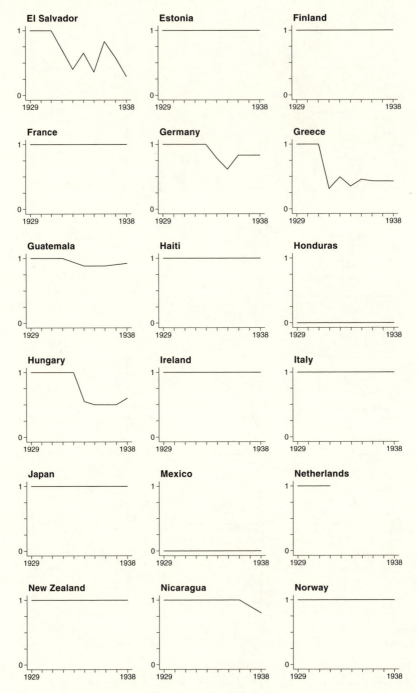

FIGURE 5.1 (continued, part B)

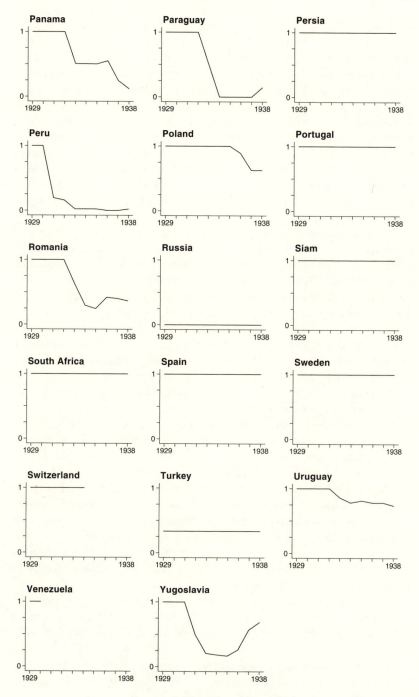

FIGURE 5.1 (continued, part C)

measure, be due to unwillingness rather than inability to pay."[20] The annual publications of bondholder councils in the United States and Britain also accused certain nations of not doing all they could to satisfy creditors.

In general, though, creditors knew the defaults had arisen from exceptional conditions. Yields of the recently defaulted sovereigns in Latin America and Eastern Europe never rose to the heights of an obvious lemon like Russia; rather, they remained at levels that suggested hope of repayment once the crisis had passed. As anticipated in the previous chapter, both analysts and investors took context into account. They inferred that the defaulters could not have been stalwarts but did not proceed to brand them as lemons. Without sufficient evidence to accuse the defaulters of bad faith, markets treated those countries as likely fair-weathers that had fallen on tough times.

Nevertheless, investors would not venture new capital to countries that remained in default. They needed a costly signal to be sure that the debtor was indeed a fair-weather, rather than a lemon. Evidence for this prediction appears in table 5.3. The rows distinguish countries that defaulted on interest payments during the years 1931–37 from those that complied in full. The columns indicate which countries issued new foreign-currency loans on international markets after 1931 but before 1939.[21] As the table shows, not a single country that defaulted during the Great Depression managed to float new bonds during 1932–38. In contrast, several payers attracted new credit even during this period of relatively tight liquidity.

Did creditors organize an embargo against the 26 defaulters in table 5.3? Documents in bank archives and articles in the popular press contain no hint of such collaboration, even though the organizers could have publicized an embargo to deter other nations from defaulting. An alternative interpretation seems more plausible: investors shied away from lending to the likes of Bolivia and Brazil for fear that such loans would not be profitable. Until those countries signaled their reliability by offering an adequate settlement, investors preferred to sit on the sidelines. This interpretation fits most closely with the investment literature of the period (as cited in this chapter and the previous one), and it does not require thousands of current and future investors to overcome collective action problems. Table 5.3 adds to other evidence in this book to form a coherent picture of how reputations work.

Many countries that serviced their debts during the 1930s managed to float new loans, but several countries in the lower right corner of table 5.3 chose not to borrow. As traditional creditors, France, Sweden, Swit-

---

[20] Royal Institute of International Affairs 1937, 247.

[21] For reasons stated earlier, I excluded any loan that was guaranteed by a foreign sovereign or placed with a private corporation.

TABLE 5.3
Relationship between Credit History and New Borrowing in the 1930s

| Credit History | Borrowed in 1932–38 | Did Not Borrow in 1932–38 |
| --- | --- | --- |
| Defaulted during 1931–37 | | Bolivia, Brazil, Bulgaria, Chile, China, Colombia, Costa Rica, Cuba, Ecuador, El Salvador, Germany, Greece, Guatemala, Honduras, Hungary, Mexico, Nicaragua, Panama, Paraguay, Peru, Poland, Romania, Russia, Turkey, Uruguay, Yugoslavia |
| Did not default during 1931–37 | Argentina, Australia, Belgium, Canada, Denmark, Finland, New Zealand, Norway, Siam, South Africa | Austria, Czechoslovakia, Dominican Republic, Egypt, Estonia, France, Haiti, Ireland, Italy, Japan, Netherlands, Persia, Portugal, Spain, Sweden, Switzerland |

*Source*: Author's compilation from Moody's Investors Service, *Moody's Manual of Investments*.

zerland, and the Netherlands turned to international markets in the 1920s only because war had led to a shortage of capital. Moody's put Ireland in the same category, calling it a creditor whose earnings from foreign investment exceeded the payments on its external debts.[22] During the 1930s, these countries typically found themselves in better economic shape than either the United States or the United Kingdom and opted to rely on domestic capital instead of seeking funds abroad. Two pieces of evidence support this interpretation. First, many of these countries repatriated their debts; they raised loans on the domestic capital market and used the proceeds to retire their foreign obligations. Second, investors in these countries actually lent to foreigners during the 1930s.[23] If such countries were truly strapped for cash, they probably would not have called in their external bonds, nor would they have permitted foreign lending. Most likely, these creditor states could have borrowed abroad but elected not to do so.

Other countries in the lower right corner probably could not borrow because creditors doubted that compliance would last. The prospect of war posed an obvious danger. As the Royal Institute of International Affairs wrote in 1937, "There has been little or no difficulty in connection with service payments on foreign investment in Japan, whose credit stand-

[22] Moody's Investors Service, *Moody's Manual of Investments* (1934), A33.
[23] Investors in Switzerland underwrote bonds for Belgium and Norway; those in Sweden lent to Belgium, Denmark, Finland, and Norway; French investors lent to Argentina, Belgium, Czechoslovakia; and the Dutch lent to Denmark and Luxembourg.

ing would consequently be very high, were it not for the continued threat of war in the Far East."[24] Impending changes in domestic politics may have raised doubts, as well. Haiti, for example, behaved like a stalwart during the 1930s, but its punctual service in the face of severe shocks was "no mystery," given the presence of U.S. Marines and a customs receiver that collected tariff revenues and remitted the proceeds to bondholders.[25] The situation changed in late 1934, when U.S. Marines withdrew and the power of the customs receiver declined. From that point forward, investors must have wondered whether they could expect the same compliance they had previously observed.[26]

In summary, investors did not allege bad faith by most countries that defaulted during the depression, but they did refrain from extending new credit until the economic crisis passed and the debtors offered acceptable settlements. At the same time, markets continued to deal with countries that paid their debts in full. These patterns are highly consistent with the theory of reputation developed in chapter 2.

## The Treatment of Surprising Payers during Bad Times

I now test an additional implication of the reputational theory: a country that pays during difficult times can establish itself as a stalwart, and thereby obtain easier credit when it returns to international markets. The improvement should be especially pronounced for countries that were not previously held in the highest regard. To test this proposition, I developed a method for identifying "surprising payers," those that honored their debts in full even though investors expected a default. I then asked whether the surprising payers received significantly easier credit when they reborrowed, and I consulted archival documents and the financial press to see how investors justified the loans they made. As we will see, surprising payers climbed the reputational ladder and gained access to better credit because they revealed themselves as stalwarts.

Which countries surprised creditors the most? For an answer, I examined the market yields of government bonds during 1931–33, the deepest phase of the depression. By that point, the economic crisis had spread

[24] Royal Institute of International Affairs 1937, 267.

[25] Díaz Alejandro 1983, 27.

[26] In a few cases, the data do not reveal whether the sovereign could have borrowed in its own name. Austria and Czechoslovakia paid their debts for all but the final years of the 1930s, and therefore appear in the lower right cell of table 5.3. Before they defaulted in 1938 and 1939, respectively, both countries floated new bonds in foreign markets. The Czech loan of 1937 carried the full guarantee of France, however, and the Austrian loan of 1934 was backed by eight foreign states.

TABLE 5.4
Bond Yields of Countries That Repaid and Reborrowed, 1931–33

| Country | Yield |
| --- | --- |
| Argentina | 10.4 |
| Finland | 9.8 |
| Australia | 7.5 |
| Belgium | 6.7 |
| Norway | 6.6 |
| Denmark | 6.6 |
| Siam | 5.7 |
| Canada | 4.8 |
| New Zealand | 4.2 |
| South Africa | 4.1 |

*Source*: Author's calculations from the *Commercial and Financial Chronicle*; and Moody's Investors Service, *Moody's Manual of Investments*.

*Note*: The countries in the table paid fully during the depression and issued new debt in 1932–38. The table gives average bond yields for the years 1931–33, and therefore measures the expectations of investors during the depths of the depression.

around the world, and investors had witnessed defaults by several debtors in Latin America. Based on their knowledge of the crisis and their prior beliefs about the resolve of debtors that remained in good standing, investors estimated the likelihood that still-compliant countries would continue to meet their obligations in full. Those estimates were reflected in bond prices and yields. If investors perceived the borrower as a fair-weather that would fold under pressure, they bid down the price of its debt, causing yields to rise. Among countries that paid in full throughout the 1930s, those with the highest yields in 1931–33 must have surprised creditors the most.

Table 5.4 reports average yields for countries that repaid their debts throughout the 1930s and reborrowed before World War II.[27] The order of the entries reflects prevailing beliefs about the probability of default. Argentina, with an average yield of 10.4 percent, was seen as the most likely candidate to suspend payments. Investors also feared that Finland and Australia would default. These three countries exceeded expectations by paying their debts to the last cent, and thus stand among the most surprising payers of the interwar period. Investors apparently had more faith in Canada, New Zealand, and South Africa, whose yields remained at fairly low levels during the trough of the depression.

If the reputational theory is correct, surprising payers such as Argentina, Finland, and Australia should have received better terms when they

[27] The list of countries comes from the lower left quadrant of table 5.3.

returned to markets in the late 1930s. I now examine these three cases in detail. As expected, all three countries refinanced their debts at significantly lower interest rates. Moreover, qualitative evidence suggests that they obtained better terms *because* of the reputation they gained by paying during difficult times.

### Argentina as a Surprising Payer

Argentina entered the depression as a reputed fair-weather, a country expected to honor its debts during good times but to default when conditions turned sour. Interwar stockbrokers believed that Argentine bonds "were not 'gilt-edged,' but quite all right as part of a varied menu."[28] The problem, as many recognized, was that Argentina remained vulnerable to external shocks that could trigger a default. The *Economist* presented this view in mid-1929: "Argentine stocks . . . are rated highly among foreign securities, but are not regarded as immune from risks. . . . An agricultural nation must expect to meet bad as well as good times, arising out of circumstances largely beyond its control, however well its several activities may be spread."[29]

The depression did not treat Argentina kindly. Between 1928 and 1932 the Argentine terms of trade, defined as the price of exports relative to imports, fell by approximately 40 percent. On top of this, severe drought led to poor harvests, reducing the quantity of wheat and other agricultural staples that Argentina could export.[30] These shocks not only made it difficult for Argentina to obtain foreign exchange, but also created a perilous fiscal situation. During the late 1920s the Argentine government had obtained more than three-fifths of its revenue from customs and harbor duties. As exports and imports fell, so too did government revenues.[31] The government thus found itself less able to bid for the increasingly scarce supply of foreign exchange. With international capital markets at a standstill, there was little hope of rolling over the government debts, and many reasonable observers expected a default.

Argentina did not bring these problems on itself through poor economic management. Rather, the country and others like it had suffered a stroke of incredible bad luck. In his 1933 report on Argentine finances, Sir Otto Niemeyer of the Bank of England wrote that "the depression

---

[28] Withers 1930, 41.

[29] *Economist*, May 11, 1929, 1054.

[30] O'Connell 1984, 196–97.

[31] "Between January 1929 and September 1930, import and export duties collected at the port of Buenos Aires fell by 10 percent and 45 percent respectively" (Alhadeff 1986, 107).

from which the Argentine is suffering, in common with all other countries of its economic type," arose from "the decline in the purchasing power of industrial countries due to universal trade depression, the disproportionate fall in the prices of agricultural products, [and] the obstruction of trade by economic nationalism." Niemeyer emphasized that these developments were "for the most part outside the influence of separate Argentine action."[32] Considering the severity of the shock and the fact that Argentines did not cause it, investors would have been right to anticipate and excuse a default.

As we have seen, investors did indeed expect a default. Yields on Argentine bonds hovered at more than 10 percent during the early 1930s, and the investment press overflowed with speculation about when the ultimate suspension would occur. While taking care not to create a situation of moral hazard, both bankers and the financial press acknowledged that they would tolerate a default. According to an editor of the *Morning Post*, "British creditors, as a class, usually have the good sense to recognize the limitations of the debtor." If Argentina were to default temporarily, "It seems unlikely that there would be any active resentment by holders of the external debt, especially if combined with a policy of strict economy in the matter of Argentine budget expenditure."[33] Baring Brothers, lead bankers to Argentina for more than a century, showed similar willingness to excuse a temporary breach of contract.[34]

Contrary to the expectations of international investors, Argentina distinguished itself from other borrowers in South America by maintaining a perfect record of debt service throughout the Great Depression, even though its terms of trade and other external indicators had dropped precipitously. Not one central government bond fell into default. Investors had not anticipated this outcome. One financial journalist wrote, "It is astonishing to many observers that the country has been able to maintain service on its national debt so faithfully. The effort and sacrifice involved have, in fact, been tremendous."[35] It seemed that Argentine leaders were displaying "almost superhuman" resolve to avoid default.[36]

How did Argentina achieve such a clean record of debt service when its neighbors were defaulting? The short explanation is that Argentine citizens tightened their belts, thereby leaving enough government revenue and foreign exchange to uphold contractual obligations to foreigners. On

[32] *Review of the River Plate*, April 7, 1933, 19.

[33] *Review of the River Plate*, January 20, 1933, 19.

[34] Letter from Baring Brothers to Argentine finance minister, reprinted in *Review of the River Plate*, January 6, 1933, 38.

[35] *Barron's*, December 26, 1932, 16.

[36] *Review of the River Plate*, August 12, 1932, 13; September 16, 1932, 23.

the fiscal side, the central government raised import duties and imposed an income tax for the first time in Argentine history; it also slashed public spending, even in the previously inviolate civil service and military sectors. These measures transformed the budget deficit of 329 million pesos in 1930 into a surplus by the year 1935.[37] In monetary affairs, the government began commandeering foreign exchange and dedicating it to debt service, thereby depriving domestic firms of the ability to import. As chapter 7 shows, leaders imposed these policies with the express goal of raising Argentina's reputation and improving its subsequent access to capital.

Creditors rewarded this perseverance: Argentina was one of the few countries that issued new bonds in London and New York during the depression, and it was able to convert its entire foreign debt into new issues at lower interest rates. Conversions began in May 1934 when the Argentine government reduced interest rates on its sterling-denominated debt from 5 percent to 4.5 percent (see table 5.5) and cut amortization payments from 1 percent to only 0.5 percent per year. At the same time, the government refinanced its local-currency debt, due largely to the enthusiasm of foreign investors who bought many of the domestic securities.[38] After completing its sterling and peso conversions, the Argentine government refinanced its 6 percent dollar bonds at a new rate of 4 percent and then borrowed $25 million in fresh capital on the New York market in November 1938. This was "the first time in the history of the republic" that internal and external bonds had been issued at such economical rates.[39] Overall, these operations reduced the government's external burden by 30 percent and allowed the government to save £5.1 million per year on its foreign and domestic debts.[40]

The behavior of creditors in response to Argentine policy closely fits the reputational theory. Once seen as a fair-weather, the country behaved like a stalwart during the depression. By doing the unexpected, Argentina bolstered its reputation in the eyes of creditors, who responded by lowering interest rates and raising credit ceilings at a time when most governments were shut out of capital markets.

The standing ovation Argentina received from foreign creditors reflected the reputation it acquired for paying during difficult times. As Sir Otto Niemeyer wrote to the Argentine finance minister in June 1934, the

[37] *Barron's*, July 15, 1935, 17.

[38] "Argentina: Bond Issues Since the Beginning of 1937," Memorandum, March 22, 1938, OV 102/8, Bank of England Archives.

[39] J. H. Leche to Anthony Eden, December 22, 1936, OV 102/6, Bank of England Archives.

[40] Alhadeff 1983, 178–79; "Argentine Conversion Savings," Memorandum of the Overseas and Foreign Department, August 7, 1937, OV 102/7, Bank of England Archives.

TABLE 5.5
Argentina's Debt Conversion, 1934–37

| Conversion Date | Bond Name | Currency | Original Interest Rate (%) | New Interest Rate (%) |
|---|---|---|---|---|
| May 1934 | City of Buenos Aires (1909) | £ | 5.0 | 4.5 |
| May 1934 | Argentine Irrigation Loan (1913) | £ | 5.0 | 4.5 |
| September 1934 | Port of Buenos Aires (1892) | £ | 5.0 | 4.5 |
| September 1934 | Buenos Aires Water Supply (1892) | £ | 5.0 | 4.5 |
| September 1934 | Internal Loan (1907) | £ | 5.0 | 4.5 |
| September 1934 | Internal Loan (1909) | £ | 5.0 | 4.5 |
| September 1934 | Internal Loan (1910) | £ | 5.0 | 4.5 |
| December 1934 | Port of the Capital (1913) | £ | 5.0 | 4.5 |
| October 1935 | Argentine Railway (1896–99) | £ | 4.0 | 3.5 |
| November 1936 | External Series B (1924) | $ | 6.0 | 4.5 |
| February 1937 | External Series A (1923) | $ | 6.0 | 4.0 |
| February 1937 | State Railway (1927) | $ | 6.0 | 4.0 |
| April 1937 | Public Works (1926) | $ | 6.0 | 4.0 |
| April 1937 | Public Works (1927) | $ | 6.0 | 4.0 |

Source: República Argentina, Presidente 1938, vol. 1, chap. 3; Moody's Investors Service, *Moody's Manual of Investments*; White, Weld & Co., *Foreign Dollar Bonds*; and Council of the Corporation of Foreign Bondholders, Newspaper Cuttings Files, Guildhall Library.

successful conversion of Argentine debt in London was "made possible by the impression created by the firm adherence of Argentina . . . to the payment of her foreign obligations. Had it not been for the reputation so gained, I am sure that the result could not have been achieved . . . the prevalence of defaults by others doubly enhances the standing of those who do not default."[41]

Articles in the London press echoed Niemeyer's view. The *Economist* noted that Argentina had enhanced its "good name" through "the exemplary manner" in which it complied with its financial obligations throughout the depression. By elevating its reputation, the nation "succeeded in penetrating the wall of fire" surrounding the London capital market and converted its sterling-denominated debt to lower rates of interest.[42] Likewise, the *Times* reported in September 1934 that "Argentina

[41] Otto Niemeyer to Alberto Hueyo, June 13, 1934, OV 102/4, Bank of England Archives.

[42] *Economist*, April 28, 1934, 933; February 8, 1936, 6. The *South American Journal* (May 25, 1935, 515), a leading source of economic data for British bankers, concurred: Argentina "as a primary producer, has been badly hit during the past five years; but the Government has maintained Argentine credit at the highest level, by steadfastly refusing to agree to any schemes of interference with the strict letter of its contractual debt obligations, and is now getting its reward." See also the *Financial News*, May 29, 1934, 1.

has throughout the severe economic depression maintained in full the service of her external debt. At times this has involved . . . considerable strain." But Argentina "has succeeded where every other South American state has failed. She is now to receive the reward for this exceptional financial record."[43]

Reactions were similar in New York, where Argentina converted its debt and then obtained new loans in 1938. *Barron's* magazine explained that investors were willing to extend cheap credit because Argentina had "demonstrated to the world how it values a satisfactory credit rating . . . with every other South American borrower and the majority throughout the world taking the easier course, [Argentina] kept its eyes fixed on the goal of meeting contractual obligations. This during the most severe and comprehensive economic dislocation the world has yet seen when so many countries seemed to feel the matter of debt honor wasn't worth the sacrifice."[44] The *New York Herald Tribune* added, "The numerous Latin-American defaulters have to stand, hat in hand, and beg for advances from the official Export-Import Bank. But Argentina stands as a shining example of probity in international financial dealings and fully deserves, on her record, the ability to borrow in the United States."[45]

Credit markets in the 1930s therefore operated as predicted by my theory of reputation. Governments that honored their debts under adverse conditions climbed the reputational ladder and gained access to foreign capital when other governments could not borrow. I now consider the experiences of two other surprising payers, Australia and Finland. Both countries, like Argentina, surpassed expectations by paying in full and subsequently refunded their debts at superior rates.

### Australia as a Surprising Payer

Throughout the 1920s, Australia satisfied its need for capital by borrowing from investors in the United States and Britain. The country used these foreign funds to meet interest on past debts and finance mounting budget and trade deficits. By mid-decade the external debt had reached staggering proportions; only France owed more money to foreign creditors on a per capita basis.[46] As long as the prosperity of the interwar period continued and the prices of Australian exports remained high, investors accepted this indebtedness. They understood, however, that Aus-

[43] *Times* (London), September 12, 1934, 17.
[44] *Barron's*, July 15, 1935, 17.
[45] *New York Herald Tribune*, March 24, 1940, Sec. II, 15.
[46] Redmond & Co. 1928.

tralia was living on borrowed funds and potentially vulnerable to an exogenous shock.

When the depression struck, Australia experienced sharp declines in the prices of wool, wheat, and other key agricultural exports. Since import prices fell more slowly, the terms of trade deteriorated by nearly 38 percent between 1928 and 1932.[47] Moreover, a severe drought hurt agricultural production, reducing the supply of exportable goods at a moment when the country needed foreign exchange. The economic crisis also caused government revenue to fall. Moody's reported that the drop in public receipts had imposed "acute strain upon the governmental exchequer" and described the situation as "undeniably grave."[48] Through the end of 1931, sources acknowledged that default remained a real possibility.[49]

To the surprise of many, Australia paid its debts throughout the Great Depression. Leaders managed this feat "only by means of the most rigid economies, which could not have been forced upon her people unless they were ready and willing to recognize their obligations to lenders in other countries."[50] The government slashed spending, raised import duties, and required citizens to accept smaller payments on domestic bonds. The government also devalued the currency and promoted exports through campaigns to grow more wheat, make more wine, and mine more gold. These measures transformed the trade balance from a £22 million deficit in 1929 to an equally large surplus in 1931 and a balance of £35 million in 1933. Market sentiment began to change, and observers stopped talking about the prospect of default.

One Australian state attempted to suspend payments, but the central government intervened to stop it. Under the leadership of Jack Lang, a left-labor politician, New South Wales resisted pressure to cut wages and balance the budget. In February 1932 the state defaulted, but actors within the state and at higher levels responded quickly. The governor of New South Wales dismissed Lang and installed a new state premier, who announced that he "unreservedly" accepted "responsibility to both internal and external bondholders."[51]

According to Eichengreen and Portes, Australia took these steps "in the hope that faithful maintenance of service might permit floating new loans in London."[52] The strategy clearly worked. Between January 1933 and December 1938, the number of Australian bonds quoted on the London

---

[47] Calculated from Bambrick 1970, 5.
[48] Moody's Investors Service, *Moody's Manual of Investments* (1931), A11.
[49] See, e.g., *Economist*, November 21, 1931, 965–66.
[50] Royal Institute of International Affairs 1937, 292–93.
[51] *Economist*, May 21, 1932, 1146.
[52] Eichengreen and Portes 1987, 20.

TABLE 5.6
Australia's Debt Conversion, 1932–37

| Conversion Date | £ Millions | Original Interest Rate (%) | New Interest Rate (%) |
|---|---|---|---|
| October 1932 | 12.4 | 5.75 | 3.50 |
| February 1933 | 9.6 | 4.00 | 4.00 |
| May 1933 | 11.4 | 6.50 | 3.50 |
| July 1933 | 17.2 | 6.00 | 4.00 |
| September 1933 | 21.0 | 5.88 | 3.75 |
| December 1933 | 16.6 | 5.25 | 3.75 |
| February 1934 | 21.6 | 5.25 | 3.50 |
| November 1934 | 14.6 | 4.00 | 3.25 |
| January 1935 | 22.4 | 5.00 | 3.25 |
| July 1935 | 13.5 | 4.00 | 3.00 |
| January 1936 | 21.7 | 5.00 | 3.00 |
| June 1936 | 16.6 | 3.75 | 2.75 |
| June 1937 | 12.4 | 3.50 | 3.50 |
| November 1937 | 11.4 | 3.50 | 3.50 |
| Total or average | 222.3 | 4.90 | 3.43 |

Source: Royal Institute of International Affairs 1937, 315; Economist, December 11, 1937, 536; and Moody's Investors Service, Moody's Manual of Investments.

Stock Exchange more than doubled, and interest rates fell to historically low levels. Table 5.6 lists the Australian conversions that took place on the London market during the 1930s. As the table makes clear, the government managed to refinance its debt on favorable terms, reducing the average contractual interest rate from 4.9 to 3.4 percent within the space of a few years. The 14 conversion issues resulted in an annual savings of more than four million Australian pounds.[53]

Australia earned this treatment by signaling its resolve during difficult times. Observers described the Australian efforts as "heroic" and praised its leaders for understanding "the psychology of overseas investment." The conversions, they noted, were "a substantial reward for courage and good faith" during difficult times.[54] As the Economist explained, Australians

have overthrown statesmen who openly stood for default and repudiation, and have elected governors [who are] four-square protagonists of a policy of honorable fulfillment. . . . Wages and salaries have fallen from 20 to 30 percent. All social services have suffered reduction, including Old Age, Invalid and even Soldiers' Pensions. In fact, practically every form of expenditure, with the ex-

[53] Economist, December 11, 1937, 536.
[54] Economist, November 21, 1931, 965; June 6, 1936, 560.

ception of interest and sinking fund on external debt, has been curtailed under the operation of the financial rehabilitation plan, which has also involved a significant increase in the burden of taxation. . . . At a time when practically every South American Republic, except Argentina, and numerous European States, are wholly or partially in default on their external indebtedness . . . every penny of Australia's loan service is being punctually met. . . . Australia's record, under her present leaders, has enhanced her credit in every way.[55]

## Finland as a Surprising Payer

Like Argentina and Australia, Finland proved its mettle during the 1930s and earned the status of a "blue chip" investment. Having emerged as a sovereign state after World War I, Finland did not have a long and unblemished credit record. Analysts and investors found it "difficult to evaluate the 'character' of the people" in this new country, and thus did not know what kind of treatment to expect.[56] Would Finland pay its debts during good times and bad, honor them only when convenient, or renounce its obligations altogether? The country needed a period of seasoning before investors could know the answer with confidence.

Finland soon proved itself in two ways. First, it continued payment to private bondholders who, judging from the yields in table 5.4, had anticipated a default. By 1937 commentators counted Finland among the countries that "regard their credit standing as a sacred heritage" and "have done everything within their power to meet their external obligations . . . in spite of the economic depression."[57] Second, Finland honored its war debts to the United States Treasury. When Congress created the World War Foreign Debt Commission to negotiate funding agreements with the various debtors, Finland stepped forward as the first to sign. From that auspicious start, it continued to service its war debts, even after every other country—including Britain, Belgium, and France—suspended payment. This act, too, signaled the resolve of Finland to meet its foreign commitments.

With these two actions, Finland dispelled any notion that it was a lemon and instead rocketed to stalwart status. As a result, Finland refunded its debt in the American market "at rates far more attractive than it would appear warranted by . . . the country's economic and fiscal position." The "promptness with which payments are being made in the face of defaults by Great Britain, France, Belgium and others, created for Fin-

[55] *Economist*, May 6, 1933, 971.
[56] Atkins 1927, 24.
[57] Madden, Nadler, and Sauvain 1937, 121.

land enough publicity and good will to enable her to borrow at attractive rates many times the amount which she paid the United States Government."[58] Interest rates on Finnish bonds fell from 6 percent to 5 percent and then to 4 percent during the 1930s.[59]

## Conclusion

Investors of the interwar period behaved as my dynamic reputational theory predicts. During the boom of the 1920s, they charged higher rates to new borrowers than to more seasoned entities and refrained from lending to countries in default. The prosperity of that decade created tremendous opportunities for foreign investment, but it also complicated the task of inference. Without an adverse shock to test debtors, investors had little basis for updating their beliefs about which countries were stalwarts and which were mere fair-weathers, since both types of countries serviced their debts during the 1920s. In contrast, it was relatively easy to separate lemons from more creditworthy types. Analysts impugned the motives of Russia, Mexico, Ecuador, and others that remained in default during the economic expansion, and private investors put this perspective into practice. At a time of massive international lending, lemons could not borrow a dime.

The 1930s presented investors with a different set of conditions. The depression destroyed many opportunities for international lending, but it also gave investors a chance to distinguish between stalwarts and less creditworthy types. Shocks of that scope and magnitude occur only rarely in international finance, a fact for which all nations can be thankful. When they strike, however, they reveal valuable information about preferences that would be hard to measure in other ways.

Throughout the depression, lenders withheld capital from countries in arrears. They noted that many countries had probably defaulted under duress, and thus did not rush to accuse defaulters of willful repudiation.

[58] Max Winkler in *Magazine of Wall Street*, January 2, 1937, 346.

[59] The payoff persisted even after World War II. Victor Schoepperle (1947, 486), vice president of National City Bank, put Finland's exemplary performance in perspective: "Some of us put willingness or determination to pay ahead of capacity to pay in our estimate of the credit standing of a borrower. The man in the street is familiar with the case of Finland, which alone of all the debtors to the United States Treasury has continued to meet her obligations arising out of the First World War" and maintained full payment on other debts. And "recently, after having been defeated in [World War II], in which she suffered heavily in loss of life as well as loss of territory, Finland has again paid all amounts due." Schoepperle praised Finland's resolve to pay debts whatever the difficulty, and markets responded by granting new credits to Finland in the late 1940s.

It was hard to be sure, though, since both the proven lemons and the apparent fair-weathers were behaving in identical ways. Investors prudently waited for an acceptable settlement, a costly signal that would allay fears of bad faith and reveal the country as an honorable—though not infallible—debtor.

Although they shied away from countries in default, investors of the 1930s refinanced the debts of countries that paid during difficult times. Consider the following passage by Edwin Kemmerer, often called the "money doctor" of the interwar period. Kemmerer had served as financial advisor to the governments of Guatemala and Mexico, and he headed financial missions to Bolivia, Chile, China, Colombia, Ecuador, Peru, Poland, South Africa, and Turkey. Kemmerer had also worked as a banking and monetary expert to the Dawes Commission on European reparations in 1924. He therefore possessed a keen understanding of international finance, based on many years of practical experience. In 1932 Kemmerer remarked:

> In this time of world economic depression investors everywhere are watching to see which nations not only demonstrate their desire to pay their legally contracted debts, but which ones also show capacity, by self-sacrifice on the part of the government and people and by the skillful administration of their public finances, to meet the debt service. The continuous payment of debt service throughout a period of world economic depression like the present would enhance [a country's] public credit standing throughout the world for many years to come, and would thereby materially reduce the cost at which she could obtain foreign loans in the future.[60]

It is hard to imagine a clearer endorsement of the reputational theory.

[60] Kemmerer in U.S. Congress, Senate Committee on Finance 1931–32, 1717.

# Chapter 6 _____

## Enforcement by Gunboats

THE PREVIOUS FOUR CHAPTERS presented and tested a reputational theory of cooperation. A country's reputation, I argued, reflects its history of compliance and the circumstances it has faced. Reputations, in turn, influence international lending and repayment. Investors lend at favorable rates to countries with good reputations, but demand extra compensation from countries with short or mixed records and avoid relationships with putative lemons. These facts give leaders a reputational incentive to repay and support cooperation in an anarchical world.

The next three chapters evaluate more punitive explanations for international cooperation. I focus in particular on issue linkage, the most prominent alternative to reputational theory. Either independently or in collaboration with their home governments, creditors could link default to nonfinancial penalties such as military reprisals or trade embargoes. If the nonfinancial consequences of default are sufficiently severe, they should deter governments from cheating and reassure otherwise nervous investors. To what extent have linkage strategies influenced international financial relations? This chapter moves us closer to an answer by exploring the possibility of linkages between sovereign debt and military power.

### The Gunboat Hypothesis

For much of history, it is argued, creditors used their militaries to extract payment from foreign countries. They blockaded, cannonaded, and even invaded nations that refused to honor financial commitments. The claim that creditors employed military linkage strategies to enforce debts can be dubbed the *gunboat hypothesis*.

The gunboat hypothesis has many adherents. Academics note that, during the nineteenth century, international norms permitted if not encouraged the armed settlement of debt defaults. Martha Finnemore, for example, writes that militarized debt collection was "accepted practice" in the 1800s, and Jack Donnelly concurs that it was "a well-accepted part of international relations."[1] "Rich countries wrote the rules," economist Rudi Dornbusch explains, and "had the gunboats to collect debts."[2]

_____

[1] Finnemore 2003, 24; Donnelly 2000, 145. Wendt (2001, 1026) agrees that "military intervention to collect sovereign debts was legitimate in the nineteenth century."

[2] Dornbusch 2000, 9. In the nineteenth century, "European or American lenders would send gunboats to collect their loans" (Fukuyama 2004, 36), and sovereign bonds therefore

Some contend that great powers intervened frequently and repeatedly on behalf of bondholders. Military reprisals were allegedly "common," "regular," and "standard," especially in Latin America.[3] Consistent with this view, Mitchener and Weidenmier estimate that "supersanctions" were a "commonly used enforcement mechanism" in the nineteenth and early twentieth centuries. "All nations that defaulted on sovereign debt," they contend, "ran the risk of gunboats blockading their ports or creditor nations seizing fiscal control of their country."[4] The image of great powers as debt collectors is even used to epitomize the 1800s, a "century of gunboat diplomacy" in which intervention against defaulters was "axiomatic."[5] Other commentators judge that gunboat diplomacy was more "sporadic" than axiomatic.[6] Creditors took up arms, they claim, in only a few spectacular instances. The most frequently cited example occurred in 1902, when Britain, Germany, and Italy imposed a naval blockade on Venezuela, which was not paying its foreign debts. Soon after the intervention, Venezuela struck a deal with foreign bondholders and began meeting its obligations.

The Correlates of War (COW) project, the leading source of data for the scientific study of war, refers to this episode as the "Venezuelan Debt Crisis,"[7] and many scholars regard it as proof that creditors employed military force to ensure repayment. In his classic book *The Export of Capital*, Hobson upholds the Venezuelan blockade as a prime example of "the terrors which can be held out against a recalcitrant government," and more recent works classify the crisis as the "best known," "most

---

"had performance guaranteed by British 'gunboat' diplomacy" (Lewis and Davis 1987, 389). Debt collectors reportedly coerced Latin American borrowers. Diehl and Goertz (2000, 25) write that "the British used their naval forces . . . to collect debts from Latin American states," and Krasner (1978, 162) explains that "the pretense for most of these actions was economic, particularly the failure of Caribbean countries to meet loan payments to European financiers." Among the many other references to militarized debt collection, see Born 1986, 13–17; De Bonis, Giustiniani, and Gomel 1999, 67; De Grauwe and Fratianni 1984, 158; Krasner 1999, chap. 5; Meetarbhan 1995, 488; Obstfeld and Rogoff 1996, 352; Reinisch 1995, 539; Rieffel 2003, 195; Soros 1998, 125; and Winkler 1933, 137.

[3] See, e.g., Hilaire 1997, 11; Philpott 2001, 34; Stewart 2003, 94; and Whitehead 1989, 234, among many others.

[4] Mitchener and Weidenmier 2005b, 2. Although the British government preferred not to intervene, "Exceptions to this policy . . . were numerous" (Mitchener and Weidenmier 2005a, 661–62).

[5] Dammers 1984, 80; Marks 1979, 20.

[6] Maxfield 1997, 159. See also Baer and Hargis 1997, 1807; Bethell 1989, 12; Frieden 1989a; Lipson 1989; Mauro, Sussman, and Yafeh 2006, 134, 156; Mosley 2003, 270; Platt 1968; Sachs 1982, 220; World Bank 2003, 57–58. Marichal (1989, 121) writes that "only at the turn of the century did military punishment for nonpayment of Latin American debts become common practice."

[7] Correlates of War 1996.

famous," and "most startling" application of military force on behalf of bondholders.[8]

Journalists, too, regularly invoke the Venezuelan case. The *Economist* opened its 2005 feature about Argentine debt by harkening back to 1902. "After Venezuela defaulted on its sovereign debt, German, British and Italian gunboats blockaded the country's ports until the government paid up."[9] The *New Yorker* mentioned the same example in an editorial about "Dealing with Deadbeats" but noted that "creditors have lightened up since then."[10]

Both academic and popular writings suggest that military linkage strategies worked; they sustained lending and repayment in the absence of a world government. In Venezuela and elsewhere, gunboats were "powerful" and "effective" enforcement mechanisms that brought defaulters "to their knees" and forced them back "into line."[11] The prospect of military intervention was "the remedy for default" and "an excellent means by which to speed loan repayment."[12] What works in theory, it seems, also worked in practice.

But despite its popularity, the gunboat hypothesis has never been tested systematically. The existing literature relies mainly on anecdotes, rather than evidence.[13] Did creditors regularly use military coercion to extract payments from foreign governments? Did the mere threat of gunboats keep payments flowing, eliminating the need for actual reprisals? The remainder of this chapter introduces several new datasets and uses them to reexamine the common hypothesis about armed enforcement of sovereign debts.

## Toward a Comprehensive Test of the Gunboat Hypothesis

My empirical analysis focuses on the years 1820 to 1913. This period is especially instructive because it offers an easy proving ground for the gunboat hypothesis. All alleged examples of bondholder wars, including the

---

[8] Hobson 1914, xxii; Dammers 1984, 80; Larkin 2005, 66; Mosley 2003, 270.

[9] *Economist*, March 3, 2005, 67.

[10] *New Yorker*, October 28, 2002, 48. The attack on Venezuela has even been the subject of poetry. See, for example, Rudyard Kipling's "The Rowers," published in the *Times* (London), December 22, 1902, 9.

[11] Arrow 2005, xii; Mitchener and Weidenmier 2005b, 2; Kaletsky 1985, 40; Rodrik 1996, 175.

[12] Gianviti 1990, 241; Chernow 1990, 131.

[13] A few excellent studies examine the British role in particular cases (e.g., Platt 1962, 1968; and Lipson 1989), and new research by Mitchener and Weidenmier (2005a, 2005b) considers the years 1870–1913. No work, however, has checked for patterns across all debtors and creditors for the entire century before World War I.

famous Venezuelan crisis, occurred in the century before World War I.[14] By the 1920s, military enforcement was already seen as "a thing of the past" and a "matter of history."[15] Today, it is widely acknowledged that creditors no longer use their militaries to collect debts.[16] Consequently, any sign of linkage—any evidence of a connection between sovereign default and military intervention—seems likely to come from the century before World War I. If the gunboat hypothesis fails during the historical era when, by all accounts, it stands the best chance of succeeding, we should reject the proposition more generally.

I begin by testing for a positive correlation between debt defaults and military disputes. Other factors equal, creditors should have threatened, displayed, or used military force more often against deadbeats than against punctual payers. It is possible, of course, that the mere prospect of gunboat diplomacy deterred debtors without ever triggering explicit threats or force deployments. I return to this possibility later in the chapter. But the literature claims that creditors did, in fact, deliver ultimatums, blockade ports, and occupy territories in response to default. Any first-order test of the gunboat hypothesis should, therefore, investigate whether creditors behaved this way.

## A Database of Lending, Defaults, and Militarized Disputes

To check for evidence of linkage, I gathered data on relations between sovereign debtors and the seven most important creditor nations of the pre–World War I period: Great Britain, France, Germany, Belgium, the Netherlands, Switzerland, and the United States. These seven nations accounted for roughly 95 percent of the world's foreign investments on the eve of World War I.[17]

The research involved three steps. First, I established who owed money to whom. Creditor nations might have intervened when their own citizens had a grievance, but presumably they would not have taken military action against countries that defaulted on someone else's loans. If a creditor

[14] My research uncovered no alleged examples of bondholder wars in the eighteenth century.

[15] Madden and Nadler 1929, 359; Sakolski 1925, 165.

[16] See, e.g., Bulow and Rogoff 1989a, 157; Chowdhry 1991, 123; Donnelly 2000, 145; Kaletsky 1985, 39; Mauro, Sussman, and Yafeh 2006, 134; and Roubini and Setser 2004, 297.

[17] Maddison 1995, 63. The United Kingdom alone was responsible for 41.8 percent of the global total. France contributed 19.8 percent, Germany contributed 12.8 percent, and the United States contributed 8.0 percent. Collectively, Belgium, the Netherlands, and Switzerland represented 12.6 percent of gross investments in foreign countries. Similar estimates appear in Bairoch 1976, 101; and United Nations 1949, 1–2.

country remained on the sidelines when its own investors were not implicated, this should not count as evidence against the gunboat hypothesis.

Who, then, owed money to each of the seven investor nations? It is hard
to know for sure because international bond markets were anonymous:
citizens bought and sold bearer bonds, and the names of individual buyers
and sellers were not recorded or have not survived. One can, however,
obtain a reasonable estimate by scrutinizing the lists of bonds that were
traded on each creditor's stock exchanges. If, for example, the bonds of
a particular country were listed on the London exchange, British citizens
probably held those bonds and would suffer if the country defaulted. Conversely, if the bonds of a particular country were not listed in London,
the British probably did not hold that country's securities in significant
quantities.[18]

Following this logic, I collected stock market price sheets for each creditor on an annual basis for the period 1820–1913.[19] Information for the
British and U.S. markets were available from published sources in the
United States; records for the other creditors came from archives and special library collections in Europe. The German and Swiss markets proved
most difficult to chronicle, because foreign borrowers issued bonds in
several financial centers (Berlin, Frankfurt, and Hamburg in Germany;
Basel, Geneva, and Zürich in Switzerland). I investigated each center separately and combined the records to create overall measures of obligations
to German and Swiss investors.

Four creditor nations (Britain, France, Germany, and the Netherlands)
had foreign claims for the entire sample period. Belgium attained international creditor status shortly after independence in the 1830s, and the

---

[18] Tax returns from the United Kingdom support this assumption. The *Report of the Commissioners of Her (His) Majesty's Inland Revenue* quantifies the dividends British investors
received from each foreign country. Countries that appeared in the tax returns were also
listed on the stock exchange, and vice versa. See Command Papers C. 8226 (1896), 120–21;
C. 8548 (1897), 136–37; C. 9020 (1898), 122–23; C. 9461 (1899), 128–29; Cd. 347 (1900),
139; Cd. 764 (1901), 129; Cd. 1216 (1902), 183; Cd. 1717 (1903), 187; Cd. 2228 (1904),
200; Cd. 2633 (1905), 205; Cd. 3110 (1906), 205; Cd. 3686 (1907), 201; Cd. 4226 (1908),
167; Cd. 4868 (1909), 151; Cd. 5308 (1910), 115; Cd. 5833 (1911), 112; Cd. 6344 (1912),
110; Cd. 7000 (1913), 107; Cd. 7572 (1914), 111; and Cd. 8116 (1915), 109.

[19] The stock market price sheets are listed in the bibliography. Additional data on Belgian
investments came from StudieCentrum voor Onderneming en Beurs 2006 and Vanderauwera 1855. Supplementary data on German investments came from Bender 1830; Berghoff
2002; Böhme 1968; Brockhage 1910; Feller 1834; Frankfurter Zeitung 1911; Germany, Statistisches Reichsamt 1900–1915; Pallmann 1898; Spangenthal 1903; Steinmetz 1913; Unger
1924; the Philipsborn Collection, Geheimes Staatsarchiv Preußischer Kulturbesitz; and the
Bethmann-Archiv, Institut für Stadtgeschichte Frankfurt. For additional data on Swiss investments, I consulted Chabloz 1899, 1907–8, 1910–11; Moynier and Dominicé 1902;
Peyrot 1895; Saugy 1913–14; and Swiss Bank Corporation 1921.

Swiss began listing foreign bonds on stock exchanges in the 1850s. The United States, in contrast, did not participate actively in foreign lending to sovereign governments until 1899, when part of an international loan to Mexico was placed in New York. Thereafter, the investment portfolios of Americans came to include an ever-larger foreign component.

The second step in the research process involved compiling data about defaults and settlements. I classified defaults as beginning when the borrower violated a loan contract by missing a coupon payment or failing to repay principal on schedule. Defaults ended when a majority of bondholders consented to a settlement package, either by voting at a bondholder meeting or by exchanging old securities for restructured ones. Information about defaults and settlements came from a wide range of bond yearbooks and the annual reports of bondholder associations, which are listed in the bibliography.

Finally, for data about the military actions of creditors, I consulted the Militarized Interstate Disputes (MIDs) dataset from the Correlates of War (COW) project.[20] This dataset contains information about disputes since 1816 "in which the threat, display or use of military force short of war by one member state is explicitly directed towards the government, official representatives, official forces, property or territory of another state."[21]

Together, these sources constitute a new dataset that reveals, for all sovereign debtors in the world, when their bonds were held and traded by investors in Britain, France, Germany, Belgium, the Netherlands, Switzerland, and the United States; when those foreign bonds were in default, thereby triggering a possible military response; and when each of the seven creditor countries threatened, displayed, or used force against the borrower.

Table 6.1 lists the debtors and years in my sample. To qualify for inclusion, a debtor had to meet both financial and political criteria. Financially, the debtor's bonds had to be listed on a creditor's stock exchange. Politically, the debtor had to be a member of the international system, as defined by the COW team. (To qualify for membership, a country must have received diplomatic missions from both France and the United Kingdom.) This second criterion is necessary because MID data are available only for countries COW regards as sovereign.

The financial and political criteria did not always coincide. Some countries satisfied the financial criteria long before meeting the political one. Argentina, for example, floated its first government bond on the London market in 1824 but did not become part of the COW system until 1841. Other countries entered the COW system well before they became bor-

---

[20] Correlates of War 2003; Ghosn and Bennett 2003; and Ghosn, Palmer, and Bremer 2004.
[21] Jones, Bremer, and Singer 1996, 169.

TABLE 6.1
Countries in the Gunboat Sample, 1820–1913

| Country | Abbreviation | Start Year | End Year |
| --- | --- | --- | --- |
| Argentina | ARG | 1841 | 1913 |
| Austria-Hungary | AUH | 1820 | 1913 |
| Baden | BAD | 1820 | 1871 |
| Bavaria | BAV | 1820 | 1871 |
| Belgium | BEL | 1831 | 1913 |
| Bolivia | BOL | 1872 | 1913 |
| Brazil | BRA | 1826 | 1913 |
| Bulgaria | BUL | 1908 | 1913 |
| Chile | CHL | 1839 | 1913 |
| China | CHN | 1876 | 1913 |
| Colombia | COL | 1831 | 1913 |
| Cuba | CUB | 1902 | 1913 |
| Denmark | DEN | 1820 | 1913 |
| Dominican Republic | DOM | 1894 | 1913 |
| Ecuador | ECU | 1854 | 1913 |
| Egypt | EGY | 1862 | 1882 |
| El Salvador | SAL | 1889 | 1913 |
| France | FRN | 1820 | 1913 |
| Germany | GMY | 1820 | 1913 |
| Greece | GRC | 1828 | 1913 |
| Guatemala | GUA | 1868 | 1913 |
| Haiti | HAI | 1859 | 1913 |
| Hanover | HAN | 1838 | 1847 |
| Hesse Electoral | HSE | 1820 | 1866 |
| Hesse Grand Ducal | HSG | 1820 | 1867 |
| Honduras | HON | 1899 | 1913 |
| Iran | IRN | 1911 | 1913 |
| Italy | ITA | 1820 | 1913 |
| Japan | JPN | 1870 | 1913 |
| Mexico | MEX | 1831 | 1913 |
| Morocco | MOR | 1862 | 1911 |
| Netherlands | NTH | 1820 | 1913 |
| Nicaragua | NIC | 1900 | 1913 |
| Norway | NOR | 1905 | 1913 |
| Papal States | PAP | 1824 | 1860 |
| Paraguay | PAR | 1876 | 1913 |
| Peru | PER | 1839 | 1913 |
| Portugal | POR | 1823 | 1913 |
| Romania | ROM | 1878 | 1913 |
| Russia | RUS | 1820 | 1913 |
| Saxony | SAX | 1867 | 1867 |
| Siam | THI | 1905 | 1913 |
| Spain | SPN | 1820 | 1913 |

TABLE 6.1 (*cont.*)
Countries in the Gunboat Sample, 1820–1913

| Country | Abbreviation | Start Year | End Year |
|---------|--------------|------------|----------|
| Sweden | SWD | 1852 | 1913 |
| Switzerland | SWZ | 1857 | 1913 |
| Tunisia | TUN | 1863 | 1881 |
| Turkey | TUR | 1852 | 1913 |
| Tuscany | TUS | 1850 | 1860 |
| Two Sicilies | SIC | 1820 | 1861 |
| United Kingdom | UKG | 1820 | 1913 |
| United States | USA | 1820 | 1913 |
| Uruguay | URU | 1882 | 1913 |
| Venezuela | VEN | 1841 | 1913 |
| Württemberg | WRT | 1848 | 1871 |
| Yugoslavia | YUG | 1882 | 1913 |

rowers. COW classifies Bolivia as a sovereign nation beginning in 1848, for example, but Bolivia did not obtain its first foreign loan until 1872.

The lack of overlap between financial and political criteria may introduce some biases. Most notably, the COW criteria exclude several Latin American defaulters in the first half of the nineteenth century, because either Britain or France did not maintain a permanent diplomatic presence. To verify that the COW criteria did not influence my conclusions, later in the chapter I examine official correspondence about Central and South American borrowers before they became COW members.

My dataset contains annual information about pairs of countries, or dyads. Given the goal of studying debtor-creditor relations, I limited the sample to dyads that contained one creditor and one debtor. Creditors were paired only with countries in which their citizens invested, and only for the years in which those investments were held. For example, Chinese government bonds first appeared on the Amsterdam exchange in 1895 and were quoted each subsequent year until the end of the sample period. I therefore included the Netherlands-China dyad only for the years 1895 to 1913. The complete dataset has 8,841 records, each corresponding to a debtor-creditor relationship in a particular year.

## The Correlation between Defaults and Militarized Disputes

With this new dataset, I computed the rates at which creditors took military action against defaulters. My analyses focus on creditor-initiated MIDs: disputes in which the creditor moved first by issuing a military

TABLE 6.2
Military Action by Creditors against Debtors, 1820–1913

| Debtor in Default | Creditor-Initiated MID | | |
|---|---|---|---|
| | No | Yes | Total |
| No | 98.3% | 1.7% | 100% |
| | (N = 7,240) | (N = 123) | (N = 7,363) |
| Yes | 97.2% | 2.8% | 100% |
| | (N = 1,437) | (N = 41) | (N = 1,478) |

*Source*: MID data are from the Correlates of War 2003. The MID data are described in Jones, Bremer, and Singer 1996 and in Ghosn and Bennett 2003. Data on debts and defaults come from the stock market price sheets and bond yearbooks listed in the bibliography.

*Note*: A creditor-initiated MID is a militarized interstate dispute in which the creditor took the first hostile action. The number of dyad-years appears in parentheses. Pearson $\chi^2_{(1)}$ = 8.2 with a $p$-value of .004. Kendall's $\tau_b$ = .03 with an asymptotic standard error of .01.

threat, deploying its forces, or attacking the debtor. This focus could miss cases in which the borrower, anticipating attack, took preemptive action against the creditor. As discussed below, though, my conclusions do not change when debtor-initiated MIDs are included in the sample.

Table 6.2 summarizes the patterns of military action by creditors against defaulters and nondefaulters. On first inspection, the data seem consistent with the gunboat hypothesis. When debtors were meeting their obligations (in 7,363 of the dyad-years in the sample), creditors threatened or used force against them approximately 1.7 percent of the time. When the debtors lapsed into default (1,478 dyad-years), the frequency of creditor-initiated MIDs increased to 2.8 percent. Thus, countries that defaulted became targets of militarized disputes at a higher rate than countries that paid. Although the absolute rates in both cases are low, the relative risk is considerable: based on these point estimates, militarized disputes were about 65 percent more likely when countries were in default than when they were faithfully servicing debts.

The difference in rates evidently did not arise by chance. The table's chi-squared statistic is 8.2 with 1 degree of freedom. Under the null hypothesis of no relationship between debt default and creditor-initiated military action, we would see a chi-squared value that large less than 1 percent of the time. Other nonparametric measures of association support the same conclusion.[22]

---

[22] For example, the $\tau_b$ statistic for this contingency table is .03, three times its asymptotic standard error. An analogous table that considered all MIDs, including ones initiated by the

I next investigated whether the positive relationship between defaults and MIDs persisted after controlling for other predictors of military disputes. Previous research has shown that power, alliances, contiguity, and domestic regime type affect the probability of MIDs.[23] MIDs are less likely when both countries in a dyad are minor powers, when the balance of forces in a dyad is lopsided, or when members of a dyad are allies. MIDs are more likely among contiguous countries and ones with dissimilar political regimes (i.e., disputes occur more often between democracies and autocracies than between two democracies, or between two autocracies.)

Using standard data from the COW project, I constructed measures for each of these risk factors.[24] The variable Both Minor Powers is coded 1 if neither member of the dyad achieved major power status in the given year, and coded 0 otherwise.[25] The Balance of Forces is the military capability score of the more powerful member of the dyad, divided by the total capabilities of both states. I measure military capability with COW's Composite Index of National Capabilities, discussed in greater detail later in this chapter.

Two countries are treated as Allied if they had a defense pact, a neutrality pact, or an entente in the given year, and they are Contiguous if either they or their colonies share a land border. Regime Dissimilarity measures the absolute value of the difference in democracy levels of countries in the dyad. Following the convention in the literature, the democracy level of a state is its democracy score minus its autocracy score, as given in the Polity IV dataset.[26] Finally, to address the problem of duration dependence (long stretches in which the dyads did not experience a militarized dispute), I constructed a restricted cubic spline function of Peace Years, the number of years since the dyad's most recent MID.[27]

I used logistic regression to estimate the effect of debt default, holding other predictors constant. As in the tabular analysis presented earlier, the unit of observation was the dyad-year, and the dependent variable was

---

debtor, would show MID rates of 3.5 percent for defaulters versus 2.5 percent for nondefaulters, implying a relative risk of around 40 percent.

[23] For a review of the literature and many novel extensions, see Bennett and Stam 2004.

[24] These variables were computed using *EUGene* software v3.1 (http://www.eugenesoftware .org), developed by Bennett and Stam (2000).

[25] Britain, France, Germany, Austria-Hungary, and Russia were classified as major powers for the entire sample period. Italy became a major military power in 1860, Japan in 1895, and the United States in 1898.

[26] The dataset, developed by Marshall, Jaggers, and Gurr (2003), is described in Jaggers and Gurr 1995. The Regime Dissimilarity variable ranges from 0 to 20.

[27] See Beck, Katz, and Tucker 1998. Knots were located at 1, 12, 26, 47, and 82 years, which represent the 5th, 27.5th, 50th, 72.5th, and 95th percentiles in the data. The spline function is linear before the first knot, a piecewise cubic polynomial between adjacent knots, and linear after the last knot. Details are given in Harrell 2001, 20–24.

TABLE 6.3
Logit Analysis of Militarized Interstate Disputes, 1820–1913

| Variable | Standard Logit | | | Conditional Logit | | |
|---|---|---|---|---|---|---|
| | Estimated Coefficient | Standard Error | t-statistic | Estimated Coefficient | Standard Error | t-statistic |
| Debt default | 0.91 | 0.27 | 3.4 | 0.97 | 0.31 | 3.1 |
| Both minor powers | −3.10 | 0.98 | 3.2 | | | |
| Balance of forces | −1.66 | 0.88 | 1.9 | −5.49 | 2.20 | 2.5 |
| Allied | −0.49 | 0.29 | 1.7 | −0.62 | 0.40 | 1.6 |
| Contiguous | 0.53 | 0.21 | 2.5 | | | |
| Regime dissimilarity | 0.04 | 0.02 | 2.1 | −0.05 | 0.03 | 1.5 |
| Peace years | −0.28 | 0.05 | 5.4 | −0.24 | 0.05 | 4.9 |
| Cubic spline 1 | 3.49 | 0.78 | 4.5 | 3.90 | 0.79 | 5.0 |
| Cubic spline 2 | −7.35 | 1.73 | 4.3 | −8.60 | 1.79 | 4.8 |
| Cubic spline 3 | 4.74 | 1.31 | 3.6 | 6.22 | 1.44 | 4.3 |
| Constant | −1.25 | 0.69 | 1.8 | | | |

*Note*: Estimates from logistic regressions with robust standard errors, clustered by dyad. The dependent variable is 1 if a creditor-initiated MID was in progress and 0 otherwise. Sample size was 8,195 in the standard logit model and 2,932 in the conditional logit model.

the presence of a creditor-initiated MID. Table 6.3 presents the estimates from two models. The first is a standard logistic regression. The second is a conditional logit, which controls for unmeasured heterogeneity across dyads.[28] In the conditional logit model, I delete dyads that never experience MIDs and drop predictors that do not vary over time.

The apparent relationship between default and militarized action is even stronger in this multivariate analysis than in the cross-tabulation presented earlier. The estimated coefficient on Default is 0.91 in the standard logit model and 0.97 in the conditional logit model. Both coefficients are three times their standard errors, giving confidence that a correlation truly exists. The coefficients imply that, other factors equal, creditors initiate MIDs about 2.5 times more often against defaulters than against nondefaulters.[29] Other variables, with the possible exception of Regime Dissimilarity, behave as expected: Both Minor Power, Balance of Forces, and Alliance all reduce the probability of MIDs, while Contiguity makes MIDs more likely. In summary, both bivariate and multivariate empirical methods seem to support the gunboat hypothesis.

[28] Chamberlain 1980; Green, Kim, and Yoon 2001.
[29] The odds ratio for the effect of default is $e^{0.91} = 2.5$ in the standard logit model and $e^{0.97} = 2.6$ in the conditional logit model. With rare events such as MIDs, the odds ratio provides a very good approximation to the risk ratio.

TABLE 6.4
Military Action by Each Creditor against Debtors, 1820–1913

| Debtor in Default | Creditor | | | | | | |
|---|---|---|---|---|---|---|---|
| | Belgium | France | Germany | Netherlands | Switzerland | United Kingdom | United States |
| No | 0.0% (1,229) | 2.7% (1,260) | 2.1% (1,266) | 0.5% (1,436) | 0.0% (370) | 2.8% (1,663) | 6.5% (139) |
| Yes | 0.0% (200) | 3.4% (234) | 5.7% (122) | 0.3% (386) | 0.0% (38) | 4.9% (490) | 12.5% (8) |

Source: Same as table 7.2.

Note: Table gives the percentage of dyad-years in which a creditor initiated a militarized interstate dispute against its debtor. The total number of dyad-years appears in parentheses. Pearson $\chi_1^2$ statistics and associated p-values are France, 0.37 ($p = .54$); Germany, 6.51 ($p = .01$); Netherlands, 0.36 ($p = .55$); United Kingdom, 5.09 ($p = .02$); United States, 0.43 ($p = .51$). The Pearson $\chi^2$ is not defined for Belgium and Switzerland, which did not initiate MIDs against debtors.

## A Deeper Look at the Militarized Disputes

### Three Reasons for Concern

A closer look suggests three reasons for concern, however. First, the absolute probability of military action against deadbeat debtors was minute, even during the supposed heyday of gunboat diplomacy. Creditors threatened or used force in less than 3 percent of default-years. If gunboats were the key to enforcing debt contracts, the evidence in table 6.2 suggests that borrowers could have defaulted with impunity 97 times out of 100. It seems unlikely that a risk of such small proportions would deter governments from defaulting and inspire the confidence of foreign investors.

Second, the positive correlation between defaults and militarism did not exist for all creditors. Table 6.4 shows that Belgium and Switzerland never threatened or used force against defaulters, and the Netherlands treated nonpayers at least as favorably as payers. France and the United States displayed more hostility toward defaulters, but we cannot be confident that their aggression was systematic. The probability that the apparent patterns for France and the United States could have arisen purely by chance was greater than .50. Among the seven major creditors, only Germany and the United Kingdom evince statistically significant patterns of militarized action against defaulters.

Third, the apparent relationship between defaults and MIDs could be spurious. Figure 6.1 provides the first hint that these MIDs had little to do with debt collection. The figure presents data for all 13 countries that

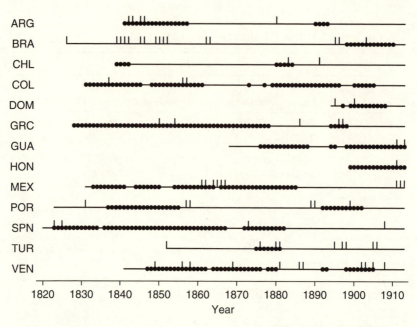

FIGURE 6.1: DEFAULTS AND MILITARIZED INTERSTATE DISPUTES, 1820–1913
Horizontal lines indicate periods in which the country was a member of the
Correlates of War system and its bonds were listed on at least one creditor's stock
exchange. Dots represent years of debt default, and vertical pipes indicate years
in which a MID took place between the debtor and at least one of its creditors.

experienced MIDs that coincided with debt default. (The remaining countries in the sample are not shown, either because they paid all creditors,
or because creditors took no military action against them during periods
of default.) Time is measured along the horizontal axis, and the vertical
axis gives a three-letter abbreviation for each debtor state, whose full
names are listed in table 6.1. The horizontal line for each country indicates periods in which the country belonged to the COW system and its
bonds were listed on a foreign stock exchange. Dots mark spells of debt
default, and vertical pipes indicate years in which a MID took place between the debtor and at least one of its creditors.

The graph shows an interesting pattern. If nineteenth-century creditors
relied on gunboats to collect debts, one would have expected prompt and
effective retaliation. Creditors should have issued threats soon after the
default, and military pressure should have led to a resumption of payments. On the contrary, the vast majority of MIDs against defaulters occurred in the middle of long default phases. Argentina, for example, began
borrowing from the British in 1824 and defaulted in 1828. Britain took
militarized action against Argentina in 1842, 1843, 1845, and 1846, but

Buenos Aires did not pay bondholders for more than a decade after the MIDs ended. If creditors intended to collect debts in Argentina and elsewhere, why were they so tardy, and why did they return home empty-handed? Figure 6.1 does not conclusively disprove the gunboat hypothesis, but it does raise enough doubt to warrant follow-up analysis.

## An Analysis of Creditor Demands

I therefore used primary and secondary sources to trace the history of every MID that coincided with a debt default. The results of this investigation are summarized in table 6.5, and sources of data are listed in the appendix to this chapter. To be conservative, the table includes not only MIDs initiated by the creditor, but also ones in which the debtor moved first. The left columns provide, for reference and replication, the unique identifying number for each MID, the debtors and creditors involved, the years in which the dispute took place, and the highest level of action by the creditor—a threat to use force, a display of force, the use of force short of war, or an interstate war. The remaining columns synthesize the demands creditors made and how long default continued after the MID was resolved.

Contrary to the gunboat hypothesis, the MIDs in table 6.5 had little if any apparent connection to debt default. The Argentine MIDs at the top of the table are representative of the larger group. During its conflicts with Argentina in the 1840s, Britain never delivered an ultimatum regarding debt repayment or even linked its naval actions to the plight of bondholders. Instead, Britain intervened to stop Argentine involvement in the Uruguayan civil war. Available documents show that "the demand of the bondholders was no part of the case against General Rosas which led to the Anglo-French intervention."[30] The MIDs ended in 1846, but default persisted for another 11 years.[31]

Table 6.5 shows many other MIDs that were triggered by contemporaneous civil or international wars, rather than bondholder interests. Additional examples, beyond the Argentine case, include British moves to end hostilities between Chile and Peru; British and French efforts to keep Greece out of the Crimean War; British, French, and German action to stabilize Crete during a period of Christian-Muslim conflict; British attempts to enforce neutrality and broker a peace agreement in the Honduran civil war; British demands that Portugal declare war on the Transvaal

---

[30] Ferns 1977, 223.
[31] The blockades may, in fact, have exacerbated the default by disrupting plans to settle with creditors. See Jenks 1927, 122.

TABLE 6.5
Analysis of Militarized Interstate Disputes That Coincided with Debt Default, 1820–1913

| Debtor | Creditor | Years | MID# | Action | Demand | Bonds Mentioned? | Years of Post-MID Default |
|--------|----------|-------|------|--------|--------|------------------|---------------------------|
| ARG | UKG | 1842 | 371 | Threat | Stop Argentine war against Uruguay, permit Anglo-French mediation, allow peaceful navigation of rivers | No | 15 |
| ARG | UKG | 1842–43 | 2055 | Display | Agree to an immediate armistice with Uruguay, withdraw Argentine forces from Uruguay, allow peaceful navigation of rivers, respect rights of foreign nationals | No | 14 |
| ARG | UKG | 1845–46 | 123 | Use | Withdraw Argentine forces from Uruguay, end Argentine blockade of Montevideo, accept Anglo-French mediation | No | 11 |
| BRA | USA | 1903 | 2005 | Threat | Respect the rights of American investors to produce rubber in the disputed territory of Acre | No | 7 |
| CHL | UKG | 1883 | 1517 | Threat | End the War of the Pacific, refrain from dismembering Peru | No | 1 |
| COL | UKG | 1837 | 2243 | Use | Release Russell (British vice-consul) from jail, compensate Russell for his imprisonment, remove responsible authorities from power, restore the British Consular office | No | 8 |
| COL | UKG | 1856–57 | 1757 | Display | Pay Mackintosh for the sale of army equipment to Gran Colombia three decades earlier, as agreed in the Colombia-U.K. conventions of 1851 and 1855 | No | 4 |
| DOM | FRN | 1900 | 68 | Threat | Pay for harm to Boismare (wrongly imprisoned) and Caccavelli (murdered), as agreed in the Dominican-French convention of 1895 | No | 8 |

TABLE 6.5 (*cont.*)
Analysis of Militarized Interstate Disputes That Coincided with Debt Default, 1820–1913

| Debtor | Creditor | Years | MID# | Action | Demand | Bonds Mentioned? | Years of Post-MID Default |
|---|---|---|---|---|---|---|---|
| GRC | UKG | 1850 | 71 | Use | Compensate Pacifico and other British citizens for destruction and seizure of property, pay indemnities to Ionians for wrongful arrest and flogging, apologize for apprehending a British naval officer | No | 28 |
| GRC[a] | UKG, FRN | 1854 | 2367 | Display | Stop Greek insurgents from attacking Turkey, avoid aligning with Russia in the Crimean War | No | 24 |
| GRC | UKG, FRN, GMY | 1896 | 2837 | Display | Stop the flow of money and weapons to Cretan Christians during a period of Christian-Muslim conflict, compel Christians to accept Turkish concessions | No | 2 |
| GRC | UKG, FRN, GMY | 1897 | 56 | Use | Withdraw Greek forces from Crete, stop supporting Cretan Christians, refrain from annexing Crete | No | 1 |
| GUA | UKG | 1911 | 1734 | Use | Remain neutral during the Honduran civil war | No | 2 |
| GUA | UKG | 1913 | 238 | Display | Use the coffee export tax to pay interest on foreign bonds held by British investors, as promised in the debt agreement of 1895 | Yes | 0 |
| HON | UKG | 1911 | 1734 | Use | Arrange an armistice in the Honduran civil war, maintain a neutral zone in which fighting would not be permitted | No | 14 |

TABLE 6.5 (*cont.*)
Analysis of Militarized Interstate Disputes That Coincided with Debt Default, 1820–1913

| Debtor | Creditor | Years | MID# | Action | Demand | Bonds Mentioned? | Years of Post-MID Default |
|--------|----------|-------|------|--------|--------|------------------|---------------------------|
| MEX | UKG[b] | 1861–62 | 135 | Use | Honor the existing treaties, conventions, and agreements between Britain and Mexico, stop the murder of British subjects in Mexico, repay money that was stolen from the British legation and the *conducta* at Laguna Seca, pay tort claimants and British bondholders, allow Britain to appoint commissioners with the power to reduce tariffs and collect customs duties | Yes | 2 |
| POR | UKG | 1899 | 1649 | Threat | Declare war on Transvaal, prevent weapons from reaching the Boers during the Anglo-Boer conflict | No | 3 |
| SPN | FRN, GMY | 1823 | 89 | War | Restore stability to Spain during civil war, reestablish Spanish monarchy | No | 11 |
| SPN | UKG | 1825 | 3233 | Use | Capture pirates on two Cuban islands | No | 9 |
| SPN[a] | UKG | 1873 | 256 | Display | Pay reparations for capture and deaths of British citizens who had been aboard the *Virginius*, halt further executions of British subjects, punish the governor of Santiago de Cuba | No | 9 |
| TUR | UKG | 1876 | 1750 | Display | Restore stability and protect Christians in Turkey following religious riots in Salonica | No | 5 |

TABLE 6.5 (cont.)
Analysis of Militarized Interstate Disputes That Coincided with Debt Default, 1820–1913

| Debtor | Creditor | Years | MID# | Action | Demand | Bonds Mentioned? | Years of Post-MID Default |
|--------|----------|-------|------|--------|--------|------------------|---------------------------|
| TUR | GMY | 1876 | 3322 | Threat | Protect Christians from Muslims, establish an armistice, resettle the insurgents | No | 5 |
| TUR[a] | FRN | 1881 | 228 | Threat | Respect French control over Tunisia | No | 0 |
| TUR | UKG, FRN, GMY | 1880–81 | 141 | Display | Respect new boundaries between Turkey and Greece | No | 1 |
| VEN[a] | NTH | 1849 | 1493 | Display | Pay indemnities for Dutch ships that had been seized | No | 13 |
| VEN | NTH | 1856 | 1495 | Display | Acknowledge Dutch ownership of Aves Islands, pay indemnities for attacks on Jewish Dutch traders in Coro | No | 6 |
| VEN | UKG | 1858 | 1628 | Use | Release former president Monagas from prison, allow him to leave the country | No | 4 |
| VEN[a] | NTH | 1869 | 1497 | Display | Release Dutch ship that had been seized, protect Dutch nationals in Venezuela | No | 7 |
| VEN | UKG, GMY | 1902–3 | 254 | Use | Pay indemnities for shipping claims and damages arising from Venezuelan civil wars, reach a settlement with foreign bondholders | Yes | 2 |
| VEN | FRN | 1905 | 310 | Display | Stop interfering with operations of French Cable Company, withdraw insulting note addressed to French chargé d'affaires in Caracas | No | 0 |

*Source:* See the appendix to this chapter.
*Note:* "Action" is the highest level of military hostility by the creditor.
[a] The debtor took the first hostile action in the MID.
[b] France also participated in the intervention, but Mexican bonds were not listed on French stock exchanges prior to 1864. That year, Maximilian, whom the French had installed as leader of Mexico, ended Mexico's long-standing default and issued bonds to French investors. When Maximilian was executed and French forces evacuated in 1866–67, the new Mexican president (Juárez) repudiated the bonds Maximilian had floated during the MID.

and prevent weapons from reaching the Boers; French and German intervention in the Spanish civil war; and British and German efforts to restore stability following religious riots in Turkey.

Other MIDs in table 6.5 arose from ongoing territorial disputes. Britain, France, and Germany took military action to enforce new boundaries between Turkey and Greece. France used its power to obtain Turkish respect for French control over Tunisia, and the United States safeguarded the rights of rubber-producers in the Acre region during a territorial conflict between Bolivia and Brazil. The Netherlands, too, resorted to coercion in territorial disputes: it sent warships when Venezuela failed to recognize Dutch ownership of the Aves Islands.

Still other MIDs occurred because the target refused to pay reparations for abuses against the property and bodily integrity of foreign nationals. In 1837, for instance, the United Kingdom blockaded the ports of Colombia until it released the British vice-consul from jail, compensated him for imprisonment, removed the perpetrators from power, and restored the British consular office. Similar cases led to British action against Greece (the Don Pacifico crisis of 1850), Colombia again (the Mackintosh affair of 1856–57), and Spain (the *Virginius* dispute of 1873). Likewise, the French took action on behalf of foreign nationals in the Dominican Republic (the Boismare-Caccavelli claims of 1900) and Venezuela (French Cable Company, 1905). Related MIDs arose in response to the seizure of ships, for example, Britain versus Spain in 1825 and the Netherlands versus Venezuela in 1849 and 1869.

Of all the MIDs in table 6.5, only three involved demands that related to bondholders. Britain applied pressure against Mexico (1861–62) and Guatemala (1913), and it collaborated with Germany in the famous Venezuelan crisis of 1902. The Mexican case is complicated, as suggested by the variety of demands in table 6.5. Britain intervened mainly to enforce international conventions between the two governments, and to protect its own citizens from violence.[32] The Venezuelan case is intricate, as well. I show later in this chapter that Britain and Germany intervened primarily to enforce tort claims, not to support private bondholders.

The Guatemalan case, in contrast, seems to be a rare example of official intervention to assist bondholders. Lionel Carden, the British minister, threatened to break diplomatic relations and depart by warship unless Guatemala started using the coffee export tax to pay investors, as promised in the debt agreement of 1895. News reports described the MID as "a new departure" in British policy. As the *South American Journal* explained, "British investors have hitherto received scant assistance from our Government in attempting to enforce the payment of their just

---

[32] See the references in the appendix to this chapter.

rights." At last, though, the Foreign Office was helping them bring a "disreputable republic to book."[33]

Why did Britain intervene in this case, after refraining in so many others? The answer is unclear. Some argue that Britain took this "almost unprecedented" action because Guatemalan president Manuel Estrada Cabrera had "deliberately flouted" the British government. After many years of debt default, Estrada Cabrera proposed a settlement in 1911 and sought to arrange it through Carden. "When, however, the agreement was presented by the British Minister to the President for his signature, the latter flatly refused to have anything to do with it, an action which was little short of an insult to the British Foreign Office." Historian Warren Kneer adds that Britain acted because of Carden's manipulations and "injured national pride."[34] Further research is needed to understand Britain's unusual behavior in this case.

Even if the Mexican, Guatemalan, and Venezuelan MIDs were all classified as bondholder MIDs, they would be exceptions, rather than the rule.[35] In the century before World War I, it is remarkably difficult to find cases in which default triggered militarism, or in which the threat, show, or use of force resolved a default. Nearly all the cases in table 6.5 arose from other grievances that happened to coincide with nonpayment of sovereign bonds. The statistical association between default and military intervention is mostly spurious.

## The 1902 Intervention against Venezuela

I now consider in detail the most famous example of a bondholder war, the 1902 intervention against Venezuela. In August 1901 Cipriano Castro, who had risen to power by overthrowing the sitting president two years earlier, suspended all payments on the foreign debt. His decision

[33] *South American Journal*, May 17, 1913, 648.

[34] *Daily Telegraph*, May 2, 1913, 3; *Financial Times*, May 1, 1913, 6; *Stock Exchange Gazette*, May 15, 1913, 851; *Times* (London), May 1, 1913, 15; Kneer 1975, 207.

[35] Two other potential exceptions, Egypt and Turkey in the 1880s, fall outside the scope of the Correlates of War MIDs dataset. In 1882, Britain bombarded Alexandria and occupied Cairo. This case does not appear in the MIDs dataset, because Egypt did not meet COW criteria for sovereignty during the years 1882–1936. There is much debate about the motives for British intervention. Platt (1968, 154–80) and Robinson and Gallagher (1981, chap. 4) argue that Britain did not intervene to defend bondholders, but Hopkins (1986) and Schölch (1976) include bondholders as one of the many spurs for the British attack. Another complex case involves the establishment of the Ottoman Public Debt Commission in 1881. This case did not appear in table 6.5 because the commission was not imposed by threat, show, or use of military force, as measured by the COW research team. For discussion of this case and the British government's role, see Blaisdell 1929; Lipson 1989; Platt 1968, 181–218; and Wynne 1951, 393–481.

hurt British and German investors. The British owned the New Consolidated Debt of 1881, which carried an annual interest rate of 3 percent, while Germans were principally invested in the 5 percent loan of 1896, which had been offered by Disconto Gesellschaft of Berlin. On the eve of the intervention, the outstanding principal on these two loans stood at £2.6 and £1.9 million, respectively.[36]

After Castro defaulted, Britain and Germany sent warships to press their claims. The U.S. minister in Caracas warned Castro, "You owe money, and sooner or later you will have to pay."[37] Britain and Germany then severed diplomatic relations with Venezuela and delivered a final ultimatum on December 7, 1901. Among other things, the ultimatum called upon Venezuela to reach a new agreement with bondholders. The powers gave Venezuela 48 hours to yield, and warned that failure to satisfy their demands would lead to immediate military action.

President Castro refused to concede, and the war began on December 9. Over the next few weeks, Britain and Germany sank several Venezuelan ships, seized others, blockaded the country's principal ports and the mouth of the Orinoco River, and bombarded forts on the Venezuelan coastline. Two Italian warships eventually joined the campaign.[38] By February, all sides agreed to American-sponsored mediation, and the powers lifted their blockade. The crisis officially ended with the Washington Protocol of February 13, 1903, in which the Venezuelan government pledged "to enter into a fresh arrangement respecting the external debt of Venezuela, with a view to the satisfaction of the claims of the bondholders."

After two years of negotiation, Venezuela reached an agreement with British and German investors. It unified the debts of 1881 and 1896 into a single issue, the so-called Diplomatic Debt of 1905, and capitalized the arrears of interest by adding them to the new debt. As security for the new bond, Venezuela pledged a share of its customs revenues.[39] Payments began in August and continued until the debt was retired in 1930.

On its face, the Venezuelan episode appears to be a rare but significant bondholder war. Venezuela owed money, and creditors forced the debtor to pay. A close examination of British and German documents shows, however, that even in this seemingly exceptional case, the powers did not send forces to defend bondholders.[40] (1) The timing of the intervention,

[36] "Memoranda on Venezuelan Loans of 1881 and 1896," January 1903, in United Kingdom Parliament 1903, 213–14.

[37] Herbert Bowen (U.S. Minister at Caracas) to John Hay (U.S. Secretary of State), November 28, 1902, quoted in Mitchell 1996, 186.

[38] Italy joined primarily to protect its nationals in Venezuela, not to enforce obligations to bondholders. For a discussion of Italy's role, see Vernassa 1980.

[39] Corporation of Foreign Bondholders, *Annual Report* 32 (1905), 14–16, 446.

[40] My analysis of British policy builds upon the important work of Platt (1962, 1968) and Lipson (1989).

(2) the content of private communications, (3) the nature of the final ultimatum, (4) the immediate outcome of the intervention, and (5) the public pronouncements of leaders are all inconsistent with the gunboat hypothesis. I consider each of these empirical implications, first for Britain and then for Germany.

## British Action against Venezuela

### THE TIMING OF THE INTERVENTION

If Britain had gone to war for bondholders, one would have expected a temporal connection between default and military intervention. Yet Venezuela had rebuffed bondholders for 54 of the previous 81 years without any sign of debt-collecting warships. Having received its first loans in 1822 and 1824 as part of the old Colombian Republic, Venezuela defaulted in 1826. When the republic split, the resulting states divided the debt among themselves, with 28.5 percent apportioned to Venezuela and the remainder to Ecuador and New Granada. In 1840 the Venezuelan president finally acknowledged his country's share of the obligations and struck an agreement to end the default. The period of good grace ended quickly, however. Venezuela reverted to default in the years 1847–62, 1864–76, 1878–80, 1882–83, and 1898–1902, when British and German forces arrived.

During these long and numerous phases of default, bondholders petitioned the British government for assistance. In 1867, for example, investors delivered a petition to Lord Stanley, the English foreign secretary. The document declared that "the time has now arrived for Her Majesty's Government to adopt active measures to enforce on the Government of Venezuela the due performance of its special obligations to British subjects." The petitioners essentially asked for "armed intervention."[41] Lord Stanley replied, however, that "Her Majesty's government do not feel justified in seeking the sanction of Parliament to adopt coercive measures which might involve this country in a war with the Republic of Venezuela."[42]

After so many years of nonintervention by British authorities, Edward Eastwick, commissioner for the Venezuelan loan of 1864, complained that "the English Government gratuitously parades its determination not to enforce the claims of its subjects." Even if authorities never wished to employ ulterior measures, they should not proclaim this fact to the rest of the world. Britain's public declarations of noninterference, Eastwick

[41] *Economist*, November 9, 1867, 1268.
[42] *Times* (London), December 3, 1867, 8.

reasoned, were "like putting up a board to warn trespassers that they will *not* be prosecuted."[43]

As Venezuela continued in default, bondholders again asked their government for help. The answer, drafted by the permanent undersecretary of the Foreign Office in 1871, is worth quoting at length because it explains why Britain scrupulously avoided punishing defaulters. British policy, the undersecretary wrote,

> has always been, and will continue to be, limited to unofficial support and friendly remonstrance. . . . Her Majesty's Government are in no way party to private loan transactions with foreign States. Contracts of this nature rest only between the Power borrowing and the capitalists who enter into them as speculative enterprises, and who are content to undertake extraordinary risks in the hope of large contingent profits. Further, it is scarcely necessary to point out the endless troubles which certainly would arise if the active intervention of England were exerted to redress the grievances of bondholders. Independently of the expense which would necessarily be incurred, and the risk of international complications, forcible measures, if adopted toward small States, which for the most part are the ones complained of, would subject this country to grievous imputations. For such and other obvious reasons . . . the parties must not expect that forcible measures, such as reprisals, and still less any of a more decidedly warlike character, will ever be resorted to by Her Majesty's government in support of their claims.[44]

Some academic commentators suggest that, in 1902, Britain finally abandoned this long-standing policy of leaving bondholders to their own devices. To political scientist John Latané, it was "perfectly apparent" that the action against Venezuela was "undertaken in the interest of bondholders." He regarded the intervention as a revolution in British and German policy, "a decided innovation in the practice of nations."[45] Historian Herbert Feis concurred that "in this episode the government had swung full circle; the whole force of the state had been put behind the foreign investor."[46]

There is, however, another explanation that more closely fits the sequence of events. The explanation centers on injuries British nationals had suffered during the years 1900–1902. Some injuries stemmed from the civil war that solidified Castro's hold on power. Venezuelan forces had bombarded and plundered the homes of British residents, wrongfully

[43] Eastwick 1868, 328.
[44] Edmund Hammond to Hyde Clarke, April 26, 1871, in United Kingdom Parliament 1874, 59–60.
[45] Latané 1906, 546.
[46] Feis 1930, 109.

arrested and court-martialed them, and expropriated their cattle and other property.[47]

By far the most important trigger, however, was the renegade behavior of the Venezuelan navy. In January 1901, Venezuelan forces sailed to Patos Island, a British possession and part of the Colony of Trinidad and Tobago. There, Venezuelan troops boarded a trading vessel, seized British cargo, captured several British subjects, and left the remaining passengers on the island without rations or means of escape. The British chargé d'affaires in Caracas protested immediately, but Castro did not respond.[48] More violations followed. Venezuelan gunboats encroached on British territorial waters in Patos Bay, landed armed forces on Patos Island, assaulted British citizens, and attacked, plundered, and burned British ships. Meanwhile, the Venezuelan government failed to answer repeated diplomatic notes about the abuses that were taking place.

The event that finally tipped the scales in favor of intervention occurred in June 1902, when a Venezuelan gunboat seized the *Queen*, a British vessel, on the high seas. The craft was pillaged and confiscated, and the crew was left stranded at Porlamar port. Legal advisors in the Foreign Office concluded that Britain finally had "clear proof of an outrage that justifies and, coupled with the other outrages, requires reprisals." Francis Villiers, the British Foreign Office advisor on Venezuela, wrote that "the time has come for strong measures against the Venezuelans," and Foreign Secretary Lansdowne agreed that "we clearly cannot let this pass."[49]

Lansdowne instructed the British minister in Caracas to deliver a stern warning. Unless the British "receive explicit assurances that incidents of this nature shall not recur, and unless the Venezuelan Government promptly pay to the injured parties full compensation . . . His Majesty's Government will take such steps as may be necessary to obtain reparation."[50] Venezuela ignored the demand, and British and German forces attacked in December 1902. As explanations for the timing of British intervention, the shipping and civil war claims seem far more plausible than debt defaults that began more than 75 years earlier.

[47] "Memorandum by Mr. [Arthur] Larcom respecting British Claims against Venezuela," February 20, 1903, in Philip 1992, *British Documents on Foreign Affairs*, 193–94.

[48] "Memorandum on Existing Causes of Complaint against Venezuela," July 20, 1902, in United Kingdom Parliament 1902, 1–4; *Times* (London), December 16, 1902, 10; and Alfred Moloney to Joseph Chamberlain, February 24, 1901, in Philip 1992, *British Documents on Foreign Affairs*, 96.

[49] Minutes by Cecil Hurst, Francis Villiers, and Lord Lansdowne on William Haggard to Lansdowne, June 30, 1902, Desp. 132 (Received F.O. July 16, 1902), FO 80/443, U.K. National Archives.

[50] Lord Lansdowne to William Haggard, July 29, 1902, in Philip 1992, *British Documents on Foreign Affairs*, 153.

THE CONTENT OF PRIVATE COMMUNICATIONS

Had Britain been acting on behalf of bondholders, discussions of their plight should have appeared prominently in internal memoranda and diplomatic correspondence. This was not the case. Spurred by the *Queen* incident, the Foreign Office prepared a list of grievances against Venezuela. The June 20 memorandum cited shipping claims but never mentioned British bonds.[51] Based on the memorandum, the British minister in Venezuela delivered demands to the Castro government and relayed identical information to the Admiralty of the British fleet. These communications, which laid the foundation for military action, did not refer to the bondholders, either.[52]

Why, then, did Britain include bondholders in the final ultimatum? Internal documents provide an explanation. In September 1902, well after the government had resolved to intervene against Venezuela, the Corporation of Foreign Bondholders asked for assistance, and the Foreign Office relented in order "to make the slate clean."[53] The first official mention of support for bondholders occurred on November 17, and their demands were delivered to Venezuelan authorities only days before the war began.[54] British bondholders were an afterthought, not an inspiration, for military intervention.

THE FINAL ULTIMATUM AND IMMEDIATE AFTERMATH

If Britain were motivated to assist bondholders, the final ultimatum should have focused on the New Consolidated Debt of 1881. In fact the opposite was true. At the behest of Germany, the intervening powers ranked their claims against Venezuela. Britain assigned first rank to shipping claims, which were nonnegotiable and had to be paid immediately. It assigned secondary importance to personal and property damages arising from the Venezuelan civil war. Britain asked Venezuela to acknowledge liability for these second-tier claims, but was prepared to enter mediation or arbitration over the exact amount of compensation. Bondholders were

[51] "Memorandum on Existing Causes of Complaint against Venezuela," July 20, 1902, in United Kingdom Parliament 1902, 1–4.
[52] Lord Lansdowne to William Haggard, July 29, 1902; Haggard to Lansdowne, August 1, 1902; and Francis Villiers to Admiralty, August 8, 1902, all in Philip 1992, *British Documents on Foreign Affairs*, 153–59.
[53] James Cooper to Foreign Office, September 23, 1902, in Philip 1992, *British Documents on Foreign Affairs*, 161–62; Francis Villiers Memorandum to Lord Lansdowne, November 13, 1902, FO 80/445, U.K. National Archives.
[54] Lord Lansdowne to George Buchanan, November 17, 1902, in United Kingdom Parliament 1902, 11; *Times* (London), December 16, 1902, 9.

relegated to the third tier, the bottom of the British hierarchy. Although grateful for any assistance at all, the Corporation of Foreign Bondholders found its bottom-rank status "undoubtedly disappointing."[55]

In the aftermath of the intervention, a bondholder-minded Foreign Office would have forced Venezuela to pay investors. The Washington Protocol, however, merely stipulated that Venezuela "undertake to enter into a fresh arrangement" with bondholders. From that point forward, neither the British military nor the Foreign Office accepted responsibility for prying open the Venezuelan coffers. Villiers reminded the CFB that the British government had always placed bondholder claims in a "wholly different category" from the other demands. Although it seemed desirable to include the loan of 1881 as part of a comprehensive settlement, official efforts on behalf of bondholders "never went further than this."[56] The British government refused to get involved in the debt negotiations.

## THE OFFICIAL RATIONALE FOR INTERVENTION

Finally, if Britain had been following a military linkage strategy, it would have publicized the linkage to deter other would-be defaulters. Instead, members of the cabinet emphasized that they were enforcing tort claims, not bonds. Prime Minister Arthur Balfour stated his position before the House of Commons in December 1902. "I doubt whether we have in the past ever gone to war for the bondholders . . . and I confess I should be very sorry to see that made a practice in this country."[57] The operations against Venezuela were "not undertaken to recover the debts of bondholders. They have been undertaken most reluctantly, and after long and patient delay, because the Venezuelans assaulted British citizens and seized British ships."[58]

Lord Cranborne, the Undersecretary of State for Foreign Affairs, was similarly insistent. The day after the fighting began, Cranborne listed for Parliament the grievances that had spurred British action. Tellingly, his speech contained no references to bondholders.[59] A few days later, in response to questioning, Cranborne explicitly repudiated the charge that Britain had gone to war for bondholders. "I can frankly tell the House," he explained, "that it is not the claims of the bondholders that bulk largest

[55] Corporation of Foreign Bondholders, *Annual Report* 30 (1903), 15.

[56] Villiers to Corporation of Foreign Bondholders, March 13, 1903, in Philip 1992, *British Documents on Foreign Affairs*, 197.

[57] *Parliamentary Debates*, 4th ser., vol. 116 (December 15, 1902), col. 1273.

[58] *Parliamentary Debates*, 4th ser., vol. 116 (December 17, 1902), col. 1491.

[59] *Parliamentary Debates*, 4th ser., vol. 116 (December 10, 1902), col. 654. See also *Financial News*, December 12, 1902, 4.

in the estimation of the Government. I do not believe the Government would ever have taken the strong measures to which they have been driven if it had not been for the attacks by Venezuela upon the lives, the liberty, and the property of British subjects."[60] Other government officials, including Selborne (First Lord of the Admiralty) and Chamberlain (cabinet minister), made similar statements before the Parliament and in meetings with members of the London community.[61]

Thus, five separate lines of analysis point to the same conclusion: even during the famous Venezuelan intervention of 1902, Britain was not implementing the kind of linkage strategy implied by the gunboat hypothesis. Tort claims better explain the timing of the intervention, and they figure more prominently in private communications, public speeches, the final ultimatum, and the Washington Protocol that resolved the MID. I now examine whether the same conclusion applies to Germany.

### German Action against Venezuela

THE TIMING OF THE INTERVENTION

The lapse between default and intervention was much shorter for Germany than for Britain, because Germans had only recently begun investing in Venezuelan bonds. German involvement began in 1887, when the Venezuelan government granted Krupp, a German industrial dynasty, a concession to build a railway between Caracas and Valencia. The following year, Krupp passed the concession to Disconto Gesellschaft and Norddeutsche Bank, which established the Great Venezuela Railway Company and began financing the construction project.[62] Work progressed slowly due to landslides, broken dams, and unforeseen difficulties in purchasing land. When the 180-kilometer line was completed in 1894, the final price tag was sixty-two million marks, more than double the original estimate.[63]

In giving the railway concession, Venezuela committed to pay interest of 7 percent per year on the building capital. Payments were scheduled to begin in 1894, when the railroad opened, but Venezuela immediately reneged. Two years later, the government capitalized the overdue and future railway guarantees into a bond, the 5 percent debt of 1896, financed by Disconto Gesellschaft. Although interest on the loan was paid briefly, Venezuelan authorities announced in November 1897 that they

---

[60] Parliamentary Debates, 4th ser., vol. 116 (December 15, 1902), col. 1263.
[61] See, e.g., Lord Selborne in Parliamentary Debates, 4th ser., vol. 118 (March 2, 1903), cols. 1085–86; and Austen Chamberlain in Times (London), February 2, 1903, 8.
[62] Forbes 1978, 319; Otto 1910, 125–27.
[63] Times (London), December 24, 1902, 3.

could not meet their commitments, and from June 1898 German creditors received nothing.[64]

Thus Germany, unlike Britain, had only endured a short phase of default before sending gunboats to Venezuela. It is, therefore, plausible that
debt default could have triggered the German intervention. Another event
coincided with the railway defaults, however, and holds equal potential
to explain both the fact and the timing of German military deployments.
This parallel event is the Venezuelan civil war.

At the turn of the century, a large number of German nationals were
living in Venezuela. Many experienced significant losses during the civil
wars of 1898–1900 and were continuing to suffer from Castro's antirebel
campaigns.[65] Venezuelan forces shelled and pillaged their homes, seized
their cattle, forced them to transport troops, and required them to make
"voluntary" contributions to the Venezuelan dictator. The German government valued these claims at about 1.7 million bolivars and had been
working to secure compensation.

In January 1901, the Venezuelan government issued a decree that pre-
cluded Germany from obtaining indemnities. The decree invalidated all
claims that predated the Castro presidency and empowered a special commission—consisting entirely of Venezuelans—to decide the status of other
claims. The decree also required that any future payments be delivered in
the form of bonds, rather than cash.[66]

Germany therefore had two significant grievances (default on the Disconto loan and losses during the civil war), both of which arose at approximately the same time and could have driven the imperial chancellor to
intervene. To judge the relative importance of these grievances, I now
turn to other types of evidence, including the private communications and
public statements of German officials.

## THE CONTENT OF PRIVATE COMMUNICATIONS

In private, German leaders placed more weight on the civil war claims
than on defaulted bonds. Shortly after the suspension of payments in
1898, investors asked the German government to intervene. Their peti-
tions were rejected. Oswald von Richthofen of the German foreign office

---

[64] Fenn, *Fenn's Compendium* (1898), 554; *Financial Times*, December 8, 1900, 4; January
1, 1902, 6; Guthrie 1983, 15; Otto 1910, 125–27; *Times* (London), December 31, 1901, 3.

[65] "Memorandum Communicated by Count Metternich," December 17, 1902, in United
Kingdom Parliament 1903, 175. Lord Lansdowne described many of the German grievances
in *Parliamentary Debates*, 4th ser., vol. 118 (March 2, 1903), col. 1064. See also Guthrie
1983, 12–13; Herwig 1986, 87–90; Kneer 1975, 46; and *Times* (London), December 6,
1902, 7.

[66] *Times* (London), December 9, 1902, 9.

"bluntly informed the Hamburg Board of Trade when it attempted to lobby the Foreign Secretary for armed intervention in Venezuela . . . that it was not the government's business to pull Disconto's chestnuts out of the fire."[67]

Although internal memoranda from as early as December 1901 cite the Disconto loan as a source of grievance,[68] Chancellor Bernhard von Bülow focused on other German claims. "The Chancellor above all desired pressure upon Castro to meet the damage claims of German nationals in Venezuela; the reclamations of the Great Venezuelan Railroad and the Disconto Bank were to be taken up only at a later date."[69]

Another indication of German intentions comes from the diplomatic correspondence of Otto von Mühlberg, undersecretary of the German Foreign Office. In instructions to his ambassador in London, Mühlberg stressed that the Disconto bonds "do not in themselves provide the basis for an insistent stance, since Venezuela does not dispute its obligations," but merely pleads that it cannot pay at the moment. "In contrast, the claims . . . stemming from the civil war have taken on a character that makes action against Venezuela urgently necessary."[70]

## THE FINAL ULTIMATUM AND IMMEDIATE AFTERMATH

Germany, like Britain, ranked its claims in the weeks before the intervention. German first-class claims concerned damages its nationals had suffered during the Venezuelan civil wars. These first-class claims were non-negotiable, and Germany demanded prompt payment in cash. Only if Venezuela refused to pay the civil war indemnities would Germany append a series of "second class" claims, including arrears on the Disconto loan. Venezuela did refuse, and Germany included bondholders in its final ultimatum to Castro. Nevertheless, the ranking of claims reveals much about their importance. The German ambassador in London explained that "Germany's 'whole action' against Venezuela had been based on its first class claims."[71]

## THE OFFICIAL RATIONALE FOR INTERVENTION

Finally, public pronouncements by German leaders undermine the gunboat hypothesis. On the eve of hostilities, Chancellor Bülow summarized his country's complaints. The chancellor stressed the harm to German

---

[67] Herwig 1986, 240.
[68] Guthrie 1983, 23.
[69] Herwig 1986, 221.
[70] Otto von Mühlberg to Paul von Metternich, July 17, 1902, in Germany Auswärtiges Amt. 1957, Venezuela 1, vol. 21.
[71] Kneer 1975, 53.

nationals, while mentioning the bondholders only briefly.[72] Later that month, in an interview with the Associated Press, Bülow dispelled the idea that Germany was "engaged in the collection of business debts." He explained that "we gave precedence to [claims] arising from the last Venezuelan civil wars. Those claims have not the character of mere business debts contracted by the Republic, but have grown out of acts of violence committed against German citizens in Venezuela."[73] In a follow-up speech to the Reichstag on March 19, 1903, Bülow again cited the civil war injuries as the main reason for the intervention.[74]

In summary, the Venezuelan crisis of 1902 is widely regarded as the most famous and shocking example of linkage between sovereign debt and military intervention. Britain and Germany sent gunboats, it is argued, to punish a country for defaulting and compel it to pay investors. A close look at primary documents from both countries suggests a different conclusion. The powers sent gunboats to vindicate the claims of foreign nationals, whose liberty and property had been compromised. Seen this way, the Venezuelan intervention belongs in the same category as the many other tort cases in table 6.5. It was not, as many have assumed, a bondholder war.

## A Survey of British Diplomatic Correspondence

I now extend the analysis by examining public speeches and diplomatic correspondence from the first half of the nineteenth century. This extension is useful for two reasons: it provides further insights into the motivations of creditors, and it helps bridge a gap in the previous analysis. The Militarized Interstate Dispute dataset omits several countries in the early 1800s, because they had not yet received permanent diplomatic missions from Britain and France. Perhaps creditors coerced debtors in the early nineteenth century, a period not well covered in the MID data. I investigated this possibility by examining official documents from the time.

In the mid-1820s, a wave of defaults in Latin America and on the Iberian Peninsula outraged bondholders, who asked British authorities to "take prompt and energetic steps to compel the governments . . . to pay."[75] At almost every turn, the government opted not to get involved.

---

[72] Bernard von Bülow, "Denkschrift uber de Reklamationen Deutschlands gegen die Vereinigten Staaten von Venezuela," December 8, 1902, in Germany Reichstag, *Stenographische Berichte über die Verhandlungen*, 10th Legis., 2nd Session, sup. 7, doc. 786, 1957–59; *Times* (London), December 9, 1902, 5.

[73] *Times* (London), December 23, 1902, 3.

[74] Bernard von Bülow, March 19, 1903, in Germany Reichstag, *Stenographische Berichte über die Verhandlungen*, 10th Legis., 2nd Session, 8719–20.

[75] George Shee to William Ewing, October 5, 1831 in United Kingdom Parliament 1847, 128.

Speaking to the House of Commons in 1824, Foreign Secretary George Canning "did not mean to throw the slightest blame on those who employed their capital in loans to the states of South America. All men had a perfect right to advance their capital in foreign governments, if they thought fit." But "parties so engaged ought not to carry with them the force and influence of the British government, in order to compel foreign states to fulfill their contracts."[76] In subsequent decades, no public address by any British prime minister or foreign secretary ever contradicted this policy of nonintervention.

As an additional step, I systematically coded a unique collection of correspondence spanning the years 1823 to 1853. The collection—520 letters involving the British government, foreign powers, and disgruntled bondholders—was presented by the Foreign Office to the House of Commons around mid-century, and provides additional insight into British policy regarding foreign loans.[77]

It is hard to verify whether the collection is comprehensive, but even if the publication contains only a sample of letters, there are two reasons to use it for empirical analysis. First, the collection is extensive not only in the sheer number of letters but also in its geographic coverage. Documents pertain to the debts of Spain, Portugal, Greece, Mexico, Central America, New Granada (Colombia), Venezuela, Ecuador, Peru, Argentina, Chile, and Uruguay, a good cross-section of sovereign borrowers. Second, any bias in the selection of correspondence would favor the linkage hypothesis. If the British government sought to deter countries from defaulting, it would have published threatening letters: ones connecting default to military retaliation.

The letters confirm that, even in the early nineteenth century, the British government would not take official action on behalf of bondholders. Table 6.6 summarizes the content of the collection. For *every* country discussed in the letters, British authorities stated at least once—and often a half-dozen times or more—that it would not link debt default to any kind of official response. As Palmerston explained in one of the letters, "No doubt an expression of the intention of the British Government authoritatively to interfere on behalf of the bondholders might be useful to them; but such a declaration would be at variance with the fixed rule of the British Government in regard to all such cases."[78] British authorities articulated the same position many times and applied it around the world.

---

[76] *Parliamentary Debates*, 2nd ser., vol. 11 (June 15, 1824), col. 1404.

[77] United Kingdom Parliament 1847, *Correspondence Relative to Loans Made by British Subjects*, Command Paper No. 839; United Kingdom Parliament 1854a, *Correspondence Relative to Loans Made by British Subjects*, House of Commons Paper 0.2.

[78] Edward Stanley to Thomas Lethbridge, March 6, 1847, in United Kingdom Parliament 1847, 11–12.

TABLE 6.6
British Refusal to Apply Pressure in Diplomatic Correspondence, 1823–53

|  | Number of Letters in which the United Kingdom | |
|---|---|---|
| Defaulting Country | Threatened or Warned the Defaulter | Refused to Threaten or Warn the Defaulter |
| Argentina | 0 | 2 |
| Central America | 0 | 1 |
| Chile | 1 | 3 |
| Colombia | 2 | 11 |
| Ecuador | 0 | 6 |
| Greece | 0 | 3 |
| Mexico | 2 | 10 |
| Peru | 1 | 2 |
| Portugal | 0 | 11 |
| Spain | 0 | 15 |
| Uruguay | 0 | 1 |
| Venezuela | 0 | 5 |
| Total | 6 | 70 |

Source: Author's analysis of correspondence in United Kingdom Parliament 1847, *Correspondence Relative to Loans Made by British Subjects*, Command Paper No. 839; and United Kingdom Parliament 1854a, *Correspondence Relative to Loans Made by British Subjects*, House of Commons Paper 0.2.

Note: The table gives the number of communications in which Britain either refused pressure or delivered what could be construed as a threat.

In a small number of cases, diplomats asserted that growing indignation in Britain might "compel the British Government to take the matter up."[79] Such threats were invariably vague, however. They never specified the consequences—military or otherwise—that might follow from continued default, nor did they give a deadline for resuming payment on defaulted bonds. Clear expressions of noninvolvement were at least 11 times more common than these vague threats, which in any case were delivered to only four of the 12 countries in the sample.

The letters describe one amusing exchange in which bondholders, frustrated by the British policy of nonintervention, requested permission to take matters into their own hands. Would Britain object, they asked, if the bondholders fitted out their own armed vessels to make reprisals on the Mexican government? After reaffirming that the defaulted bonds were

[79] Richard Pakenham to Jose María Ortiz Monasterio, September 18, 1836; April 18, 1837; William Turner to Lino de Pombo, November 7, 1836; Daniel O'Leary to Joaquín Acosta, April 19, 1844; Belford Wilson to Ramón Castilla, April 15, 1839; and John Walpole to Diego Portales, December 13, 1836, all in United Kingdom Parliament 1847, 70–73, 144–46, 167, 214–16, 260.

"private transactions which do not admit . . . of any official or authoritative interference," the Foreign Office addressed the bondholders' creative proposal. The proposition, Palmerston explained, "cannot possibly be sanctioned or allowed by His Majesty's Government."[80] In Mexico and elsewhere, Britain not only refused to take action, but also prohibited the bondholders from practicing their own vigilante justice.

Although the British government eschewed official involvement, its diplomats assumed an unofficial role, expressing investors' feelings of disappointment and hopes for repayment. Diplomats also argued that continued default would undermine countries' reputations in the eyes of capital markets, making it unlikely that investors would offer new loans.

In correspondence with the leaders of New Granada, for example, the British representative openly acknowledged that "His Majesty's Government cannot exercise any authoritative interference . . . in behalf of the bondholders." He nonetheless pointed out "the injurious effect" of default on "the credit of their country." Renewed payment, he contended, would give "proof of the earnest intention of New Granada" and help achieve "high public credit," which would confer "incalculable advantages" on the nation.[81]

British representatives offered similar advice to the government of Peru. According to the British consul, Peru had the opportunity "of proving by acts" its "desire to restore the national credit" and its "honesty of intention towards the British bondholders." A debt settlement would reveal Peru as a good type; it would "give to the world the assurance that Peru . . . cherishes the intention and possesses the means of rigidly fulfilling her engagements, of whatever kind they may be."[82]

British representatives in Chile and Venezuela made analogous reputational arguments. "Any further delay in the discharge of their just claims" would "inevitably destroy the confidence" of investors. Regular payments, on the other hand, would help "convince the bondholders how sacredly it regarded its obligations toward them." Public credit would then be "preserved and augmented to an extraordinary degree," with "salutary effects" that would "soon be apparent as well as most advantageously felt by every citizen of the Republic."[83]

[80] John Backhouse to T. Warrington, February 24, 1836, in United Kingdom Parliament 1847, 69.

[81] William Turner to José Francisco Pereira, January 20, 1832; Turner to Alejandro Vélez, November 20, 1832, both in United Kingdom Parliament 1847, 131, 134–35.

[82] Belford Wilson to José María de Pando, July 1, 1833; Wilson to Manuel del Río, October 30, 1833, both in United Kingdom Parliament 1847, 199–200, 202–3.

[83] Robert Ker Porter to Guillermo Smith, April 25, 1840; John White to Carlos Rodríguez, July 7, 1830, both in United Kingdom Parliament 1847, 181–82, 252–53.

Frederick Chatfield, the British representative to Guatemala and other Central American states, succinctly summarized the reputational logic. A fair arrangement with bondholders, Chatfield argued, would "attract the notice of European capitalists, who are ever disposed to embark their property and industry in a State, whose Government shows the inclination and an ability to maintain its credit by adhering to the principles of good faith and probity on which all character is founded."[84] The consistent line during this period was an appeal to reputation, not the threat of coercion.

## Did Creditors have an Implicit Deterrence Policy?

Creditors, we have seen, generally avoided making threats and deploying troops to defend bondholders. Is it nonetheless possible that the gunboat mechanism worked silently? Perhaps the gunboat hypothesis was an influential myth, a misperception that default would trigger intervention, even though rich-country governments had no intention of rescuing bondholders. Or perhaps the hypothesis was an unstated truth: creditors would have used force but felt no need to articulate or demonstrate threats that were already widely believed.

To see if implicit military threats played a role in nineteenth-century finance, I investigated whether people behaved *as if* the gunboat hypothesis were true. If investors thought gunboats were necessary and sufficient for debt enforcement, they should have lent only to countries they could have coerced militarily. This condition imposed few constraints on British, French, German, and American investors, whose governments were strong enough to project power around the globe and outgun almost any debtor. The geographic distribution of British, French, German, and U.S. investment therefore reveals little about the gunboat hypothesis.

The behavior of investors in countries with middle-rank militaries is much more informative. Before World War I, Belgium, the Netherlands, and Switzerland played significant roles in international finance. These three countries collectively represented around 12.5 percent of the world's gross foreign investment, and on a per capita basis their foreign holdings ranked among the highest in the world.[85] Did citizens of these countries invest only where they could have applied military pressure, or did they lend even where gunboat diplomacy was not an option?

---

[84] Frederick Chatfield to the Government of Guatemala, July 15, 1839, in United Kingdom Parliament 1847, 116–17.

[85] Bairoch (1976, 101) estimates that, on the eve of World War I, the Swiss achieved the highest rate of foreign investment per capita, followed by the British, the Dutch, and the Belgians.

My first test concerns the ability to deploy force, a prerequisite for gunboat diplomacy. Any creditor could attack countries on its border, but striking against farther-flung areas would be more difficult. The aggressor would need a navy to move forces by water, or allies that would grant permission to march troops through their territories en route to the target. Before World War I, this kind of long-distance projection would have been moderately difficult for the Netherlands and almost impossible for Belgium and Switzerland. None of these states had formal allies during the period under study, and neither Belgium nor Switzerland had a seafaring navy.[86] Consequently, Belgium and Switzerland could not have coerced countries beyond their borders, and the Netherlands, though equipped with a modern navy, could not have attacked countries in the European interior.[87]

These facts did not seem to influence the geographical distribution of international investment. As table 6.7 shows, investors held bonds from many countries out of military reach. Belgium and Switzerland lent to noncontiguous European countries, and to nations in the Americas, Africa, Asia, and the Mideast. The Dutch, who could not have waged war in many parts of Europe, nonetheless lent throughout the continent. These investment patterns belie the proposition that military linkage was the key to contract enforcement.[88]

My second test concerns the ability to win wars. Even if forces from Belgium, the Netherlands, or Switzerland could have reached foreign shores, they would have been outgunned and outmanned by many debtors. The COW project provides, for most countries, an index of military capability that takes six factors into account: military expenditure, military personnel, energy consumption, iron and steel production, urban population, and total population. This composite indicator of national capability, or CINC, is the most widely used measure of military power in the international relations literature. Here, I use the CINC to estimate whether the balance of power in a militarized dispute would have favored the debtor.

Table 6.8 lists debtors that were at least twice as powerful as their foreign creditors. Austria-Hungary, for example, owed money to Belgian in-

[86] Belgium had a naval organization but no warships. See, e.g., Chesneau and Kolesnik 1979, 415; Gray 1985, 411; and United Kingdom War Office Intelligence Division 1882, 10.

[87] The historical record is consistent with this assumption. During the entire period 1820–1913, Belgium was involved in MIDs against only one opponent, its neighbor the Netherlands, and Switzerland experienced a MID with only one nation, neighboring Germany. Beyond the wars of Belgian Independence, the Dutch engaged in MIDs against only two other countries, Japan and Venezuela, both of which were sea-accessible targets.

[88] Did Belgium, the Netherlands, and Switzerland "free ride" on the military linkage policies of stronger nations? I found no evidence to support this possibility. On the contrary, governments in Britain and other creditor nations refused to intervene for their *own* bondholders. It therefore seems unlikely that they would have intervened for someone else's.

TABLE 6.7
Foreign Bond Listings in Belgium, the Netherlands, and Switzerland, 1820–1913

| Geographic Location of Debtor | Creditor | | |
|---|---|---|---|
| | Belgium | Netherlands | Switzerland |
| Europe, contiguous to the creditor | France, Germany, Luxembourg, Netherlands, United Kingdom[b] | Belgium, Denmark[a], France[b], Germany, Norway[b], Sweden[b], United Kingdom[a] | Austria-Hungary, France, Germany, Italy |
| Europe, not contiguous to the creditor | Austria-Hungary, Bulgaria, Denmark, German States[c], Greece, Italy[d], Norway, Poland, Portugal, Romania, Russia, Serbia, Spain, Sweden, Switzerland, Turkey | Austria-Hungary, Bosnia, Bulgaria, Finland, German States[c], Greece, Italy[d], Poland, Portugal, Romania, Russia, Serbia, Spain, Switzerland | Bosnia, Bulgaria, Denmark, Finland, Norway, Portugal, Romania, Russia, Serbia, Spain, Sweden |
| Americas | Argentina, Brazil, Chile, Dominican Republic, Ecuador, Haiti, Honduras, Mexico, Peru, Uruguay, United States, Venezuela | Argentina, Brazil, Chile, Colombia, Cuba, Dominican Republic, Ecuador, Haiti, Mexico, Nicaragua, Peru, Uruguay, United States, Venezuela | Argentina, Brazil, Canada[e], Peru, Uruguay, United States |
| Africa, Asia, and Mideast | China, Egypt, Japan | China, Egypt, Japan, Liberia, Ottoman Empire, South Africa, Tunisia | China, Egypt, Japan, Morocco, Ottoman Empire, Transvaal |

*Source:* Stock market price sheets, as listed in the bibliography.
*Note:* The table gives the names and geographic locations of sovereign debtors whose bonds were listed on Belgian, Dutch, or Swiss stock exchanges at some point during 1820–1913.

[a] Contiguous by less than 150 miles of water.
[b] Contiguous by less than 400 miles of water.
[c] Includes Baden, Hamburg, Hanover, Hessen, Hesse Gran Ducal, Nassau, and Saxony.
[d] Includes Holy See, Naples, Piemont, Sardinia, Sicily, and Unified Italy.
[e] Quebec.

TABLE 6.8
Military Power of Debtors Relative to Creditors, 1820–1913

| Creditor and Debtor | Military Power Ratio (Debtor/Creditor) | | | |
|---|---|---|---|---|
| | Median | 10th Percentile | 90th Percentile | N |
| Belgium | | | | |
| Austria-Hungary | 2.8 | 2.0 | 3.3 | 82 |
| China | 8.2 | 7.5 | 9.7 | 19 |
| France | 5.3 | 4.7 | 5.9 | 73 |
| Germany | 4.9 | 1.8 | 9.2 | 75 |
| Japan | 2.4 | 2.2 | 3.5 | 12 |
| Russia | 5.3 | 3.7 | 8.2 | 82 |
| United Kingdom | 11.5 | 10.4 | 12.8 | 59 |
| United States | 6.3 | 1.9 | 15.2 | 69 |
| Netherlands | | | | |
| Austria-Hungary | 5.6 | 2.5 | 7.0 | 94 |
| Belgium | 2.2 | 2.0 | 2.6 | 69 |
| China | 16.7 | 15.1 | 20.5 | 19 |
| France | 11.3 | 3.8 | 13.4 | 94 |
| Germany | 8.2 | 1.3 | 19.0 | 94 |
| Italy | 3.9 | 0.3 | 4.7 | 82 |
| Japan | 5.2 | 4.5 | 7.5 | 12 |
| Ottoman Empire | 2.5 | 2.2 | 2.9 | 52 |
| Russia | 11.1 | 4.5 | 16.3 | 94 |
| Spain | 2.2 | 0.9 | 2.6 | 94 |
| United Kingdom | 16.1 | 8.0 | 24.7 | 28 |
| United States | 12.7 | 1.0 | 29.5 | 94 |
| Switzerland | | | | |
| Argentina | 2.2 | 1.5 | 2.5 | 25 |
| Austria-Hungary | 23.3 | 18.4 | 41.4 | 50 |
| Brazil | 4.5 | 4.3 | 4.7 | 15 |
| China | 55.6 | 53.3 | 58.2 | 15 |
| Egypt | 2.9 | 2.7 | 3.2 | 2 |
| France | 108.6 | 90.9 | 125.1 | 4 |
| Germany | 59.3 | 55.7 | 61.5 | 13 |
| Italy | 18.9 | 11.5 | 33.2 | 59 |
| Japan | 14.5 | 14.1 | 23.4 | 9 |
| Ottoman Empire | 9.0 | 7.4 | 20.4 | 44 |
| Romania | 2.1 | 1.9 | 2.2 | 20 |
| Russia | 49.0 | 41.1 | 52.2 | 26 |
| Spain | 7.3 | 6.5 | 21.2 | 7 |
| Sweden | 3.0 | 2.9 | 3.3 | 6 |
| United States | 99.9 | 77.8 | 103.3 | 11 |

*Source*: Author's calculations from Correlates of War 2005. The data are described in Singer, Bremer, and Stuckey 1972 and in Singer 1987.

*Note*: Table gives the Correlates of War CINC Index for the debtor, divided by the CINC Index for the creditor. Values are calculated for all years in which a debtor-creditor relationship existed and both countries were members of the COW system.

vestors for 82 years in our sample. During that time, the median value of the military power ratio—the CINC index for Austria-Hungary divided by the CINC index for Belgium—was 2.8, making the debtor 2.8 times more powerful than the creditor. China, France, Germany, Japan, Russia, the United Kingdom, and the United States also owed money to Belgians. If any of these nations defaulted, the Belgian army could not have collected the arrears. Dutch and Swiss investors were outmatched to an even greater degree, by an even larger number of debtors.

In summary, most loans by Belgian, Dutch, and Swiss investors were militarily unenforceable. Even if the armies of these small nations could have reached defaulters, they typically would not have prevailed in war. Nonetheless, these three nations achieved some of the highest per capita foreign investment rates in the world by lending to countries they had no prospect of coercing. Creditors did not behave as if gunboats provided the principal guarantee of repayment. Their investment activities were more consistent with reputational theory, which can sustain cooperation regardless of disparities in military power.

### Did Debtors and Investment Advisors Expect Military Intervention?

Investment advisors did not seem to expect military intervention, either. If advisors believed in the debt-collecting power of gunboats, this theme should have appeared prominently in bond advertisements and nineteenth-century investment manuals such as *Fortune's Epitome of the Stocks and Public Funds* and *Fenn's Compendium of the English and Foreign Funds*. On the contrary, these texts never reassured investors that military power would keep their money safe, nor did they mention enforceability by gunboat as a criterion for investment. Apparently the gunboat hypothesis was of little importance, not only to private investors who purchased foreign bonds, but also to nineteenth-century analysts and banks that recommended or sold them to the public.

Did debtors expect military intervention? A few probably did.[89] Three lines of analysis suggest, however, that debtors typically did not behave

---

[89] Some Japanese leaders, for example, might have feared military intervention by creditors. See Metzler 2006, 24; and Lindert and Morton 1989, 54. Leaders in Central America may have expected intervention after the attacks on Venezuela and the announcement of the Roosevelt Corollary; for a detailed analysis of this period, see Mitchener and Weidenmier 2005a, 2005b. Argentine jurist Luis Drago expected intervention and drafted his famous Drago Doctrine to outlaw it. But, as Venezuelan president Antonio Guzmán Blanco explained in 1879, it was "well known that Great Britain never intervened on behalf of bondholders" and that England would "do nothing" in response to defaults. See Robert Bunch to Marquis of Salisbury, December 29, 1879, in Philip 1992, *British Documents on Foreign Affairs*, 17–18.

as if gunboats were looming. First, debtors defaulted no less often against strong creditors than against weak ones. Table 6.4 shows that borrowers failed to pay British investors 23 percent of the time, even though Britain was the most powerful nation in the nineteenth century. The only other country in the table with a comparable default rate is the Netherlands, against whom borrowers suspended payments in 21 percent of dyad-years. Defaults were less common against France and Belgium (16 and 14 percent, respectively), and were lowest for Germany, Switzerland, and the United States. Overall, there is no clear correlation between the military power of creditors and the default rates they experienced.

Second, when countries owed money to multiple creditors, such as the United Kingdom and Switzerland, they did not discriminate based on military power. Under the gunboat hypothesis, countries in default should have channeled all their available funds to British, French, and German investors, at the expense of investors in weaker nations such as Belgium, the Netherlands, and Switzerland. In fact, debtors of the nineteenth century treated creditors equally, even though some had vastly stronger militaries than others.

Finally, if debtors feared gunboat diplomacy, defaults should have surged when creditors stopped collecting debts by force. Proponents of the gunboat hypothesis identify the early twentieth century as a turning point, a moment when creditors stopped going to war for bondholders. Martha Finnemore dates the change to 1907. "The immediate result of the Hague Conference" of 1907, she writes, "was a change in military intervention norms. Previously, it had been acceptable for states to collect debts owed to their nationals by force. After the Hague conference it was not."[90]

Even after the supposed demise of gunboat diplomacy, lending and repayment continued. As shown in chapter 5, only a handful of countries defaulted on their debts during the 1920s, while more than 50 countries paid their obligations in full (see table 5.1). Creditors, in turn, extended new loans to countries around the globe. Thus, at precisely the moment when collection by gunboat was no longer an option, international capital markets flourished. This is not the pattern one would expect if changes in international norms deprived creditors of an important enforcement tool.

## Conclusion

Overall, we have found surprisingly little evidence of a systematic link between sovereign debt and military intervention. Prior to World War I, countries that defaulted became targets of military action at a higher rate

[90] Finnemore 2003, 49.

than countries that paid. However, detailed historical analysis shows that the apparent relationship between default and militarized action is mostly spurious. Debt default and military intervention coincided, not because creditors were taking up arms on behalf of bondholders, but because defaulters happened to be involved in other disputes (civil wars, territorial conflicts, tort claims) that attracted the attention of major powers. Even the famous intervention against Venezuela in 1902 was a tort case, not a bondholder war.[91]

Analysis of official correspondence from the early nineteenth century reinforces these conclusions. Britain, the principal creditor of the era, systematically refused to apply official pressure on behalf of bondholders. Rather than threatening the arrival of warships, diplomats emphasized the reputational consequences of default. Patterns of lending and repayment are also at odds with the gunboat hypothesis. Investors lent to countries they had no chance of coercing, and debtors repaid strong creditors no more often than weak ones.

Contrary to popular belief, creditor governments typically did not use—or even threaten to use—force on behalf of bondholders, and neither investors nor borrowers generally expected that default would lead to military intervention. The next chapter considers whether creditors used commercial, rather than military, threats to enforce debt contracts.

## Appendix: Sources for Table 6.5

**ARG vs. UKG, 1842 (MID 371):** Lord Aberdeen to John Henry Mandeville, March 12, 1842, FO 6/82, U.K. National Archives. See also Cady 1929, 99; Ferns 1977, 257–58; and McLean 1995, 32–33.

---

[91] Some countries, especially in Central America and the Caribbean in the early twentieth century, invited foreigners to manage their customshouses or collect and administer other sources of revenue. They thereby created a mixed authority structure, combining elements of anarchy and hierarchy (Lake 1996 and 2006). The arrangements were generally voluntary; they were not examples of debt enforcement against the will of the borrower. As international lawyer Ernst Feilchenfeld (1934, 231) explains, "Financial control . . . has never been unilaterally imposed, but has always been created through agreements with the debtor state." Countries that invited financial controllers willingly did so to tie their own hands, and thereby increase their perceived creditworthiness in international markets. Two other facts underscore the voluntariness of these arrangements: several countries declined bankers' offers to manage fiscal affairs, and the cases do not appear in the MIDs dataset because no explicit threat, show, or use of force occurred. A related and interesting issue is how colonialism affected the volume and price of loans. Important studies of the relationship between colonialism and lending include Atkin 1977; Davis and Huttenback 1986; Ferguson 2005a; Ferguson and Schularick 2006; and Flandreau 2006.

**ARG vs. UKG, 1842–43 (MID 2055)**: John Henry Mandeville to Felipe Arana, December 16, 1842; December 18, 1842, FO 6/84, U.K. National Archives. See also Cady 1929, 104; Calógeras and Martin 1939, 168; Ferns 1977, 262; Kirkpatrick 1931, 154; and McLean 1995, 33–35.

**ARG vs. UKG, 1845–46 (MID 123)**: Lord Aberdeen to William Gore Ouseley, February 20, 1845, in *British and Foreign State Papers* 33 (1844–45), 930–38; Ouseley to Felipe Arana, May 21, 1845, FO 6/103; July 8, 1845, FO 6/104; July 16, 1845, FO 6/104; July 19, 1845, FO 6/104; July 21, 1845, FO 6/104, U.K. National Archives. See also Cady 1929, 152; Calógeras and Martin 1939, 178; Ferns 1977, 270–73; Hogan 1908, 99–100; and McLean 1995, 64, 67, 71–72.

**BRA vs. USA, 1903 (MID 2005)**: Bandeira 1997, 142; and Burns 1966, 79, 227.

**CHL vs. UKG, 1883 (MID 1517)**: Alfred St. John to Earl Granville, January 22, 1883; February 13, 1883, FO 61/346, U.K. National Archives. See also Burr 1965, 160; Dennis 1931, 181–83; Evans 1927, 115; and Millington 1948, 134.

**COL vs. UKG, 1837 (MID 2243)**: Lord Palmerston to William Turner, August 31, 1836; Turner to Granadian Minister of Foreign Affairs, November 28, 1836, both in *British and Foreign State Papers* 26 (1837–38), 183–84, 195–98. Additional primary documents are available in Deas and Sánchez 1991. See also Hogan 1908, 84; Lemaitre 1983, 4:96–97; and *Times* (London), March 6, 1837, 6.

**COL vs. UKG, 1856–57 (MID 1757)**: Philip Griffith to Lino de Pombo, September 15, 1856; September 23, 1856; September 30, 1856; October 6, 1856; October 8, 1856, FO 55/126, U.K. National Archives. See also *New York Times*, November 14, 1856, 3; and Lemaitre 1983, 4:161. For the origins of the Mackintosh claims in the 1820s, see Dawson 1990, 48–49.

**DOM vs. FRN, 1900 (MID 68)**: *New York Times*, January 7, 1900, 6; and Welles 1928, 2:504–7, 556–59.

**GRC vs. UKG, 1850 (MID 71)**: Thomas Wyse to M. Anastasios Londos, January 17, 1850; April 26, 1850; Wyse to Lord Palmerston, April 27, 1850, all in *British and Foreign State Papers* 39 (1849–50), 491, 871–74, 875–77. Many other informative documents appear in *British and Foreign State Papers* 39 (1849–50), 332–932. See also Hannell 1989, 497; Hogan 1908, 106–7; and Woodhouse 1968, 164.

**GRC vs. UKG, FRN, 1854 (MID 2367)**: Lord Cowley to Earl of Clarendon, February 11, 1854; Clarendon to Thomas Wyse, February 16, 1854; Cowley to Clarendon, February 22, 1854; Wyse to Clarendon,

February 13, 1854; Clarendon to Cowley, March 3, 1854; Clarendon to Wyse, March 6, 1854, and many other communications in United Kingdom Parliament 1854b, 48, 50–51, 55, 67–69, 80, 83. See also Stavrianos 1958, 294; and *Times* (London), April 6, 1854, 8; May 30, 1854, 5, 8.

**GRC vs. UKG, FRN, GMY, 1896 (MID 2837):** Frédéric Bourée to Gabriel Hanotaux, July 7, 1896, in France, Ministère des Affaires Étrangères 1897a, 114–15. See also Dakin 1972, 150. It is not clear why the Correlates of War classifies this event as a MID against Greece. Crete was Turkish territory, and the powers (Austria, France, Germany, Italy, Russia, and the United Kingdom) sent warships after Turkish troops massacred Cretan Christians. The powers then demanded that Turkey suspend hostilities, declare an amnesty, convene the assembly, and restore the Helpa Constitution with a Christian governor. The fighting in Crete is described in Alfred Biliotti to Marquis of Salisbury, June 1, 1896, FO 78/4736, U.K. National Archives. Military deployments by the powers are described in the *Washington Post*, May 26, 1896, 1; and in France, Ministère des Affaires Étrangères 1897a. The demands of the powers against Turkey are summarized in the *Times* (London), June 4, 1896, 5; June 24, 1896, 7. Greeks only became involved at a later point, when they provided material support to the Cretan Christians.

**GRC vs. UKG, FRN, GMY, 1897 (MID 56):** Edouard Pottier to Armand Besnard, February 13, 1897; and Frédéric Bourée to Gabriel Hanotaux, February 28, 1897, both in France, Ministère des Affaires Étrangères 1897b, 52–53, 120–21. Additional documents include Marquis of Salisbury to Philip Currie, February 10, 1897; and Salisbury to Nicholas O'Conor, February 15, 1897, both in *British and Foreign State Papers* 90 (1897–98), 1229, 1314–15. See also *Annual Register for the Year 1897* (1898), 308–9; and Dakin 1972, 151–52.

**GUA vs. UKG, 1911 (MID 1734):** *New York Times*, January 16, 1911, 5; *Times* (London), January 17, 1911, 5; *Washington Post*, January 16, 1911, 3; and Langley and Schoonover 1995, chap. 5.

**GUA vs. UKG, 1913 (MID 238):** Calvert 1971; Jones 1940, 83–85; Kneer 1975, 202–7; and Munro 1964, 244.

**HON vs. UKG, 1911 (MID 1734):** Philander Knox to Fenton McCreery, January 31, 1911, in U.S. Department of State, *Foreign Relations of the United States* (1911), 298; *Times* (London), January 23, 1911, 5; January 27, 1911, 7; and *Washington Post*, January 3, 1911, 1; January 23, 1911, 1; January 31, 1911, 3; February 2, 1911, 1; February 4, 1911, 1. It is not clear that this event should be classified as a MID against Honduras. The Honduran president requested the intervention of the United States and Britain to terminate the civil war. He further offered to deliver the Honduran presidency to any person designated by the United States. See, e.g., the correspondence in *Foreign Relations of the United States* (1911), 297–98; and the discussion in Langley and Schoonover 1995, 142–43. American and British forces did, however, limit the Honduran army's ability to fight the insurrection.

**MEX vs. UKG, 1861–62 (MID 135):** Lord John Russell to Charles Wyke, March 30, 1861; Wyke to Russell, June 25, 1861; Russell to Lord Cowley, September 23, 1861; September 27, 1861; and Wyke to Manuel María de Zamacona, November 24, 1861, among many other documents in *British and Foreign State Papers* 52 (1861–62), 237–42, 269–71, 326–31, 413–14; and Wyke to Manuel Doblado, January 12, 1862, in *British and Foreign State Papers* 53 (1862–63), 410–11. See also *Parliamentary Debates*, 3rd ser., vol. 168 (July 15, 1862), cols. 364–66. For a detailed study of the intervention and British motives, see Bock 1966. Other useful treatments of this complex case include Aggarwal 1996, 128–37; Bazant 1968, chap. 5; Turlington 1930, 126–70; Villegas Revueltas 2005, chap. 2; and Wynne 1951, 14–30.

**POR vs. UKG, 1899 (MID 1649):** Marquis of Salisbury to Luis de Soveral, October 4, 1899, in United Kingdom, Foreign Office 1927, 1:92–93. See also Costa 1998, 102–3; Grenville 1964, 260–62; and Lains and Costa 2001, 150. I corrected the date of this MID, which is listed in the COW database as occurring in 1897.

**SPN vs. FRN, GMY (MID 89):** *Annual Register for the Year 1823* (1824), 19–20, 148–52, 180–82, 189–210; Clarke and Hutton 1906, 65; and Nichols 1971.

**SPN vs. UKG, 1825 (MID 3233):** Isaac McKeever to Lewis Warrington, April 1, 1825, in U.S. Congress 1825, 2:107–8; Earle 2003, 243; and U.S. Department of State 1967, 17.

**SPN vs. UKG, 1873 (MID 256):** *Times* (London), November 18, 1873, 12; December 22, 1873, 5; October 21, 1874, 5. British demands also appear in "Correspondence between Great Britain and Spain, respecting the Capture, on the High Seas, of the American Steamer *Virginius*, by the Spanish Man-of-War *Tornado*, and the execution at St. Jago de Cuba of British Subjects taken on board the *Virginius*," *British and Foreign State Papers* 65 (1873–74), 98–229.

**TUR vs. UKG, 1876 (MID 1750):** *Atlanta Constitution*, May 12, 1876, 1; *New York Times*, May 19, 1876, 1.

**TUR vs. GMY, 1876 (MID 3322):** "Proposals of Austria, Germany, and Russia for the Pacification of Bosnia and the Herzegovina," May 13, 1876, in *British and Foreign State Papers* 67 (1875–76), 1230–33; *Times* (London), May 13, 1876, 7; May 15, 1876, 7; and Langer 1972, 779.

TUR vs. FRN, 1881 (MID 228): *New York Times*, March 5, 1881, 4; April 3, 1881, 2; *Times* (London), April 5, 1881, 5; Pakenham 1991; and Zouari 1998.

TUR vs. UKG, FRN, GMY, 1880–81 (MID 141): Charles Joseph Tissot to Charles de Freycinet, August 3, 1880, in France, Ministère des Affaires Étrangères 1880, 332–35; Tissot to Jean Bernard Jauréguiberry, August 31, 1880 in France, Ministère des Affaires Étrangères 1881, 113; *Annual Register for the Year 1880* (1881), 206; Dakin 1972, 136; Miller 1966, 782; and *Times* (London), July 9, 1880, 5; August 31, 1880, 6; September 9, 1880, 3.

VEN vs. NTH, 1849 (MID 1493): Goslinga 1990, 112; and Vandenbosch 1959, 214.

VEN vs. NTH, 1856 (MID 1495): *Times* (London), March 28, 1856, 5; April 14, 1856, 9; Gray 1949; and Ireland 1938, 247.

VEN vs. UKG, 1858 (MID 1628): Morón 1964, 166; and *New York Times*, May 27, 1858, 2; June 5, 1858, 5; August 31, 1858, 1.

VEN vs. NTH, 1869 (MID 1497): Vandenbosch 1959, 219; Goslinga 1990, 390; and *Times* (London), June 24, 1870, 11. This MID may have occurred in 1870, rather than 1869.

VEN vs. UKG, GMY, 1902–3 (MID 254): See text.

VEN vs. FRN, 1905 (MID 310): McBeth 2001, 135–37; Sullivan 1974, 442–49; and *Times* (London), October 5, 1905, 3; October 19, 1905, 9; October 25, 1905, 3; November 2, 1905, 3; December 20, 1905, 5.

# Chapter 7

## Enforcement through Trade Sanctions

IN MANY THEORIES of sovereign debt, the strength of creditors arises from their ability to link debt with trade. Creditors, it is argued, use the threat of commercial sanctions to compel foreign governments to meet their financial obligations. The trade sanction hypothesis is widely accepted among economic theorists and offers an important alternative to reputational theories. Empirical research about the link between debt and trade remains limited, however. This chapter systematically tests the trade sanction hypothesis.

### Three Kinds of Trade Sanctions

The literature mentions three steps creditors could take to interfere with the trade of a foreign state: they could seize its foreign assets, withhold short-term credit for imports and exports, or impose protectionist measures. All three forms of retaliation are conceivable, but the first has been illegal for much of financial history. Creditor countries have traditionally adhered to the absolute doctrine of sovereign immunity, which prohibits investors from suing a sovereign in foreign courts without the sovereign's consent. Over the centuries, the doctrine of sovereign immunity prevented investors from attaching a defaulter's assets (taking them in a lawsuit).

After the Peruvian default of 1875, for example, bondholders sought in the Court of Chancery to seize the proceeds from guano shipments. Peru had pledged the proceeds as collateral, and commercial representatives in London were holding the money. If bondholders could have succeeded anywhere, they should have prevailed in this case. Instead, the court followed its predecessors in rejecting the petition on grounds of sovereign immunity. According to the Master of the Rolls:

> These so-called bonds amount to nothing more than engagements of honour, binding, so far as engagements of honour can bind, the government which issues them, but are not contracts enforceable before the ordinary tribunals of any foreign government, or even by the ordinary tribunals of the country which issued them, without the consent of the government of that country.[1]

[1] *Twycross v. Dreyfus*, 5 Ch. D. 605, 616 (C.A. 1877) (Jessel, M.R.).

The situation prevailed well into the twentieth century. As Edwin Borchard, professor of law at Yale, wrote in 1951, "The various attempts that have been made to sue defaulting states in the creditor's country, even where on occasion security has been attachable," had failed because of "the elementary principle that a foreign state cannot in principle, under established rules of international law, be sued in municipal courts."[2] The threat to seize assets in a lawsuit cannot, therefore, explain why countries have attracted loans and repaid their debts for centuries.

Lawsuits against foreign governments became more plausible in the 1970s, when both the United States and Britain relaxed the doctrine of sovereign immunity. In a comprehensive review of litigation since the immunity doctrine was relaxed, though, Sturzenegger and Zettelmeyer find that "creditors have in general been relatively unsuccessful in devising legal strategies that have allowed them to obtain payment from defaulting nations. If anything . . . defaulting countries . . . have substantially improved their legal tactics to avert litigation losses." Moreover, even if creditors could obtain a judgment in court today, they would have trouble finding assets to seize. Most developing-country governments do not hold significant physical assets abroad, and they could repatriate vulnerable investments prior to default. Sturzenegger and Zettelmeyer therefore conclude that today, as in previous historical periods, "a realistic model of sovereign debt must include the fact that no sanctions are possible."[3]

The second form of retaliation, involving trade-related credit, has also been historically unimportant. For most of modern history the primary long-term creditors (private bondholders) had little ability to withhold trade credits, which were supplied by separate actors with distinct and often opposing interests. Governments nonetheless repaid their debts. The situation changed during the 1970s and 1980s, a period that inspired much of the sanctioning literature. During that unique moment, commercial banks provided not only short-term trade credits but also long-term sovereign loans, making the debt-trade linkage more feasible. I show in chapter 8, however, that banks fare no better than bondholders in enforcing debt contracts. If anything, the evidence in chapter 8 shows that governments default on bank loans at a higher rate than bonds. The failure of governments to favor banks, the only creditors with the ability to withhold commercial credit, counts as strong evidence against the trade credit hypothesis.

The third form of linkage is harder to dismiss. Although private bondholders and commercial banks cannot impose trade embargoes themselves, they may persuade their own governments to retaliate against for-

---

[2] Borchard 1951, 166.
[3] Sturzenegger and Zettelmeyer 2006b, 3–4.

eign defaulters. The home government could, for example, raise tariffs against the defaulter or prohibit the export of essential products to the offending state. Perhaps debtors honor their obligations to avoid retaliation, not by private investors, but by the politicians who serve them through control over trade policy.

Economist Jeffrey Sachs writes that "most debtor governments pay their debts not out of fear of the banks, but out of fear of a foreign policy rupture with the United States." In particular, the debtor government "might fear retaliation in the form of hostile trade policies."[4] Political scientist Laurence Whitehead echoes this view: "In the long term the most powerful . . . influence available to the creditors is the ability to offer or to withhold market openness." Defaulters, Whitehead claims, "could easily slip into a trade war" due to their "uncooperative behavior on debt servicing."[5]

I examine this possibility by studying patterns of default and repayment during the 1930s. The period is especially informative for two reasons. First, it offers a relatively easy proving ground for the trade embargo hypothesis. Investors had few coercive alternatives to a trade embargo during the 1930s. They could not block the supply of commercial credit in response to default, nor could they attach the assets of a sovereign. The only trade-related weapon in their arsenal would have been an embargo, which investors (if punitively minded) should have used to maximum capacity. Kenneth Oye contends that nations "commonly constructed tactical linkages between market access and debt servicing" in the 1930s, but emphasizes that such linkages are rare in financial bargaining today.[6] If the trade sanctions hypothesis fails during the 1930s, when such linkage supposedly reached a historical peak, the hypothesis in general should probably be rejected.

Second, the interwar period offers a unique opportunity for empirical analysis because there were two major groups of international creditors, both from large trading nations. In the 1920s the United States emerged as the leading supplier of international capital, and investors from Wall Street and Main Street funneled enormous sums to sovereigns in Latin America, Europe, and the Far East. British investors continued to offer new loans as well, albeit at a slower pace, and many sterling bonds with long maturities remained on the books. The coexistence of lenders from the United States and the United Kingdom, each with its own patterns of international trade, allows a test for discrimination across creditors.

---

[4] Sachs 1988, 710.

[5] Whitehead 1989, 238. For additional discussion of the trade sanctions hypothesis, see the references in chapter 1 and Alexander 1987, 44; Kletzer 1988, 588; Lindert 1989, 256; Nunnenkamp and Picht 1989, 683; Özler and Tabellini 1991, 16; and Picht 1988, 350.

[6] Oye 1992, 11, 80.

When deciding who should bear the burden of default, did sovereigns of the 1930s pay more money to their principal trading partner, or did they treat American and British lenders equally?

My analysis of the interwar period proceeds in two steps. I begin with a detailed examination of the Argentine case, which many scholars have used to illustrate the importance of trade sanctions. According to the conventional wisdom, Argentina repaid its debts during the 1930s to avert a trade war with Britain. Using several types of data, I show that Argentina paid to bolster its reputation in capital markets, not to avoid trade sanctions. I then explore evidence across a wider range of cases. Quantitative analysis of compliance with dollar and sterling bonds during the 1930s lends very little support to the sanctioning hypothesis. Apparently, neither borrowers nor lenders used the prospect of a trade embargo as a basis for debt policy.

## Did Argentina Pay to Avert a Trade War?

Historians widely believe that Argentina was an "informal dependency" of the United Kingdom during the early twentieth century, when the British market served as the primary outlet for Argentine exports of beef and grain.[7] By the 1930s reliance on Britain had reached such acute proportions that, in the words of one scholar, Argentine foreign policy became a mere "corollary" of U.K. policy.[8] The perception of Argentina as an appendage of Britain so captivated intellectuals that it contributed to the rise of Peronism and inspired much of the "dependency" literature that emerged from Latin America after the Great Depression.[9]

Cognizant of this dependence, many scholars have argued that Britain coerced Argentina into repaying its debts during the Great Depression by threatening to impose a trade embargo in the event of default.[10] Argentina depended upon Britain as a destination for exports during the 1920s and 1930s. On the eve of the depression, Britain absorbed about one-third of Argentine exports, a level three times higher than either Belgium or

[7] In his study of imperialism, Lenin (1917) identified Argentina as a British dependency. Modern historians have developed and documented this perspective. See, e.g., Gallagher and Robinson (1953) and the vast literature they inspired, some of which is reviewed by Miller (1999).

[8] Abreu 1984, 153.

[9] Valenzuela and Valenzuela (1978) and Packenham (1992) review this dependency literature.

[10] See, for example, Díaz Alejandro 1983, 28–29; Eichengreen 1992, 260; Eichengreen and Portes 1989, 80; Fishlow 1985, 428; Jorgensen and Sachs 1989, 66; Oye 1992, 87; and Skiles 1988, 24. Della Paolera and Taylor (1999, 2001) offer a contrary view that is closer to my own.

Germany, the next-largest consumers of Argentine products.[11] Further-more, the dependence was asymmetric, giving Britain considerable lever-age in the relationship. As the *Financial Times* observed, "The United Kingdom market is much more essential to Argentina than the Argentine market is to the United Kingdom, for whereas she takes about 14 percent of her imports from [us], she sells 36 percent of her total exports to this country."[12]

Above all, Argentina needed Britain as an outlet for chilled beef. In the early twentieth century refrigeration technology became advanced enough to allow transatlantic shipments of chilled beef that would not spoil in transit. Exports of chilled meats, which carried higher profit mar-gins than canned or frozen varieties, consequently rose to represent nearly 70 percent of total Argentine beef exports by 1930.[13] Argentina sold 99 percent of this chilled beef (and more than half of its frozen meats) to Great Britain, and many observers felt that there was no real alternative to the British market.[14] Only relatively rich countries could afford to buy chilled meat on a large scale, but as discussed below, the United States had banned Argentine beef, and other countries had "placed almost pro-hibitive restrictions on meat imports."[15] This left Britain as the only obvi-ous outlet. Quite rightly, then, Argentines often referred to Britain as the *mercado único* (the only market), thereby recognizing that "the depen-dence was *absolute*."[16]

The distribution of political power in Argentina seemed to reinforce this dependence, since cattle ranchers played a central role in Argentine politics and society. Of the eight presidents that led Argentina between 1910 and the outbreak of World War II, five were members of the Socie-dad Rural (Rural Society), an elite group of ranchers involved in livestock trade. In addition, more than 40 percent of cabinet positions went to members of the Rural Society.[17] Ranchers played an especially prominent role after 1930, when a military coup toppled the Radicales. The ensuing government and its successors were backed by the *concordancia*, a coali-tion of political parties that included cattle ranchers.[18] Given the political prominence of ranchers, one student of Argentine history has dubbed this

---

[11] *Economist*, February 8, 1936, 6.

[12] *Financial Times*, April 5, 1933, 5.

[13] Smith 1969, 84.

[14] United Kingdom, Department of Overseas Trade 1930, 21.

[15] Major W. A. McCallum, Chairman of British Chamber of Commerce in Argentina, *Review of the River Plate*, May 22, 1936, 11–13.

[16] O'Connell 1986b, 23; Fodor and O'Connell 1973, 11.

[17] Smith 1969, 48–49.

[18] Rock 1987, chap. 6.

period *gobierno de las vacas* ("the government of the cows").[19] Thus, Argentina depended heavily upon the United Kingdom in an economic sector of great significance to policymakers.

During the depression, however, this precious access to the British market was thrown into question. As agricultural producers around the world struggled to cope with sharp declines in the prices of their exports, negotiators for the United Kingdom and its dependencies met in Ottawa to discuss trade. There, Australia and New Zealand lobbied the British to establish imperial preferences for beef. Britain agreed not to import more chilled beef from nonimperial sources than it had purchased in the year ending June 1932, when Argentine shipments to Britain had dipped to their lowest levels in nearly a decade. Although Argentina retained access to the British market, the new quantitative restriction raised a red flag: if not careful, Argentine ranchers could lose access to their most valuable client.[20] In this context, politicians in Buenos Aires debated whether to continue paying the foreign debt, a large portion of which had been contracted in London.

Leading scholars contend that Argentina honored its debts to avert a trade embargo, which Britain would have imposed in the event of default. According to Carlos Díaz Alejandro, the dean of Argentine economic history, "Tampering with the normal servicing of the Argentine debt would have involved not only a bruising commercial clash with the United Kingdom, but also probably a major restructuring of the Argentine domestic political scene, at the expense of groups linked with Anglo-Argentine trade."[21] Economist Barry Eichengreen concurs: "Britain was Argentina's most important export market, and the British Government was more inclined than its American counterpart to impose trade sanctions in retaliation against default. This combination of forces induced Argentina to maintain debt service throughout the 1930s."[22]

## A Test of the Traditional View

Although the traditional view seems plausible, further analysis indicates that the apparent correlation between commercial dependence and debt repayment is spurious. Argentina did depend heavily on the British mar-

---

[19] Drosdoff 1972.

[20] Smith 1969, 140–41; Gravil 1985, 183.

[21] Díaz Alejandro 1983, 29.

[22] Eichengreen 1992, 260. According to Jorgensen and Sachs (1989, 66), "The government must have believed that any tampering with debt service was sure to be commercially and politically costly." Skiles (1988, 24) adds that "any deviation by Argentina . . . such as a suspension of debt servicing, could have led to retaliatory trade action by the U.K."

ket during the 1930s, but this dependence did not motivate the country to repay. Argentina honored its debt obligations not to protect itself from commercial sanctions, but instead to build its reputation in global capital markets. Put simply, Argentina paid to obtain *finance*, not trade.

Four lines of analysis, discussed in detail below, support this conclusion. First, Argentina repaid not only the British but also the Americans, even though the United States had almost no capacity to impose trade sanctions against Argentina. Second, Argentina met its obligations by increasing taxes on beef exporters, the very group debt repayment was supposed to protect in the conventional account. Third, beef-exporting provinces of Argentina were no more committed to repayment than regions that did not participate in the beef trade. Finally, Argentine leaders justified their decision to repay, not by arguing that default would jeopardize access to foreign markets, but by pointing out the reputational benefits of repayment during hard times. Thus in four key areas—Argentina's treatment of dollar debt, its policy of taxation, the behavior of provincial borrowers, and the statements of key decision makers—the evidence points to concerns about reputation, rather than fear of trade sanctions, as the impetus for repayment.

TREATMENT OF DOLLAR DEBT

Before the depression, Argentina owed money to both British and American investors. The British had long served as bankers to Argentina, beginning with the first sterling-denominated loan to the newly independent state in 1824. In the aftermath of World War I, however, new British lending slowed to a crawl, and the United States became Argentina's leading supplier of fresh capital. Throughout the 1920s, Argentina floated millions of dollars in foreign bonds through investment banks in New York, principally to finance public works, improve sanitation, develop state railways, and cover treasury deficits, at a time when the government was amortizing its prewar sterling bonds. By the end of 1931 more than 60 percent of the central government's foreign debt was denominated in dollars, whereas only 37 percent had to be paid in sterling. The remaining 3 percent, owed to scattered creditors in France and Spain, is too trivial to merit attention.[23]

Dollar bonds carried higher nominal interest rates than their sterling counterparts. Every Argentine dollar bond required an annual interest payment of at least 5.5 percent, with a mean rate of 6 percent across all New York issues. Sterling debts, issued in a prewar era when the cost of capital was lower, were cheaper to service: the average coupon rate was

---

[23] Calculated from Alhadeff 1983, 153.

4.6 percent, and no issue had an interest obligation that exceeded 5 percent per annum. Thus, not only was the stock of dollar debt larger as a share of the central government's external obligations, but the nominal burden of interest payments was considerably heavier for dollar bonds than for sterling ones.

Continued U.S. adherence to the gold standard only exacerbated the burden of repayment for Argentina. During the 1920s many countries had pegged their currencies to gold in an effort to stabilize exchange rates, only to abandon this policy when the Great Depression struck. Britain suspended convertibility in September 1931, thereby devaluing the pound relative to gold. This departure from gold made it less costly for debtors like Argentina to acquire British currency necessary to service their sterling-denominated debts.[24] The United States, however, remained committed to gold for an additional 19 months, which deprived Argentina of relief during some of the worst years of the depression. Thus, the confluence of three factors—larger stocks of debts, higher interest rates, and a more expensive currency—made repayment to the Americans considerably more expensive than repayment to the British.

If the threat of trade sanctions had motivated Argentina to repay, the government should have defaulted on its extremely costly dollar debt while maintaining punctual service to creditors in the United Kingdom. The reason is straightforward: U.S.-Argentine trade relations, particularly in the area of beef, were already wretched. Commercial intercourse between the two countries had never been particularly friendly, given a lack of economic complementarities. The United States exported the same agricultural commodities as Argentina, leaving little scope for gains from trade. Relations turned especially sour during the 1920s, when leaders in Washington raised tariffs on agricultural goods and banned the importation of Argentine beef. U.S. policymakers therefore entered the depression with an empty quiver: having already embargoed Argentine products for reasons unrelated to the foreign debt, they had no sanctions to apply in the event of default.

A brief analysis of U.S. tariff policy reveals why relations had become so acrimonious. U.S. duties on Argentine goods climbed steadily between the two world wars. The Fordney-McCumber Act, approved by the U.S. Congress in September 1922, increased tariffs on agricultural products such as beef and linseed (two crucial Argentine exports), and the Smoot-Hawley Act of 1930 exacerbated tensions by raising taxes on an even wider range of Argentine commodities. Outraged Argentines warned that reprisals might follow, but their threats failed to stop the march of protec-

---

[24] Vázquez-Presedo (1978, 149) shows the improved exchange rate.

tion. The Agricultural Adjustment Act of 1933 subsidized U.S. farmers, and subsequent legislation blocked agricultural imports that were less expensive than domestic equivalents, thereby robbing Argentina of any remaining comparative advantage.[25]

The greatest irritant to commercial relations, however, came in the form of a U.S. "sanitary embargo" on Argentine beef. In 1927 the U.S. Department of Agriculture banned imports of meat from Argentina and other countries where livestock showed signs of hoof-and-mouth disease.[26] Argentines viewed the embargo as a form of protectionism, and the cattle barons strongly resented it.[27] In response to the new trade barriers, the president of the Argentine Rural Society spearheaded a movement against U.S. products under the slogan "comprar a quien nos compra," or "buy from those who buy from us." From February 1927 onward, this slogan appeared on the cover of every issue of the Rural Society's monthly newsletter.

The combination of high tariffs and the sanitary embargo effectively closed the U.S. market to Argentine products, including beef, which meant Argentina could default on dollar bonds without fear of commercial reprisal. Although Argentina imported some manufactured goods—mainly cars, trucks, and machines—from the United States, there was no risk of retaliation in that area, either. By the depths of the depression, purchases of U.S. goods accounted for only 12 percent of Argentine imports, half the British level. If for some reason the United States undermined its own industry in a time of need by prohibiting exports to Argentina, industrial nations such as Britain and Italy could have filled the gap.[28]

Clearly, if the threat of trade sanctions had been the main motivation for honoring foreign debts, the Argentine government would have repaid the British while defaulting against Americans. On the contrary, the Argentine central government repaid American bondholders, even though the dollar debt was considerably larger, carried a higher interest rate, and could only be serviced by purchasing a currency that was more expensive in real terms than British sterling. The behavior of the Argentine govern-

[25] O'Connell 1986a, 80, 86; Peterson 1964, 351–60; Rock 1987, 242–43.

[26] Although initially an administrative measure, the embargo became U.S. law in 1930, when it was incorporated into the Tariff Act, "stalling all possibilities of convincing inspectors to make a change" (García-Mata 1941, 6).

[27] John Whitaker (1940, 148), explained the Argentine view: "American sanitary regulations are designed, the Argentine believes, not because the United States needs protection from the hoof-and-mouth disease but because American cattle growers are needlessly protecting their home markets against better and cheaper meats. This is what the Argentine believes—every Argentine, all Argentines." Subsequent analysis by O'Connell (1986b) suggests that the embargo probably had scientific merit, however.

[28] *Economist*, February 8, 1936, 6; *Barron's*, June 12, 1933, 9.

ment demonstrates that the threat of trade sanctions—particularly the threat of an embargo on beef—did not motivate the decision to repay.

Is it possible, however, that creditors on both sides of the Atlantic united to extract payment from Argentina? Perhaps the British did the Americans a favor by threatening to retaliate in the commercial arena if any bonds—dollar or sterling—fell into default. Archival evidence actually suggests the opposite. The British, annoyed that Argentina was repaying U.S. bondholders at the expense of English exporters (who had sold to Argentina and were not getting paid for their goods), wanted Argentina to default on dollar debts and redirect the savings to the United Kingdom.

This British-American competition arose from the problem of blocked exchange. During the 1930s, Argentina owed money to several types of British creditors: bondholders, firms that exported to Argentina, and English who held property in Argentina and remitted profits to the motherland. To ensure enough foreign exchange for bondholders, the government prohibited British merchants and property owners from converting their pesos into sterling and taking the money out of the country. The freeze on exchange adversely affected more than 20,000 English merchants, whose blocked accounts in 1932 exceeded the annual service of the foreign debt.[29]

The British were especially upset about Argentina's decision to repay the Americans, because Argentina earned the foreign exchange to service dollar debts by running a trade surplus with Britain. For most of the interwar period, Argentina sold more than it bought in relations with Britain, while accumulating a trade deficit with the United States. When the supply of international loans dried up in 1929, trade became the only source of foreign exchange for external debt payments. Argentina therefore used the profits it earned from trade with Britain to pay bondholders in America, while at the same time blocking payments to British merchants. The British found this practice "galling."[30] When the British Board of Trade met with bankers and merchants to discuss the situation, it concluded that British exporters should get priority over American bondholders, even if this required defaulting on the dollar debt.[31] Far from extending a favor to the United States, the British preferred a dollar-bond default "to provide larger scope for Anglo-Argentine trade."[32]

[29] Alhadeff 1985, 371; Gravil 1985, 189.

[30] The overseas files in the Bank of England Archives are replete with such complaints. See, e.g., Robert Craigie to Herbert Brittain, October 31, 1932, OV 102/2; Harry Siepmann to Brittain, November 9, 1932, OV 102/2; John Simon to Ronald Macleay, January 27, 1933, OV 102/208; "Memorandum on Argentina," November 29, 1933, OV 102/4; Eric Lingeman, "United Kingdom Exchange Quota May/December 1933," May 7, 1934, OV 102/4.

[31] Frederick Leith-Ross to Charles Hambro, December 20, 1932, OV 102/2, Bank of England Archives.

[32] Fishlow 1989, 328.

To summarize, the conventional wisdom holds that Argentina paid its debts during the 1930s to avert a trade war. Yet Argentina honored its commitments to bondholders in the United States (a country that could not impose sanctions), while violating its commitments to merchants in the United Kingdom (the country with potential sanctioning power). This pattern of behavior contradicts the logic of the trade sanctions hypothesis.

## THE POLICY OF EXCHANGE CONTROL

We can learn more about Argentina's motives by examining how the government acquired foreign exchange to pay bondholders. The Argentine government introduced exchange controls in October 1931. Under the new regulations, exporters were required to surrender foreign exchange at officially authorized banks, which acted as intermediaries for the central government. Although exporters received payment in pesos, all transactions occurred at an "official" rate that understated the true value of the exchange. Any exporter who refused to comply with the regulation lost authorization to ship additional merchandise out of the country.[33]

These controls helped the government honor its commitments to bondholders in two ways. First, they gave the government privileged access to increasingly scarce foreign exchange. In the early years of the depression some exporters hoarded their exchange, hoping to gain a profit by deferring sales at a time when the value of the Argentine peso was falling. Other exporters immediately sold their bills of exchange abroad.[34] Such behavior, in the context of a global contraction that had depressed the volume and value of trade, led to an acute shortage of foreign currency. The government responded by commandeering exchange and allocating it according to a rigid hierarchy, with foreign debts heading the list of priorities. After taking enough to pay foreign bondholders, the government sold the remaining foreign exchange to importers.

Second, the government realized a profit from its controls and spent the extra revenue on debt payments. The possibility of profits arose because the government collected more foreign currency than it actually needed to service the debt. Prior to 1933, it resold the balance at the official purchase price, but in 1933 the government began auctioning the surplus to the highest bidder. Taking advantage of a considerable margin between buying and selling rates, the government realized a profit of 1 billion pesos (a sum larger than the annual Argentine budget) between 1934 and 1940.

---

[33] Beveraggi Allende 1954; Institute of International Finance 1936.
[34] Alhadeff 1983, 125.

The government used a large percentage of the profit to meet debt payments, which had increased due to a depreciation of the peso.[35]

Surprisingly, beef producers bore the brunt of this exchange rate "tax." The exchange control system originally included exemptions for exporters of hides, guano, yerba maté, tobacco, fruit, honey, wine, butter, and eggs. Eventually the set of exemptions expanded to include wool, but the government refused to release beef and grain exporters from the obligation to sell exchange at the official rate. To some extent, the government compensated grain exporters by establishing a system of price supports for wheat, corn, and linseed. Profits from exchange control financed the price supports, after deducting a portion for service on the foreign debt. Thus, the policy of exchange control amounted to a tax on exporters, but the government returned some profits to grain producers in the form of price subsidies. It offered no similar program for beef producers, who therefore suffered the most from exchange control.[36]

Was this tax on ranchers a "necessary evil," a price the government had to inflict to avoid default and a beef embargo? The answer seems to be no, for two reasons. First, the Argentine government had other sources of foreign exchange that would have imposed less pain on beef exporters. In particular, the government could have used its foreign reserves. Argentina entered the depression with a large reserve of gold, which the conversion office held to support the paper currency in circulation. Beginning in 1929, the country shipped gold to cover its debt payments and other obligations, but this policy came to a halt with the imposition of exchange control.

Many observers (London and New York bankers, British exporting firms, and the financial press at home and abroad) in the early 1930s recommended that Argentina pay its debts with foreign reserves. They argued that Argentina could safely let the gold cover fall without jeopardizing the currency.[37] Paying the debt with gold reserves would have lightened the burden on beef exporters by reducing if not eliminating the need to take ranchers' foreign exchange at below-market rates. Nevertheless, the government remained committed to its policy of exchange control, which amounted to a tax on ranchers.

[35] "Memorandum on Exchange Control in 1935," OV 102/6, Bank of England Archives; Rock 1987, 223.

[36] "Argentine Exchange Profits," Memorandum, May 10, 1935, OV 102/5, and "Argentina: How the Exchange Control Works," Memorandum, October 10, 1935, OV 102/6, Bank of England Archives. See also Institute of International Finance 1936.

[37] *Review of the River Plate*, April 8, 1932, 7–8; August 12, 1932, 7; September 9, 1932, 25; *Barron's*, September 26, 1932, 23; *Financial News*, October 26, 1932, 4; and Emilio Schweiger to Harry Goschen, December 5, 1932, OV 102/2, Bank of England Archives.

Second, if Argentina had failed to remit enough foreign exchange to repay foreign bondholders, British authorities almost certainly would not have retaliated by cutting trade. If anything, Britain used its clout to expand the scope for trade, not to promote bondholders' interests. Lord Luke of Pavenham aptly summarized the view in London: "The whole Argentine trading and financial structure is being inconvenienced and endangered so that the bondholder may have his full annual 'pound of flesh.'"[38] Sharing this perspective, the British Board of Trade recommended that Argentina default on foreign bonds, including sterling bonds if necessary, to alleviate the problem of blocked exchange.[39] British bankers and traders, as well as influential figures within the Bank of England, agreed.[40] "Even when confronted with outright suggestions of suspension by the British authorities," however, Argentina maintained full payment.[41]

The evidence to this point can be summarized as follows. Argentina imposed a heavy tax on beef exporters in an effort to pay both U.S. and British bondholders. This policy is especially surprising because the United States did not have the ability to impose trade sanctions, and because British leaders recommended default as a way to *stimulate* trade, rather than viewing default as a trigger for trade sanctions. Moreover, if the threat of trade sanctions were somehow credible, Argentina could have met its obligations by using its foreign currency reserves and taxing industries other than beef. These facts contradict the conventional view that Argentina repaid its debts as a concession to ranching interests.

THE BEHAVIOR OF ARGENTINE PROVINCES

Thus far my analysis has focused on debts of the central government, but many Argentine provinces and municipalities issued their own bonds in New York and London. Some of these subnational borrowers participated actively in the beef trade, whereas others specialized in different aspects of economic life. If Argentines feared losing the British beef market in the wake of default, beef-exporting provinces should have been

[38] *Times* (London), June 22, 1932, 19.

[39] Confidential Minutes of Meeting (January 25, 1933) of the Subcommittee on Exchange Restrictions in South and Central America, February 1, 1933, OV 102/208; Board of Trade, Draft of First Report of the Subcommittee on Exchange Restrictions in South and Central America, February 2, 1933, OV 102/2, Bank of England Archives.

[40] See Frederick Leith-Ross to Charles Hambro, December 20, 1932, OV 102/2; Harry Siepmann to Otto Niemeyer, January 27, 1933, OV 102/208; Bank of England to Everard Meynell, January 31, 1933, OV 102/208; and Bank of England to Meynell, February 8, 1933, OV 102/208, Bank of England Archives. Niemeyer, however, favored debt repayment to protect the reputation of Argentina. See Niemeyer to Hambro and Edward Peacock, February 2, 1933, OV 102/208, Bank of England Archives.

[41] O'Connell 1984, 204.

TABLE 7.1
Compliance by Argentine Provinces, 1930s

| Province | Number of Bonds | Average Compliance Rate (%) |
|---|---|---|
| Buenos Aires | 9 | 85 |
| Capital Federal | 4 | 100 |
| Córdoba | 2 | 88 |
| Corrientes | 1 | 0 |
| Mendoza | 1 | 67 |
| Santa Fe | 4 | 50 |
| Tucumán | 1 | 100 |

Source: Author's calculations from the database of provincial bonds, as described in the text.

Note: The table refers to dollar-denominated and sterling-denominated bonds issued or guaranteed by Argentine provinces. For each bond, compliance is measured as the nominal value of interest payments the borrower actually made during the years 1930–39, as a percentage of payments the debtor would have made if the bond had been honored in full. The average compliance rate of each province is the unweighted mean across all the province's bonds.

particularly scrupulous in repaying their debts and encouraging other borrowers to do the same.

To test this hypothesis, I collected data on all Argentine provinces that owed debts denominated in dollars or sterling on the eve of the Great Depression.[42] The sample included 20 provincial bonds, as well as two municipal loans that were guaranteed by provincial authorities and could therefore be regarded as provincial debts. For each bond I calculated an "ideal" cash flow, which the investor would have received if the borrower had remained in full compliance during the period 1930–39, and compared it with the amount of money the borrower actually paid.[43] The new variable, Compliance, is actual payments as a percentage of ideal payments in nominal terms. Table 7.1 summarizes the data by province.

I then measured the role each province played in the beef trade. My principal measure was the province's share of the national stock of cattle, on the assumption that provinces with more cattle would participate more actively in exports. A secondary measure involved chilled beef, 99 percent of which was sold to Britain. Argentines typically converted their best

[42] In Argentina, the municipality of Buenos Aires (often called the Capital Federal) has a status similar to the District of Columbia in the United States. Consistent with investment literature from the 1920s, I treat the Capital Federal as a separate province, even though in land area it is much smaller than the others.

[43] Data on ideal and actual cash flows, as well as other features of the indentures, came from Moody's Investors Service, Moody's Manual of Investments; and White, Weld & Co., Foreign Dollar Bonds.

cattle into chilled beef while reserving lower grades for frozen and canned meat. Before sending these "chillers" to the slaughterhouse, ranchers fattened the top-grade calves on special alfalfa pastures in east-central Argentina. The fatteners, who controlled the regions where alfalfa flourished, belonged to the upper class and enjoyed more economic and political influence than mere breeders.[44] Given their specialization in the chilled beef trade, these fatteners probably would have suffered the most if Britain closed its market to Argentine beef. To identify the location of fatteners, I measured the acreage of alfalfa pastureland in each province as a percentage of the national total. The linkage hypothesis implies that provinces with more cattle or alfalfa should have complied at a higher rate, on average.

Finally, I measured the wealth of each province, to guard against the possibility of omitted variable bias. If beef-exporting provinces were relatively poor and, therefore, more likely to default due to lack of financial resources, then analyses that failed to control for wealth would understate the positive effect of beef on compliance. If, on the other hand, the beef industry flourished in wealthy regions of the country, omitting wealth would lead to an overestimate of the relationship between beef and compliance. No systematic data on provincial wealth exist for the interwar period, but I use the provincial illiteracy rate (the percentage of residents over the age of 13 who could not read or write) as a proxy.[45] Other factors equal, illiteracy rates should have been negatively correlated with compliance.

I regressed compliance on cattle stock, with and without controlling for illiteracy.[46] The unit of observation in these regressions was the bond, rather than the province, giving a sample size of 22. Since some provinces issued more than one bond, intraprovincial observations were not fully

[44] Smith 1969, 36–46.

[45] Illiteracy data are from Vázquez-Presedo 1978, 212, and are averaged over the years 1914 and 1943. Similar results are obtained by using the literacy rates of registered voters in 1930, as given in Díaz Alejandro 1970, 50. I tried other proxies, such as infant mortality rates (Díaz Alejandro 1970, 50) and provincial revenue per capita (Banco de la Nación Argentina, Oficina de Investigaciónes Económicas, January 13, 1933, OV 102/209, Bank of England Archives), supplemented with data from Moody's Investors Service, *Moody's Manual of Investments* (1934). Results were qualitatively similar but even less favorable to the linkage hypothesis.

[46] The compliance variable is bounded between 0 and 100, whereas OLS assumes that the dependent variable has no theoretical bounds. One might obtain better estimates with a model designed for limited dependent variables, though such models work best with a larger sample. I estimated a fractional probit model (discussed later in this chapter) and a two-limit Tobit regression (censoring at 0 and 100) of compliance on cattle stock. Although qualitatively similar to the results in this chapter, the fractional probit and Tobit estimates provided even stronger evidence against sanctioning: beef was negatively associated with compliance.

TABLE 7.2
Regression Analysis of Compliance of Argentine Provinces, 1930s

| Variable | Model 1 | | | Model 2 | | |
| | Estimated Coefficient | Standard Error | t-statistic | Estimated Coefficient | Standard Error | t-statistic |
| --- | --- | --- | --- | --- | --- | --- |
| Cattle | 0.12 | 0.45 | 0.3 | 0.02 | 0.25 | 0.1 |
| Illiteracy rate | | | | −2.15 | 0.99 | 2.2 |
| Constant | 75.37 | 16.20 | 4.7 | 127.68 | 18.97 | 6.7 |

*Source*: Author's calculations from República Argentina, Dirección de Economía Rural y Estadística 1935, 157; Vázquez-Presedo 1978, 212; and the database of provincial bonds as described in the text.

*Note*: Estimates from ordinary least squares (OLS) regression with robust standard errors, clustered by province. The unit of observation in both models is the provincial bond. The dependent variable, Compliance, measures the nominal value of interest that was paid on the bond during the years 1930–39, as a percentage of the interest that would have been paid if the bond had been honored in full. The regressions are based on 22 bonds from the 7 Argentine provinces listed in table 7.1. Cattle is the number of cattle in the province as a percentage of the national total. Illiteracy Rate is the percentage of the provincial population over the age of 13 that cannot read or write. In model 1, $R^2 = .01$ and the standard error of the regression is 27.4. In model 2, $R^2 = .35$ and the standard error of the regression is 22.7.

independent. I computed robust standard errors, clustered by province, to account for statistical dependence among bonds of the same province.

Table 7.2 shows that major beef-producing provinces did not comply at a higher rate than provinces that specialized in other economic activities. The coefficient on Cattle in model 1 is positive, as hypothesized, but carries a standard error nearly four times as large. Thus, the marginal effect is statistically indistinguishable from zero at conventional levels of confidence. Even if we take the point estimate at face value, though, the substantive effect is trivial. On a scale from 0 to 100, compliance is predicted to be only four points higher in the most beef-intensive province (with 32 percent of the national stock of cattle) than in areas with no cattle at all. Finally, the $R$-squared statistic for model 1 signifies that, at most, participation in the beef trade explains only 1 percent of the variation in provincial debt service. Alfalfa, an alternative measure of participation in the beef trade (not shown to save space), performs similarly but exhibits an even larger standard error and a smaller $R$-squared.[47]

After controlling for illiteracy, the estimated effect of beef becomes even more miniscule and statistically insignificant. The coefficient on Cattle in model 2 falls to 0.02, implying a difference of less than one percentage point in the predicted compliance rates of the most and least beef-intensive

[47] The estimated coefficient on alfalfa was 0.12 with a standard error of 0.73, and the $R^2$ was less than .01.

provinces.[48] The illiteracy coefficient, on the other hand, is large and statistically significant. Each percentage point of illiteracy reduces compliance by approximately two points. Considering that provincial illiteracy rates ranged from 14 to 45 percent in our sample, the overall effect is enormous. Moreover, given the small standard error, it is almost certain that the negative effect of illiteracy did not arise by chance. Finally, illiteracy alone accounts for 35 percent of the variation in compliance. Thus, even with a relatively small sample, our data and methods can deliver strong results. The contrast in explanatory power between the beef and illiteracy variables is striking. Overall, the regressions in table 7.2 count as strong evidence against the trade linkage hypothesis.

I conclude this section by considering how legislators from cattle-raising provinces attempted to shape national policy. By far the most important cattle-raising province was Buenos Aires, represented in the Argentine senate by Matías Sánchez Sorondo. As a deputy in the lower chamber of the national legislature during the 1920s, Sánchez Sorondo had earned a reputation as an energetic defender of ranching interests. He continued this advocacy in the 1930s in his new role as senator. If default on the external debt had endangered beef exporters, surely this senator would have lobbied for strict repayment. Instead, Sánchez Sorondo authored and sponsored a bill that would have required the central government to suspend amortization and reduce interest payments on the national debt. This was the only prodefault bill introduced into the national legislature during the 1930s.[49]

A second important cattle center was the province of Santa Fe, located just north of Buenos Aires. Lisandro de la Torre, lead senator from Santa Fe, had served as president of the Rural Society in the city of Rosario. Nevertheless, when the province of Santa Fe suspended payment on its foreign debt, Senator de la Torre argued that the moratorium should extend nationwide. He complained that "Argentina's obstinate insistence on meeting her foreign debt," particularly in a period of depression and with depreciated exchange rate, was "materially prejudicial to the immediate interests of the country" and, with respect to the future, "little if anything better than a beau geste." Such behavior by leading senators from the most important beef-producing provinces seriously undermines the claim that Argentina repaid its debts at the behest of ranching interests.[50]

[48] The alfalfa measure performs even worse. After controlling for illiteracy, the coefficient on alfalfa is −0.03, suggesting a negative relationship between chilled beef and compliance. The estimate has a standard error of 0.33, however, so we cannot reject the null hypothesis that the effect is zero.

[49] *La Nación*, May 31, 1933, 1; República Argentina, Congreso de la Nación, Senado de la Nación 1933, 233; Smith 1969, 94–95, 105–6, 129.

[50] *Barron's*, December 26, 1932, 16. Similar behavior, albeit at a popular rather than an elite level, occurred in the cattle provinces of Corrientes and Entre Ríos, where a mass meeting of cattle breeders, farmers, and industrialists was held in 1932 to call for default on the

## THE STATEMENTS OF KEY DECISION MAKERS

Finally, the statements of key decision makers in the Argentine central government shed light on Argentina's motivations. If the link between debt service and trade relations were salient, interlocutors would have presented the debate in these terms. Proponents of repayment would have warned that Britain would retaliate against a lapse of payments by restricting access to the English market. Meanwhile, advocates of default would have stated, both publicly and privately, that the country should lighten the burden of austerity by suspending payments, even if it meant losing an important foreign client.

The silence on these issues is deafening. In transcripts of the debates, I could not find a single reference to the threat of trade sanctions as a reason for repaying the foreign debt. Instead, major players in the debate focused on reputation, asking how default might affect the image of Argentina in the eyes of investors and, therefore, the country's ability to borrow anew when the global economy recovered. The notion that Argentina repaid to avert a hypothetical sanction that no one bothered to mention, when so many speeches were delivered and so much ink was spilt on the theme of reputation, strains the limits of credulity.

Consider the views of General Justo, president of Argentina from 1932 until 1938. Justo emphatically believed that "it would be madness not to maintain the debt service . . . at a time when almost every other South American state was defaulting," since repayment would enhance the reputation of the country, while default would "throw away the future benefits of cheap borrowing."[51] In a national radio broadcast in 1933 the president justified the policy of repayment as a way to "save the good name of Argentina and consequently its credit."[52]

Alberto Hueyo, who served as finance minister during the first two years of the Justo administration, viewed the issue in much the same way. Hueyo insisted that the country continue paying, even if it meant "demanding a strenuous sacrifice from the inhabitants of the country," because he viewed compliance as "the fundamental basis of credit." Like many of his contemporaries in government, Hueyo thought the global economy would eventually recover, and he deemed it "vital that our country should arrive at that hour with its prestige unabated" so it could "immediately take advantage" of the increased supply of capital.[53]

---

foreign debt. See *Review of the River Plate*, August 19, 1932, 21–22; September 2, 1932, 11; *New York Times*, August 22, 1932, 6.

[51] *Financial News*, September 28, 1932, 5; October 26, 1932, 4.

[52] The broadcast, delivered on November 16, 1933, is reprinted in República Argentina, Ministerio de Hacienda de la Nación 1934, 5–6.

[53] *Review of the River Plate*, January 22, 1932, 17.

The finance minister elaborated these views during a particularly revealing debate in the Argentine senate. In May 1933 Sánchez Sorondo, who had recently formalized his proposal for default, asked Hueyo to defend the government's policy before the senate. If the linkage argument had merit, there could not have been a more opportune time to invoke it. But Hueyo never mentioned the risk of commercial sanctions as a reason for repayment, even though he was being interpellated by the senator of the largest beef-exporting province. Rather, Hueyo argued that the country would need to borrow again, especially for transportation, irrigation, and sanitation, and for this reason identified Argentina as one of the countries in the world "that most requires the safeguarding of its credit." Default would be "short-sighted," since it would not convey Argentina's determination to carry out the weight of contractual obligations. Hueyo held out the prospect of converting the outstanding debt into new issues at lower interest rates, but insisted that conversion would not occur if Argentina sullied her credit.[54]

In fact, the theme of reputation seemed central to all discourse about debt, while the prospect of sanctions was conspicuously absent. Federico Pinedo, who succeeded Hueyo as minister of finance, perceived the debate in these terms.[55] So too did the National Association of Importers, which pointed out that the world was marching slowly toward an economic recovery, and that Argentina would benefit from its "reputation of having complied with all obligations. The destruction of this favorable situation must not be permitted."[56] *La Prensa* and *La Nación*, the two leading newspapers in Buenos Aires, often rehearsed the reputational theme, though they sometimes questioned whether a stalwart image was worth the cost.[57] Even the advocates of default, such as Matías Sánchez Sorondo and Lisandro de la Torre, couched their arguments in reputational terms, asserting that the Great Depression gave the country an excuse to default without hurting its reputation.[58]

As chapters 4 and 5 showed, both sides were right. Default probably would not have undermined the reputation of Argentina, which investors regarded as a fair-weather payer on the eve of the depression. Nevertheless, the decision to repay during a period of extreme difficulty allowed

---

[54] Alberto Hueyo in República Argentina, Congreso de la Nación, Senado de la Nación 1933, 210. Hueyo presented similar arguments to the Argentine Chamber of Deputies.

[55] See, e.g., his radio broadcast on November 16, 1933, reprinted in *Review of the River Plate*, November 24, 1933, 15.

[56] *Review of the River Plate*, March 18, 1932, 7–8.

[57] In early August 1932 the editors of *La Nación* advocated default because they believed that creditors would excuse a moratorium, given the dire circumstances.

[58] See, e.g., Matías Sánchez Sorondo in República Argentina, Congreso de la Nación, Senado de la Nación 1933, 223–24.

Argentina to climb the reputational ladder and obtain special access to new credit. Years later, Hueyo reflected that Argentina had succeeded by showing its resolve to pay not only in times of bonanza but also during periods of extreme poverty: "Cumplir los compromisos contraídos es sumamente honroso, pero hacerlo cuando todo el mundo falla y en momentos de penuria . . . tiene mil veces más valor" [To fulfill one's contracted obligations is extremely honorable, but to do so when everyone is defaulting and in times of crisis is a thousand times more valuable].[59]

### Synopsis of the Argentine Case

The evidence strongly shows that Argentina repaid its debts, not to avoid a costly trade war, but to facilitate additional borrowing. The desire for a positive reputation led decision makers to take the remarkable step of maintaining payments during the depths of the depression. All four patterns—the treatment of dollar debt, the policy of exchange control, the behavior of Argentine provinces, and the statements of key decision makers—lead to the same conclusion, increasing confidence in the importance of reputation.

Although the evidence in this section points overwhelmingly in the direction of reputation rather than sanctioning, it is understandable why scholars might have thought otherwise. The correspondence between commercial dependence and debt repayment is eye-catching, especially for authors predisposed to view the world through *dependendista* lenses. The story of a conspiratorial alliance between British investors and Argentine ranchers makes for interesting fiction but has little basis in fact.

If the prospect of trade sanctions did not shape the debt policies of interwar Argentina, it seems unlikely to be potent elsewhere. Even in an extreme case of dependency, the risk of a trade embargo did not figure prominently in the decision to repay. The evidence is particularly damning because it contradicts the main example researchers have supplied to illustrate the payment-inducing power of trade sanctions.

The results are not merely negative, however. In casting doubt on the importance of trade sanctions, the data also show the overriding importance of reputation. Debate in Argentina centered on how default would affect the image of Buenos Aires in the eyes of foreign investors. The desire for a better reputation, even at great cost, probably motivated other peripheral countries to repay during the Great Depression, though we cannot verify this without in-depth studies of the national debates in other

[59] Alberto Hueyo, October 1, 1937, at El Colegio Libre de Estudios Superiores, reprinted in Hueyo 1938, 307.

countries. For now, we can be highly confident that what seemed the strongest example of the power of trade sanctions is actually a testament to the importance of reputation.

## Cross-Country Analysis of Trade Sanctions

In this section I cast the empirical net more broadly by conducting a cross-country statistical analysis of debtor behavior during the 1930s. If the prospect of trade embargoes motivates sovereigns to repay, two patterns should appear in the data. First, countries that depend heavily on trade with creditor nations should repay their bonds at a higher rate than countries that depend less on commercial relations with creditors. Second, when defaults take place, debtors should discriminate in favor of their senior trading partners, which have the greatest potential to impose trade sanctions. I investigate both of these propositions below.

### *The Level of Compliance*

To test the first hypothesis, I measured each government's compliance with dollar and sterling debts. As in the Argentine case study, my measure was the nominal value of interest payments the government made as a proportion of its contractual obligations. Suppose, for example, that a government paid $200 million in interest on its dollar bonds in 1934, even though by right it should have paid $500 million that year. The government would earn a compliance score of 200/500 = .4 in 1934. Using the database described in chapter 5, I calculated an average compliance score for each government and denomination of bond (dollar vs. sterling) during the period 1933–38. Those dates offered the greatest variation in the dependent variable while avoiding the potential problems imposed by World War II.

The key explanatory variable was trade—the sum of exports plus imports—with the creditor country as a proportion of gross domestic product in 1928. I chose 1928 to minimize the risk of a reciprocal relationship between dependent and explanatory variable. If creditors did indeed slap trade sanctions on countries that defaulted during the 1930s, the value of trade with creditors during that decade would have been, at least in part, a consequence rather than a cause of the decision to repay or default. To determine whether the prospect of a trade embargo deterred default, it was essential to measure the threat of trade sanctions at a moment before the defaults took place.

This same concern with endogeneity led me to exclude known lemons from the sample. China, Ecuador, Mexico, and Russia had all initiated default before 1928 and remained in default throughout the depression. Assuming that lenders did retaliate commercially, lemons would have had atypically low levels of trade with creditors in 1928, due perhaps to default decisions that were taken many years earlier.[60] For reasons of logical consistency, then, I dropped the proven lemons from the sample, leaving only those countries that were honoring their debts before the Great Crash.

Trade was measured for all countries and reported in standard sources, such as the *Statistical Yearbook* of the League of Nations, but the level of GDP in 1928–29 was more difficult to find. A comprehensive literature search uncovered estimates for most sovereigns, but in a few cases the data were simply not available, despite the best efforts of economic historians to calculate them.[61] To overcome this problem I collected auxiliary variables that correlated closely with GDP per capita. Several performed well, including movie theaters per capita, trade per capita, radio sets per person, life expectancy, illiteracy rates, and infant mortality, each of which explained at least 50 percent of the variation in GDP levels. Ultimately I settled on motor vehicles per capita, which was available for all sovereign countries and tightly related to GDP.[62] I used this auxiliary information to fill holes in the dataset via the technique of multiple imputation.

In the final sample, compliance scores ranged from 0 to 1 with a mean of .73 for sterling bonds and .68 for dollar bonds. I analyzed the sterling and dollar bonds separately, since it seemed implausible that, say, the United States would use trade sanctions to retaliate against defaults on sterling bonds. Trade with the United Kingdom as a proportion of GDP ran from .007 to .31, with an average value of .08. Trade with the United States, in turn, was .10 on average, with a minimum of .004 and a maximum of .71. I included GDP per capita as a control variable, since it

[60] This effect is not readily apparent in the data. Mexican trade with the United States, for example, was no lower or more restricted in the late 1920s than before the revolution, even though Mexico had *repudiated* its financial obligations to U.S. investors in 1914. Trade with creditors remained equally buoyant for China, Ecuador, and Russia, despite their defaults. These observations themselves should cast doubt on the trade sanction hypothesis.

[61] The principal sources of GDP data were Bulmer-Thomas 1987, 1994; Butlin 1984; Buyst 1997; Chakalov 1946; Eckstein 1955; Ercolani 1969; Fremdling 1995; Hansen and Marzouk 1965; Hansen 1974; Hjerppe 1989; Kostelenos 1995; Krantz and Nilsson 1975; Leacy 1983; Lethbridge 1985; Mitchell 1998a, 1998b; National Industrial Conference Board 1939; Neves 1994; Österreichisches Institut für Wirtschaftsforschung 1965; Rankin 1992; Toutain 1987; Turkey, State Institute of Statistics 1996; United Nations 1948, 1950, 1952; and Yuru 1992.

[62] Data on motor vehicles per capita came from League of Nations 1931, 18–23, 186–88. A bivariate regression of GDP on motor vehicles, both measured in natural logs per capita at their 1928–29 levels, produced an $R^2$ of nearly .80, suggesting that this was an excellent predictor of the missing data.

should have influenced compliance and might have covaried with dependence on trade.

For each type of bond (dollar or sterling), I estimated a fractional probit model in which the log likelihood for country $i$ is

$$y_i \ln\pi_i + (1 - y_i) \ln(1 - \pi_i),$$

where $y_i$ is the observed rate of compliance for country $i$ during the period 1933–38, $\pi_i = F(\beta'x_i)$ is the expected rate of compliance conditional on the explanatory variables $(x_i)$ and their coefficients $(\beta)$, and $F$ is the cumulative standard normal distribution. The model is similar to a probit regression, but modified to allow values of $y$ anywhere in the $[0,1]$ interval. For cases in which $y_i$ is 1 or 0, the likelihood is governed by either $\pi_i$ or $1 - \pi_i$, just as in a probit model. In cases where $y_i$ takes on an intermediate value, the likelihood amounts to a weighted average of the probability of full compliance $(\pi_i)$ and the probability of full default $(1 - \pi_i)$.

The results for sterling and dollar bonds appear in table 7.3.[63] Against the trade embargo hypothesis, dependence on trade with the United Kingdom did not lead countries to honor their sterling debts at a higher rate. The estimated coefficient on trade with the lender is negative, the reverse of what one would expect if countries repaid to avoid a trade embargo. Nevertheless, the standard error is more than 50 times the point estimate, so for all practical purposes the estimate is indistinguishable from zero. Results for dollar bonds are similar. The coefficient on trade with the lender is slightly positive, but once again the large standard error and miniscule $t$-statistic inspire no confidence that the effect differed from zero. Apparently, trade dependence did not provide systematic protection to either British or American investors during the interwar years.[64]

Could measurement error have caused this resoundingly null result? The key explanatory variable, trade with lender as a share of GDP, was probably measured with error, which—if random—could have biased the estimated coefficient toward zero. By the 1920s, the United States and Britain had been collecting detailed trade statistics for a century. Gross

[63] The following countries were included in both the dollar and sterling samples: Argentina, Australia, Austria, Belgium, Brazil, Bulgaria, Canada, Chile, China, Colombia, Costa Rica, Czechoslovakia, Denmark, El Salvador, Estonia, Finland, Germany, Greece, Guatemala, Hungary, Italy, Japan, Norway, Peru, Poland, Romania, Sweden, Uruguay, Yugoslavia. The dollar sample also included Bolivia, Cuba, Dominican Republic, France, Haiti, Ireland, Panama, and Switzerland; and the sterling sample included Ecuador, Egypt, Iran, New Zealand, Nicaragua, Paraguay, Portugal, Siam, South Africa, and Turkey.

[64] My analysis focuses on trade with the lender. Using different data and methods, Eichengreen and Portes (1986, 616) reach a complementary conclusion: exports as a share of GDP had no significant effect on compliance with dollar and sterling debt during the years 1934–38.

TABLE 7.3
Compliance as a Function of Trade with the Lender, 1933–38

| | Sterling Bonds | | | Dollar Bonds | | |
|---|---|---|---|---|---|---|
| Variable | Estimated Coefficient | Standard Error | t-statistic | Estimated Coefficient | Standard Error | t-statistic |
| Trade with lender | −0.04 | 2.28 | 0.02 | 0.04 | 1.59 | 0.02 |
| GDP per capita | 0.77 | 0.27 | 2.84 | 0.70 | 0.18 | 3.92 |
| Constant | −0.44 | 0.35 | 1.26 | -0.68 | 0.37 | 1.83 |

*Source*: Author's calculations from the database of sovereign bonds and economic indicators described in the text.

*Note*: Estimates from a fractional probit regression, as described in the text. The unit of observation is the country, with $N = 39$ for sterling bonds and $N = 37$ for dollar bonds. In the sterling bonds model, the dependent variable is the nominal value of interest payments the country made on its sterling bonds during the years 1933–38, as a proportion of the interest payments that were contractually required. The dependent variable in the dollar bonds model is analogous, but measures compliance with dollar rather than sterling bonds.

domestic product, in contrast, was a fairly new concept that only reached full development by economists around the time of World War II. The estimates of GDP at 1929 levels were, for the most part, obtained through retrospective calculation by historians, rather than systematic work by researchers at the time. Were measures of GDP so riddled with error that they obscured the effects of trade with the lender?

The quality of the parameter estimate for GDP per capita suggests otherwise. If GDP per capita suffered from severe measurement error, it would not have proved so consequential in the statistical analysis. To the contrary, the coefficients on GDP per capita in table 7.3 carried the anticipated sign and were estimated with a considerable degree of precision. Simulations from this quasi-probit model reveal that, holding trade with the lender at its mean, GDP per capita exhibits positive but diminishing effects on compliance, and that higher income not only increases the expected level of compliance but also increases certainty about the amount the borrower will pay. If the variable were plagued with measurement error, we probably would not have observed such clean and intuitive results. Thus, measurement error does not seem serious enough to alter our conclusion that trade with the lender exerted no effect on compliance.

A related concern is the paucity of data during the 1930s. If interwar leaders did not have measures of national income, could they really be expected to base decisions on trade with the lender as a share of GDP? There are two answers. First, policymakers probably had a good intuition about how extensively their economies depended on trade with lenders, even if they could not quantify it to several decimal points. (If leaders could not gauge their level of dependence, then the embargo hypothesis should be rejected immediately.) Second, the conclusions in this section do not depend on any one measure of trade reliance. In addition to trade as a share of GDP, I considered trade with the creditor as a percentage of all trade, and trade with the creditor in dollars per capita. For both the sterling and dollar bonds, the estimated coefficients on these alternative measures were slightly negative (the opposite of the embargo hypothesis) but statistically indistinguishable from zero.

Finally, readers might attribute the null result to selection bias. Perhaps investors refrained from lending to countries that had little commercial intercourse with the United Kingdom or the United States, such that the ones that actually attracted capital were satisfactorily vulnerable to trade sanctions. If this objection is valid, it might explain the absence of a relationship between trade and debt in the sample of borrowers.

Three pieces of evidence argue against this possibility. First, as detailed in chapter 4, investment primers of the interwar period almost never mentioned the direction of trade or the prospect of an embargo as a factor in lending decisions. It therefore seems unlikely that investors rationed credit on the basis of trade sanctions. Second, the wide range on trade with the lender provides a considerable degree of reassurance. British and American investors lent to countries that conducted less than 1 percent of their foreign trade with the motherland and would therefore have been relatively invulnerable to an embargo. Third, countries that borrowed from the British actually conducted *less* trade with the United Kingdom, on average, than countries that did not attract sterling loans. The behavior of U.S. lenders seemed slightly more consistent with rationing: American investors showed a slight preference for countries that traded extensively with the United States. The difference was not statistically significant, however, either in a *t*-test of means or in a probit regression that explored whether dependence on the United States could explain which countries attracted dollar loans. Thus, investors of the interwar period did not use dependence on trade as a criterion for allocating credit.

## Patterns of Discrimination

For additional evidence I turned to the subset of countries that defaulted. If the threat of an embargo truly loomed, defaulters should have pushed the cost of noncompliance onto their junior trading partners, thereby minimizing the commercial penalty. Did governments behave in this way? To answer this question, I identified all sovereigns that owed money to both British and U.S. bondholders during the 1930s. Of these sovereigns, I disqualified 13 that had paid their creditors in full and three that defaulted on both dollar and sterling obligations before the Great Depression.[65] That left 16 sovereigns who, having borrowed on both sides of the Atlantic, violated their debt contracts during the 1930s.

For each of the 16, I checked for discrimination by comparing compliance rates on similar sterling and dollar bonds during period 1933–38. I focused on similar obligations for two reasons. First, some debt contracts are harder to honor than others. A government must exert more effort to honor a debt with an 8 percent interest rate than to service one with an annual burden of only 4 percent, for example. When testing for discrimination, it seemed crucial to hold constant the degree of difficulty that the obligations posed. Second, certain types of bonds traditionally enjoy higher standing than others. During moments of crisis, governments usually prioritize "funding" or "adjustment" bonds that were issued to compensate lenders for past defaults. This practice not only seems fair, but also signals that the government is serious about the settlement offered to bondholders.

Whenever possible, then, I paired sterling and dollar debts that bore approximately the same interest rate and security, and I tried not to mix funding bonds with new issues. Sometimes the pairings were obvious, as when a sovereign issued identical bonds in two tranches, one in London and the other in New York. In other cases it proved impossible to find an exact match, so I opted for as close an approximation as possible. Each pairing received a letter grade ranging from A, which signified a perfect match on all characteristics except the issue market, to D, which meant that the closest pair differed in type, interest rate, and other features. Details about the grading scheme appear in the notes at the bottom of table 7.4.

I created at least one pairing for each of the 16 defaulters, calculated separate compliance rates for sterling and dollar debts, and then computed the disparity in treatment, if any. In cases where more than one pairing was possible, I opted for the one with the highest grade. Heavy borrowers such as Austria, Bulgaria, Chile, Germany, and Greece had several grade-A pairs. Rather than pick one arbitrarily, I used them all to compute the average gap in compliance between sterling and dollar bonds. A difference of zero means that the government afforded equal treatment to creditors in the United States and the United Kingdom. A positive difference implies that the borrower gave priority to sterling bonds, whereas a negative difference indicates that dollar bonds received preferential treatment.

---

[65] The nondefaulters were Argentina, Australia, Belgium, Canada, Czechoslovakia, Denmark, Estonia, Finland, Italy, Japan, Newfoundland, Norway, and Sweden. The three predepression defaulters were China, Mexico, and Russia.

TABLE 7.4
Compliance and Trade of 16 Defaulters, 1933–38

|            | Trade (%) | | | Compliance (%) | | | |
|------------|------|------|------------|------|------|------------|------------------|
| Defaulter  | U.K. | U.S. | Difference | U.K. | U.S. | Difference | Quality of Match |
| Colombia   | 10   | 60   | −51        | 28   | 28   | 0          | B                |
| Guatemala  | 5    | 55   | −50        | 100  | 54   | 46         | D                |
| El Salvador| 7    | 34   | −28        | 56   | 43   | 13         | D                |
| Brazil     | 12   | 36   | −24        | 32   | 32   | 0          | A                |
| Peru       | 21   | 33   | −12        | 0    | 0    | 0          | A                |
| Costa Rica | 35   | 40   | −5         | 14   | 14   | 1          | D                |
| Chile      | 28   | 33   | −5         | 5    | 5    | 0          | A                |
| Greece     | 14   | 18   | −4         | 40   | 40   | 0          | A                |
| Germany    | 8    | 11   | −3         | 100  | 70   | 30         | A                |
| Uruguay    | 19   | 21   | −2         | 58   | 63   | −5         | B                |
| Austria    | 3    | 5    | −2         | 99   | 99   | 0          | A                |
| Hungary    | 3    | 2    | 1          | 61   | 61   | 0          | A                |
| Yugoslavia | 4    | 3    | 1          | 38   | 34   | 4          | C                |
| Poland     | 9    | 8    | 1          | 86   | 85   | 1          | A                |
| Romania    | 6    | 3    | 4          | 41   | 18   | 24         | A                |
| Bulgaria   | 6    | 2    | 5          | 36   | 37   | −1         | A                |

*Source*: Author's calculations from the League of Nations 1929 and 1932; United Kingdom Customs and Excise Department 1930; U.S. Department of Commerce 1931; and the database of loans, as described in the text.

*Note*: Trade is the defaulter's trade with the lender (either the U.K. or the U.S.), as a percentage of the defaulter's total trade in 1928. Apparent discrepancies between U.K.-U.S. and "Difference" are due to rounding. Compliance is defined as in previous tables, and is computed for sterling bonds (U.K.) and dollar bonds (U.S.) that are as similar as possible. Quality of match measures the degree of similarity between the dollar and sterling bonds.

Quality of match is "A" if the comparison involves sterling and dollar tranches of identical loans. This grade applies to Austria (7% loan of 1930 and 6% loan of 1923), Brazil (6.5% loan of 1927), Bulgaria (7% loan of 1926 and 7.5% loan of 1928), Chile (6% loans of 1928 and 1929), Germany (7% loan of 1924 and 5.5% loan of 1930), Greece (7% loan of 1924 and 6% loan of 1928), Hungary (7.5% loan of 1924), Peru (6% loan of 1928), Poland (7% loan of 1927), and Romania (4% loan of 1922). Quality of match is "B" if the loans differ in some respects but have identical interest rates, and if both are new issues rather than funding bonds. This grade applies to Colombia (6% sterling loan of 1913 versus 6% dollar loan of 1927) and Uruguay (5% sterling loan of 1914 versus 5% dollar loan of 1915). Quality of match is "C" if the loans have different interest rates, *or* if one is a readjustment bond, whereas the other is a new issue. This grade applies to Yugoslavia (5% sterling loan of 1909 versus 7% dollar loan of 1922/27). Quality of match is "D" if the loans have different interest rates *and* one is a readjustment bond, whereas the other is a new issue. This grade applies to Costa Rica (5% sterling readjustment loan of 1911 versus 7% dollar loan of 1926), El Salvador (6% sterling readjustment loan of 1923 versus 7% dollar loan of 1924), and Guatemala (4% sterling readjustment loan of 1927 versus 8% dollar loan of 1927).

Table 7.4 asks whether patterns of favoritism were related to levels of trade. The first set of columns in table 7.4 gives each country's trade with the United Kingdom and the United States as a percentage of total trade in 1928. The second set reports compliance rates on sterling and dollar bonds during the 1930s. Finally, the rightmost column reports the quality of the match between sterling and dollar obligations. Rows with a grade of C or lower involved incommensurable obligations, which should be given little weight.

The countries in table 7.4 appear in order of their dependence on the United States versus the United Kingdom. Colombia, which heads the list, conducted 60 percent of its foreign trade with the United States versus only 10 percent with the United Kingdom, an enormous disparity that could have aided U.S. bondholders. Likewise, Guatemala, El Salvador, Brazil, and Peru depended much more on commerce with the United States than with the United Kingdom. Conversely, a few European countries, such as Romania and Bulgaria, appear at the bottom of the list, since they traded more intensively with the British than with the Americans.

The largest commercial asymmetries in table 7.4 favored the Americans for reasons that are easy to understand. The wave of defaults that began in 1931 confined itself mainly to Latin America and Eastern Europe, where debtors were relatively poor and suffered sharp declines in their terms of trade. As a "gravity" model of commerce would predict, most Latin American countries traded heavily with their nearest developed neighbor, the United States. The nations of Eastern Europe, in contrast, could interact with any number of large developed markets on the Continent, and therefore relied less on either the United States or the United Kingdom. Thus, the 16 defaulters in the sample fell into two categories: Latin American states, which for reasons of geography depended heavily on the United States, and east European countries, whose trade was more diversified.

The "difference" columns show that defaulters did not discriminate in favor of their senior trading partners. The modal difference in compliance (United Kingdom minus United States) was 0, and the next most common value was 1 percentage point. In all but four cases, discrimination amounted to no more than 5 percent of contractual obligations, a gap that could have arisen from slightly different terms of contract. Overall, the average defaulter paid nearly the same amount to British and U.S. bondholders, regardless of its dependence on trade.

Not all defaulters treated their creditors equally, however. Table 7.4 shows that Guatemala, El Salvador, Germany, and Romania serviced their sterling debts more fully than their dollar obligations, sometimes by a wide margin. The behavior of the first two countries runs contrary to the embargo hypothesis: Guatemala and El Salvador favored their sterling bonds, even though they relied more extensively on the U.S. market. How can we explain this perplexing result? The apparent discrimination by Guatemala and El Salvador arose from an inability to match dollar and sterling obligations, rather than any coercive actions by lenders. British investors held funding bonds with interest rates of 4 to 6 percent, whereas U.S. citizens had invested in new securities with interest rates of 7 to 8 percent. The higher rates on dollar debt were meant to compensate for the risk of default, especially since investors understood that the funding bonds would receive priority. Based purely on the nature of the obligations, without any reference to trade, Guatemala and El Salvador should have treated their sterling bonds more scrupulously than their dollar debt.

This leaves only two genuine cases of discrimination: Germany and Romania. Both countries received match grades of A, meaning the disparities in table 7.4 were not due to incommensurate bonds. Instead, the two countries explicitly elevated British bondholders over American ones. The German government honored all debts through mid-1934, when it changed course by offering full service to British investors but only partial payment to Americans. Agents implemented this policy of discrimination by stamping each bond to indicate "U.K. domicile" or "U.S.A. domicile." Likewise, the Romanian government serviced bonds that were British-owned, while withholding payment from American investors.

Although unusual, these two examples demonstrate that governments could have favored some bondholders over others. The fact that most governments did *not* discriminate, despite the German and Romanian precedents, counts as powerful evidence against the embargo hypothesis. Moreover, the two cases of discrimination probably did not arise from the threat of an embargo, though they did originate from tense trade relations between Britain and the borrowers. Later in this section I explain why Germany and Romania slighted the Americans. For now, though, it bears emphasizing that neither country depended heavily on British trade, and Germany actually conducted more commerce with the United States than with the United Kingdom.

If the threat of an embargo truly had been credible, we would have expected discrimination not from Germany and Romania, but from nations closer to the top of the dependency scale. Brazil, for example, should have favored American bondholders. During the interwar period, Brazil conducted more than one-third of its trade with the United States and sent half of its exports to the U.S. market. Perhaps more importantly, it sold up to 70 percent of its most politically sensitive export, coffee, to U.S. buyers. In contrast, Brazil relied on the British for only 12 percent of trade and less than 5 percent of exports. Considering these differences in the direction of trade, an embargo-minded U.S. government could have extracted preferential treatment from Brazil.

Apparently it did not. On the matched bonds in table 7.4, Brazil paid exactly the same amount to British and American creditors. This outcome arose from a strong commitment to treating all creditors equally. As early as 1933, Brazilian officials announced that they would "in no way discriminate between different nations" in the repayment of their foreign debt. Instead, they strove to classify bonds "solely on their respective merits," including "relative security, previous funding, debtors solvency or capacity to pay, differing rates of contractual interest, and actual market values."[66]

In the debt renegotiation act of 1933–34, Brazil classified its foreign debts into eight categories and indicated how much it would pay for each. A few sterling bonds stood alone in the top tier and received full service at a time when other loans were in default. This policy should not be viewed as discriminatory, however. The sterling bonds in the top tier were *funding* loans, which Brazil had offered to British bondholders in settlement of previous defaults. The holders had made great sacrifices, Brazil argued, and it seemed fair to give them special consideration. These sterling loans did not affect the calculations in table 7.4, because they had no dollar equivalent.

U.S. observers apparently agreed. The Foreign Bondholders Protective Council (FBPC) had hired Allen Dulles to investigate the situation and opine on the fairness of the Brazilian plan. After a thorough investigation, he concluded that "the privileged position given these two funding loans in the Brazilian plan should be maintained," even though the bonds belonged to British investors.[67] The FBPC signaled its approval by recommending the plan to bondholders.

Colombia, too, chose not to discriminate, despite its potential vulnerability to trade sanctions. Between the world wars, Colombia conducted 60 percent of its trade with the United States, which absorbed almost 90 percent of Colombian coffee exports. By comparison, the United Kingdom played only a minor role in Colombian commerce. U.S. bondholders understood the situation and urged officials to link debt with trade. For example, a committee of Colombian bondholders appeared before the U.S. Tariff Commission to demand repayment as a precondition for a

[66] Hugh Gibson to Secretary of State, November 10, 1933, enclosure 2, 2, Brazil Files, Archives of the Foreign Bondholders Protective Council, Stanford University Library.

[67] Allen Dulles, "Memorandum on the Proposed Plan for the Adjustment of Brazilian National, State, and Municipal External Loans," December 26, 1933, 9, 12, Brazil Files, Archives of the Foreign Bondholders Protective Council, Stanford University Library.

reciprocal trade treaty with Colombia.[68] U.S. officials refused to hold trade hostage, however. Sumner Welles, as Assistant Secretary of State, relayed the official view:

> The position of the Department is that the primary purpose of the trade agreements negotiated under the Act of June 12, 1934, is the revival of international trade, and the agreement with Colombia does not, therefore, contain provisions specifically relating to the resumption of service of Colombian dollar obligations. However, inasmuch as the decline in international trade was one of the principal causes of financial difficulties in many countries, it is to be expected that the revival of international trade which the trade agreement program seeks to foster will aid in remedying conditions which have led to defaults.[69]

The same U.S. policy applied to other debtors.[70] At various points bondholders asked policymakers to use trade as a weapon, but Secretary of State Cordell Hull "would [not] consider it for a moment; he [was] thinking only of his trade agreements and extending them and not of bringing in any economic pressure on those countries."[71] Thus, an authoritative report by the Securities and Exchange Commission found "no case on record" in which the United States had threatened or imposed "trade sanctions for the purpose of concluding a debt settlement."[72]

This firm U.S. policy may explain the null statistical results that appeared earlier in this chapter. I found that governments did not pay in proportion to their commercial dependence on the United States, nor did they discriminate in favor of U.S. bondholders. Perhaps they ignored trade because sanctions were not credible. Whatever its capacity to slap trade sanctions on countries that violated their debt contracts, the U.S. government clearly lacked the will, a reality that debtors and bondholders understood all too well.

Even without the threat of trade sanctions, though, the United States secured payment from most countries. Twenty nations paid their debts in

[68] U.S. Securities and Exchange Commission 1937, 445. The FBPC also sent a thinly veiled threat to the Colombian government: although it had "not as yet" urged the U.S. government to employ "coercive measures" against Colombia, it had received "many requests" to that effect and implored Colombia to settle before such steps became necessary. Minutes of Meeting of the Executive Committee, August 7, 1934, Box 45, Minute Book, vol. 1, 1933–34, Archives of the Foreign Bondholders Protective Council, Stanford University Library.

[69] U.S. Securities and Exchange Commission 1937, 446.

[70] Eichengreen 1991, 159–60; Fishlow 1985, 429.

[71] Francis White, Memorandum, April 5, 1938, Box 29, Province of Mendoza (Argentina) Folder, Document 25–1, Archives of the Foreign Bondholders Protective Council, Stanford University Library.

[72] U.S. Securities and Exchange Commission 1937, 445.

full to American investors during the 1930s,[73] and others honored a high proportion of their obligations. Only two countries, Bolivia and Peru, made no transfers to U.S. bondholders between 1933 and 1938. Clearly, then, the threat of a trade embargo cannot explain why countries repaid their debts to the Americans or why so many nations treated British and American investors equitably. Moreover, if the United States lacked the will to apply sanctions during one of the most discriminatory moments in the history of international trade, it seems unlikely to have linked trade and debt during other periods. As an explanation for U.S. foreign investment and repayment, the embargo hypothesis is seriously deficient.

The British were only slightly more willing to flex their commercial muscle on behalf of bondholders. In relations with Romania and Germany, the two discriminators identified earlier, the U.K. government did indeed apply commercial leverage, though in the form of a clearing arrangement rather than a trade embargo. Parties to a clearing agreement required their importers to pay for goods in domestic currency, which accumulated in a domestic clearing office instead of being shipped abroad. Exporters, in turn, were paid in their own currency from funds in the clearing office. Thus, clearing agreements allowed countries to trade without transferring foreign funds, except to settle the account. The country with a trade deficit invariably accumulated a surplus in its clearing office, and under some agreements could redirect the surplus to bondholders.

By threatening or imposing clearing arrangements, Britain secured preferential treatment from Romania and Germany. Britain and Romania established a clearing arrangement in the late 1930s. Under the terms of the agreement, any surplus sterling that piled up in the British clearing office could be transferred to British holders of Romanian bonds. The United States had no such agreement with Romania, which explains why British bondholders fared better than American ones. A similar situation arose with Germany. When Germany declared a moratorium on all long-term government bonds in June 1934, Britain threatened to impose a clearing. It proved unnecessary to carry out the threat, however. Under the Anglo-German transfer agreement of 1934, the British pledged not to establish a clearing, and Germany committed to pay full interest to British holders of Dawes and Young bonds.

This British behavior smacks of trade sanctions, but it is important to keep the evidence in perspective. First, Britain never threatened to sever or even reduce trade with Romania and Germany in response to default. Instead, it sequestered the surplus exchange that accumulated when those

---

[73] The countries were Argentina, Australia, Belgium, Canada, Czechoslovakia, Denmark, Dominican Republic, Estonia, Finland, France, Haiti, Ireland, Italy, Japan, Netherlands, Newfoundland, Norway, Sweden, Switzerland, and the United Kingdom.

two debtors ran a trade surplus with Britain. Thus, the discrimination arose from a special form of currency rationing, rather than traditional trade sanctions. Second and more importantly, the Romanian and German cases were unique. As Barry Eichengreen emphasizes, they "were exceptions to the rule. British officials generally rejected bondholders' calls for commercial retaliation," and American policymakers uniformly refused.[74] Nevertheless, many countries paid in full. Thus, evidence for the embargo hypothesis is surprisingly thin.

## Evidence from Other Historical Periods

Having found little evidence of linkage during the interwar period, when it was most likely to occur, I briefly consider data from other historical periods.

### Evidence from Diplomatic Correspondence and the Financial Press

After the Napoleonic Wars, nearly all countries around the world issued bonds on the London capital market. Did the British government use the threat of trade sanctions to deter these countries from defaulting? We can gain valuable insight by analyzing the correspondence of the Foreign Office, discussed in chapter 6. As noted in that chapter, the British government laid 520 pieces of bondholder-related correspondence before Parliament in the middle of the nineteenth century. Even though many countries depended heavily on trade with Britain, not one of the letters in the collection mentions trade sanctions.

If the threat of trade sanctions sustained lending and repayment, discussion of this enforcement mechanism should have appeared not only in diplomatic correspondence, but also in the financial press. To test this hypothesis I examined a unique collection of newspaper articles compiled by the British Corporation of Foreign Bondholders (CFB), which was founded in the late 1860s to monitor foreign debtors and negotiate with them when defaults took place. The CFB kept abreast of debt-related policies at home and abroad by maintaining a massive collection of scrapbooks, with clippings from dozens of domestic and foreign newspapers.

Working with a team of research assistants, I analyzed all newspaper clippings during the period 1870–1914 for the 45 countries and regions listed in table 7.5. The table gives the number of pages we read and classified, which ranged from 29 for Bosnia to 10,324 for Turkey. In total we

---

[74] Eichengreen 1991, 160.

TABLE 7.5
References to Trade Sanctions in the Newspaper Files of the Corporation of Foreign Bondholders, 1870–1914

| Country or Region | Number of Pages Analyzed | References to Trade Sanctions | Country or Region | Number of Pages Analyzed | References to Trade Sanctions |
|---|---|---|---|---|---|
| Austria | 1,151 | 0 | Liberia | 391 | 0 |
| Belgium | 227 | 0 | Mexico | 8,293 | 0 |
| Bolivia | 1,802 | 0 | Morocco | 44 | 0 |
| Bosnia | 29 | 0 | Netherlands | 231 | 0 |
| Brazil | 4,859 | 0 | Nicaragua | 1,288 | 0 |
| Bulgaria | 431 | 0 | Norway | 108 | 0 |
| Central and South America | 1,221 | 0 | Panama | 389 | 0 |
| Chile | 2,795 | 0 | Paraguay | 3,351 | 0 |
| China | 1,272 | 0 | Peru | 6,089 | 1 |
| Colombia | 3,811 | 0 | Portugal | 3,599 | 0 |
| Costa Rica | 2,558 | 0 | Romania | 581 | 0 |
| Cuba | 1,022 | 0 | Russia | 3,504 | 0 |
| Cyprus | 215 | 0 | Serbia | 236 | 0 |
| Denmark | 172 | 0 | South Africa | 1,007 | 0 |
| Dominican Republic | 2,081 | 0 | South America | 720 | 0 |
| Ecuador | 2,381 | 0 | Spain | 4,637 | 0 |
| Egypt | 7,409 | 0 | Sweden | 317 | 0 |
| El Salvador | 1,472 | 0 | Switzerland | 155 | 0 |
| Greece | 3,089 | 1 | Tunisia | 134 | 0 |
| Guatemala | 1,881 | 0 | Turkey | 10,324 | 0 |
| Honduras | 2,194 | 0 | Uruguay | 3,559 | 0 |
| Hungary | 432 | 0 | Venezuela | 4,310 | 0 |
| Japan | 490 | 0 | | | |

Total pages analyzed: 96,261
Total references to trade sanctions: 2

Source: Council of the Corporation of Foreign Bondholders, Newspaper Cuttings Files, Guildhall Library.

checked more than 96,000 scrapbook pages, each containing between one and five newspaper articles.

In all those pages, we found only two references to a possible link between debt repayment and trade sanctions. The first example concerned the Peruvian default discussed at the beginning of this chapter. Peru defaulted in 1876, and bondholders immediately tried to seize the guano Peru had pledged as collateral. When British courts prevented this action on grounds of sovereign immunity, bondholders proposed to achieve the same result through tariffs.

The proposal came from James Croyle, president of the International Committee of Peruvian Bondholders, which had failed on previous occasions to obtain aid from the British government. In a new and somewhat desperate letter to the British foreign secretary, Croyle explained that the bondholders "are still in hopes of getting some support from H.M. Government." His earlier recommendations rebuffed, Croyle wrote that "there is still another mode of dealing with the Peruvian Government which would . . . probably in a very short time rectify the whole position, viz., to place an import duty on Peruvian guano of, say, £6 per ton—£5 of this to be appropriated to the redemption of the Bonds."[75] The British government never levied the tariff, and the issue was never mentioned again in the CFB scrapbooks on Peru.

The second reference to trade sanctions was stronger, since it involved an actual threat by a German diplomat, rather than a mere petition by a disaffected bondholder. In 1893 Greece defaulted on its debts to foreign bondholders, most of whom resided in England and Germany. The following July, the German minister in Athens threatened that his government would support the bondholders by suspending the commercial treaty between Germany and Greece.[76] News of the threat appeared in the London *Times* on August 1, 1894.

Over the next two days, though, the *Times* downplayed the significance of the threat. The "premature" threat had not been authorized by Berlin, and the *Times* deemed it "unlikely that the German government will take any immediate steps to support the claims of the bondholders."[77] Moreover, Greece could "without much hesitation return a polite refusal" because the rupture of commercial relations would hurt Germany more than

---

[75] James Croyle to Marquis of Salisbury, April 30, 1878, printed in Council of the Corporation of Foreign Bondholders, Newspaper Cuttings Files, Reel 146, Guildhall Library.

[76] *Times* (London), August 1, 1894, in Council of the Corporation of Foreign Bondholders, Newspaper Cuttings Files, Reel 21, Guildhall Library.

[77] *Times* (London), August 2 and 4, 1894, in Council of the Corporation of Foreign Bondholders, Newspaper Cuttings Files, Reel 21, Guildhall Library.

Greece.[78] The threat came to nothing: the German government did not suspend its commercial treaty, and Greek exports to Germany nearly doubled between 1891 and 1895.[79]

Other than these two references—a petition by a disgruntled bondholder, and an unauthorized threat that was never carried out—we found no discussion of trade sanctions in more than 96,000 pages of newspaper articles.

### Three Additional Findings

Three additional pieces of evidence strengthen the conclusion that loans are not enforced via the threat of trade sanctions. First, the leading investment texts of the interwar period never counseled readers to consider the prospect of a trade embargo or other types of commercial sanctions. A systematic search of the investment literature, detailed in chapter 4, uncovered only one contemporary reference to trade sanctions, which the commentator offered as a curiosity rather than a general piece of investment advice. In contrast, nearly all the commentators—drawn from professions as diverse as banking, journalism, law, accounting, public administration, and academia—cited reputation as an important, if not the key, consideration when lending to foreign governments.

Second, at various points in history, investors have extended loans to borrowers that were invulnerable to trade embargoes. One telling example comes from the nineteenth century, when Massachusetts, Pennsylvania, New York, and other U.S. states borrowed from British investors.[80] In the event of default, an individual state could have evaded British trade sanctions by transshipping goods through neighboring states. To apply effective pressure, then, Britain would have needed to embargo the entire union in response to default by one of its members. It is highly unlikely that Britain would have followed such a course. Despite their invulnerability to trade sanctions, though, the U.S. states managed to borrow, and most of them repaid their debts. Even the ones that defaulted did not experience a trade embargo, but they did tarnish their reputations and lose access to capital markets, at least until they settled their defaults.

---

[78] *Times* (London), October 25, 1894, in Council of the Corporation of Foreign Bondholders, Newspaper Cuttings Files, Reel 21, Guildhall Library.

[79] *Financial Times*, May 17, 1897, in Council of the Corporation of Foreign Bondholders, Newspaper Cuttings Files, Reel 21, Guildhall Library.

[80] English (1996) discusses the impossibility of trade sanctions against the U.S. states, and Sylla and Wallis (1998) identify cross-state variation in the sources of public revenue as the main reason why some states defaulted whereas others did not. See also Wallis, Sylla, and Grinath 2004.

Thus, the U.S. experience provides further support for a reputation-based theory, rather than one premised on trade sanctions.

Finally, investors from commercially insignificant states have supplied capital to foreign governments, even though their governments could do little damage to defaulters. Throughout history, loans have flowed not only from Britain and the United States but also from small states such as Switzerland, Belgium, Denmark, and the Netherlands. It is hard to believe countries would repay to maintain access to Swiss-sized markets, yet citizens of small states repeatedly risk their capital abroad. Moreover, as shown in chapter 6, investors from small states experience no higher default rates than investors from larger (and more commercially powerful) countries such as Britain, France, Germany, and the United States.

### *Why Have Trade Sanctions Played Such a Small Role?*

Why have governments so consistently avoided making commercial relations contingent on debt repayment? There are several possibilities. First, such linkage may not be in the interests of creditors. A sovereign debtor needs foreign currency to service its external debts, and practically the only way to obtain such funds over the long run is through earnings from foreign trade. In fact, it is reasonable to think about foreign loans as advances on future exports. Sanctions reduce the earnings from trade, and in this sense they are counterproductive.

Even if sanctions could help bondholders and commercial banks, though, the creditor government may have other priorities that argue against using trade as a weapon. Trade sanctions would damage the lending economy, especially if trade with the debtor is an important source of gains from exchange. Sanctions would also have distributional consequences, hurting exporters and selected importers in the lending country. The linkage hypothesis requires the central government to side consistently with bondholders and banks at the expense of trading interests. This seems unlikely, given that exporters and importers have been relatively concentrated throughout history, whereas bondholders—the principal lenders to foreign governments—have been more atomized and vulnerable to problems of collective action.

Finally, the political representatives of bondholders and banks may avoid trade sanctions on purely practical grounds. In many cases, a defaulting government could minimize its punishment by finding new commercial partners or transshipping products through other states. Knowing that sanctions would be largely ineffective in the presence of third parties, it makes sense for the lenders' government to avoid them.

## Conclusion

This chapter has shown that the threat of trade sanctions probably does not sustain lending and repayment. Between the two world wars, governments did not service debts in proportion to their dependence on trade with creditors, nor did they offer preferential treatment to the specific creditors that were most capable of imposing a trade embargo. I uncovered only two examples of a debt-trade connection (Germany and Romania), and many more instances in which it played no role at all. Moreover, careful investigation revealed that Argentina, long upheld as exemplar of the embargo hypothesis, paid out of concern for reputation, not trade. Thus, the chapter not only showed via statistical analysis that commercial threats were of little significance during the 1930s, the decade when linkages between debt and trade supposedly reached their height, but also disproved the Argentine case that helped inspire the hypothesis in the first place.

Other types of evidence, from other historical periods, support the same conclusion. I uncovered no hint of trade sanctions in diplomatic correspondence and found only two references of the possibility in more than 96,000 pages of newspaper clippings about foreign lending. One reference came from a private bondholder who petitioned but received no satisfaction from the British government; the other involved an unauthorized threat that was never carried out.

Other examples may eventually turn up, perhaps in the late twentieth century (a period only briefly covered by the data in this chapter), but it seems that governments rarely, if ever, link finance with trade in an effort to enforce private loan contracts. Although plausible in theory, the embargo hypotheses and other trade-related mechanisms have not proven particularly relevant in practice. Reputation-based theory provides a more reliable guide to the behavior of debtors and creditors.

# Chapter 8

## Enforcement through Collective Retaliation

PREVIOUS CHAPTERS not only tested the predictions of reputational theory, but also searched for signs of other cooperation-promoting mechanisms. I found little evidence that creditors enforce commitments by linking debt default to nonfinancial penalties, such as trade sanctions and military intervention. This chapter presents additional tests of the idea that retaliation, rather than reputation, underpins cooperation. The chapter examines an intuitive and widely cited measure of retaliatory power: the international cohesion of creditors.

A rock-solid creditor cartel could impose penalties that are beyond the reach of more atomized lenders. Economic sanctions, in particular, stand the greatest chance of success when creditors collaborate to deprive a defaulter of new loans or international trade. Without extensive collaboration, a debtor could exploit holes in a financial or commercial embargo and play some creditors against others. Diplomatic and military sanctions are also more likely when creditors form a tight coalition. Although private investors cannot sever diplomatic ties or launch military assaults, they can solicit support from their home government. The more cohesive the creditor lobby, the higher the probability of winning support from politicians who could order a retaliatory strike. Thus, cohesion among creditors should widen the range and improve the efficacy of threats to punish a defaulting state.

As explained in detail below, banks are more cohesive than bondholders, and should therefore have more retaliatory power. Groups can organize most easily when they have a small number of members that are long-lived, readily identifiable, geographically concentrated, and relatively homogenous.[1] Institutions can also make organization easier, as can a hegemon that cajoles others into doing their share. Banks rank higher than bondholders on all these organizational dimensions.

To the extent that creditor cohesion matters, three patterns should be evident. First, investors should prefer lending through banks, rather than purchasing bonds on an open market. Second, governments should default less often against banks than against bondholders. Third, interest rates and other protections against risk should decline as the cohesion of creditors increases. The evidence in this chapter is at odds with all three predictions.

---

[1] Olson 1965.

## Why Banks Can Punish More Effectively Than Bondholders

Banks possess an organizational and retaliatory advantage over bond-holders for many reasons. The first is group size. Tens of thousands of investors hold the bonds of developing countries. In contrast, only a few hundred commercial banks supply credit to foreign governments, and less than a dozen take the lead in arranging almost all sovereign loans. Members of this exclusive community interact regularly in domestic and international affairs. Their small numbers imply that, in comparison with bondholders, banks can "more easily engage in group action and threaten the borrower with penalties" in the event of default.[2]

Second, banks are more visible and long-lived than bondholders, and therefore more capable of initiating and sustaining collective action. The leading commercial lenders to sovereign governments—Bank of America, Chase Manhattan, Citicorp, Morgan Guarantee, Wells Fargo, and the like—have existed for decades and are household names. These actors have no trouble identifying each other, and they can conceivably work together over the long run. In contrast, most sovereign bonds belong to anonymous investors who trade their holdings in a fluid market, making it practically impossible to track down the relevant actors and establish ongoing relationships among them.[3]

Third, international banks cluster in major financial centers, facilitating face-to-face communication that bondholders cannot match. Nearly all banks that participate in international lending maintain branches in Manhattan or London, but bondholders are scattered far and wide. Because of the anonymous nature of securities trading, no precise information exists on the whereabouts of bondholders. One indication comes from the 1940s, when all U.S. citizens were required by executive order to report their holdings of foreign bonds. Although the census "failed to reach a large fraction of bondholders," the Treasury concluded from responses it received that foreign dollar bonds were "very widely distributed geographically." Residents of all 48 states and the District of Columbia held foreign bonds, typically in small blocks averaging about $3,000 per investor.[4]

---

[2] De Grauwe and Fratianni 1984, 159. See also Lessard and Williamson (1985, 41), who argue that the "concentration" of loans "in relatively few lending institutions" has "enhanced the enforceability of developing-country obligations"; Edwards (1986, 568), who says that the cohesiveness of banks "gives them an additional advantage to impose sanctions on those countries that default"; and Gersovitz (1985, 73), who claims that the prospect of imposing sanctions declines when ownership of debt is more dispersed.

[3] Prior to World War II, more than 99 percent of bonds were bearer bonds, meaning that investors did not register with the debtor, the underwriter, or any other party (Lisman 1934, 24). Even today most emerging market bonds are bearer instruments (Eichengreen and Rühl 2001, 9).

[4] U.S. Department of the Treasury 1947, 38, 41. See also Morrow 1927.

Fourth, banks are more homogenous than bondholders. Most banks have a common organizational structure and arrange loans with similar characteristics. For these reasons, Lessard and Williamson expect "relatively little conflict of interest among banks" in choosing a collective response to default, "such as a cutoff of future trade or finance."[5] The bondholder community is more diverse. Heterogeneity among the private investors, brokers, banks, hedge funds, pension funds, and insurance companies that buy foreign securities only aggravates the organizational problems bondholders face.[6]

Fifth, banks can draw on a wider range of cooperation-promoting mechanisms than bondholders. Commercial banks form syndicates to share the risk of lending. These syndicates, which always include a lead bank, provide a chain of communication and command that can be invoked in the event of default.[7] Since bondholders purchase securities on the open market, rather than organizing to grant loans, they lack prefabricated structures that could make collective action easier. Banks can also enforce seniority and cross-default clauses between each other more successfully than bondholders, which further "enhances their abilities to impose penalties on reluctant debtors."[8]

Sixth, hegemonic actors are more likely to facilitate cooperation among banks than among bondholders. One potential hegemon, the lenders' home government, pays close attention to the balance sheets of banks, since defaults against those institutions could imperil the domestic financial system. If collective action failed to emerge spontaneously in response to default, regulators and central bankers might pressure uncooperative banks. Governments presumably would devote less attention to bondholders, who could suffer losses without putting the financial system at risk. At any rate, it would be difficult to twist the arms of many thousands of bond owners. As U.S. Treasury secretary Lawrence Summers noted, "Governments have far fewer powers of suasion" over bondholders than over commercial banks.[9]

Other potential hegemons are unlikely to assist bondholders. The most obvious candidates, underwriting houses, have legal and economic conflicts of interest. Bond contracts typically treat the underwriter as an agent of the *borrower*, not the lender.[10] Furthermore, underwriters earn commis-

---

[5] Lessard and Williamson 1985, 42.

[6] Spiegel 1996.

[7] Lipson 1981, 1985; Uppal and Van Hulle 1997.

[8] Kletzer 1988, 594.

[9] Summers in *Economist*, December 23, 1995–January 5, 1996, 48. See also Eichengreen 1999, 66.

[10] This has been the case for centuries. See Riley 1980, 206.

sions not only for floating new loans but also for serving as fiscal agents of foreign governments.[11] My own analysis of 637 foreign bonds launched during the 1920s reveals that the underwriter served as a fiscal agent in 84 percent of the cases.[12] Helping bondholders punish a defaulter might bring this profitable business to an end. *Forbes* magazine drew the appropriate conclusion: in the area of foreign bonds, "Neither the American [underwriter] nor the American government is likely to undertake effective action to secure the return of the investor's money. The only element of protection which is open to him, therefore, is the privilege of looking before he leaps."[13]

Seventh, banks not only enjoy an organizational advantage over bondholders, but they also control more retaliatory weapons. Banks dispense short-term credits that grease the wheels of international commerce. They could, therefore, punish a defaulter by depriving its exporters and importers of working capital. Bondholders cannot use the same linkage strategy, because they do not supply short-term trade credits. This fact gives banks "a comparative advantage in imposing sanctions."[14]

Overall, then, banks can retaliate far more effectively than bondholders. Table 8.1 summarizes the reasons. If this retaliatory advantage is important, bank loans should be preferred by investors, be subject to lower default rates, and be offered on more attractive terms than bonds. I test these hypotheses in the remainder of the chapter.

## Do Investors Prefer Bank Loans?

If sanctions are needed to keep debtors in line, it makes little sense to purchase bonds on the open market, thereby forgoing any serious chance of collective retaliation. Instead, investors should lend through well-orga-

---

[11] Dulles 1932, 478–79.

[12] This figure probably understates the overlap, since the apparent disconnect between the underwriter and the fiscal agent could have been an artifact of bank mergers and name changes that were difficult to track.

[13] *Forbes*, October 1, 1929, 30.

[14] Gersovitz 1985, 73. Bird and Snowden (1997, 210) argue that "one problem confronting bond markets . . . arises in connection with the sanctions for non repayment available to such investors." They emphasize that banks "through their provision of trade credit were able to enforce sanctions . . . it is much less certain that bond investors could have done so." Lessard and Williamson (1985, 41–42) maintain that bank debt is relatively more enforceable, since banks can withhold trade credit in response to default on long-term loans. Many mathematical models of debtor-creditor relations rest on the premise that banks penalize countries that do not repay by restricting access to credit that would facilitate trade. See, e.g., Fernández and Glazer 1990, 300.

TABLE 8.1
Why Banks Can Sanction More Effectively Than Bondholders

|  | Banks | Bondholders |
|---|---|---|
| Is the number of actors small? | Yes | No |
| Are the actors easy to identify? | Yes | No |
| Are the actors geographically concentrated? | Yes | No |
| Do the actors have homogeneous interests? | Yes | No |
| Do institutions exist to organize the actors? | Yes | No |
| Are hegemons willing to organize the actors? | Yes | No |
| Do the actors have many retaliatory options? | Yes | No |

nized intermediaries such as commercial banks that could conceivably force a defaulter to pay.

Scholars invoke this logic to explain bank-based lending. According to economist Kenneth Kletzer, "The domination of syndicated bank lending over bond lending" and other strategies "can be seen as outcomes of the enforceability problem in sovereign lending."[15] David Folkerts-Landau, too, attributes the large share of development finance flowing through banks to "comprehensive advantages gained by international bank lenders over more traditional sources of development finance." Banks, he claims, are "better equipped" than bondholders to deal with the risk of default, because banks can "form credible coalitions" against delinquent borrowers.[16] If sanctions are important, bank lending should be the norm, rather than the exception.

### Historical Rates of Bond and Bank Lending

The historical record reveals the opposite pattern. During the past half millennium, private investors financed foreign governments almost entirely through bonds, while commercial banks traditionally confined themselves to facilitating trade among private companies. The situation changed only in the late 1960s, when commercial banks began lending to foreign governments on a large scale.[17] Although it may be etched in the

---

[15] Kletzer 1988, 590.

[16] Folkerts-Landau 1985, 318. See also De Grauwe and Fratianni 1984, 158–59. Alexander (1987, 91–92) theorizes that not only investors but also borrowers should prefer bank lending, due to the enforcement advantages of bank-based lending.

[17] To find a precedent for the bank-centered lending of the 1970s and 1980s, one must look back more than 400 years to the era of Genoese financial dynasties. My understanding of sovereign lending since the 1960s has been aided by many studies, including Aggarwal 1987, 1996; Cline 1995; Cline and Barnes 1997; Cohen 1985, 1986; Cohen 1991; Cuddington 1989; Devlin 1985, 1989; Díaz Alejandro 1984, 1986; Dooley 1995; Eichengreen and Mody 2000; Frieden 1991; Haggard 2000; Helleiner 1994; Kahler 1985; Kapstein 1994;

memories of scholars and practitioners who lived through the 1980s, the recent episode of bank lending to foreign sovereigns is a historical blip.

Moreover, the tide has again turned in favor of bonds. The Brady initiative of 1989 converted many bank loans into bonds, and now most new sovereign lending involves tradable securities. Figure 8.1 quantifies bond and bank loans to public borrowers in developing countries since 1970. The top panel shows gross lending (disbursements), and the bottom panel depicts net lending (disbursements minus amortization). The panels show that, on both measures, bonds have outstripped banks in every year since the mid-1990s. Neither the historical dominance of bond-based lending, nor its return after a brief interregnum, seems consistent with sanction-based theories of enforcement.

Nevertheless, the rise and fall of bank lending in the late twentieth century seems puzzling. Why, exactly, did commercial banks corner the sovereign lending market during the 1970s, and why did they recede in importance only a few years later?

If enforcement problems were especially severe in the 1970s, investors might have turned to banks to meet their unprecedented retaliatory needs. To test this hypothesis, one requires a long-run measure of enforcement problems in international lending. Real interest rates provide one plausible index. The temptation to default increases with real interest rates, which increase the potential windfall from default (the opportunity cost of paying). As interest rates rise, lenders in a sanction-based world would need ever more powerful punishment options to deter governments from defaulting.

On the contrary, figure 8.2 shows that real interest rates were low during the 1970s, the decade when bank lending exploded. In fact, real rates fell below zero for much of the period, due to inflation in creditor countries such as the United States and the United Kingdom. Thus, lenders with the greatest capacity to impose sanctions dominated the market at a time when, from the standpoint of deterrence, they were least necessary.

If enforceability problems do not explain why bank lending expanded during the 1970s, what encouraged the atypical lending pattern? In part, Persian Gulf countries poured money into banks during the oil shocks of the 1970s, giving liquidity to actors that had not previously participated in sovereign lending. Banks "recycled" much of the money in the form of loans to the third world. At the same time, loan guarantees and tax loop-

Kapur, Lewis, and Webb 1997; Kaufman 1988; Lindert 1989; Lindert and Morton 1989; Lipson 1979, 1981, 1985; Lissakers 1991; Mauro, Sussman, and Yafeh 2006; Obstfeld and Taylor 2004; Sachs 1982, 1985, 1986, 1989; Sachs and Huizinga 1987; Sobel 1999; Stallings 1987; Stone 2002; Sturzenegger and Zettelmeyer 2006a; Verdier 2003, chap. 8; and Wellons 1987.

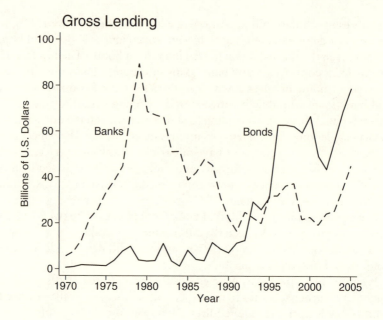

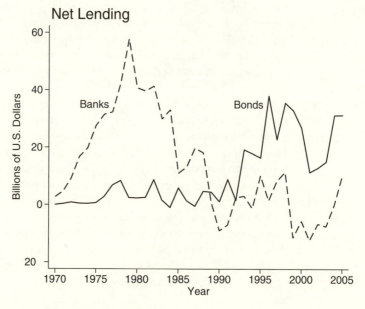

FIGURE 8.1: GROSS AND NET LENDING TO PUBLIC BORROWERS IN DEVELOPING COUNTRIES, 1970–2005
Data are in billions of U.S. dollars at year 2005 prices.
*Source*: Loan data are from World Bank 2006, deflated by the U.S. GDP price index from U.S. Department of Commerce, Bureau of Economic Analysis 2006.

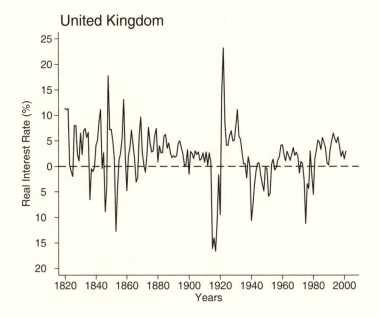

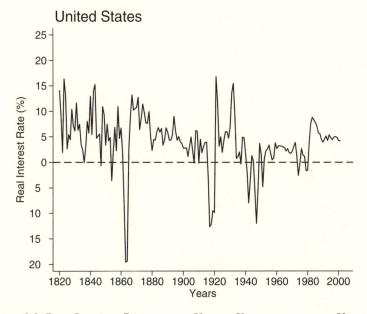

FIGURE 8.2: REAL INTEREST RATES IN THE UNITED KINGDOM AND THE UNITED
STATES, 1820–2005
*Source*: United Kingdom and United States long-term interest rates from Officer 2006,
deflated by inflation rates in McCusker 2006.

holes began to favor banks over bonds. The guarantees and loopholes were partially closed after the debt crisis of the 1980s, allowing bonds to regain their traditional role as the principal vehicles for sovereign lending. This little-known story is worth telling, because it helps explain a phenomenon that some have mistakenly interpreted as an outgrowth of the need for sanctions.

### Guarantees, Regulations, and Bank Lending

Bank lending surged, in part, because monetary authorities appeared increasingly willing to guarantee bank loans. In 1974 the U.S. Federal Reserve bailed out Franklin National Bank, which had supplied euroloans through its London office. A few months later, central bankers from the Group of Ten nations issued a public statement that many interpreted as a promise to supply lender-of-last-resort facilities not only to resident parent banks, but also to overseas branches. With this step, the G10 "provided the financial marketplace with the safety net that it needed before [petrodollar] recycling could proceed."[18] The bond market had not been included in this "broadening implicit insurance scheme."[19]

At the same time, banks were given considerable latitude to participate in sovereign lending. When operating domestically, banks are required to meet capital adequacy requirements, such as maintaining a sufficient ratio of reserves to loans and limiting their exposure to risky borrowers. These requirements not only enhance the safety of the domestic banking system, but also give public authorities a way to control the money supply. Banks faced far fewer restraints on their international operations during the 1960s and 1970s. During that period, many banks opened offshore branches to evade the reach of domestic regulators. Those branches, operating in what became known as the euromarket, lent to foreigners without the reserve requirements and other constraints that governed domestic banking.[20] The combination of light regulations and implicit loan guarantees helped banks rise to prominence in sovereign lending.[21]

Regulations tightened in the 1980s, partly in response to the Latin American debt crisis that had destabilized the international banking system. The U.S. Congress passed the International Lending Supervision Act of 1983, which required banks to increase their ratio of capital to total

---

[18] Kapstein 1994, 66.

[19] Edwards 1986, 569.

[20] Surveillance and control of the euromarket was so light that, for much of the 1970s, the U.S. Federal Reserve did not even have reliable data on the foreign claims and liabilities of international banks.

[21] McKinnon 1986, 334–35.

assets and establish loan-loss reserves for problem debt. The act also reduced secrecy by compelling banks to disclose details of their less-developed country (LDC) lending on a quarterly basis. Moreover, the act limited the fees banks could charge to restructure outstanding loans, and it authorized regulators to apply stricter criteria when assessing the safety of international portfolios. According to the chairman of the Senate Committee on Banking, Congress imposed the regulations to show that it "didn't bail out those big banks" and to ensure that banks would never again overlend to the developing world.[22]

Banks warned that the new regulations would stifle international lending. A top officer from First Boston predicted that the measures would have a "chilling effect" on bank participation in international credit markets, while the vice chairman of Chase Manhattan maintained that supervision would "diminish the ability of banks to furnish needed new credit." These predictions apparently came to pass. When Congress revisited the legislation three years later, experts testified that "tighter regulation of international lending, including the 1983 Lending Supervision Act, and the continuing problems of the debtors, mean that banks view cross-border lending to LDCs not as an area for future growth but a problem of cost containment."[23] Thus, bank involvement in sovereign lending waxed and waned in response to changes in regulations, rather than the need for retaliation against debtors.

### Tax Loopholes and Bank Lending

Tax laws also contributed to the surge of bank lending during the 1970s. At the time, banks in the United States, the United Kingdom, and other financial centers exploited tax loopholes that made sovereign lending highly profitable.

Banks were able to evade taxes on foreign loans because fiscal authorities in Washington and London assessed taxes on *profits* while granting tax credits in proportion to *revenues*. To see how the process worked, suppose that Manufacturers Hanover collected $250 million in revenue from loans to Brazil.[24] After deducting operating expenses and the cost of funds, the bank might have realized a $20 million profit, which during the 1970s would have been taxed in the United States at a rate of 46 percent. In theory, then, Manufacturers Hanover would owe $9 million

---

[22] Jake Garn in U.S. Congress, Senate Committee on Banking 1983, 95.

[23] Peter Read in U.S. Congress, House Committee on Banking 1983, 109; William Ogden in *New York Times*, February 10, 1983, D1; Karin Lissakers in U.S. Congress, Senate Committee on Banking 1986b, 45–46.

[24] The example comes from *American Banker*, May 15, 1986, 23.

to the U.S. Internal Revenue Service. Further suppose that the government of Brazil taxed the bank by withholding 25 percent of the bank's total revenues. To avoid double taxation, the IRS would have allowed the bank to claim a credit for $63 million (25 percent of $250 million).

"The real genius of the arrangement," according to Karin Lissakers, former U.S. executive director of the International Monetary Fund, was that "banks in most instances didn't actually pay the withholding taxes that generated the valuable credits."[25] Loan contracts typically stipulated that banks would receive the stated interest rate *net* of any withholding taxes. In other words, borrowers were required to pay not only the interest but also the taxes in their own jurisdictions. Banks nonetheless received credits as if they, rather than the borrowers, had paid the foreign taxes. In the previous example, Manufacturers Hanover would have received a net tax credit of $54 million ($63 million less the $9 million that would have been its U.S. liability), which it could have used to offset taxes on income from loans in other countries.

Developing countries began "grossing up" the interest rate to compensate for withholding taxes around 1974. Within two years every developing country except the Philippines adopted the procedure to attract foreign loans.[26] Former members of the British Empire achieved the same effect through less intricate means. Under U.K. law, banks could claim tax credits for loans to ex-colonies, even when the borrower had completely waived its right to levy a tax.[27] Thus, one way or another, banks received credits for taxes they never paid.

Tax credits from LDC loans rose to enormous proportions during the 1970s and were "probably the most important tax shelter for large banks."[28] With the help of such credits, leading financial institutions paid an effective U.S. tax rate of only 3.8 percent, compared with the nominal federal rate of 46 percent.[29] Intentionally or inadvertently, tax authorities in the United States and other financial centers subsidized bank lending to developing countries. One way to quantify the subsidy is to measure its

[25] Lissakers 1991, 119.

[26] Lissakers 1991, 125–26. Some countries achieved a similar result through a system of subsidies. In the case of Brazil, the borrower paid the withholding tax on behalf of the foreign bankers, but it also received a matching rebate from the Brazilian government, thereby reducing the tax to a mere bookkeeping entry. Nevertheless, banks got receipts as if the tax had been paid in full. The Brazilian tax-and-rebate system stemmed from an effort the government began in 1974 to stimulate investment by reducing the interest cost on loans by foreign banks. See *Washington Post*, June 9, 1978, F1; *American Banker*, December 24, 1985, 2; *Bankers Magazine*, January–February 1986, 76–79.

[27] These tax-spared loans were of special benefit to Malaysia, India, and Pakistan.

[28] *American Banker*, June 13, 1985, 3.

[29] U.S. Congress, Joint Committee on Taxation 1984, 22.

effect on the profitability of transactions. On average, foreign tax credits doubled the return on loans to LDCs.[30] Credits proved so lucrative that some banks lent at negative spreads (interest rates that would not even cover their costs), knowing they could turn a profit thanks to tax loopholes. Clearly, tax credits provided a major incentive for banks to lend to the developing world.

In 1982 the banks narrowly averted a threat to their privileged tax position. That year, the British Chancellor of the Exchequer announced his intention to curb the tax credits, which had enabled banks to lend at much lower interest rates than otherwise would have been the case. The proposal ignited a "storm of protest" from the British Bankers' Association, which argued that the change would make banks uncompetitive and force them to renegotiate existing loans. In the face of these protests, the British Treasury agreed to water down the reforms, and the final measure produced "little effective change" in policy.[31] For the moment the banks were spared.

The devastating blow occurred across the Atlantic only four years later, when the U.S. Congress severely restricted the use of foreign tax credits. Since the 1960s the U.S. government had allowed banks to offset the income they earned in one foreign country with tax credits from another. Banks took advantage of this opportunity by applying credits from the developing world to wipe out taxes in more advanced regions, where credits were typically unavailable.[32] In 1986 Congress sought to change the rules by requiring banks to allocate credits on a country-by-country basis, instead of putting all foreign income and credit in a common pool. Under the proposed rules, credits earned in Brazil would offset income only from Brazil, and any surplus Brazilian credits would go to waste.[33]

Banks objected that the proposed rule would remove their incentive to lend at a time when the Baker plan called for new money. The plan, proposed by U.S. Treasury secretary James Baker in October 1985, sought

---

[30] Lissakers 1991, 116, 125, 127, 131. A senior vice president of Bankers Trust corroborated these estimates: at a time when the average spread on syndicated loans was 1 percent, he estimated that banks would have to raise overseas rates by 1–2 percent if the tax credits suddenly disappeared (*Business Week*, January 28, 1980, 120; November 9, 1981, 84).

[31] *Financial Times*, March 15, 1982, sec. II, 17; March 19, 1982, sec. I, 9; May 29, 1982, sec. I, 4; September 27, 1982, sec. III, xii.

[32] Governments in western Europe and Japan conventionally did not withhold taxes on bank income, and therefore did not provide U.S. banks with receipts that would reduce the bill to the IRS.

[33] It is hard to know exactly how much this reform would have cost the banks. One estimate, based on annual reports and interviews with tax counsels, suggests that the annual loss to Manufacturers Hanover alone would have been $30–70 million. See *American Banker*, May 15, 1986, 23.

to increase flows of private and official capital to debtor countries.[34] The president of the American Bankers Association, whose members represent more than 95 percent of assets in the industry, testified that banks had lent "to borrowers in Latin America and less developed countries . . . under the assumption that the U.S. tax rules would continue to allow full credit for all gross withholding taxes." The proposed reforms would undermine the profitability of the loans.[35] Top executives from Chase Manhattan, Chemical Bank, Manufacturers Hanover, Mellon, Marine Midland, Morgan Guarantee, and other large institutions warned that the reforms would discourage new lending to less-developed countries and force banks to renegotiate old loans at higher spreads.[36]

Fearing that rapid reform would "torpedo" the Baker initiative, the Treasury urged legislators to phase in the reforms gradually.[37] Congress relented: income from loans to 33 developing countries would remain exempt from the new limitations on tax creditability until 1990. Nevertheless, the new law dissuaded forward-looking banks from getting more deeply involved in sovereign lending, particularly to the third world. According to Eli Fink, partner with the accounting firm of Deloitte, Haskins & Sells, the 1986 tax reform created "tax disincentives to operating overseas. The earnings reasons aren't there anymore."[38] About the same time, the United Kingdom reduced tax breaks for its own banks.[39]

Banks suffered another blow in May 1989, when an IRS ruling further undermined the usefulness of foreign tax credits. Under U.S. law, banks can apply foreign tax credits against domestic liabilities, but only to the extent that foreign operations are profitable. Some big banks had been applying a large portion of their foreign loan losses against *domestic* income to make foreign profits as large as possible. The bigger the foreign

[34] In return for new loans, debtors would be required to adopt economic policy reforms.

[35] Senterfitt in U.S. Congress, Senate Committee on Banking 1986a, 178.

[36] Shipley in U.S. Congress, Senate Committee on Banking 1986a, 220, 231; Esposito in U.S. Congress, House Committee on Ways and Means 1985, 7450–51; Petty in U.S. Congress, House Committee on Ways and Means 1985, 7376–77; *American Banker*, May 19, 1986, 1; August 19, 1986, 1; *Christian Science Monitor*, July 15, 1986, 19.

[37] *American Banker*, April 14, 1986, 47; June 2, 1986, 1.

[38] *American Banker*, March 7, 1988, 2.

[39] Inland Revenue, the British equivalent of the IRS, contended that banks were sheltering unreasonable amounts of U.K.-derived income by aggressively exploiting loopholes in the tax law. An extensive investigation led to new rules that were even more restrictive than their U.S. counterparts. Starting in 1987, banks were forced to allocate credits on a transaction-by-transaction basis, such that credits from one loan would apply only to profits from that loan, and could not offset other income from that country or from any other. The new rules increased the cost of borrowing for many third world nations and deterred banks from extending new loans. See *American Banker*, December 22, 1986, 1; March 27, 1987, 2; *Wall Street Journal*, March 25, 1987, 1; *Financial Times*, June 11, 1987, sec. I, 9.

profits, the more they could use foreign tax credits to reduce their U.S. tax bills. With its new ruling, the IRS required each bank to apply loan losses against income in proportion to the split between the bank's foreign and domestic business. According to one estimate, banks lost about $20 billion in credits as a result of the new IRS ruling.[40]

Thus, in a series of momentous steps, authorities closed the tax loopholes that banks had exploited during the 1970s. The loopholes had attracted banks to the third world; their elimination had the opposite effect. Writing in the early 1990s, Lissakers observed that "many of the tax benefits of lending to LDCs have disappeared, accelerating the pace of bank disengagement from sovereign lending."[41]

In summary, bank lending rose to prominence as a result of several interrelated factors: excess bank liquidity during the oil shocks of the 1970s, a regulatory environment that encouraged banks to undertake risky loans, and tax laws that made bank loans artificially profitable. When liquidity returned to more normal levels and the regulatory and tax loopholes disappeared, banks withdrew from sovereign lending and bonds regained their historically prominent position. Investors throughout history have not used bank intermediaries to maximize their collective retaliatory power. Instead they have purchased bonds directly, knowing that reputation creates powerful incentives even in atomized capital markets.

## Do Bank Loans Experience Lower Default Rates?

If collective retaliation is important, bank loans should not only be preferred by investors, but should also experience lower rates of default. I tested this hypothesis by analyzing how sovereign governments treated creditors between 1970 and 2004. I first identified all country-years in which governments owed money to *both* foreign bondholders and commercial banks.[42] I then limited the sample for each sovereign to years in which it had defaulted on at least some obligations, and therefore faced a choice between treating all creditors equally or repaying some but not others.[43] The final sample included 292 annual observations from 39 developing countries.

[40] *American Banker*, May 2, 1989, 1, 15; May 3, 1989, 3; *Wall Street Journal*, May 4, 1989, B5; *Financial Times*, May 5, 1989, sec. I, 34; *Magazine of Bank Management*, July 1989, 10.

[41] Lissakers 1991, 136.

[42] Data on debts owed by governments (and by private entities with sovereign guarantees) came from World Bank 2006.

[43] Standard & Poor's (2004, 22) provided the data on defaults, defined as "the failure to meet a principal or interest payment on the due date" specified in "the original terms of the

TABLE 8.2
Defaults on Bonds and Bank Loans, 1970–2004

| | Defaulted on Bonds | Did Not Default on Bonds | Total |
|---|---|---|---|
| Defaulted on bank loans | 7% (N = 21) | 84% (N = 246) | 91% (N = 267) |
| Did not default on bank loans | 9% (N = 25) | | 9% (N = 25) |
| Total | 16% (N = 46) | 84% (N = 246) | 100% (N = 292) |

Source: Evidence of indebtedness to banks and bondholders comes from World Bank 2006. Dates of defaults are given in Standard & Poor's 2004.

Note: The table contains annual entries for countries that owed money to *both* banks and bondholders, and were in default on at least some of these obligations. The data pertain to 39 countries.

Table 8.2 summarizes the decisions these countries made. The table shows 246 country-years in which countries favored the *weaker* creditor, by repaying bondholders but defaulting against banks. In contrast, the sample contained only 25 country-years in which the stronger creditor secured payment while the weaker one did not. This is not the pattern one would expect from sanction-focused debtors.[44]

Bondholders may have escaped default because their holdings were small, especially in the 1970s and 1980s.[45] To see whether this was the case, I conducted an ordered probit analysis of repayment decisions. Did countries treat bondholders more favorably, I asked, after controlling for the composition of external debt? Put another way, would governments have discriminated if they had owed equal amounts to bondholders and banks?

The ordered probit model in figure 8.3 is designed to answer this question. The model involves a continuous latent variable $(y^*)$ that measures how strongly the sovereign prefers bondholders over bankers. Researchers cannot observe exactly where a government sits on this spectrum, but they can see the resulting behavior and summarize it with the discrete variable $y$. Governments with a strong predilection for bondholders $(y^* > \tau_{bond})$ will pay bonds but default on banks, resulting in the observed outcome $y = 1$. Governments with a keen preference for banks $(y^* < \tau_{bank})$ will do the reverse, leading to $y = -1$, and governments between these extremes will treat both classes equally, such that $y = 0$.

---

debt issue." Thus, default on commercial bank loans occurred when the government did not pay in full on time, or when it rescheduled "at less favorable terms than the original loan." Likewise, a default on bonds occurred when the government underpaid or swapped existing debt for new issues with less attractive terms.

[44] Summarizing the data by countries leads to a similar conclusion: 29 countries always favored bondholders, 7 countries favored bondholders in some years and banks in other years, and only 3 always gave preference to banks.

[45] Buchheit 1995, 49; *Financial Times*, February 18, 1999, 6.

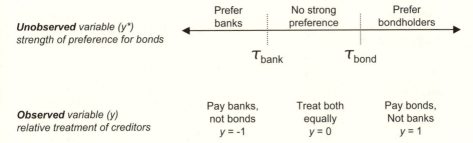

FIGURE 8.3: ORDERED PROBIT MODEL OF DISCRIMINATORY REPAYMENT BY BORROWERS

The key explanatory variable in the model is bonded debt as a proportion of total obligations to bondholders and banks. The model also includes lagged indicators of default against bonds and banks, to control for dynamic effects. Finally, the model includes a dummy variable for a structural shift in debtor behavior, beginning with the Mexican crisis of 1995. The complete model for country $i$ in time $t$ is

$$y_{i,t}^* \sim N(\mu_{i,t}, 1)$$

$$\mu_{i,t} = \beta_1 \frac{\text{Bond}_{i,t}}{\text{Bond}_{i,t} + \text{Bank}_{i,t}} + \beta_2(\text{Year} > 1994) + \beta_3 \text{BondDefault}_{i,t-1} + \beta_4 \text{BankDefault}_{i,t-1}$$

$$y_{i,t} = \begin{cases} 1 \text{ if } y_{i,t}^* > \tau_{bond} \\ -1 \text{ if } y_{i,t}^* < \tau_{bank} \\ 0 \text{ otherwise} \end{cases}$$

I estimated the unknown parameters (the $\beta$'s and the $\tau$'s) via maximum likelihood, computed robust standard errors (clustered by country) to adjust for dependence among observations from the same country, and used simulation to interpret the results.

The probit analysis confirms that bondholders received special treatment partly because they represented a small share of the capital account. In table 8.3, the estimated coefficient on "bond debt as a proportion of total debt" is negative and highly significant. This estimate implies that, as bonds increase in importance, governments are less likely to pay bondholders while defaulting on banks. The table also shows a temporal shift: governments are now less likely to favor bondholders than they were in earlier years. Other coefficients in the equation carry the expected signs and are statistically different from zero.

To further interpret the coefficients in table 8.3, I considered a hypothetical country that initiated a default after having paid all creditors in the previous year. Figure 8.4 displays the predicted relationship between the composition of debt and discrimination against banks, computed as

TABLE 8.3
Ordered Probit Analysis of Discrimination in Favor of Bondholders, 1970–2004

| Variable | Estimated Coefficient | Standard Error | t-statistic |
|---|---|---|---|
| Bond debt as proportion of total debt | –1.36 | 0.31 | 4.4 |
| Years after 1994 | –0.58 | 0.30 | 1.9 |
| Default on bonds in previous year | –2.33 | 0.32 | 7.3 |
| Default on banks in previous year | 1.24 | 0.23 | 5.4 |

Source: Same as in table 6.2.

Note: The sample is the same as in table 6.2, with $N = 292$ annual observations involving 39 countries. The dependent variable measures discrimination in favor of bondholders. It takes on a value of 1 if the borrower paid bonds but defaulted on bank loans, 0 if the borrower defaulted on both types of debt, and –1 if the borrower paid bank loans but defaulted on bonds. Standard errors are robust and clustered by country. The cutpoint $\tau_{bank}$ was estimated to be –2.35 with a standard error of 0.30, and the cutpoint $\tau_{bond}$ was estimated to be –1.32 with a standard error of 0.24.

the probability that the borrower would repay bondholders but not banks. The top panel shows that, before 1995, debtors discriminated against banks, even after controlling for the composition of the debt. A hypothetical country with a 50–50 split between bond and bank debt favored bondholders roughly 75 percent of the time. The bottom panel shows that discrimination has become less likely since 1995. Today, countries with a 50–50 split do not systematically discriminate against banks.

Overall, the behavior of borrowers contradicts an important implication of sanctioning theory. During debt crises, sanction-fearing countries should repay the strongest creditors while withholding funds from weaker ones. I find, however, that debtors have either favored bondholders or treated both classes of creditors equally, even though banks possess vastly more retaliatory potential.

## Does Creditor Cohesion Make Loans Less Expensive?

Sanctioning theory also predicts a negative relationship between retaliatory power and risk premiums. The ability to punish lowers the risk of default, allowing investors to lend at terms that approach the "risk-free" rate. Conversely, lenders with relatively little punishment power must charge higher rates. As Kenneth Schultz and Barry Weingast explain, "The harder it is to sanction the government for default, the riskier are loans to the sovereign. Consequently, lenders demand a risk premium when lending to a sovereign that cannot be readily punished."[46]

---

[46] Schultz and Weingast 1998, 20.

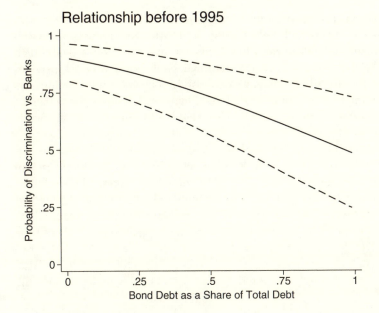

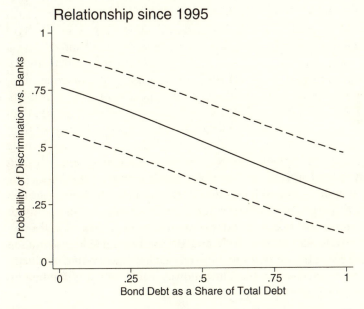

FIGURE 8.4: PREDICTED RELATIONSHIP BETWEEN COMPOSITION OF DEBT AND DISCRIMINATION AGAINST BANKS

Dashed lines are 95 percent confidence intervals.

*Source*: Calculated from the ordered probit estimates in table 8.3.

To test this prediction, I first compared the terms on bank loans with the terms on sovereign bonds. During the 1990s, bank loans to sovereign governments did indeed carry lower interest rates than bonds. The spread (over the risk-free rate) on international bank loans was 1.1 percent, whereas the spread on bonds was almost 2.6 percent.[47] But bondholders were willing to offer significantly longer maturities (8–10 years versus 3–4 for banks). On balance, it is not clear that banks offered more attractive terms to sovereign borrowers.

Moreover, three factors unrelated to sanctioning could explain the difference in interest rates. First, bondholders and banks charge for risk in different ways. Bondholders rely entirely on interest rates, whereas banks cover risks via front-end fees and commissions, in addition to interest rates. Systematic data on bank fees are difficult to obtain. Researchers with access to such data have found, however, that banks impound the risk of default/renegotiation into front-end fees, while charging low interest rates that are relatively insensitive to economic fundamentals.[48] Consequently, tests that focus on interest rates systematically underestimate the price of bank loans, relative to sovereign bonds.

Second, interest rates on bonds and bank loans are set relative to different benchmarks. Sovereign bonds usually involve fixed interest rates, such as 5 percent per annum. Banks loans, on the other hand, typically have floating interest rates: the borrower pays a predetermined spread over a variable base, such as the London interbank offered rate (LIBOR). Through this practice, banks transfer "the risk inherent in fluctuation of international interest rates" to the borrower, instead of bearing it themselves.[49] Without this element of risk, bank loans carry lower spreads than bonds. Moreover, the spreads on fixed-rate sovereign bonds are traditionally expressed relative to U.S. Treasury bills, which are significantly cheaper benchmarks than LIBOR. This reporting convention helps explain why quoted spreads are higher for bonds than for bank loans.

Third, bondholders and banks are subject to different regulations and tax laws. In particular, monetary authorities sometimes stand ready to bail out banks, and tax authorities sometimes offer banks special privileges, as was the case in the 1970s and 1980s. These regulatory and tax differences affect the profitability of sovereign lending, making it difficult to separate the effects of punishment power from other confounding influences on the prices of bonds versus bank loans.

[47] Eichengreen and Mody 2000, 14.

[48] Hallak 2003; Lissakers 1991, 107; Mills and Terrell 1984; and personal interview with Jorge Gallardo Zavala, Former Finance Minister of Ecuador, Cambridge, MA, April 16, 1999.

[49] Cline and Barnes 1997, 10.

I overcome these problems of incommensurability by estimating the effects of retaliatory power *within* the category of bank loans. My analysis centers on the presence, size, and composition of the banking syndicate. A syndicate is a group of banks that jointly lend to a single borrower. Typically one bank, the "lead," manages the operation by reviewing the creditworthiness of the borrower, negotiating the terms of the loan, and recruiting other banks to participate. After closing the deal, the lead bank oversees cash flows and monitors whether parties are honoring their obligations. In exchange for these services the lead manager receives a commission. During the 1960s commercial banks almost never used syndicates for loans to developing countries, because the flow of new money was low. By the 1970s, however, syndications became commonplace, accounting for approximately three-quarters of capital that banks lent to less-developed countries.

Philip Wellons of Harvard asserts that "syndication became popular because, compared to other types of finance, it adds value by . . . deterring default."[50] Syndicates increase the retaliatory power of banks in three ways. First, they make it easier for banks to impose a financial embargo on the borrower. An effective embargo requires the cohesion of many creditors, who must join forces to prohibit the defaulter from tapping international capital markets. Syndicated loan contracts contain features, such as sharing and cross-default clauses, that strengthen the creditor coalition.[51]

Second, syndication increases the probability that lenders could interfere with international trade. To a much greater extent than a single bank, a multinational syndicate could block a country from obtaining normal access to trade credit, and could force a country to ship its products covertly or indirectly to avoid seizure. "Indeed," write economists Jeremy Bulow and Kenneth Rogoff, "it is no accident that syndicated bank loans generally involve banks from all the borrower's major trading partners."[52] Finally, a syndicate could be more effective than a single bank in lobbying policymakers to impose official sanctions, such as the suspension of diplomatic relations. For all these reasons, syndication is said to "strengthen

[50] Wellons 1987, 175.

[51] See, e.g. Sundaram (1989, 453), who claims that syndications "arise basically as a mechanism for credible enforcement of penalties"; and Folkerts-Landau (1985, 327), who asserts that syndications and cross-default clauses "raise the cost of defaulting on any loan," since they help "ensure that a borrower in default will be denied access to the international banking markets and have its external economic relations interrupted."

[52] Bulow and Rogoff 1989a, 175. See also Boehmer and Megginson (1990, 1524), who say that "most problem debtors owe money to banks in all major industrialized countries. Therefore, in the case of default a country would be excluded from trading with virtually all of the industrialized world."

the deterring powers" of banks, thereby providing "additional protection against defaults."[53]

By this logic, the potential for punishment increases with the number of banks that participate in a loan. Syndicates possess more retaliatory power than a single bank, and larger syndicates are more formidable than smaller ones. Smith and Walter highlight the "reduced risk of borrower default against a syndicate of banks as compared to any single bank," since the syndicate is better able to deprive the borrower of access to financial markets.[54] The intuition that syndicates deter default has now been expressed in formal models of lending. These models predict that borrowers who use large syndicates are "a better credit risk, causing the interest rate charged to be lower" than for borrowers with small syndicates or bilateral banking relationships.[55]

Sanction-based theories also imply that the potential for punishment increases with the geographic scope of the lending coalition. When all lenders hail from one country, the threat to punish a defaulter could ring hollow, since financial institutions in other countries could thwart an embargo. The more countries that are implicated in the syndicate, the greater the degree of international cohesion and the greater the punishment power should be.

Under sanctioning theory, a multinational syndicate would not only increase the credibility of financial and trade embargoes, but might also raise the specter of diplomatic pressure. One economist reasons that "a widely syndicated loan from banks in several nations" would "magnify the penalty" associated with default, since "unwillingness to repay debts would bring political pressure from several countries as opposed to only one or two."[56] Thus, the terms of credit should improve not only as the cartel of lenders becomes larger, but also as it becomes more international.

To test these hypotheses, I draw on a unique study conducted by the Center for Transnational Corporations at the United Nations. Precise information about the terms of bank loans to developing countries is notoriously difficult to find. Banks operate on the principle of confidentiality, and they do not disclose the full details of loan transactions. UN researchers managed to lift the veil of secrecy, however, not by extracting information from commercial banks, but by asking borrowers in Latin America to reveal the terms of their loan contracts.

The UN initiated its project in Peru, which ranked among the top 10 LDC borrowers during the 1970s. In an extremely laborious effort, a team

---

[53] Pecchioli 1983, 32.
[54] Smith and Walter 2003, 103; Esty and Megginson 2003.
[55] Chowdhry 1991, 140; see also Uppal and Van Hulle 1997.
[56] Goodman 1983, sec. 3.4, 5.

TABLE 8.4
Terms of Syndicated and Single-Bank Loans to Peru, 1972–76

| Year | Spread over LIBOR | | Flat Fees (%) | | Maturity in Years | |
|---|---|---|---|---|---|---|
| | Syndicates | Single Banks | Syndicates | Single Banks | Syndicates | Single Banks |
| 1972 | 2.1 | 2.0 | | | 6.3 | 6.0 |
| 1973 | 1.7 | 1.6 | 0.5 | 0.1 | 8.8 | 8.1 |
| 1974 | 1.1 | 1.2 | 0.3 | 0.1 | 9.6 | 8.7 |
| 1975 | 1.8 | 1.7 | 1.0 | 0.4 | 5.6 | 6.4 |
| 1976 | 2.2 | 2.0 | 1.4 | 0.3 | 5.0 | 3.2 |
| Average | 1.8 | 1.7 | 0.8 | 0.2 | 7.1 | 6.5 |

Source: Devlin 1985, 132.

of researchers inspected every nonmilitary loan contract on file with the Peruvian Ministry of Economy and Finance from the period 1965 to 1976. Using standardized data collection sheets, the team recorded the name of the borrower, the amount contracted, the pricing and maturity of the loan, the composition of the banking syndicate, and the guarantor (if any) for all medium and long-term financial flows. The result was an unusually comprehensive database covering more than 740 individual commercial loan contracts to the Peruvian public sector.[57]

Data from the UN study show that syndicates did not offer better terms than single banks, despite differences in punishment power. Raw data from this remarkable study have not survived, but summary statistics were published for the years 1972–76, a period covering more than 635 loan contracts.[58] Approximately one-quarter of the money came from single banks; the balance was mobilized via syndication. Table 8.4 shows virtually no difference in the terms of these two kinds of bank loans.

The first set of columns summarizes the interest rate premium, or spread. During the 1970s, nearly all bank loans to developing countries involved a fixed premium over LIBOR, the interest rate at which commercial banks lend to each other. Table 8.4 shows that the average spread over LIBOR for single-bank credits was 1.7 percent, a tad less than the spread of 1.8 percent for syndicated credits. Thus, in the dimension of interest rates, syndicated loans were no cheaper than single-bank loans.

The next set of columns reports transaction fees. In the 1970s, sovereign borrowers paid fees to the lead bank and other members of the syndicate. Negotiated in each case, the fees sometimes rose as high as 2 percent

[57] Devlin 1985, 10, 277.
[58] This estimate is based on the fact that Peru had more than 740 individual loan transactions during the period 1965–76, and 86 percent of these took place during the years 1972–76 (Devlin 1989, 284).

of the principal on the loan. Banks were tight-lipped about fees, some-times at the behest of the borrower, who was willing to pay a higher fee in exchange for a lower interest spread, the one piece of information that is sometimes publicized as a signal of creditworthiness. Nevertheless, the UN team succeeded in obtaining comprehensive data on fees beginning in 1973. Table 8.4 shows that syndicated loans, not single-bank loans, carried higher fees. The difference probably arose from the transaction costs of recruiting many banks, rather than the additional riskiness of syndicated credits.

Finally, table 8.4 reports the average maturity of loans in years. Syndi-cated loans did have longer maturities, but the difference may not be re-lated to punishment power. The average bank contributed $2.8 million to each syndicated loan, versus $5 million when lending in isolation. Single lenders probably favored shorter maturities to compensate for the fact that they were taking bigger stakes and had less opportunity to share risk over the life of the loan.[59] UN researchers interpreted the data in precisely this way.

In summary, the price of bank loans does not seem to be a function of organizational strength. A rare study—containing unusually comprehen-sive information on hundreds of loan contracts to a major sovereign bor-rower—shows that interest rates and fees were slightly more attractive for single-bank loans, whereas syndicates afforded borrowers somewhat more time to repay. We cannot conclude from table 8.4 that syndicates offered cheaper credit than single banks. On the contrary, the terms of credit were roughly equal, despite substantial differences in punishment power.

## Conclusion

This chapter has examined an oft-cited source of creditor power, the cohe-sion of a retaliatory cartel, and found no clear support for the sanctioning mechanism. Banks enjoy many organizational and retaliatory advantages over bondholders. Nonetheless, over the centuries, almost all medium- and long-term loans from private creditors to foreign governments took the form of bonds that were traded in Amsterdam, London, New York, and other capital markets. Commercial banks played an active role in foreign trade by arranging short-term credits for importers and exporters, but they almost never granted multiyear loans to sovereigns.

The late twentieth century stands as a unique moment in the history of international finance, when governments owed large sums to both bond-holders and commercial banks. At that time, borrowers defaulted against

[59] Devlin 1985, 133.

organized creditors at least as often as against disorganized ones. Moreover, single banks lent on the same terms as syndicates, suggesting that
creditors did not use cohesion as a guide for setting interest rates or other
features of loan contracts. In short, the cohesion of creditors, so central
in theories of sanctioning, has had remarkably little effect on the behavior
of borrowers and lenders. The next chapter concludes the book by discussing the theoretical and practical implications of these findings.

# Part III

## IMPLICATIONS

# Chapter 9 _____

## Reputation and Cooperation under Anarchy

HOW DOES COOPERATION emerge in a condition of international anarchy? The question is both ancient and modern, and remains fundamental to world affairs. Long before the era of sovereign nations, international actors searched for ways to cooperate in the absence of a central authority. City-states and territorial rulers sought alliances for protection and mutual prosperity. Individuals pursued trade with people of foreign lands, and financial dynasties endeavored to lend and borrow. All these actors recognized the potential benefits of political and economic exchange, yet they faced the challenge of working together without the help of an overarching power. Today, the need for international cooperation is no less pressing than it has been for centuries.

Much modern scholarship in the field of international relations examines the conditions and mechanisms that promote cooperation in an anarchical world. Interest in this topic cuts across traditional disciplinary boundaries such as security studies and political economy, and it provides common ground for researchers from a variety of methodological traditions. Whether the subject is war, arms races, international trade, debt crises, exchange rates, or environmental degradation, scholars aim to understand why cooperation emerges and when it breaks down. How states achieve cooperation under anarchy is a core puzzle that unites scholars in an otherwise diverse field.

In this book, I have approached the question of cooperation under anarchy by examining relations between sovereign governments and foreign investors. The book opened by describing the central problem of international lending. Governments seek foreign loans for a variety of purposes, such as consumption, investment, and national defense. After receiving the money, though, debtors may be tempted not to repay. Default, after all, can be economically advantageous, especially in the short run. With no global Leviathan to enforce contracts, why do governments ever honor their foreign debts, and what gives private investors the confidence to lend billions of dollars abroad each year?

The answer, I argue, is reputation. In previous chapters, I developed a reputational theory that involves incomplete information and political change. I then used the theory to explain not only international lending and repayment, but also the dynamics of debtor-creditor relations. I now summarize the theory and findings and discuss their implications for public policy. I also indicate how the reputational arguments in this book could apply beyond sovereign debt, shedding further light on the problem of cooperation under anarchy.

## The Theory in Brief

The theory in this book builds upon, and extends, the work of other scholars. I begin with the now-familiar insight that the shadow of the future can give leaders an incentive to cooperate today. I then add two elements, incomplete information and political change, that have not received sufficient attention in existing models, yet are realistic and salient features of international relations. Taking them into account transforms the standard repeat-play theory into a dynamic model of reputation in which investors regularly update their beliefs about the preferences of foreign borrowers. The evolving beliefs of investors, which represent the borrower's reputation in foreign eyes, are fundamental to both lending and repayment.

Investors must make decisions under conditions of incomplete information: they cannot fully know the preferences of a foreign government. They do, however, understand that some governments assign a higher value than others to maintaining good relations with creditors. Stalwart governments benefit the most from future access to foreign capital, relative to the short-term costs of repayment. They stand ready to service their debts in good times and bad. Lemons, on the other hand, find the costs of keeping faith with creditors too much to bear. They default in bad times and may even do so when economic conditions are favorable. Finally, fair-weather governments have intermediate preferences. The net value they attach to future loans is sufficient to motivate repayment in good times but not during bad ones. Investors further understand the possibility of political change: a government in office today may have different preferences from its predecessors.

At each moment, investors hold beliefs about whether they are dealing with a stalwart, a fair-weather, or a lemon, and revise their beliefs through a process of contextual inference. They gather information about the borrower's type by noting how it behaves given economic circumstances. Knowing this, debtors that place a high value on future loans (relative to the immediate costs of debt service) have a reputational incentive to honor their commitments. They pay either to avoid being classified as unreliable and screened out of capital markets, or to improve their international image and borrow more cheaply in the future. Investors, in turn, willingly engage in international lending, especially to foreign borrowers with long and unblemished records.

My theory not only illuminates a reputational basis for cooperation, but also generates concrete predictions about the allocation of capital and the incidence of defaults. Investors charge higher interest rates to new borrowers than to more established entities, to cover the risk of lending to a potential lemon. As borrowers acquire a record, investors update their beliefs and recalibrate the terms of credit. Countries that pay, thereby distinguishing themselves from bad types, see their risk premiums decline asymptotically toward a baseline rate for reliable borrowers. Those that default, on the other hand, find themselves unable to borrow until they signal through a costly compensation package that they are serious about foreign commitments. In short, my theory predicts *uncertainty premiums* for newcomers, *seasoning effects* for consistent payers, *market exclusion* for defaulters, and *market reentry* when compensation is offered.

The theory also implies that investors and analysts pay close attention to context. They have especially low regard for borrowers that default without a valid economic excuse, such as a shock to commodity prices or global interest rates. No reasonable investor would lend to such lemons, for fear that they would not repay. Investors do not disparage debtors for defaulting during hard times, but neither do they hazard more capital while conditions are bad and defaults continue. Finally, investors upgrade low-rated debtors that confound expectations by servicing their debts under extreme hardship. Thus, I predict *contextual inference*, in which countries ascend and descend the reputational ladder based not only on their behavior but also—when available—data about the circumstances they faced.

Borrowers understand this logic and apply it to their own decisions. The desire for a positive reputation motivates many countries to repay their debts, especially during good times. But the reputational incentive does not work for all countries in all conditions. Some nations, such as ones in which the political and economic costs of debt service outweigh the benefits of future credit, prefer to default. The reputational mechanism encourages, but does not guarantee, rosy relations.

In my theory, unlike many others, defaults occur in equilibrium. Defaults are by-products of incomplete information, political change, and economic shocks. Under conditions of incomplete information, investors sometimes advance money to borrowers that have not yet been identified as lemons. And with the possibility of political change, bad types occasionally inherit loans that were offered to their good-type predecessors. Defaults arise most often in bad times, when the reputational consequences of noncompliance are lowest, but in a world with lemons, some defaults take place in good times, as well. My theory, therefore, anticipates a mix of *faithful repayment, excusable defaults*, and *inexcusable defaults*. Each type of behavior triggers a different response from creditors.

The theory further predicts that cooperation can emerge without collective action by lenders. In standard models of debt, creditors threaten to bar defaulters from future loans or trade. These retaliatory strategies require a high degree of creditor coordination and are vulnerable to free-riding. Kenneth Schultz and Barry Weingast succinctly summarize the problem: "Credit boycotts are difficult to organize and sustain." The sovereign "will be able to play some [creditors] off against others," and each lender has "significant incentives to defect from a boycott in order to become the state's sole source of credit."[1]

Ironically, collusion is unnecessary under conditions of incomplete information. In a world where investors cannot fully know the preferences of foreign leaders, default conveys an important message: it signals that the borrower is not a stalwart. Investors independently update their beliefs and adjust their plans. Each opts not to lend until the debt is settled, and subsequently charges a risk premium that reflects the settler's sullied history. Investors need not collude with each other, or even know each other, to respond in this way. Reputational theory explains lending and repayment even with completely *atomized creditors*.

Finally, my theory accounts for cooperation even when some actors are short-lived. In classic repeat-play models of international relations, two players interact over long periods. Each understands that, by cheating today, it may forgo the fruits of cooperation for many years, if not for eternity as implied by the "grim trigger" punishment. The incentive to cooperate weakens when players interact only briefly. Robert Axelrod explains, "If you are unlikely to meet the other [player] again . . . you might as well defect now and not worry about the consequences for the future."[2] Standard theories of cooperation work best when players survive and interact over the long run.

---

[1] Schultz and Weingast 2003, 11. Eaton and Gersovitz (1981) address the problem of potential embargo-busters by assuming that investors earn zero profits and therefore suffer no costs when they withhold future loans. As Kletzer (1988, 589) points out, however, "this equilibrium can be difficult to support under noncooperative behavior among lenders. If all other creditors refrain from lending in the future to a defaulter, then any particular lender can provide a profitable loan." Kletzer and Wright (2000) and Wright (2002) propose creative solutions to this credibility problem, including "cheat the cheater" strategies in which each lender not only threatens to punish the borrower, but also threatens to punish lenders who fail to implement the retaliatory strategy. Wright (2004a, 2005) explains how institutions and government intervention can facilitate cooperation among creditors, and Martin (1992) shows that international institutions can help countries collude in the application of trade sanctions. My solution is different, because it requires no collusion on the part of lenders.

[2] Axelrod 1984, 15.

The theory developed here, however, applies to ephemeral as well as long-lived investors.[3] Once again, the presence of incomplete information contributes to a cooperative outcome. Each cohort of creditors consults the records to learn how the borrower treated their predecessors. An unfavorable record suggests that the borrower is a bad type, and investors respond by charging higher interest rates, requiring contractual protections, or withholding credit altogether. It should not matter whether each investor participates in the market for a century or for only a year. Governments service their debts to reassure future, as well as current, generations of lenders. Concerns about reputation can, therefore, sustain cooperation involving even *short-lived creditors*.

Although my theory works for short-lived creditors, the same is not necessarily true for short-lived debtors. If the borrower's preferences are highly unstable—at the extreme, if types change randomly in every period—past behavior conveys no reliable information about the borrower's current preferences, and the reputational mechanism breaks down. History can be a guide only when types are somewhat sticky. And yet types cannot be permanent. As chapter 2 explained, theories with permanent types raise a paradox: eventually the history of play grows so long that each new act of repayment or default has only an infinitesimal effect on beliefs about the borrower. The reputational mechanism is most powerful when investors assume that government preferences are persistent but not immutable.

## Findings from Three Centuries

I found strong support for my reputational theory across three centuries of financial history. As predicted, investors required a substantial uncertainty premium from first-time borrowers. Bond yields in Amsterdam, London, and New York were significantly higher for newcomers than for countries that had borrowed and repaid repeatedly. Moreover, the yield premium persisted, even after controlling for economic fundamentals that might have been correlated with the length of borrowing experience. I confirmed these patterns not only via statistical analysis, but also through qualitative studies of investment manuals and the popular press. Authors commented that new borrowers faced higher yields *because* they had not yet demonstrated, through years of service, their willingness to honor debt contracts.

---

[3] The seminal work of Kreps and Wilson (1982) and Milgrom and Roberts (1982) has a similar feature: a small dose of incomplete information helps monopolists deter challengers from entering, even when actors play the game for a small number of rounds. Alt, Calvert, and Humes (1988) apply this insight to international relations by developing a reputational theory of hegemonic stability.

My analysis also uncovered strong evidence of seasoning effects. Countries that paid consistently over the years increased their standing in foreign eyes and received progressively cheaper credit. As their yields approached the levels of highly experienced borrowers, diminishing returns set in. Each additional interest payment or principal reimbursement had smaller reputation-enhancing effects. This pattern, well illustrated by the asymptotic trajectory of Brazilian and Japanese bond yields in the 1800s, was evident in all three centuries on three different capital markets.[4]

Data throughout history also supported the market exclusion hypothesis. Countries could not issue new bonds while in default on previous ones. The only significant nineteenth-century exception, Greece, borrowed in the 1830s even though it was not meeting prior commitments to British investors. As noted in chapter 3, however, the new loan was guaranteed by England, France, and Russia, which had just intervened to liberate Greece from Turkey. The reputation of these guaranteeing powers helped Greece obtain funds it could not have attracted in its own name. I found similar patterns in other periods, including the interwar years, when the exclusion mechanism operated during both good times and bad.

Market reentry, too, occurred as predicted by the reputational theory. Countries regained access to financial markets by settling with creditors. Not just any settlement package would do, however. Creditors judged the fairness of offers, given the borrower's economic and political circumstances. For much of the nineteenth and twentieth centuries, bondholder councils performed this auditing function; they advised investors about whether the borrower was negotiating in good faith. When borrowers did settle, they were put on probation. Bond yields were, therefore, higher for recent settlers (countries that had just made amends) than for borrowers with unblemished records. Settlers, like new borrowers, then underwent a seasoning process; their bond yields fell with years of faithful service.

Evidence also supported the contextual inference hypothesis. Investors adjusted their beliefs and their loans as new information arrived during good times and bad. I tested this proposition by examining the formation of reputations during the roaring 1920s and the Great Depression. Most countries paid their debts in the 1920s, but a few—Russia, Mexico, and Ecuador, for example—defaulted when external conditions did not justify a lapse. These apparent lemons could not borrow in the 1920s, a decade when more than 40 other countries issued new debt in New York or London.

---

[4] Özler (1992) found a similar pattern in the late twentieth century. Spreads on commercial bank loans began at high levels for borrowers with little experience, and trended downward asymptotically as the borrower consistently repaid.

The Great Depression offered investors an opportunity to study behavior in a different context, and thereby distinguish stalwarts from mere fair-weathers. Many presumed fair-weathers around the world defaulted in the 1930s, but a handful met their obligations in full. Argentina, Australia, and Finland, in particular, stunned the world by repaying in dire circumstances. These surprising payers gained esteem in the eyes of foreign investors and refinanced their debts at low rates.

The effects of reputation were evident not only in the behavior of investors, but also in the writings of experts who advised them. As shown in chapter 4, bankers, financial analysts, and rating agencies consistently identified reputation as a top consideration when investing in foreign securities, and they articulated a reputational logic that closely matched the theory in this book. A content analysis of bond advertisements, rating manuals, and stock market disclosure regulations further supported the reputational theory, as did interviews with international bankers.

Borrowers, too, behaved according to reputational theory. Most countries repaid their debts most of the time. Defaults did occur, however, as expected in a model with incomplete information, political change, and economic shocks. In any given year, some 10 percent of countries in the world failed to satisfy private foreign lenders, and the figure soared to nearly 50 percent during exogenous shocks such as the Great Depression. Furthermore, the most egregious cases of opportunistic default (Russia, Mexico, and Cuba, for example) arose when political revolutions brought antiforeign or anticapitalist leaders to power. The mix of faithful repayment, excusable default, and inexcusable repudiation was consistent with my reputational model.

Finally, governments articulated a reputational rationale for repaying their loans. Underrated countries (epitomized by Argentina in the 1930s) that paid despite great hardship did so with the express aim of raising their reputations. Moreover, diplomatic correspondence in the nineteenth century abounded with discussion of reputation, not only by diplomats from creditor countries but also by presidents and finance ministers in the borrowing states.

The breadth and depth of these empirical tests, across three centuries of financial history, gives confidence in the reputational theory. Uncertainty premiums, seasoning effects, equilibrium default, market exclusion, market entry, contextual inference, and other predictions are clearly evident in both quantitative and qualitative data. From the Amsterdam market of the 1700s, through the rise of London and New York as financial centers, to the euromarkets of today, reputations have formed and influenced behavior in a remarkably consistent way.

Evidence from the past three centuries not only fits my reputational theory, but also challenges alternative accounts of reputation in world affairs. Desire-based theory, described in chapter 2, contends that people draw systematically biased lessons from history. When a foreign government acts against their interests, observers assume it is a bad type. The converse is not true, however; desirable behavior does not impress outside observers. Jonathan Mercer, the leading proponent of desire-based theory, argues that observers attribute desirable behavior to situational forces, and therefore give the foreign government no reputational credit. "Only undesirable behavior," Mercer writes, "can generate a reputation."[5]

I uncovered no clear evidence, however, that desires systematically distort the formation of reputations. On the contrary, chapters 3–5 showed that investors made dispositional attributions not only when countries defaulted, but also when they repaid. Countries that broke obligations were branded as lemons and lost access to foreign loans, whereas countries that met commitments were classified as good types and received easier access to external capital. *Both* undesirable and desirable behavior had reputational consequences.

I also found, contra desire-based theory, that investors used situational data to sharpen their inferences. When a government repaid in hard times, such as the Great Depression, investors did not invent situational explanations for the desirable behavior. Rather, they noted that normal countries would have defaulted under the circumstances, and concluded that the payer must have been a stalwart type. I detected these rational patterns of inference not only in statistical analysis of bond yields and loan access, but also in statements by bankers, investment advisors, and the popular press. Data from debt markets were more consistent with my rationalist theory of reputation than with the desire-based alternative.

Another alternative to my own argument is current calculus theory, in which past behavior has no impact on present beliefs. According to Daryl Press, people use historical analogies for mundane decisions but abandon them in favor of "systematic reasoning" when the stakes are high.[6] Systematic thinkers, it is argued, judge the credibility of foreign governments by analyzing fresh intelligence about capabilities and interests, not past records of commitments honored or broken. Applied to global finance, where trillions of dollars change hands daily and financial survival depends on prudent decisions, current calculus theory implies that past actions should have little explanatory power.

I found, however, that even in the high-stakes world of global finance, history had profound effects. The beliefs of investors, and therefore the quantity and price of loans, depended on the borrower's record, even after adjusting for current information about the borrower's economy. Experts, moreover, regarded experience as one of the first tests of a gov-

[5] Mercer 1996, 46.
[6] Press 2005, 6.

ernment bond. Far from ignoring history, investors and their advisors consistently treated the past as an indicator of future risk.

While highlighting the importance of reputation, my evidence in no way denied the relevance of current conditions. A borrower's economic health unquestionably affected its access to capital. Chapters 3 and 5 found a significant correlation between bond yields and economic indicators, such as debt levels and wealth. Moreover, experts in chapter 4 often stressed the relevance of current economic conditions. But only one investment advisor from the interwar period referred to present conditions without citing past actions. The remaining 96 percent of experts in the sample cited the borrower's record as an important, if not the most crucial, variable in the credit equation.

The theory of reputation presented in this book stresses that current calculations and historical analyses can, in fact, be complementary. Actors in international relations engage in both activities to gain a better understanding of the scope for cooperation. In the area of debt, investors use data about economic conditions—when available—to put current and past behavior in context. When money is on the line, investors and their advisors use both sources of information to draw inferences, rather than relying on one while ignoring the other.

The same evidence that contradicts current calculus theory also challenges the prevailing academic belief that creditors ignore history. As noted in chapter 1, many careful studies by distinguished scholars have failed to find reputational effects. This body of research has contributed to the (mistaken) impression that creditors rely on direct sanctions, such as trade embargoes, asset seizures, and gunboat diplomacy, to enforce contracts. I found that creditors actually pay close attention to repayment records, giving borrowers an incentive to service their debts.

Why did I find clear and consistent evidence of reputation, when so many other scholars had not? The discovery, I believe, stemmed from a combination of new data and improved theory. The detailed data in this book were not available to previous researchers. I gathered the empirical material over many years from archives and libraries in nine countries. The resulting information, including inventories of loans, defaults, settlements, and bond yields across the centuries, allowed more definitive statistical tests than were previously possible. Likewise, the case studies and content analyses in the book drew on previously untapped sources. With this new array of quantitative and qualitative data, I uncovered stronger reputational effects than earlier scholars had been able to document.

The theory in chapter 2 contributed to this discovery by suggesting where and how to look for evidence of reputation. Most previous empirical work compared interest rates on loans to countries that defaulted versus ones that did not. My theory suggested additional and more precise tests. For example, uncertainty premiums and seasoning effects should be present within the subset of countries that have not defaulted; default should not only affect interest rates but also lead to credit rationing (market exclusion); and the reputational consequences of default and repayment should vary with context. Theory pointed me to these and many other empirical implications. In summary, my theory indicated where and how concerns about reputation should be manifest, and new data made it possible to judge the accuracy of those predictions.

Previous chapters not only built a case for reputation but also questioned the importance of extrinsic sanctions. According to many researchers, lenders deter defaults by threatening to retaliate in nonfinancial issue areas. This idea is widely invoked to explain lending and repayment over the long run. The evidence in this book demonstrates, however, that what works in theory may prove relatively unimportant in practice.

Specifically, my findings challenge a common view about the historical importance of gunboat diplomacy. Many argue that, before World War I, the fear of gunboat diplomacy motivated countries to repay their debts. The apparent correlation between sovereign default and military intervention is mostly spurious, however. Militarized disputes between creditors and debtors arose not because creditors were using arms to defend bondholders, but because default happened to coincide with other disputes (civil wars, territorial conflicts, and tort claims) that attracted the involvement of foreign powers. Even the so-called bondholder war against Venezuela in 1902 was really about torts, not bonds. Analyses of diplomatic correspondence, geographic patterns of investment, and default rates against strong and weak creditors were also inconsistent with the gunboat hypothesis. Although there were exceptions, creditor governments generally did not use—or even threaten to use—force on behalf of bondholders, and neither investors nor borrowers expected default to trigger military intervention. The consistent line then, as now, was an appeal to reputation, not the threat of coercion.

This book also disputes the relevance of enforcement via trade sanctions. During the interwar period, often regarded as the heyday of tactical linkage between debt and trade, the countries most exposed to international commerce did not repay at a higher rate than more insular counterparts. Moreover, defaulters did not discriminate in favor of their major trading partners, as trade sanction theory might expect. Researchers cite interwar Argentina as the prime instance of using trade to bully borrowers. Close inspection of archival evidence showed that even in the Argentine case, however, the government repaid to enhance its reputation, not to avert a trade war. I found only two references to trade sanctions in more than 96,000 newspaper clippings about sovereign debt. Likewise, my systematic survey of investment commentary from the 1920s found almost no trace of the trade sanctions hypothesis. In a large sample of texts, only one analyst even mentioned the potential linkage between debt and trade, and he did not include it among factors investors should consider when lending to a foreign government.

Finally, my data raise doubts about the need for collective action in enforcing loan contracts. For centuries, money flowed to sovereign borrowers via atomized bond markets, even though bank lending would have provided more punishment power. When investors finally began to lend through commercial banks in the late twentieth century, neither the terms of lending nor the patterns of repayment matched the predictions of sanctioning theory. Single banks lent on the same terms as well-organized syndicates, and governments that had borrowed from both bondholders and banks did not treat the latter more favorably, despite the enormous disparity in retaliatory power. These patterns, though odd from the standpoint of sanctioning theory, are consistent with my reputational argument, which supports lending and repayment even when investors are atomized and short-lived.

The evidence in this book demonstrates that across the centuries and around the world, extrinsic sanctions have played an insignificant role in debtor-creditor relations. Future researchers should, therefore, devote more attention to reputational theories, especially ones incorporating incomplete information and political change.[7] We can learn much about international relations by placing reputation at the center of analysis.

## Policy Implications

The arguments in this book have practical as well as theoretical significance. During the 1980s and 1990s, many sovereigns defaulted on their debts to foreigners, and others maintained payment only with emergency assistance from the International Monetary Fund and other public bodies.

---

[7] I have examined how informational asymmetries between governments and *foreign* investors affect the prospects for international cooperation. One could also study the international effects of *domestic* informational asymmetries. Two excellent examples are Milner 1997, which proposes a model in which the domestic legislature does not have complete information about agreements the executive has negotiated with foreign countries, and Sandleris 2006, which develops a theory of sovereign debt in which the government has information about the economy that is not available to domestic firms. Future research could also examine the effects of domestic political institutions. A large literature, beginning with North and Weingast 1989, argues that liberal democratic institutions reduce the risk of default on domestically held debt. In several important studies, Stasavage amends this insight by showing that the effect of political institutions on debt is conditional on the constellation of domestic interest groups. See, for example, Stasavage 2003, 2007a, 2007b. Even if democratic institutions increase the credibility of debts owed to domestic citizens, though, it is an open question whether such institutions enhance the credibility of debts to foreigners. For recent theory and evidence on this issue, see Schultz and Weingast 1998, 2003; and Saiegh 2005.

Defaults continued in the early twenty-first century, most spectacularly in Argentina. Few developing nations escaped the crises, which not only struck the poorest economies but also grounded previous high-fliers in Latin America and East Asia. These shocking events have spurred what former IMF director Stanley Fischer calls "the most serious rethinking of the structure of the international financial system since breakdown of the Bretton Woods system in 1971."[8]

This book could inform the ongoing and important policy discussion. In his survey of international financial reforms, economist Kenneth Rogoff asks: "Why, exactly, are debtor countries willing to make repayments of any kind, partial or full?" The question is "the crux of understanding international debt markets," and "it is quite dangerous to think about grand plans to restructure the world financial system without having a concrete view of it."[9] To build a better financial architecture, one less susceptible to shocks and panics, reformers must know what motivates governments to repay and gives investors the confidence to lend. Only with that knowledge can leaders build a system that plays to the incentives of key actors.

Reforms could, for example, seek to reinforce the reputational mechanism that sustains cooperation between debtors and creditors. One positive step might be the reestablishment of bondholder councils.[10] The American and British units, known respectively as the Foreign Bondholders Protective Council and the Corporation of Foreign Bondholders, went defunct in the 1970s and officially closed their doors a decade later. The decision now seems shortsighted, since bondholders recently regained their historically dominant role as the primary suppliers of foreign loans. As the volume of bond-based lending increased, so too did exposure to the risk of defaults. Ecuador, the country with the dubious distinction of most years in default since 1820, soon made the risk a reality. In 1999 it became the first country to suspend payment on Brady Bonds, which had been issued to restructure commercial bank loans. The Argentine moratorium of 2002 further underscores the vulnerability of foreign bondholders.

Evidence in this book shows the potential value of resurrecting bondholder committees, not necessarily to facilitate debt restructuring, but to help investors distinguish between excusable defaults and inexcusable ones. For centuries, bondholder committees supplied valuable information to capital markets. They investigated defaults to determine whether

[8] Fischer 1999, 85.

[9] Rogoff 1999, 31.

[10] See, e.g., Eichengreen and Portes 1995; Macmillan 1995a, 1995b; and *Financial Times*, August 15, 1995, 11. Esteves (2006) and Mauro, Sussman, and Yafeh (2006, chap. 7) analyze the functions of bondholder committees before World War I.

each borrower acted in good faith given the circumstances, and they served as clearinghouses of information to help differentiate stalwarts from fair-weathers and lemons. Today, as before, bondholder committees could strengthen the reputational basis for lending and repayment.

Reforms could also set stricter limits on international bailouts. Traditionally, sovereign lending and repayment occurred in the absence of supranational organizations such as the IMF and the World Bank. Without the prospect of multilateral bailouts, investors followed the *caveat emptor* (buyer beware) principle: they studied past behavior and current economic conditions to identify—and avoid—potential lemons.[11] Today, sovereign lending occurs in the shadow of supranational organizations. Some experts worry that the IMF, through its rescue packages, is signaling a willingness to guarantee sovereign debts, and is thereby encouraging reckless borrowing and lending.

In light of these concerns, should the IMF be abolished? Most believe the answer is no; the organization can play a constructive role in international finance. As a potential lender of last resort, the IMF can reassure investors, thereby preventing a rush to the exits at the first sign of an impending default.[12] At the same time, IMF-type organizations can assist countries that are already suffering from liquidity crises or debt overhang.[13] Yet the organization must take care not to offer seemingly unconditional bailouts, which undermine the power of reputation by reducing the incentive for borrowers to pay, and by lowering the risk of lending to unreliable types.

The challenge reformers now face is how to strike an appropriate balance—how to preserve the reputational mechanism while, at the same time, reducing the incidence and the cost of defaults. Aggarwal and Granville succinctly pose the dilemma: reformers must "devise a successful debt-rescue package without encouraging investors to engage in unduly risky ventures and . . . debtors to pursue irresponsible economic policies."[14] The search for an appropriate solution will occupy reformers for many years. It seems clear, however, that stricter limits on bailouts would help address moral hazard problems in a world of multilateral organizations.[15]

---

[11] Flandreau (2003) develops this point in an insightful study of the sovereign risk analysis department at Crédit Lyonnais, the largest French underwriter in the late nineteenth century.

[12] Cohen and Portes (2006) argue that it may even be beneficial for the IMF to act as a lender of *first* resort to prevent self-fulfilling crises.

[13] See, e.g., Sachs 1995, 1999; and Fischer 1999.

[14] Aggarwal and Granville 2003, 281.

[15] Such limits may be difficult to enforce in practice, however. Stone (2002, 2004) shows that, when dealing with large or politically important borrowers, the IMF has trouble limiting its bailouts and enforcing its loans-for-policy contracts. For further analysis of the

A similar dilemma confronts reformers who seek to streamline the process of debt restructuring.[16] Until recently, many sovereign bond contracts could not be altered without the unanimous consent of all holders.[17] These provisions created a potential for maverick investors to obstruct settlements. To address this apparent problem, some scholars and policymakers have recommended the broad use of majority-voting, sharing, and collective-representation clauses in bond contracts.[18] The standard objection is that such clauses, by making it easier for borrowers to restructure their debts, increase the temptation to default, leading investors to raise interest rates and reduce loan sizes.

Recent research shows that both sides of the debate may be right. In an innovative study, Eichengreen and Mody compare interest rates on emerging market bonds with and without collective action clauses. They find that collective action clauses reduce the cost of borrowing for more creditworthy countries, but have the opposite effect on countries with higher ex ante probabilities of default. Investors apparently believe that, when dealing with good types, collective action clauses are, on balance, beneficial: the gains from orderly restructuring outweigh the increased risk of default. But in relations with less reliable borrowers, "The advantages of orderly restructuring are offset by the moral hazard and default risk associated with the presence of renegotiation-friendly loan provisions."[19] This suggests an even more general lesson for reformers to consider. Changes in the feasibility of renegotiation may have different effects on highly reputed borrowers than on less esteemed ones.

## Extensions

Beyond its implications for international debt, this book sheds light on the fundamental problem of cooperation under anarchy. Scholars and practitioners of international relations often cite reputation as a motive for keeping one's word. A government that honors its commitments can acquire a reputation for reliability, which should help it attract partners for cooperative endeavors, whereas a government that breaks its commit-

---

political forces that affect IMF lending and constrain the potential for reforms, see Broz 2005; Broz and Hawes 2006; Gould 2006; Thacker 1999; and Vreeland 2007. On the political evolution of the IMF and its mandate, see Pauly 1997.

[16] For an overview of proposals in this area, see Eichengreen 2002, 2003; Krueger 2003; and Tirole 2002.

[17] There is some disagreement among scholars about the proportion of bonds that require unanimous consent. For various estimates, see Eichengreen and Mody 2004; Gugiatti and Richards 2004; and Richards and Gugiatti 2003.

[18] Eichengreen and Portes 1995; International Monetary Fund 2002; and Taylor 2002.

[19] Eichengreen and Mody 2004, 247.

ments may signal that it cannot be trusted, prompting others to exclude it from beneficial agreements. This argument appears in classical works of international relations as well as modern analyses of military and economic affairs, and it suggests a plausible mechanism for international cooperation.

Notwithstanding the importance of reputation, Robert Jervis wrote in the 1980s that "scholars know remarkably little" about the topic. "It is not clear how these reputations are established and maintained or how important they are compared to the other influences on credibility. . . . On these points we have neither theoretically grounded expectations nor solid evidence."[20] Jervis's assessment of the field still holds. How do people form beliefs about the reliability of prospective partners? What causes reputations to change, and when do they remain the same? In what contexts will concerns about reputation exert the greatest effect on international behavior, and when are they less likely to matter? Existing literature does not offer clear, convincing answers to these questions.

This book begins to fill the knowledge gap. It shows how reputations form under conditions of incomplete information and political change, and how they affect patterns of cooperation and conflict. Building on the theory developed here, scholars might now find reputation to be a crucial but overlooked factor in areas other than international debt. The opportunities for extension are perhaps as ubiquitous as the problem of cooperation itself. I mention just a few areas of scholarship that might profit from a closer look at reputation.

Foreign direct investment (FDI), like loans, creates the potential for conflict as well as cooperation. Corporations often acquire factories and other property in foreign lands. Once the investment is sunk, though, the host country may decide to nationalize the entire firm or seize some of its assets. Alternatively, the host could tax the firm, block its ability to remit profits, or otherwise change the regulatory environment in ways that make the enterprise less profitable. Any of these acts might be considered parallel to default on a foreign debt contract. Investors therefore need information about the government's willingness to expropriate.

As with debt, investors cannot directly observe a foreign government's preferences regarding expropriation, but they can begin to infer the government's type by studying its behavior in context. Applying the theory in this book, we might expect new host countries to incur an uncertainty premium: other factors equal, they should receive less FDI, on less favorable terms, than countries with a long history of respect for direct investments. The reputational logic in this book also implies seasoning, in

[20] Jervis 1982–83, 8–9.

which governments that refrain from interfering with FDI attract progressively larger investments on better terms.

If a government did expropriate foreign factories and firms, the reputational consequences would depend on the circumstances that motivated the seizure and the amount of compensation offered to investors. A host that expropriated outside the context of a severe external shock or national emergency, and that refused to offer adequate compensation to investors, would quickly acquire a lemonlike reputation. Investors would shy away from purchasing additional property in the host country, out of fear that new acquisitions would suffer a similar fate.

A host that expropriated in response to shocks and offered fair compensation to investors would acquire an intermediate reputation. The costly act of compensation would signal to investors a preference profile more typical of a fair-weather than a lemon. In time, investors might be willing to acquire more property in the host country, but only with enhancements and safeguards to address the risk of further expropriation. Finally, a host that refrained from nationalization and other forms of expropriation over many years, during fair and foul weather, would establish itself as a stalwart and attract new investment on good terms. Just as in debt, then, I would expect market exclusion in response to expropriation, market reentry after the provision of compensation, and contextual inference: a conditional relationship between the expropriation record of a country and its access to FDI.

It might also be fruitful to examine the reputational spillovers from FDI to debt, and vice versa. We now know that lenders update their beliefs about the creditworthiness of a borrower after examining its history of payment versus default. Perhaps lenders also consider how the government has treated other international commitments, including pledges not to expropriate factories and firms. This intuition rests on a plausible but untested assumption: countries have general traits that affect their behavior across a wide range of interactions. Most of us do, in fact, draw inferences across issues in everyday life. We observe how individuals respond to certain commitments and judge whether they are likely to uphold others. We buy the products of a diversified firm and, based on our experience with some goods, infer the likely quality of other items the company produces. Research could reveal whether actors make similar connections across issues in international affairs.[21]

---

[21] Cole and Kehoe (1997, 1998) propose a theory of "general reputations," in which governments that misbehave in one area of international relations tarnish their reputations in other areas. Downs and Jones (2002) argue, in contrast, that reputations are likely to be compartmentalized. More theoretical and empirical work is needed to understand whether, and under what conditions, countries acquire general rather than issue-specific reputations.

Another potential application of reputational theory involves international monetary commitments. Countries often peg their currencies to a visible and widely accepted standard, such as the U.S. dollar or the value of gold. In less rigid cases, they commit to float their currency within a target zone, as was the case in Europe before the advent of the euro. Countries that honor such commitments despite severe external shocks could rise to the top of the reputational scale and achieve stalwart standing in monetary affairs. Those that maintain the peg during good times but devalue when conditions turn sour, on the other hand, might get categorized as fair-weathers, while countries that devalue without reasonable justification would lose the trust of international observers and sink to the level of lemons. As with FDI, there may also be reputational spillovers from monetary commitments to international debt. Recent work on both the classical gold standard and the European monetary union provides preliminary support for these propositions and suggests the potential payoff from future research.[22]

Students of international trade, too, could refine and apply the reputational theory. In trade negotiations, we might expect interlocutors to treat newcomers differently from seasoned partners that have shown their reliability (or unreliability) over a number of years. When dealing with an unfamiliar partner, policymakers may demand more safeguards, enter into shallower agreements, and float trial balloons that, if successful, could lead to more comprehensive cooperation later on. From that point, reputations should evolve in response to surprising and unsurprising behavior. Countries that maintain low trade barriers in the face of balance-of-payments crises, especially when "escape clauses" would have permitted a reversion to protectionism, will earn the admiration and trust of partners. At the opposite extreme, those that raise trade barriers without sufficient cause, and without compensating their partners adequately, will get categorized as lemons in the international marketplace.

Researchers could also devote more attention to the institutions that support reputation in world trade. How, for example, do the countries and firms that participate in international commerce obtain reliable information about their partners? At various points in history, institutions have served this function. A classic example concerns the Lex Mercatoria, or Law Merchant, a system of legal codes and private judges that facilitated commercial transactions in medieval Europe. Under the system, mer-

---

[22] See, e.g., Bordo, Edelstein, and Rockoff 2003; Bordo and Rockoff 1996; Bordo and Schwartz 1996; Chen and Giovannini 1994; and Holden and Vikøren 1996. Simmons (2000) and Simmons and Hopkins (2005) offer important studies of reputation in a different financial area, capital account liberalization, and Guzman (2002) examines the reputational incentive to uphold international legal commitments, more generally.

chants could file grievances against other traders, judges would determine
whether the claims were legitimate, and the outcomes were recorded for
future reference. The judges in this system had "only limited powers to
enforce judgments against merchants from distant places." If a party failed
to perform as promised, "no physical sanction or seizure of goods could
then be applied." Nevertheless, judges and notaries fostered cooperation
by keeping track of which traders had cheated.[23] Like the bondholder
councils in this book, the Law Merchant system separated lemons from
more reliable types. Future research might identify how the World Trade
Organization and other institutions support cooperation via reputation.[24]

Reputation-based theories could also shed light on topics in international security, such as military deterrence. A number of distinguished
scholars, working with qualitative and quantitative data, have failed to
confirm that reputations affect the outcome of military crises.[25] Paul Huth
aptly summarizes the state of our scientific knowledge: "There is a substantial gap between the intuitive belief that reputations are an important
cause of international conflict and the development of a compelling logical argument and empirical evidence to support such a conclusion." Consequently, "there is a considerable need for further theoretical and empirical work on reputations."[26]

The arguments in this book suggest several potentially fruitful lines of
analysis. In particular, it may be useful to integrate external circumstances
more explicitly into studies of reputation and military deterrence. The
behavior of a country should affect its reputation, I hypothesize, after
taking into account exogenous factors that might have caused the country
to stand firm or back down. So far, scholars have not tested this more
qualified view of deterrence. Huth regards this as "an important gap in
the empirical literature," because the qualified view rests on "a stronger
logical foundation" than theories scholars have been testing to date.[27]

Future work should also explore more thoroughly the connection between reputation and general, as distinct from immediate, military deterrence. Most empirical work has examined the impact of past behavior on

[23] Milgrom, North, and Weingast 1990, 2.

[24] For the seminal discussion of international institutions as organizations that supply
information and contribute to reputational processes, see Keohane 1984. See also Katzenstein, Keohane, and Krasner 1998.

[25] See, e.g., Snyder and Diesing 1977, 187; Hopf 1994; Mercer 1996; and Press 2005.

[26] Huth 1997, 97. For examples of the best new work in this area, see Guisinger and
Smith (2002) and Sartori (2005), who argue that the desire to maintain a reputation for
honesty deters leaders from bluffing; and Walter (2006), who argues that governments fight
separatist groups to build a reputation for nonaccommodation and thereby deter future
challenges.

[27] Huth 1999, 43.

crises that have already begun, but past actions are perhaps more likely to affect whether crises erupt in the first place. In debt markets, investors will not interact with governments they regard as lemons, but they will sign agreements with putative fair-weathers and stalwarts. There is a parallel in military deterrence: challengers will not bully countries they regard as tough, though they may threaten countries they perceive as soft. Thus, just as investors use reputation to look before they leap, countries may take reputation into account *before* issuing a military challenge. Future research on the reputational sources of crisis initiation could confirm this hypothesis.

Finally, the theory presented in this book could deepen our understanding of alliance politics. It seems intuitive that reputations play a critical role in military alliances, just as in personal or business relationships, yet we know surprisingly little about this important issue. In his review of the alliance literature, James Morrow urged scholars to train their attention on the question of reputation: "Is it possible for one state to infer another state's present degree of resolve from a past case, and is there a plausible model that incorporates this foreign reputation argument?" Developing and testing a theory of reputation in alliances would, in Morrow's judgment, represent "a major advance."[28]

Throughout this book, I have used reputational theory to address the puzzle of cooperation under anarchy. Starting from the fundamental insights of others, I attempted to explain how actors form beliefs and make decisions when information is imperfect and preferences can change. Participants in international relations update their beliefs, I argue, by studying behavior in context: they use data about past actions and—when available—external circumstances to learn about the disposition of a foreign government. The resulting beliefs summarize the government's reputation in foreign eyes and affect the course of international relations. With this reputational approach, I was able to account for patterns of cooperation and conflict across three centuries of international finance. I hope the theory and evidence in this book will contribute to a deeper understanding of reputation, debt, and international cooperation.

---

[28] Morrow 2000, 80–81. For recent efforts to develop and test hypotheses about reputations and alliances, see Leeds 2003 and Miller 2003.

# Bibliography

## Manuscript Sources

Archive historique de la Bourse de Paris auprès de Euronext de Paris. Paris, France. *Cours authentique* collection.

Archivo General de Simancas. Simancas, Spain. Sección de Estado.

Bank of England Archive. London, England. Records of the Overseas Department pertaining to Argentina (OV 102).

Geheimes Staatsarchiv Preußischer Kulturbesitz. Berlin, Germany. Philipsborn Collection.

Gemeentearchief. Amsterdam, The Netherlands. Ketwich & Voombergh (PA 600), Huijsinga (PA 836), and Bibliotheekcollectie Brochures leningen.

Guildhall Library. London, England. Correspondence and Newspaper Cuttings Files of the Council of the Corporation of Foreign Bondholders.

Institut für Stadtgeschichte Frankfurt. Frankfurt, Germany. Bethmann-Archiv.

Nederlandsch Economisch-Historisch Archief (NEHA). Amsterdam, The Netherlands. Algemeene Maatschappij voor Levensverzekering en Lijfrente (Bijzondere collecties 491) and Huijsinga (Bijzondere collecties 523).

Stanford University Library. Stanford, California. Country Files and Minutes of Meetings of the Executive Committee of the Foreign Bondholders Protective Council.

United Kingdom National Archives. Kew, England. Records of the Foreign Office pertaining to Argentina (FO 6), Chile (FO 61), Colombia (FO 55), the Ottoman Empire (FO 78), and Venezuela (FO 80).

## Stock Market Price Sheets

Belgium (Antwerp and Brussels)
    *Cours authentique de la Bourse de Bruxelles*
    *Moniteur belge prix courant*
    *Recueil financier*
France (Paris)
    *Cours authentique*
    *Tableaux des cours des principales valeurs négociées et cotées aux bourses des effets publics de Paris, Lyon et Marseille*
Germany (Berlin, Frankfurt, and Hamburg)
    *Aktionär*
    *Berliner Börsen-Zeitung*
    *Berliner Cours-Anzeiger*
    *Börsen-Coursblatt* (Sulzbach)
    *Cours-Bericht der Berliner Börse* (Hertel)
    *Course Fremde Staatspapiere* (Philipsborn)

*Frankfurter Cours-Blatt* (Berlyn)
*Frankfurter Zeitung*
*Öffentliches Börsen-Coursblatt* (Wechselmakler-Syndikat)
Netherlands (Amsterdam)
    *Amsterdamsch Effectenblad*
    *Maandelijksche Nederlandsche Mercurius*
    *Nieuw Algemeen Effectenblad*
    *Prys-Courant der Effecten*
Switzerland (Basel, Geneva, Zurich)
    *Cote des agents de change réunis* (Geneva)
    *Cote journalière de la Bourse de Genève*
    *Cote officielle de la Société des Agents de Change* (Geneva)
    *Cours des effets publics* (Geneva)
    *Kursblatt der Zürcher Effektenbörse*
    *Öffentliches Kursblatt der Basler Effektenbörse*
    *Öffentliches Kursblatt der beeidigten Sensalen* (Basel)
    *Öffentliches Wechsel- und Effekten-Cursblatt von Zürich*
    *Zürcher Kursblatt*
United Kingdom (London)
    *Bankers' Price Current*
    *Circular to Bankers*
    *Course of the Exchange*
    *Investors' Monthly Manual*
United States (New York)
    *Commercial and Financial Chronicle*
    *New York Times*

**Bond Yearbooks**

Ayres, Henry. *Ayres's Financial Register of British and Foreign Funds*. London.
Chaix. *Annuaire–Chaix: Les principales sociétés par actions*. Paris.
Committee of the Stock Exchange. *The Stock Exchange Official Intelligence*. London.
Corporation of Foreign Bondholders. *Annual Report*. London.
Courtois, Alphonse. *Manuel des fonds publics et des sociétés par actions*. Paris.
Desfosses, E. *Manuel des valeurs cotées hors parquet à la Bourse de Paris*. Paris.
———. *Manuel des valeurs cotées en coulisse à la Bourse de Paris*. Paris.
———. *Annuaire Desfossés*. Paris.
Fenn, Charles. *Fenn's Compendium of the English and Foreign Funds*. London.
Fitch Publishing Company. *The Fitch Bond Book*. New York.
Foreign Bondholders Protective Council. *Annual Report*. New York.
Fortune, Thomas. *Fortune's Epitome of the Stocks and Public Funds*. London.
Iselin, A. *Foreign Bonds Issued in the United States*. New York.
Kimber, Albert W. *Kimber's Record of Government Debts*. New York.
Moody's Investors Service. *Moody's Manual of Investments, American and Foreign: Government Securities*. New York.

Saling, A. *Saling's Börsen-Jahrbuch: Ein Handbuch für Bankiers und Kapitalisten.* Berlin.
White, Weld & Co. *Foreign Dollar Bonds.* New York.


**Newspapers and Magazines**

*American Banker*
*Atlanta Constitution*
*Bankers Magazine*
*Barron's*
*Business Week*
*Christian Science Monitor*
*Commercial and Financial Chronicle*
*Daily Telegraph* (London)
*Economist* (London)
*Financial News* (London)
*Financial Times* (London)
*Forbes*
*Foreign Securities Investor*
*Magazine of Bank Management*
*Magazine of Wall Street*
*Morning Chronicle* (London)
*La Nación* (Buenos Aires)
*New Yorker*
*New York Herald Tribune*
*New York Times*
*Review of the River Plate* (Buenos Aires)
*Sentinel* (Glasgow)
*South American Journal* (London)
*Stock Exchange Gazette* (London)
*Times* (London)
*Wall Street Journal*
*Washington Post*


**Books, Articles, and Scholarly Papers**

Abreu, Marcelo de Paiva. 1984. "Argentina and Brazil during the 1930s: The Impact of British and American International Economic Policies." In *Latin America in the 1930s: The Role of the Periphery in World Crisis*, ed. Rosemary Thorp, 144–62. New York: St. Martin's.
Aggarwal, Vinod K. 1987. *International Debt Threat: Bargaining among Creditors and Debtors in the 1980s.* Berkeley: Institute of International Studies, University of California.
———. 1996. *Debt Games: Strategic Interaction in International Debt Rescheduling.* Cambridge: Cambridge University Press.

———. 1998. *Institutional Designs for a Complex World: Bargaining, Linkages, and Nesting*. Ithaca, NY: Cornell University Press.

Aggarwal, Vinod K., and Brigitte Granville. 2003. "Sovereign Debt Management: Lessons and Policy Implications." In *Sovereign Debt: Origins, Crises and Restructuring*, ed. Vinod K. Aggarwal and Brigitte Granville, 281–87. London: Royal Institute of International Affairs.

Aizenman, Joshua. 1989. "Country Risk, Incomplete Information and Taxes on International Borrowing." *Economic Journal* 99, no. 394: 147–61.

———. 1991. "Trade Dependency, Bargaining and External Debt." *Journal of International Economics* 31, nos. 1–2: 101–20.

Akerlof, George A. 1970. "The Market for Lemons: Qualitative Uncertainty and the Market Mechanism." *Quarterly Journal of Economics* 84, no. 3: 488–500.

Alesina, Alberto. 1988. "The End of Large Public Debts." In *High Public Debt: The Italian Experience*, ed. Francesco Giavazzi and Luigi Spaventa, 34–79. Cambridge: Cambridge University Press.

Alexander, Lewis Suverkrop. 1987. "Three Essays on Sovereign Default and International Lending." Ph.D. diss., Yale University.

Alhadeff, Peter. 1983. "Finance and the Economic Management of the Argentine Government in the 1930s." Ph.D. diss., St. Antony's College, Oxford University.

———. 1985. "Dependency, Historiography and Objections to the Roca Pact." In *Latin America, Economic Imperialism and the State: The Political Economy of the External Connection from Independence to the Present*, ed. Christopher Abel and Colin M. Lewis, 367–78. London: Athlone.

———. 1986. "The Economic Formulae of the 1930s: A Reassessment." In *The Political Economy of Argentina, 1880–1946*, ed. Guido di Tella and D.C.M. Platt, 95–119. New York: St. Martin's.

Alt, James E., Randall L. Calvert, and Brian D. Humes. 1988. "Reputation and Hegemonic Stability: A Game-Theoretic Analysis." *American Political Science Review* 82, no. 2: 445–66.

Amador, Manuel. 2002. "A Political Model of Sovereign Debt Repayment." Working paper, Stanford University.

American Institute of Banking. 1924. *Investments*. New York: American Institute of Banking.

*Annual Register*. Various issues. London.

Arrow, Kenneth J. 2005. "Globalisation and its Implications for International Security." In *Economics of Globalisation*, ed. Partha Gangopadhyay and Manas Chatterji, xi–xiv. Aldershot: Ashgate.

Atkin, John Michael. 1977. *British Overseas Investment, 1918–1931*. New York: Arno Press.

Atkins, Paul M. 1926. *Foreign Investment Securities: The Merchandising of Foreign Securities*. Chicago: H. N. Stronck.

———. 1927. "Factors Underlying the Purchase of Foreign Securities." *Bankers Magazine* 114, no. 1: 23–27.

Axelrod, Robert. 1981. "The Emergence of Cooperation among Egoists." *American Political Science Review* 75, no. 2: 306–18.

———. 1984. *The Evolution of Cooperation*. New York: Basic Books.

Axelrod, Robert, and Robert O. Keohane. 1985. "Achieving Cooperation under Anarchy: Strategies and Institutions." *World Politics* 38, no. 1: 226–54.

Badger, Ralph Eastman. 1928. *Badger on Investment: Principles and Practices.* New York: Prentice Hall.

Baer, Werner, and Kent Hargis. 1997. "Forms of External Capital and Economic Development in Latin America: 1820–1997." *World Development* 25, no. 11: 1805–20.

Bairoch, Paul. 1976. *Commerce extérieur et développement économique de l'Europe au XIXe siècle.* Paris: Mouton.

Bambrick, Susan. 1970. "Australia's Long-Run Terms of Trade." *Economic Development and Cultural Change* 19, no. 1: 1–5.

Bandeira, Moniz. 1997. *Relações Brasil-EUA no contexto da globalização.* 2nd ed. São Paulo: Editora Senac São Paulo.

Baxter, Robert Dudley. 1871. *National Debts, Partly Read before the British Association, at Liverpool, September, 1870.* London: Robert John Bush.

Bazant, Jan. 1968. *Historia de la deuda exterior de México (1823–1946).* Mexico City: El Colegio de México.

Beck, Nathaniel, Jonathan N. Katz, and Richard Tucker. 1998. "Taking Time Seriously: Time-Series-Cross-Section Analysis with a Binary Dependent Variable." *American Journal of Political Science* 42, no. 4: 1260–88.

Bender, Johann Heinrich. 1830. *Der Verkehr mit Staatspapieren im In- und Auslande- 2., umfassendere und überall berichtigte Ausg.* Göttingen: Vandenhoeck and Ruprecht.

Bennett, D. Scott, and Allan C. Stam. 2000. "EUGene: A Conceptual Manual." *International Interactions* 26, no. 2: 179–204.

———. 2004. *The Behavioral Origins of War.* Ann Arbor: University of Michigan Press.

Berghoff, Hartmut. 2002. "Der Berliner Kapitalmarkt im Aufbruch (1830–1870)." In *Geschichte des Finanzplatzes Berlin,* ed. Hans Pohl, 55–102. Frankfurt am Main: Knapp.

Bethell, Leslie. 1989. "Britain and Latin America in Historical Perspective." In *Britain and Latin America: A Changing Relationship,* ed. Victor Bulmer-Thomas, 1–24. Cambridge: Cambridge University Press.

Beveraggi Allende, Walter Manuel. 1954. *El servicio del capital extranjero y el control de cambios: La experiencia argentina de 1900 a 1943.* Mexico City: Fondo de Cultura Económica.

Bird, Graham, and Nicholas Snowden. 1997. "From Banks to Bonds: A Problem Resolved? A Perspective from the LDC Debt Literature." *Journal of International Development* 9, no. 2: 207–20.

Blaisdell, Donald C. 1929. *European Financial Control in the Ottoman Empire: A Study of the Establishment, Activities, and Significance of the Administration of the Ottoman Public Debt.* New York: Columbia University Press.

Bock, Carl H. 1966. *Prelude to Tragedy: The Negotiation and Breakdown of the Tripartite Convention of London, October 31, 1861.* Philadelphia: University of Pennsylvania Press.

Boehmer, Ekkehart, and William L. Megginson. 1990. "Determinants of Secondary Market Prices for Developing Country Syndicated Loans." *Journal of Finance* 45, no. 5: 1517–40.

Böhme, Helmut. 1968. *Frankfurt und Hamburg.* Frankfurt am Main: Europäische Verlagsanstalt.

Bonner, Francis A. 1925. "A General Classification of Bonds." In *Fundamentals of Investment,* ed. Samuel O. Rice, 64–92. Chicago: A. W. Shaw.

Boot, Arnoud W. A., and George Kanatas. 1995. "Rescheduling of Sovereign Debt: Forgiveness, Precommitment and New Money." *Journal of Money, Credit and Banking* 27, no. 2: 363–77.

Borchard, Edwin. 1951. *State Insolvency and Foreign Bondholders.* Vol. 1: *General Principles.* New Haven, CT: Yale University Press.

Bordo, Michael D., Michael Edelstein, and Hugh Rockoff. 2003. "Was Adherence to the Gold Standard a 'Good Housekeeping Seal of Approval' during the Interwar Period?" In *Finance, Intermediaries, and Economic Development,* ed. Stanley L. Engerman et al., 288–318. Cambridge: Cambridge University Press.

Bordo, Michael D., Barry Eichengreen, and Douglas A. Irwin. 1999. "Is Globalization Today Really Different from Globalization a Hundred Years Ago?" *Brookings Trade Forum,* ed. Susan M. Collins and Robert Z. Lawrence, 1–50. Washington, DC: Brookings Institution Press.

Bordo, Michael D., and Hugh Rockoff. 1996. "The Gold Standard as a Good Housekeeping Seal of Approval." *Journal of Economic History* 56, no. 2: 389–428.

Bordo, Michael D., and Anna J. Schwartz. 1996. "The Operation of the Specie Standard: Evidence for Core and Peripheral Countries, 1880–1990." In *Currency Convertibility: The Gold Standard and Beyond,* ed. Jorge Braga de Macedo, Barry Eichengreen, and Jaime Reis, 11–83. London: Routledge.

Borensztein, Eduardo, and Paolo Mauro. 2004. "The Case for GDP-Indexed Bonds." *Economic Policy* 19, no. 38: 165–216.

Born, Karl Erich. 1986. "Erfahrungen aus internationalen Finanzkrisen der Vergangenheit." In *Die Internationale Schuldenkrise: Ursachen, Konsequenzen, historische Erfahrungen,* ed. Peter Bernholz and Armin Gutowski, 9–29. Berlin: Duncker & Humblot.

Brockhage, Bernhard. 1910. "Zur Entwicklung des Marktes für ausländische Wertpapiere für langfristige Exportkapitalien in Berlin." Ph.D. diss., Friedrich-Wilhelms-Universität zu Berlin.

Broz, J. Lawrence. 2005. "Congressional Politics of International Financial Rescues." *American Journal of Political Science* 49, no. 3: 479–96.

Broz, J. Lawrence, and Michael Brewster Hawes. 2006. "Congressional Politics of Financing the International Monetary Fund." *International Organization* 60, no. 1: 367–99.

Buchheit, Lee C. 1995. "Cross-Border Lending: What's Different This Time?" *Journal of International Law and Business* 16, no. 1: 44–56.

Buist, Marten G. 1974. *At Spes Non Fracta: Hope & Co., 1770–1815.* Amsterdam: Martinus Nijhoff.

Buiter, Willem H. 1988. "Comments on External Borrowing by LDCs: A Survey of Some Theoretical Issues." In *The State of Development Economics*, ed. Gustav Ranis and T. Paul Schultz, 613–18. Oxford: Basil Blackwell.

Bulmer-Thomas, Victor. 1987. *The Political Economy of Central America since 1920*. Cambridge: Cambridge University Press.

———. 1994. *The Economic History of Latin America since Independence*. Cambridge: Cambridge University Press.

Bulow, Jeremy, and Kenneth Rogoff. 1989a. "A Constant Recontracting Model of Sovereign Debt." *Journal of Political Economy* 97, no. 1: 155–78.

———. 1989b. "Sovereign Debt: Is to Forgive to Forget?" *American Economic Review* 79, no. 1: 43–50.

Burns, E. Bradford. 1966. *The Unwritten Alliance: Rio-Branco and Brazilian-American Relations*. New York: Columbia University Press.

Burr, Robert N. 1965. *By Reason or Force: Chile and the Balancing of Power in South America, 1830–1905*. Berkeley and Los Angeles: University of California Press.

Butlin, N. G. 1984. *Select Comparative Economic Statistics, 1900–1940: Australia and Britain, Canada, Japan, New Zealand and USA*. Source Papers in Economic History No. 4. Canberra: Australian National University.

Buyst, Erik. 1997. "New GNP Estimates for the Belgian Economy during the Interwar Period." *Review of Income and Wealth* 43, no. 3: 357–75.

Cady, John Frank. 1929. *Foreign Intervention in the Rio de la Plata, 1835–50*. Philadelphia: University of Pennsylvania Press.

Calógeras, João Pandiá, and Percy Alvin Martin. 1939. *A History of Brazil*. Chapel Hill: University of North Carolina Press.

Calvert, Peter. 1971. "The Last Occasion on which Britain Used Coercion to Settle a Dispute with a Non-Colonial Territory in the Caribbean: Guatemala and the Powers, 1909–1913." *Inter-American Economic Affairs* 25, no. 3: 57–75.

Calvo, Guillermo A. 1989. "A Delicate Equilibrium: Debt Relief and Default Penalties in an International Context." In *Analytical Issues in Debt*, ed. Jacob A. Frenkel, Michael P. Dooley, and Peter Wickham, 172–93. Washington, DC: International Monetary Fund.

Cardoso, Eliana A., and Rudiger Dornbusch. 1989. "Brazilian Debt Crises: Past and Present." In *The International Debt Crisis in Historical Perspective*, ed. Barry Eichengreen and Peter H. Lindert, 106–39. Cambridge, MA: MIT Press.

Carlson, John A., Aasim M. Husain, and Jeffrey A. Zimmerman. 1997. *Debt Reduction and New Loans: A Contracting Perspective*. IMF Working Paper WP/97/95. Washington, DC: International Monetary Fund.

Cavanaugh, Eleanor S. 1929. *Some Sources of Information on Stocks and Bonds: Prepared for the Annual Meeting of the Financial Group of the Special Libraries Association, Washington, D.C., May 15, 1929*. New York: Standard Statistics Company.

Chabloz, Edouard. 1899. *Manuel des valeurs cotées aux Bourses de Bâle et Zurich*. Geneva: Kündig & fils.

———. 1907–8. *Vade-Mecum des Bourses de Bâle, Zurich et Genève*. Zurich: Orell Füssli.

———. 1910–11. *Vade-Mecum des Bourses de Bâle, Zurich et Genève*. Zurich: Orell Füssli.

Chakalov, Asen Khristov. 1946. *Natsionalniiat dokhod i razkhod na Bulgariia, 1924–1945* (The National Income and Outlay of Bulgaria, 1924–1945). Sofia: Pechatnitsa knipegraf.

Chamberlain, Gary. 1980. "Analysis of Covariance with Qualitative Data." *Review of Economic Studies* 47, no. 1: 225–38.

Chamberlain, Lawrence, and George W. Edwards. 1927. *The Principles of Bond Investment*. Rev. ed. New York: Henry Holt.

Chancellor, Edward. 1999. *Devil Take the Hindmost: A History of Financial Speculation*. New York: Farrar, Straus and Giroux.

Chen, Zhaohui, and Alberto Giovannini. 1994. "The Determinants of Realignment Expectations under the EMS: Some Empirical Regularities." In *The Monetary Economics of Europe: Causes of the EMS Crisis*, ed. Christopher Johnson and Stefan Collignon, 113–40. London: Pinter.

Chernow, Ron. 1990. *The House of Morgan: An American Banking Dynasty and the Rise of Modern Finance*. New York: Atlantic Monthly Press.

Chesneau, Roger, and Eugène M. Kolesnik, eds. 1979. *Conway's All the World's Fighting Ships, 1860–1905*. New York: Mayflower Books.

Chowdhry, Bhagwan. 1991. "What Is Different about International Lending?" *Review of Financial Studies* 4, no. 1: 121–48.

Clarke, Henry Butler, and William Holden Hutton. 1906. *Modern Spain, 1815–1898*. Cambridge: Cambridge University Press.

Clarke, Hyde. 1878. "On the Debts of Sovereign and Quasi-Sovereign States, Owing by Foreign Countries." *Journal of the Statistical Society* 51, no. 2: 299–347.

Clay, Paul 1920. *Sound Investing*. New York: Moody's Investors Service.

Clemens, Michael A., and Jeffrey Williamson. 2004. "Wealth Bias in the First Global Capital Market Boom, 1870–1913." *Economic Journal* 114, no. 2: 304–37.

Cline, William R. 1995. *International Debt Reexamined*. Washington, DC: Institute for International Economics.

Cline, William R., and Kevin J. S. Barnes. 1997. *Spreads and Risk in Emerging Markets Lending*. Research Paper 97-1. Washington, DC: Institute of International Finance.

Cohen, Benjamin J. 1985. "International Debt and Linkage Strategies: Some Foreign-Policy Implications for the United States." *International Organization* 39, no. 4: 699–727.

———. 1986. *In Whose Interest? International Banking and American Foreign Policy*. New Haven, CT: Yale University Press.

Cohen, Daniel. 1991. *Private Lending to Sovereign States: A Theoretical Autopsy*. Cambridge, MA: MIT Press.

Cohen, Daniel, and Richard Portes. 2006. "Toward a Lender of *First* Resort." IMF Working Paper WP/06/66. Washington, DC: International Monetary Fund.

Cole, Harold L., James Dow, and William B. English. 1995. "Default, Settlement, and Signalling: Lending Resumption in a Reputational Model of Sovereign Debt." *International Economic Review* 36, no. 2: 365–85.

Cole, Harold L., and Patrick J. Kehoe. 1997. "Reviving Reputation Models of International Debt." *Federal Reserve Bank of Minneapolis Quarterly Review* 21, no. 1: 21–30.

———. 1998. "Models of Sovereign Debt: Partial versus General Reputations." *International Economic Review* 39, no. 1: 55–70.

Correlates of War. 1996. *Militarized Interstate Disputes Data Set*, Version 2.1. http://cow2.la.psu.edu/.

———. 2003. *Militarized Interstate Disputes Data Set*, Version 3.02. http://cow2 .la.psu.edu/.

———. 2005. *National Material Capabilities Data Set*, Version 3.02. http://cow2 .la.psu.edu/.

Costa, Fernando. 1998. *Portugal e a Guerra Anglo-Boer: Política externa e opinião pública (1899–1902)*. Lisbon: Edições Cosmos.

Crawford, Vincent P. 1987. "International Lending, Long-Term Credit Relationships, and Dynamic Contract Theory." *Princeton Studies in International Finance* No. 59. Princeton, NJ: International Finance Section, Department of Economics, Princeton University.

Cripps, Martin W., George J. Mailath, and Larry Samuelson. 2004. "Imperfect Monitoring and Impermanent Reputations." *Econometrica* 72, no. 2: 407–32.

Cuddington, John T. 1989. "The Extent and Causes of the Debt Crisis of the 1980s." In *Dealing with the Debt Crisis*, ed. Ishrat Husain and Ishac Diwan, 15–44. Washington, DC: World Bank.

Dakin, Douglas. 1972. *The Unification of Greece, 1770–1923*. New York: St. Martin's.

Dammers, Clifford. 1984. "A Brief History of Sovereign Defaults and Rescheduling." In *Default and Rescheduling: Corporate and Sovereign Borrowers*, ed. David Suratgar, 77–84. Washington, DC: Euromoney.

Davies, Albert Emil. 1927. *Investments Abroad*. Chicago: A. W. Shaw.

Davis, Christina L. 2003. *Food Fights over Free Trade: How International Institutions Promote Agricultural Trade Liberalization*. Princeton, NJ: Princeton University Press.

———. 2004. "International Institutions and Issue Linkage: Building Support for Agricultural Trade Liberalization." *American Political Science Review* 98, no. 1: 153–69.

Davis, Lance E., and Robert A. Huttenback. 1986. *Mammon and the Pursuit of Empire: The Political Economy of British Imperialism*. Cambridge: Cambridge University Press.

Dawson, Frank Griffith. 1990. *The First Latin American Debt Crisis: The City of London and the 1822–25 Loan Bubble*. New Haven, CT: Yale University Press.

Deas, Malcolm D., and Efraín Sánchez. 1991. *Santander y los ingleses, 1832–1840*. Bogotá: Fundación para la Conmemoración del Bicentenario del Natalicio y el Sesquicentenario de la Muerte del General Francisco de Paula Santander.

De Bonis, Riccardo, Alessandro Giustiniani, and Giorgio Gomel. 1999. "Crises and Bail-Outs of Banks and Countries: Linkages, Analogies, and Differences." *World Economy* 22, no. 1: 55–86.

De Grauwe, Paul, and Michele Fratianni. 1984. "The Political Economy of International Lending." *Cato Journal* 4, no. 1: 147–70.

della Paolera, Gerardo, and Alan M. Taylor. 1999. "Economic Recovery from the Argentine Great Depression: Institutions, Expectations, and the Change of Macroeconomic Regime." *Journal of Economic History* 59, no. 3: 567–99.

———. 2001. *Straining at the Anchor: The Argentine Currency Board and the Search for Macroeconomic Stability, 1880–1935*. Chicago: University of Chicago Press.

Dennis, William Jefferson. 1931. *Tacna and Arica: An Account of the Chile-Peru Boundary Dispute and of the Arbitrations by the United States*. New Haven, CT: Yale University Press.

Devlin, Robert. 1985. *Transnational Banks and the External Finance of Latin America: The Experience of Peru*. Santiago: United Nations.

———. 1989. *Debt and Crisis in Latin America: The Supply Side of the Story*. Princeton, NJ: Princeton University Press.

De Vries, Jan, and Ad van der Woude. 1997. *The First Modern Economy: Success, Failure, and Perseverance of the Dutch Economy, 1500–1815*. Cambridge: Cambridge University Press.

Diamond, Douglas W. 1989. "Reputation Acquisition in Debt Markets." *Journal of Political Economy* 97, no. 4: 828–62.

Díaz Alejandro, Carlos F. 1970. *Essays on the Economic History of the Argentine Republic*. New Haven, CT: Yale University Press.

———. 1983. "Stories of the 1930s for the 1980s." In *Financial Policies and the World Capital Market: The Problem of Latin American Countries*, ed. Pedro Aspe Armella, Rudiger Dornbusch, and Maurice Obstfeld, 5–35. Chicago: University of Chicago Press.

———. 1984. "Latin American Debt: I Don't Think We Are in Kansas Anymore." *Brookings Papers on Economic Activity* 1984, no. 2: 335–403.

———. 1986. "The Early 1980s in Latin America: The 1930s One More Time?" In *Theory and Reality in Development: Essays in Honour of Paul Streeten*, ed. Sanjaya Lall and Frances Stewart, 154–64. Houndmills, Basingstoke, Hampshire: Macmillan.

Diehl, Paul F. and Gary Goertz. 2000. *War and Peace in International Rivalry*. Ann Arbor: University of Michigan Press.

Diwan, Ishac. 1990. "Linking Trade and External Debt Strategies." *Journal of International Economics* 29, nos. 3–4: 293–310.

Donnelly, Jack. 2000. *Realism in International Relations*. Cambridge: Cambridge University Press.

Dooley, Michael P. 1995. "A Retrospective on the Debt Crisis." In *Understanding Interdependence: The Macroeconomics of the Open Economy*, ed. Peter B. Kenen, 262–87. Princeton, NJ: Princeton University Press.

Dornbusch, Rudi. 2000. *Keys to Prosperity: Free Markets, Sound Money, and a Bit of Luck*. Cambridge, MA: MIT Press.

Downs, George W., and Michael A. Jones. 2002. "Reputation, Compliance, and International Law." *Journal of Legal Studies* 31, no. 1, pt. 2: S95–S114.

Drosdoff, Daniel. 1972. *El gobierno de las vacas (1933–1956): Tratado Roca-Runciman*. Buenos Aires: Ediciones La Bastilla.

Dulles, Allen W. 1932. "The Protection of American Foreign Bondholders." *Foreign Affairs* 10, no. 3: 474–84.

Earle, Peter. 2003. *The Pirate Wars*. New York: St. Martin's Griffin/Thomas Dunne.

Eastwick, Edward B. 1868. *Venezuela: Or, Sketches of Life in a South American Republic*. London: Chapman and Hall.

Eaton, Jonathan. 1990. "Debt Relief and the International Enforcement of Loan Contracts." *Journal of Economic Perspectives* 4, no. 1: 43–56.

———. 1996. "Sovereign Debt, Reputation and Credit Terms." *International Journal of Finance and Economics* 1, no. 10: 25–35.

Eaton, Jonathan, and Mark Gersovitz. 1981. "Debt with Potential Repudiation: Theoretical and Empirical Analysis." *Review of Economic Studies* 48, no. 2: 289–309.

Eaton, Jonathan, Mark Gersovitz, and Joseph E. Stiglitz. 1986. "The Pure Theory of Country Risk." *European Economic Review* 30, no. 3: 481–513.

Eckstein, Alexander. 1955. "National Income and Capital Formation in Hungary, 1900–1950." In *Income and Wealth*, ed. Simon Kuznets, 152–223. London: Bowes and Bowes.

Edelstein, Michael. 1982. *Overseas Investment in the Age of High Imperialism: The United Kingdom, 1850–1914*. New York: Columbia University Press.

Edwards, George W. 1926. *Investing in Foreign Securities*. New York: Ronald Press.

Edwards, Sebastian. 1986. "The Pricing of Bonds and Bank Loans in International Markets: An Empirical Analysis of Developing Countries' Foreign Borrowing." *European Economic Review* 30, no. 3: 565–89.

Egli, Dominick. 1997. "Optimal Debt Relief under Threat of Trade Punishments." *Review of International Economics* 5, no. 2: 272–83.

Eichengreen, Barry. 1991. "Historical Research on International Lending and Debt." *Journal of Economic Perspectives* 5, no. 2: 149–69.

———. 1992. *Golden Fetters: The Gold Standard and the Great Depression, 1919–1939*. New York: Oxford University Press.

———. 1999. *Toward a New International Financial Architecture: A Practical Post-Asia Agenda*. Washington, DC: Institute for International Economics.

———. 2002. *Financial Crises: And What to Do about Them*. Oxford: Oxford University Press.

———. 2003. "Restructuring Sovereign Debt." *Journal of Economic Perspectives* 17, no. 4: 75–98.

Eichengreen, Barry, and Ashoka Mody. 2000. "Lending Booms, Reserves and the Sustainability of Short-Term Debt: Inferences from the Pricing of Syndicated Bank Loans." *Journal of Development Economics* 63, no. 1: 5–44.

———. 2004. "Do Collective Action Clauses Raise Borrowing Costs?" *Economic Journal* 114, no. 495: 247–64.

Eichengreen, Barry, and Richard Portes. 1986. "Debt and Default in the 1930s: Causes and Consequences." *European Economic Review* 30, no. 3: 599–640.

———. 1987. "The Anatomy of Financial Crises." In *Threats to International Financial Stability*, ed. Richard Portes and Alexander K. Swoboda, 10–66. Cambridge: Cambridge University Press.

———. 1989. "Dealing with Debt: The 1930s and the 1980s." In *Dealing with the Debt Crisis*, ed. Ishrat Husain and Ishac Diwan, 69–86. Washington, DC: World Bank.

———. 1995. *Crisis? What Crisis? Orderly Workouts for Sovereign Debtors*. London: Centre for Economic Policy Research.

Eichengreen, Barry, and Christof Rühl. 2001. "The Bail-In Problem: Systematic Goals, Ad Hoc Means." *Economic Systems* 25, no. 1: 3–32.

English, William B. 1996. "Understanding the Costs of Sovereign Default: American State Debts in the 1840s." *American Economic Review* 86, no. 1: 259–75.

Ercolani, Paolo. 1969. "Documentazione statistica di base." In *Lo sviluppo economico in Italia: Storia dell'economia italiana negli ultimi cento anni*, ed. Giorgio Fuà, 380–460. Milan: Franco Angeli Editore.

Esteves, Rui Pedro. 2006. "Quis custodiet quem? Sovereign Debt and Bondholders' Protection Before 1914." Working paper, Simon Fraser University.

Esty, Benjamin C., and William L. Megginson. 2003. "Creditor Rights, Enforcement, and Debt Ownership Structure: Evidence from the Global Syndicated Loan Market." *Journal of Financial and Quantitative Analysis* 38, no. 1: 37–59.

Evans, Henry Clay. 1927. *Chile and Its Relations with the United States*. Durham, NC: Duke University Press.

Fafchamps, Marcel. 1996. "Sovereign Debt, Structural Adjustment, and Conditionality." *Journal of Development Economics* 50, no. 2: 313–35.

Feilchenfeld, Ernst H. 1934. "Rights and Remedies of Foreign Bondholders." In *Bonds & Bondholders: Rights & Remedies*, ed. Sylvester E. Quindry, vol. 2: 130–239. Chicago: Burdette Smith.

Feis, Herbert. 1930. *Europe: The World's Banker, 1870–1914*. New Haven, CT: Yale University Press.

Feller, Friedrich E. 1834. *Archiv der Staatspapiere, enthaltend den Ursprung, die Einrichtung und den jetzigen Zustand der Staats-Anleihen: Nebst die Berechnung der Staats-Effecten und den darin vorkommenden Geschäften*. 2nd ed. Leipzig: I. Müller.

Ferguson, Niall. 1998. *The House of Rothschild: Money's Prophets, 1798–1848*. New York: Viking.

———. 1999. *The House of Rothschild: The World's Banker, 1849–1999*. New York: Viking.

———. 2005a. "The City of London and British Imperialism: New Light on an Old Question." In *London and Paris as International Financial Centres in the Twentieth Century*, ed. Youssef Cassis and Éric Bussière, 57–77. Oxford: Oxford University Press.

———. 2005b. "The First 'Eurobonds': The Rothschilds and the Financing of the Holy Alliance, 1818–1822." In *The Origins of Value: The Financial Innovations that Created Modern Capital Markets*, ed. William N. Goetzmann and K. Geert Rouwenhorst, 313–35. Oxford: Oxford University Press.

———. 2006. "Political Risk and the International Bond Market between the 1848 Revolution and the Outbreak of the First World War." *Economic History Review* 59, no. 1: 70–112.

Ferguson, Niall, and Moritz Schularick. 2006. "The Empire Effect: The Determinants of Country Risk in the First Age of Globalization, 1880–1913." *Journal of Economic History* 66, no. 2: 283–312.

Fernández, Raquel, and Jacob Glazer. 1990. "The Scope for Collusive Behavior among Debtor Countries." *Journal of Development Economics* 32, no. 2: 297–313.

Fernández, Raquel, and Şule Özler. 1999. "Debt Concentration and Bargaining Power: Large Banks, Small Banks, and Secondary Market Prices." *International Economic Review* 40, no. 2: 333–55.

Ferns, Henry S. 1977. *Britain and Argentina in the Nineteenth Century.* New York: Arno Press.

Finnemore, Martha. 2003. *The Purpose of Intervention: Changing Beliefs about the Use of Force.* Ithaca, NY: Cornell University Press.

Fischer, Stanley. 1999. "On the Need for an International Lender of Last Resort." *Journal of Economic Perspectives* 13, no. 4: 85–104.

Fishlow, Albert. 1985. "Lessons from the Past: Capital Markets during the 19th Century and the Interwar Period." *International Organization* 39, no. 3: 383–439.

———. 1989. "Hard Times: Latin America in the 1930s and 1980s." In *Interactions in the World Economy: Perspectives from International Economic History*, ed. Carl-Ludwig Holtfrerich, 314–37. New York: New York University Press.

Flandreau, Marc. 2003. "Caveat Emptor: Coping with Sovereign Risk under the International Gold Standard, 1871–1913." In *International Financial History in the Twentieth Century: System and Anarchy*, ed. Marc Flandreau, Carl-Ludwig Holtfrerich, and Harold James, 17–50. Cambridge: Cambridge University Press.

———. 2006. "Home Biases, Nineteenth Century Style." *Journal of the European Economics Association* 4, nos. 2–3: 634–43.

Flandreau, Marc, Jacques Le Cacheux, and Frédéric Zumer. 1998. "Stability without a Pact? Lessons from the European Gold Standard, 1880–1914." *Economic Policy* 13, no. 26: 115–62.

Flandreau, Marc, and Frédéric Zumer. 2004. *The Making of Global Finance, 1880–1913.* Paris: Organisation for Economic Co-operation and Development.

Fodor, Jorge G., and Arturo A. O'Connell. 1973. "La Argentina y la economía atlántica en la primera mitad del siglo XX." *Desarrollo económico* 13, no. 49: 3–65.

Folkerts-Landau, David. 1985. "The Changing Role of International Bank Lending in Development Finance." *IMF Staff Papers* 32, no. 2: 317–63.

Forbes, Ian L. D. 1978. "The German Participation in the Allied Coercion of Venezuela, 1902–1903." *Australian Journal of Politics and History* 34, no. 3: 317–31.

France. Ministère des Affaires Étrangères. 1880. *Documents diplomatiques: Affaires du Monténégro no. 1.* Paris: Imprimerie Nationale.

———. 1881. *Documents diplomatiques: Affaires de Grèce en 1880.* Paris: Imprimerie Nationale.

———. 1897a. *Documents diplomatiques: Affaires d'Orient, affaire de Crète: June 1894–February 1897.* Paris: Imprimerie Nationale.

———. 1897b. *Documents diplomatiques: Affaires d'Orient, affaire de Crète: February-May 1897.* Paris: Imprimerie Nationale, 1897.

Frankfurter Zeitung. 1911. *Geschichte der Frankfurter Zeitung.* Frankfurt am Main: Frankfurter Societätsdruckerei.

Fremdling, Rainer. 1995. "German National Accounts for the 19th and Early 20th Century." *Scandinavian Economic History Review* 43, no. 1: 77–100.

Frieden, Jeffry A. 1988. "Classes, Sectors, and Foreign Debt in Latin America." *Comparative Politics* 21, no. 1: 1–19.

———. 1989a. "The Economics of Intervention: American Overseas Investments and Relations with Underdeveloped Areas, 1890–1950." *Contemporary Studies in Society and History* 31, no. 1: 55–80.

———. 1989b. "Winners and Losers in the Latin American Debt Crisis: The Political Implications." In *Debt and Democracy in Latin America*, ed. Barbara Stallings and Robert R. Kaufman, 23–37. Boulder, CO: Westview Press.

———. 1991. *Debt, Development, and Democracy: Modern Political Economy and Latin America, 1965–1985*. Princeton, NJ: Princeton University Press.

———. 1999. "Actors and Preferences in International Relations." In *Strategic Choice and International Relations*, ed. David A. Lake and Robert Powell, 39–76. Princeton, NJ: Princeton University Press.

Friedman, James W. 1971. "A Non-cooperative Equilibrium for Supergames." *Review of Economic Studies* 38, no. 1: 1–12.

Fukuyama, Francis. 2004. *State-Building: Governance and the World Order in the 21st Century*. Ithaca, NY: Cornell University Press.

Gallagher, John, and Ronald Robinson. 1953. "The Imperialism of Free Trade." *Economic History Review* 6, no. 1: 1–15.

García-Mata, Carlos. 1941. "The Problem of Beef in United States—Argentine Relations: Lecture Given at Harvard University on the 23rd of April, 1941." Lecture, Harvard University.

Gelman, Andrew, John B. Carlin, Hal S. Stern, and Donald B. Rubin. 2004. *Bayesian Data Analysis*. 2nd ed. Boca Raton, FL: Chapman & Hall/CRC.

Germany. Auswärtiges Amt. 1957. *German Foreign Ministry Archives, 1867–1920*. Microfilm edition. Washington, DC: American Committee for the Study of War Documents.

Germany. Reichstag. Various issues. *Stenographische Berichte über die Verhandlungen des Reichstages*.

Germany. Statistisches Reichsamt. Various issues. *Vierteljahrshefte zur Statistik des Deutschen Reichs*. Berlin.

Gersovitz, Mark. 1983. "Trade, Capital Mobility and Sovereign Immunity." Research Program in Development Studies, Discussion Paper No. 108. Princeton, NJ: Woodrow Wilson School, Princeton University.

———. 1985. "Banks' International Lending Decisions: What We Know and Implications for Future Research." In *International Debt and Developing Countries*, ed. Gordon W. Smith and John T. Cuddington, 61–78. Washington, DC: World Bank.

Ghosn, Faten, and Scott Bennett. 2003. *Codebook for the Dyadic Militarized Interstate Incident Data*, Version 3.0. http://cow2.la.psu.edu.

Ghosn, Faten, Glenn Palmer, and Stuart Bremer. 2004. "The MID3 Data Set, 1993–2001: Procedures, Coding Rules, and Description." *Conflict Management and Peace Science* 21, no. 2: 133–154.

Gianviti, François. 1990. "The International Monetary Fund and External Debt."
In *Recueil des cours: Collected Courses of the Hague Academy of International
Law 1989–III*, 205–86. Boston: Martinus Nijhoff.

Gibson, Rajna, and Suresh Sundaresan. 2005. "A Model of Sovereign Borrowing
and Sovereign Yield Spreads." Working paper, University of Zurich and Columbia University.

Glick, Reuven. 1986. *Economic Perspectives on Foreign Borrowing and Debt
Repudiation: An Analytic Literature Review*. New York: Salomon Brothers
Center for the Study of Financial Institutions, Graduate School of Business Ad-
ministration, New York University.

Goodman, Laurie S. 1983. "Syndicated Eurolending: Pricing and Practice." In
*International Finance Handbook*, ed. Abraham M. George and Ian H. Giddy
sec. 3.4, 3–29. New York: John Wiley and Sons.

Goslinga, Cornelis Ch. 1990. *The Dutch in the Caribbean and in Surinam 1791/
5–1942*. Assen: Van Gorcum.

Gould, Erica R. 2006. *Money Talks: The International Monetary Fund, Conditionality and Supplementary Financiers*. Stanford, CA: Stanford University
Press.

Gravil, Roger. 1985. *The Anglo-Argentine Connection, 1900–1939*. Boulder, CO:
Westview Press.

Gray, Randal, ed. 1985. *Conway's All the World's Fighting Ships, 1906–1921*.
Annapolis, MD: Naval Institute Press.

Gray, William H. 1949. "The Human Aspect of Aves Diplomacy: An Incident in
the Relations between the United States and Venezuela." *The Americas* 6, no.
1: 72–84.

Green, Donald P., Soo Yeon Kim, and David H. Yoon. 2001. "Dirty Pool." *International Organization* 55, no. 2: 441–68.

Gregg, Richard T. 1999. *Gregor MacGregor, Cazique of Poyais: 1786–1845*. London: International Bond and Share Society.

Greif, Avner, Paul Milgrom, and Barry R. Weingast. 1994. "Coordination, Commitment and Enforcement: The Case of the Merchant Guild." *Journal of Political Economy* 102, no. 4: 745–76.

Grenville, J.A.S. 1964. *Lord Salisbury and Foreign Policy: The Close of the Nineteenth Century*. London: University of London, Athlone Press.

Grossman, Herschel I., and John B. Van Huyck. 1988. "Sovereign Debt as a Contingent Claim: Excusable Default, Repudiation, and Reputation." *American
Economic Review* 78, no. 5: 1088–97.

Gugiatti, Mark, and Anthony Richards. 2004. "The Use of Collective Action
Clauses in New York Law Bonds of Sovereign Borrowers." *Georgetown Journal of International Law* 35, no. 4: 815–35.

Guisinger, Alexandra, and Alastair Smith. 2002. "Honest Threats: The Interaction of Reputation and Political Institutions in International Crises." *Journal
of Conflict Resolution* 46, no. 2: 175–200.

Guthrie, Wayne Lee. 1983. "The Anglo-German Intervention in Venezuela, 1902–
03." Ph.D. diss., University of California, San Diego.

Guzman, Andrew T. 2002. "A Compliance-Based Theory of International Law."
*California Law Review* 90, no. 6: 1823–87.

Haas, Ernst B. 1980. "Why Collaborate? Issue-Linkage and International Regimes." *World Politics* 32, no. 3: 357–405.

Haggard, Stephan. 2000. *The Political Economy of the Asian Financial Crisis.* Washington, DC: Institute for International Economics.

Hallak, Issam. 2003. "Bank Loans Non-linear Structure of Pricing: Empirical Evidence from Sovereign Debts." CFS Working Paper 2003/33. Center for Financial Studies, Goethe-Universität Frankfurt.

Hallinan, Charles T. 1927. *American Investments in Europe.* London: Europa.

Hannell, David. 1989. "Lord Palmerston and the 'Don Pacifico Affair' of 1850: The Ionian Connection." *European History Quarterly* 19, no. 4: 495–508.

Hansen, Bent, and Girgis A. Marzouk. 1965. *Development and Economic Policy in the UAR (Egypt).* Amsterdam: North-Holland.

Hansen, Svend Aage. 1974. *Økonomisk vækst i Danmark.* Copenhagen: Akademisk Forlag.

Harrell, Frank E. 2001. *Regression Modeling Strategies: With Applications to Linear Models, Logistic Regression, and Survival Analysis.* New York: Springer.

Hasbrouck, Alfred. 1927. "Gregor McGregor and the Colonization of Poyais, Between 1820 and 1824." *Hispanic American Historical Review* 7, no. 4: 438–59.

Helleiner, Eric. 1994. *States and the Reemergence of Global Finance: From Bretton Woods to the 1990s.* Ithaca, NY: Cornell University Press.

Hellwig, Martin. 1986. "The Pure Theory of Country Risk: Comments." *European Economic Review* 30, no. 3: 521–27.

Herschel, Arthur Hobart. 1925. *The Selection and Care of Sound Investments.* New York: H. W. Wilson.

Herwig, Holger H. 1986. *Germany's Vision of Empire in Venezuela, 1871–1914.* Princeton, NJ: Princeton University Press.

Hilaire, Max. 1997. *International Law and the United States Military Intervention in the Western Hemisphere.* Boston: Kluwer Law International.

Hjerppe, Riitta. 1989. *The Finnish Economy, 1860–1985: Growth and Structural Change.* Helsinki: Bank of Finland and Government Printing Centre.

Hobson, C. K. 1914. *The Export of Capital.* New York: Macmillan.

Hogan, Albert E. 1908. *Pacific Blockade.* Oxford: Clarendon Press.

Holden, Steinar, and Birger Vikøren. 1996. "The Credibility of a Fixed Exchange Rate: How Reputation Is Gained or Lost." *Scandinavian Journal of Economics* 98, no. 4: 485–502.

Honaker, James, Anne Joseph, Gary King, Kenneth Scheve, and Naunihal Singh. 2001. *Amelia: A Program for Missing Data.* Gauss Version. Cambridge, MA: Harvard University.

Hopf, Ted. 1994. *Peripheral Visions: Deterrence Theory and American Foreign Policy in the Third World, 1965–1990.* Ann Arbor: University of Michigan Press.

Hopkins, A. G. 1986. "The Victorians and Africa: A Reconsideration of the Occupation of Egypt, 1882." *Journal of African History* 27, no. 2: 363–91.

Hueyo, Alberto. 1938. *La Argentina en la depresión mundial, 1932–1933: Discursos—conferencias.* Buenos Aires: Librería y Editorial "El Ateneo."

Huth, Paul K. 1997. "Reputations and Deterrence: A Theoretical and Empirical Assessment." *Security Studies* 7, no. 1: 72–99.

———. 1999. "Deterrence and International Conflict: Empirical Findings and Theoretical Debates." *Annual Review of Political Science* 2: 25–48.

Institute of International Finance. 1936. *Credit Position of Argentina.* New York: Institute of International Finance.

International Monetary Fund. 2002. "Collective Action Clauses in Sovereign Bond Contracts—Encouraging Greater Use." Washington, DC: International Monetary Fund.

Ireland, Gordon. 1938. *Boundaries, Possessions, and Conflicts in South America.* Cambridge, MA: Harvard University Press.

Jaggers, Keith, and Ted Robert Gurr. 1995. "Tracking Democracy's Third Wave with the Polity III Data." *Journal of Peace Research* 32, no. 4: 469–82.

Jenks, Leland Hamilton. 1927. *The Migration of British Capital to 1875.* New York: Alfred A. Knopf.

Jervis, Robert. 1976. *Perception and Misperception in International Politics.* Princeton, NJ: Princeton University Press.

———. 1982–83. "Deterrence and Perception." *International Security* 7, no. 3: 3–30.

Jones, Chester Lloyd. 1940. *Guatemala: Past and Present.* Minneapolis: University of Minnesota Press.

Jones, Daniel M., Stuart A. Bremer, and J. David Singer. 1996. "Militarized Interstate Disputes, 1816–1992: Rationale, Coding Rules, and Empirical Patterns." *Conflict Management and Peace Science* 15, no. 2: 163–215.

Jones, Edward D. 1919. *Investment.* New York: Alexander Hamilton Institute.

Jordan, David F. 1929. *Jordan on Investments.* 1st ed. New York: Prentice Hall.

———. 1934. *Jordan on Investments.* 3rd ed. New York: Prentice Hall.

Jorgensen, Erika, and Jeffrey Sachs. 1989. "Default and Renegotiation of Latin American Foreign Bonds in the Interwar Period." In *The International Debt Crisis in Historical Perspective,* ed. Barry Eichengreen and Peter H. Lindert, 48–85. Cambridge, MA: MIT Press.

Kahler, Miles. 1985. "Politics and International Debt: Explaining the Crisis." *International Organization* 39, no. 3: 357–82.

Kaletsky, Anatole. 1985. *The Costs of Default.* New York: Priority Press.

Kapstein, Ethan B. 1994. *Governing the Global Economy: International Finance and the State.* Cambridge, MA: Harvard University Press.

Kapur, Devesh, John P. Lewis, and Richard Webb. 1997. *The World Bank: Its First Half Century.* Washington, DC: Brookings Institution.

Katzenstein, Peter J., Robert O. Keohane, and Stephen D. Krasner. 1998. "*International Organization* and the Study of World Politics." *International Organization* 52, no. 4: 645–85.

Kaufman, Robert R. 1988. *The Politics of Debt in Argentina, Brazil, and Mexico: Economic Stabilization in the 1980s.* Berkeley: Institute of International Studies, University of California.

Kelly, Trish. 1998. "Ability and Willingness to Pay in the Age of Pax Britannica, 1890–1914." *Explorations in Economic History* 35, no. 1: 31–58.

Keohane, Robert O. 1984. *After Hegemony: Cooperation and Discord in the World Political Economy.* Princeton, NJ: Princeton University Press.

Keohane, Robert O., and Lisa L. Martin. 1995. "The Promise of Institutionalist Theory." *International Security* 20, no. 1: 39–61.

Keohane, Robert O., and Joseph S. Nye. 1977. *Power and Interdependence: World Politics in Transition.* Boston: Little, Brown.

Kimber, Albert W. 1919. *Foreign Government Securities: A Text-Book for Banker and Statistician.* New York: A. W. Kimber.

Kindleberger, Charles P. 1986. *The World in Depression, 1929–1939.* Berkeley and Los Angeles: University of California Press.

———. 1993. *A Financial History of Western Europe.* 2nd ed. New York: Oxford University Press.

King, Gary, James Honaker, Anne Joseph, and Kenneth F. Scheve. 2001. "Analyzing Incomplete Political Science Data: An Alternative Algorithm for Multiple Imputation." *American Political Science Review* 95, no. 1: 49–69.

King, Gary, Michael Tomz, and Jason Wittenberg. 2000. "Making the Most of Statistical Analyses: Improving Interpretation and Presentation." *American Journal of Political Science* 44, no. 2: 347–61.

Kirkpatrick, F. A. 1931. *A History of the Argentine Republic.* Cambridge: Cambridge University Press.

Kirshman, John Emmett. 1924. *Principles of Investment.* September 1926 ed. Chicago: A. W. Shaw.

Kletzer, Kenneth M. 1988. "External Borrowing by LDCs: A Survey of Some Theoretical Issues." In *The State of Development Economics: Progress and Perspectives,* ed. Gustav Ranis and T. Paul Schultz, 579–612. Oxford: Basil Blackwell.

Kletzer, Kenneth M., and Brian D. Wright. 2000. "Sovereign Debt as Intertemporal Barter." *American Economic Review* 90, no. 3: 621–39.

Klimenko, Mikhail M. 2002. "Trade Interdependence, the International Financial Institutions, and the Recent Evolution of Sovereign-Debt Renegotiations." *Journal of International Economics* 58, no. 1: 177–209.

Kneer, Warren G. 1975. *Great Britain and the Caribbean, 1901–1913.* East Lansing: Michigan State University Press.

Kostelenos, George C. 1995. *Money and Output in Modern Greece, 1858–1938.* Athens: Centre of Planning and Economic Research.

Krantz, Olle, and Carl-Axel Nilsson. 1975. *Swedish National Product 1861–1970: New Aspects on Methods and Measurement.* Lund, Sweden: LiberLäromedel/Gleerup.

Krasner, Stephen D. 1978. *Defending the National Interest: Raw Materials Investments and U.S. Foreign Policy.* Princeton, NJ: Princeton University Press.

———. 1999. *Sovereignty: Organized Hypocrisy.* Princeton, NJ: Princeton University Press.

Kreps, David M., and Robert Wilson. 1982. "Reputation and Imperfect Information." *Journal of Economic Theory* 27, no. 2: 253–79.

Krueger, Anne. 2003. "Sovereign Debt Restructuring: Messy or Messier?" *American Economic Review* 93, no. 2: 70–74.

Lagerquist, Walter Edwards. 1921. *Investment Analysis: Fundamentals in the Analysis of Investment Securities.* New York: Macmillan.

Lains, Pedro, and Fernando Costa. 2001. "Portugal and the Boer War." In *The International Impact of the Boer War,* ed. Keith M. Wilson, 140–57. New York: Palgrave.

Lake, David A. 1996. "Anarchy, Hierarchy, and the Variety of International Relations." *International Organization* 50, no. 1: 1–33.

———. 2006. "Hierarchy in International Relations: Authority, Sovereignty, and the New Structure of World Politics." Unpublished manuscript, University of California, San Diego.

Lamont, Thomas W. 1920. "Foreign Government Bonds." *Annals of the American Academy of Political and Social Science* 88, no. 177: 121–29.

Lane, Philip R. 2004. "Empirical Perspectives on Long-Term External Debt." *Topics in Macroeconomics* 4, no. 1: 1–21.

Langer, William L. 1972. *An Encyclopedia of World History.* Boston: Houghton Mifflin.

Langley, Lester D., and Thomas Schoonover. 1995. *The Banana Men: American Mercenaries and Entrepreneurs in Central America, 1880–1930.* Lexington: University Press of Kentucky.

Larkin, Charles. 2005. "The History of Debt Conditionality." In *Innovative Solutions to the Debt Problem,* ed. Charles Kearney, 60–77. Institute for International Integration Studies, Trinity College, Dublin.

Latané, John H. 1906. "The Forcible Collection of International Debts." *Atlantic Monthly,* October, 542–50.

Leacy, F. H. 1983. *Historical Statistics of Canada.* 2nd ed. Ottawa: Statistics Canada.

League of Nations. 1929. *Review of World Trade, 1926–1928.* Geneva: League of Nations.

———. 1931. *Statistical Yearbook of the League of Nations, 1930/31.* Geneva: League of Nations.

———. 1932. *International Trade Statistics, 1930.* Geneva: League of Nations.

Leeds, Brett Ashley. 2003. "Alliance Reliability in Times of War: Explaining State Decisions to Violate Treaties." *International Organization* 57, no. 4: 801–27.

Lemaitre, Eduardo. 1983. *Historia general de Cartagena.* Bogotá: Banco de la República.

Lenin, Vladimir Il'ich. 1917. *Imperialism: The Last Stage of Capitalism.* London: Communist Party of Great Britain.

Lessard, Donald R., and John Williamson. 1985. *Financial Intermediation Beyond the Debt Crisis.* Washington, DC: Institute for International Economics.

Lethbridge, E. 1985. "National Income and Product." In *The Economic History of Eastern Europe, 1919–1975,* vol. 1: *Economic Structure and Performance between the Two Wars,* ed. M. C. Kaser and E. A. Radice, 532–97. Oxford: Clarendon Press.

Levandis, John Alexander. 1944. *The Greek Foreign Debt and the Great Powers, 1821–1898.* New York: Columbia University Press.

Lewis, Cleona. 1938. *America's Stake in International Investments.* Washington, DC: Brookings Institution.

Lewis, Mervyn K., and Kevin T. Davis. 1987. *Domestic and International Banking.* Cambridge, MA: MIT Press.

Lincoln, Edmond E. 1926. *Testing before Investing.* Chicago: A. W. Shaw.

Lindert, Peter H. 1989. "Response to the Debt Crisis: What Is Different about the 1980s?" In *The International Debt Crisis in Historical Perspective,* ed. Barry Eichengreen and Peter H. Lindert, 227–75. Cambridge, MA: MIT Press.

Lindert, Peter H., and Peter J. Morton. 1989. "How Sovereign Debt Has Worked." In *Developing Country Debt and Economic Performance*, vol. 1: *The International Financial System*, ed. Jeffrey D. Sachs, 39–106. Chicago: University of Chicago Press.

Lipson, Charles. 1979. "The IMF, Commercial Banks, and Third World Debts." In *Debt and the Less Developed Countries*, ed. Jonathan David Aronson, 317–33. Boulder, CO: Westview Press.

———. 1981. "The International Organization of Third World Debt." *International Organization* 35, no. 4: 603–31.

———. 1984. "International Cooperation in Economic and Security Affairs." *World Politics* 37, no. 1: 1–23.

———. 1985. "Bankers' Dilemmas: Private Cooperation in Rescheduling Sovereign Debts." *World Politics* 38, no. 1: 200–25.

———. 1989. "International Debt and National Security: Comparing Victorian Britain and Postwar America." In *The International Debt Crisis in Historical Perspective*, ed. Barry Eichengreen and Peter H. Lindert, 189–226. Cambridge, MA: MIT Press.

Lisman, F. J. 1934. "Protective Committees for Security Holders." *Harvard Business Review* 13, no. 3: 19–32.

Lissakers, Karin. 1991. *Banks, Borrowers, and the Establishment: A Revisionist Account of the International Debt Crisis*. New York: Basic Books.

Lohmann, Susanne. 1997. "Linkage Politics." *Journal of Conflict Resolution* 41, no. 1: 38–67.

Lyon, Hastings. 1926. *Investment*. Boston: Houghton Mifflin.

Macmillan, Rory. 1995a. "The Next Sovereign Debt Crisis." *Stanford Journal of International Law* 31, no. 2: 305–58.

———. 1995b. "The New Latin American Debt Regime—Towards a Sovereign Debt Work-out System." *Journal of International Law and Business* 16, no.1: 57–106.

Madden, John T., and Marcus Nadler. 1929. *Foreign Securities: Public and Mortgage Bank Bonds—An Analysis of the Financial, Legal and Political Factors*. New York: Ronald Press.

Madden, John T. , Marcus Nadler, and Harry C. Sauvain. 1937. *America's Experience as a Creditor Nation*. New York: Prentice Hall.

Maddison, Angus. 1995. *Monitoring the World Economy, 1820–1992*. Paris: Development Centre of the Organisation for Economic Co-operation and Development.

Mailath, George J., and Larry Samuelson. 2001. "Who Wants a Good Reputation?" *Review of Economic Studies* 68, no. 2: 415–41.

———. 2006. *Repeated Games and Reputations: Long-Run Relationships*. Oxford: Oxford University Press.

Marichal, Carlos. 1989. *A Century of Debt Crises in Latin America: From Independence to the Great Depression, 1820–1930*. Princeton, NJ: Princeton University Press.

Marin, Dalia, and Monika Schnitzer. 2003. "Creating Creditworthiness through Reciprocal Trade." *Review of International Economics* 11, no. 1: 159–74.

Marks, Frederick W. 1979. *Velvet on Iron: The Diplomacy of Theodore Roosevelt*. Lincoln: University of Nebraska Press.

Marshall, Monty G., Keith Jaggers, and Ted Robert Gurr. 2003. *Polity IV Data Set: Political Regime Characteristics and Transitions, 1800–2002*. Center for

International Development and Conflict Management, University of Maryland. http://www.cidcm.umd.edu/polity/.

Martin, Lisa L. 1992. *Coercive Cooperation: Explaining Multilateral Economic Sanctions*. Princeton, NJ: Princeton University Press.

Martinez, Jose Vicente, and Guido Sandleris. 2006. "Is It Punishment? Sovereign Defaults and the Decline in Trade." Working paper, Johns Hopkins University.

Mauro, Paolo, Nathan Sussman, and Yishay Yafeh. 2006. *Emerging Markets and Financial Globalization: Sovereign Bond Spreads in 1870–1913 and Today*. Oxford: Oxford University Press.

Maxfield, Sylvia. 1997. *Gatekeepers of Growth: The International Political Economy of Central Banking in Developing Countries*. Princeton, NJ: Princeton University Press.

McBeth, Brian S. 2001. *Gunboats, Corruption, and Claims: Foreign Intervention in Venezuela, 1899–1908*. Westport, CT: Greenwood Press.

McCusker, John J. 2006. "What Was the Inflation Rate Then?" Economic History Services. EH.Net. http://eh.net/hmit/inflation (accessed October 9, 2006).

McGinnis, Michael D. 1986. "Issue Linkage and the Evolution of International Cooperation." *Journal of Conflict Resolution* 30, no. 1: 141–70.

McKinnon, Ronald I. 1986. "Issues and Perspectives: An Overview of Banking Regulation and Monetary Control." In *Pacific Growth and Financial Interdependence*, ed. Augustine H. H. Tan and Basant Kapur, 319–36. Boston: Allen and Unwin.

McLean, David. 1995. *War, Diplomacy and Informal Empire: Britain and the Republics of La Plata, 1836–1853*. London: British Academic Press.

Meetarbhan, Milan J. N. 1995. "Vers un droit international de la dette extérieure?" In *La dette extérieure / The External Debt*, ed. Dominique Carreau and Malcolm N. Shaw. Boston: Martinus Nijhoff.

Mercer, Jonathan. 1996. *Reputation and International Politics*. Ithaca, NY: Cornell University Press.

Metzler, Mark. 2006. *Lever of Empire: The International Gold Standard and the Crisis of Liberalism in Prewar Japan*. Berkeley and Los Angeles: University of California Press.

Milgrom, Paul R., Douglass C. North, and Barry R. Weingast. 1990. "The Role of Institutions in the Revival of Trade: The Law Merchant, Private Judges, and the Champagne Fairs." *Economics and Politics* 2, no. 1: 1–23.

Milgrom, Paul, and John Roberts. 1982. "Predation, Reputation, and Entry Deterrence." *Journal of Economic Theory* 27, no. 2: 280–312.

Miller, Gregory D. 2003. "Hypotheses on Reputation: Alliance Choices and the Shadow of the Past." *Security Studies* 12, no. 3: 40–78.

Miller, Rory. 1999. "Informal Empire in Latin America." In *The Oxford History of the British Empire*, vol. 5, ed. Robin W. Winks, 437–49. Oxford: Oxford University Press.

Miller, William. 1966. *The Ottoman Empire and Its Successors*. London: Frank Cass.

Millington, Herbert. 1948. *American Diplomacy and the War of the Pacific*. New York: Columbia University Press.

Mills, Rodney H., and Henry S. Terrell. 1984. "The Determination of Front-End Fees on Syndicated Eurocurrency Credits." International Finance Discussion

Papers No. 250. Washington, DC: Board of Governors of the Federal Reserve System.

Milner, Helen V. 1997. *Interests, Institutions, and Information: Domestic Politics and International Relations.* Princeton, NJ: Princeton University Press.

Mitchell, Brian R. 1998a. *International Historical Statistics: Africa, Asia and Oceania, 1750–1993.* Basingstoke, U.K.: Macmillan.

———. 1998b. *International Historical Statistics: Europe, 1750–1993.* Basingstoke, U.K.: Macmillan.

Mitchell, Nancy. 1996. "The Height of the German Challenge: The Venezuela Blockade, 1902–3." *Diplomatic History* 20, no. 2: 185–209.

Mitchener, Kris James, and Marc D. Weidenmier. 2005a. "Empire, Public Goods, and the Roosevelt Corollary." *Journal of Economic History* 65, no. 3: 658–92.

———. 2005b. "Supersanctions and Sovereign Debt Repayment." NBER Working Paper No. 11472. Cambridge, MA: National Bureau of Economic Research.

Montgomery, Robert H. 1925. *Financial Handbook.* 1st ed. New York: Ronald Press.

———. 1933. *Financial Handbook.* 2nd ed. New York: Ronald Press.

Moody, John. 1925. *Profitable Investing: Fundamentals of the Science of Investing.* New York: B. C. Forbes.

Morón, Guillermo. 1964. *A History of Venezuela.* London: George Allen and Unwin.

Morris, Ray. 1928. "American Investments in South America." *Proceedings of the Academy of Political Science in the City of New York* 12, no. 4: 29–44.

Morrow, Dwight W. 1927. "Who Buys Foreign Bonds?" *Foreign Affairs* 5, no. 2: 219–32.

Morrow, James D. 2000. "Alliances: Why Write Them Down?" *Annual Review of Political Science* 3: 63–83.

Mosley, Layna. 2003. *Global Capital Markets and National Governments.* Cambridge: Cambridge University Press.

Moynier, Adolphe, and Frédéric Dominicé. 1902. *Manuel des valeurs cotées à la Bourse de Genève.* Geneva: Ch. Eggimann & Cie.

Munro, Dana G. 1964. *Intervention and Dollar Diplomacy in the Caribbean, 1900–1921.* Princeton, NJ: Princeton University Press.

National Industrial Conference Board. 1939. *Conference Board Studies in Enterprise and Social Progress.* New York: National Industrial Conference Board.

Neves, João Luís César das. 1994. *The Portuguese Economy: A Picture in Figures, XIX and XX Centuries with Long Term Series.* Lisbon: Universidade Católica Editora.

Nichols, Irby Coghill. 1971. *The European Pentarchy and the Congress of Verona, 1822.* The Hague: Nijhoff.

Nisbett, Richard, and Lee Ross. 1980. *Human Inference: Strategies and Shortcomings of Social Judgment.* Englewood Cliffs, NJ: Prentice-Hall.

North, Douglass C., and Barry R. Weingast. 1989. "Constitutions and Commitment: The Evolution of Institutions Governing Public Choice in Seventeenth-Century England." *Journal of Economic History* 49, no. 4: 803–32.

Nunnenkamp, Peter, and Hartmut Picht. 1989. "Willful Default by Developing Countries in the 1980s: A Cross-Country Analysis of Major Determinants." *Weltwirtschaftliches Archiv* 125, no. 4: 681–702.

Obstfeld, Maurice, and Kenneth Rogoff. 1996. *Foundations of International Macroeconomics*. Cambridge, MA: MIT Press.

Obstfeld, Maurice, and Alan M. Taylor. 2003. "Sovereign Risk, Credibility and the Gold Standard: 1870–1913 vs. 1925–1931." *Economic Journal* 113, no. 2: 241–75.

———. 2004. *Global Capital Markets: Integration, Crisis, and Growth*. Cambridge: Cambridge University Press.

O'Connell, Arturo. 1984. "Argentina into the Depression: Problems of an Open Economy." In *Latin America in the 1930s: The Role of the Periphery in World Crisis*, ed. Rosemary Thorp, 188–222. Oxford: Macmillan.

———. 1986a. "Free Trade in One (Primary Producing) Country: The Case of Argentina in the 1920s." In *The Political Economy of Argentina, 1880–1946*, ed. Guido di Tella and D. C. M. Platt, 74–94. New York: St. Martin's.

———. 1986b. "La fiebre aftosa, el embargo sanitario norteamericano contra las importaciones de carne y el triángulo Argentina-Gran Bretaña-Estados Unidos en el período entre las guerras mundiales." *Desarrollo económico* 26, no. 101: 21–50.

Officer, Lawrence H. 2006. "What Was the Interest Rate Then?" Economic History Services, EH.Net. http://eh.net/hmit/interest_rate (accessed October 9, 2006).

Olson, Mancur. 1965. *The Logic of Collective Action: Public Goods and the Theory of Groups*. Cambridge, MA: Harvard University Press.

O'Rourke, Kevin H., and Jeffrey G. Williamson. 1999. *Globalization and History: The Evolution of a Nineteenth-Century Atlantic Economy*. Cambridge, MA: MIT Press.

Österreichisches Institut für Wirtschaftsforschung. 1965. *Österreichs Volkseinkommen 1913 bis 1963*. Vienna: Österreichisches Institut für Wirtschaftsforschung.

Otto, Walter. 1910. *Anleiheübernahme-, Gründungs- und Beteiligungsgeschäfte der Deutschen Grossbanken in Übersee*. Berlin: Borussia Druck-und Verlagsanstalt.

Oudermeulen, Cornelis van der. 1791. *Recherches sur le commerce, ou, idées rélatives aux intérêts des différens peuples de l'Europe*. Vol. 2, part 2. Amsterdam: Chaz D. J. Changuion.

Oye, Kenneth A. 1985. "Explaining Cooperation under Anarchy: Hypotheses and Strategies." *World Politics* 38, no. 1: 1–24.

———, ed. 1986. *Cooperation under Anarchy*. Princeton, NJ: Princeton University Press.

———. 1992. *Economic Discrimination and Political Exchange: World Political Economy in the 1930s and 1980s*. Princeton, NJ: Princeton University Press.

Özler, Şule. 1992. "The Evolution of Credit Terms: An Empirical Study of Commercial Bank Lending to Developing Countries." *Journal of Development Economics* 38, no. 1: 79–97.

———. 1993. "Have Commercial Banks Ignored History?" *American Economic Review* 83, no. 3: 608–20.

Özler, Şule, and Guido Tabellini. 1991. "External Debt and Political Instability." NBER Working Paper No. 3772. Cambridge, MA: National Bureau of Economic Research.

Packenham, Robert A. 1992. *The Dependency Movement: Scholarship and Politics in Development Studies*. Cambridge, MA: Harvard University Press.

Pakenham, Thomas. 1991. *The Scramble for Africa*. London: Weidenfeld and Nicolson.

Pallmann, Heinrich. 1898. *Simon Moritz von Bethmann und seine Vorfahren*. Frankfurt am Main: Carl Wallau.

Patterson, Ernest Minor. 1928. *Tests of a Foreign Government Bond*. New York: Payson and Clarke.

Pauly, Louis W. 1997. *Who Elected the Bankers: Surveillance and Control of the World Economy*. Ithaca, NY: Cornell University Press.

Pecchioli, R. M. 1983. *The Internationalisation of Banking: The Policy Issues*. Paris: Organisation for Economic Co-operation and Development.

Peterson, Harold F. 1964. *Argentina and the United States, 1910–1960*. New York: State University of New York.

Peyrot, Edouard. 1895. *Manuel des valeurs cotées à la Bourse de Genève*. Geneva: E. Peyrot.

Phelan, Christopher. 2006. "Public Trust and Government Betrayal." *Journal of Economic Theory* 130, no. 1: 27–43.

Philip, George. 1992. *British Documents on Foreign Affairs: Reports and Papers from the Foreign Office Confidential Print*. Part 1, Series D, vol. 6: *Venezuela, 1879–1908*. Bethesda, MD: University Publications of America.

Philpott, Daniel. 2001. *Revolutions in Sovereignty: How Ideas Shaped Modern International Relations*. Princeton, NJ: Princeton University Press.

Picht, Hartmut R. 1988. "The Political Economy of Debt Repudiation and Expropriation in LDCs." In *Monetary Theory and Policy: Proceedings of the Fourth International Conference on Monetary Economics and Banking*, ed. Didier Laussel, William Marois, and Antoine Soubeyran, 329–83. Berlin: Springer-Verlag.

Platt, Desmond Christopher Martin. 1962. "The Allied Coercion of Venezuela, 1902–3—A Reassessment." *Inter-American Economic Affairs* 15, no. 4: 3–28.

———. 1968. *Finance, Trade, and Politics in British Foreign Policy, 1815–1914*. Oxford: Clarendon Press.

Press, Daryl G. 2005. *Calculating Credibility: How Leaders Assess Military Threats*. Ithaca, NY: Cornell University Press.

Rankin, Keith. 1992. "New Zealand's Gross National Product: 1859–1939." *Review of Income and Wealth* 38, no. 1: 49–69.

Raymond, William L. 1925. *National Government Loans*. Boston: Barron's.

Redmond & Co. 1928. *World Economics 1927*. New York: Redmond.

Reinisch, August. 1995. "Debt Restructuring and State Responsibility Issues." In *La dette extérieure / The External Debt*, ed. Dominique Carreau and Malcolm N. Shaw. Boston: Martinus Nijhoff.

República Argentina. Congreso de la Nación. Senado de la Nación. 1933. *Diario de sesiones de la Cámara de Senadores*. Vol. 1. Buenos Aires: Cuerpo de Taquígrafos del Honorable Senado de la Nación.

República Argentina. Dirección de Economía Rural y Estadística. 1935. *Anuario agropecuario: Año 1935*. Buenos Aires: Ministerio de Agricultura de la Nación.

República Argentina. Ministerio de Hacienda de la Nación. 1934. *El plan de acción económica nacional.* Buenos Aires: Talleres Gráficos de la Penitenciaría Nacional.

República Argentina. Presidente. 1938. *Poder ejecutivo nacional, período 1932–1938: Presidente de la nación, Agustín P. Justo, vicepresidente de la nación, Julio A. Roca.* Buenos Aires: Talleres de G. Kraft.

Richards, Anthony, and Mark Gugiatti. 2003. "Do Collective Action Clauses Influence Bond Yields? New Evidence from Emerging Markets." *International Finance* 6, no. 3: 415–47.

Rieffel, Lex. 2003. *Restructuring Sovereign Debt: The Case for Ad Hoc Machinery.* Washington, DC: Brookings Institution.

Riley, James C. 1980. *International Government Finance and the Amsterdam Capital Market, 1740–1815.* Cambridge: Cambridge University Press.

Rippy, J. Fred. 1959. *British Investments in Latin America, 1822–1949: A Case Study in the Operations of Private Enterprise in Retarded Regions.* Minneapolis: University of Minnesota Press.

Robinson, Ronald, and John Gallagher. 1981. *Africa and the Victorians: The Official Mind of Imperialism.* 2nd ed. London: Macmillan.

Rock, David. 1987. *Argentina, 1516–1987: From Spanish Colonization to Alfonsín.* Berkeley and Los Angeles: University of California Press.

Rodrik, Dani. 1996. "Why Is There Multilateral Lending?" In *Annual World Bank Conference on Development Economics 1995,* ed. Michael Bruno and Boris Pleskovic, 167–93. Washington, DC: World Bank.

Rogoff, Kenneth. 1999. "International Institutions for Reducing Global Financial Instability." *Journal of Economic Perspectives* 13, no. 4: 21–42.

Rollins, Montgomery. 1926. *Money and Investments: A Reference Book for the Use of Those Desiring Information in the Handling of Money or the Investment Thereof.* London: George Routledge and Sons.

Ronald, James H. 1935. "National Organizations for the Protection of Holders of Foreign Bonds." *George Washington Law Review* 3, no. 4: 411–53.

Rose, Andrew K. 2005. "One Reason Countries Pay Their Debts: Renegotiation and International Trade." *Journal of Development Economics* 77, no. 1: 189–206.

Rose, Andrew K., and Mark M. Spiegel. 2004. "A Gravity Model of Sovereign Lending: Trade, Default and Credit." *IMF Staff Papers* 51, special issue: 50–63.

Roubini, Nouriel, and Brad Setser. 2004. *Bailouts or Bail-Ins? Responding to Financial Crises in Emerging Economies.* Washington, DC: Institute for International Economics.

Royal Institute of International Affairs. 1937. *The Problem of International Investment.* London: Oxford University Press.

Sachs, Jeffrey D. 1982. "LDC Debt in the 1980s: Risk and Reforms." In *Crises in the Economic and Financial Structure,* ed. Paul Wachtel, 197–243. Lexington, MA: Lexington Books.

———. 1985. "External Debt and Macroeconomic Performance in Latin America and East Asia." *Brookings Papers on Economic Activity* 1985, no. 2: 523–43.

———. 1986. "Managing the LDC Debt Crisis." *Brookings Papers on Economic Activity* 1986, no. 2: 397–431.

———. 1988. "Comprehensive Debt Retirement: The Bolivian Example." *Brookings Papers on Economic Activity* 1988, no. 2: 705–13.

———, ed. 1989. *Developing Country Debt and Economic Performance*. 3 vols. Chicago: University of Chicago Press.

———. 1995. "Do We Need an International Lender of Last Resort?" Frank D. Graham Lecture, Princeton University, April 20.

———. 1999. "The International Lender of Last Resort: What Are the Alternatives?" In *Rethinking the International Monetary System*. Conference Proceedings Series No. 43. Boston: Federal Reserve Bank of Boston, June 1999.

Sachs, Jeffrey D., and Harry Huizinga. 1987. "U.S. Commercial Banks and the Developing-Country Debt Crisis." *Brookings Papers on Economic Activity* 1987, no. 2: 555–601.

Saiegh, Sebastian M. 2005. "Do Countries Have a 'Democratic Advantage'?" *Comparative Political Studies* 38, no. 4: 366–87.

Sakolski, Aaron M. 1925. *Principles of Investment*. New York: Ronald Press.

Sandleris, Guido. 2006. "Sovereign Defaults: Information, Investment and Credit." Working paper, Johns Hopkins University.

Sartori, Anne E. 2005. *Deterrence by Diplomacy*. Princeton, NJ: Princeton University Press.

Saugy, Ernest de. 1913–14. *Vade-Mecum des Bourses de Bâle, Zurich et Genève*. Zurich: Orell Füssli.

Schoepperle, Victor. 1947. "Foreign Bonds and Direct Foreign Investment." In *Fundamentals of Investment Banking*, ed. John F. Fennelly, Nathan D. McClure, and Robert W. Clark, Jr., 484–94. Chicago: Investment Bankers Association of America.

Schölch, Alexander. 1976. "The 'Men on the Spot' and the English Occupation of Egypt in 1882." *Historical Journal* 19, no. 3: 773–85.

Schultz, Kenneth A., and Barry R. Weingast. 1998. "Limited Governments, Powerful States." In *Strategic Politicians, Institutions, and Foreign Policy*, ed. Randolph M. Siverson, 15–49. Ann Arbor: University of Michigan Press.

———. 2003. "Institutional Foundations of Financial Power in International Competition." *International Organization* 57, no. 1: 3–42.

Simmons, Beth A. 1994. *Who Adjusts? Domestic Sources of Foreign Economic Policy during the Interwar Years*. Princeton, NJ: Princeton University Press.

———. 2000. "International Law and State Behavior: Commitment and Compliance in International Monetary Affairs." *American Political Science Review* 94, no. 4: 819–35.

Simmons, Beth A., and Daniel J. Hopkins. 2005. "The Constraining Power of International Treaties: Theory and Methods." *American Political Science Review* 99, no. 4: 623–31.

Sinclair, David. 2003. *Sir Gregor MacGregor and the Land that Never Was: The Extraordinary Story of the Most Audacious Fraud in History*. London: Headline Book Publishing.

Singer, J. David. 1987. "Reconstructing the Correlates of War Dataset on Material Capabilities of States, 1816–1985." *International Interactions* 14, no. 2: 115–32.

Singer, J. David, Stuart Bremer, and John Stuckey. 1972. "Capability Distribution, Uncertainty, and Major Power War, 1820–1965" In *Peace, War, and Numbers*, ed. Bruce Russett, 19–48. Beverly Hills: Sage.

Skiles, Marilyn E. 1988. "Latin American International Loan Defaults in the 1930s: Lessons for the 1980s?" New York: Federal Reserve Bank of New York.

Smalley, George W. 1912. *Anglo-American Memories*. 2nd ser. London: Duckworth.

Smith, Peter H. 1969. *Politics of Beef in Argentina: Patterns of Conflict and Change*. New York: Columbia University Press.

Smith, Roy C., and Ingo Walter. 2003. *Global Banking*. 2nd ed. Oxford: Oxford University Press.

Snidal, Duncan. 1985. "Coordination versus Prisoners' Dilemma: Implications for International Cooperation and Regimes." *American Political Science Review* 79, no. 4: 923–42.

Snyder, Glenn H., and Paul Diesing. 1977. *Conflict among Nations: Bargaining, Decision Making, and System Structure in International Crises*. Princeton, NJ: Princeton University Press.

Sobel, Andrew C. 1999. *State Institutions, Private Incentives, Global Capital*. Ann Arbor: University of Michigan Press.

Soros, George. 1998. *The Crisis of Global Capitalism*. New York: Public Affairs.

Spangenthal, S. 1903. *Die Geschichte der Berliner Börse*. Berlin: Spangenthal's Verlag.

Special Libraries Association Exhibit Committee. 1930. *Sources of Investment Information, Compiled for the Investment Bankers Association of America by Exhibit Committee, Financial Group, Special Libraries Association*. Rev. ed. Chicago: Educational Department of the Investment Bankers Association of America.

Spiegel, Mark. 1996. "Collective Action Difficulties in Foreign Lending: Banks and Bonds." *FRBSF Economic Letter* no. 1996-24, August 23. San Francisco: Federal Reserve Bank of San Francisco.

Stallings, Barbara. 1987. *Banker to the Third World: U.S. Portfolio Investment in Latin America, 1900–1986*. Berkeley and Los Angeles: University of California Press.

Standard & Poor's. 2004. "Sovereign Defaults Set to Fall Again in 2005." *Standard & Poor's RatingsDirect*.

Stasavage, David. 2003. *Public Debt and the Birth of the Democratic State: France and Great Britain, 1688–1789*. Cambridge: Cambridge University Press.

———. 2007a. "Cities, Constitutions, and Sovereign Borrowing in Europe, 1274–1785." Forthcoming, *International Organization*.

———. 2007b. "Partisan Politics and Public Debt: The Importance of the Whig Supremacy for Britain's Financial Revolution." *European Review of Economic History* 11, no. 1: 123–53.

*Statesman's Yearbook*. Various issues. London: Macmillan.

Stavrianos, Leften Stavros. 1958. *The Balkans since 1453*. New York: Rinehart.

Stein, Arthur A. 1980. "The Politics of Linkage." *World Politics* 33, no. 1: 62–81.

Steinmetz, Will. 1913. *Die Deutschen Grossbanken im Dienste des Kapitalexports*. Luxembourg: Druckerei der St. Pauleusgesellschaft.

Stewart, Taimoon. 2003. "Debt and Resurrection: Prognosis for the Periphery in the 21st Century." In *Emerging Issues in the 21st Century World System*, ed. Wilma A. Dunaway, vol. 2, 91–108. Westport, CO: Praeger.

Stone, Irving. 1999. *The Global Export of Capital from Great Britain, 1865–1914*. New York: St. Martin's.

Stone, Randall W. 2002. *Lending Credibility: The International Monetary Fund and the Post-Communist Transition*. Princeton, NJ: Princeton University Press.

———. 2004. "The Political Economy of IMF Lending in Africa." *American Political Science Review* 98, no. 4: 577–91.

Strangeways, Thomas. 1822. *Sketch of the Mosquito Shore, Including the Territory of Poyais, Descriptive of the Country: With Some Information as to Its Productions, the Best Mode of Culture, &c., Chiefly Intended for the Use of Settlers*. Edinburgh: William Blackwood.

StudieCentrum voor Onderneming en Beurs. 2006. *Cours authentique de la Bourse de Bruxelles electronic database*. University of Antwerp, Belgium.

Sturzenegger, Federico, and Jeromin Zettelmeyer. 2006a. *Debt Defaults and Lessons from a Decade of Crises*. Cambridge, MA: MIT Press.

———. 2006b. "Has the Legal Threat to Sovereign Debt Restructuring Become Real?" Working Paper 04/2006. Centro de Investigación en Finanzas, Universidad Torcuato Di Tella.

Sullivan, William M. 1974. "The Rise of Despotism in Venezuela: Cipriano Castro, 1899–1908." Ph.D. diss., University of New Mexico.

Sundaram, Anant K. 1989. "Syndications in Sovereign Lending." *Journal of International Money and Finance* 8, no. 3: 451–64.

Sussman, Nathan, and Yishay Yafeh. 2000. "Institutions, Reforms, and Country Risk: Lessons from Japanese Government Debt in the Meiji Era." *Journal of Economic History* 60, no. 2: 442–67.

Suter, Christian. 1990. *Schuldenzyklen in der Dritten Welt: Kreditaufnahme, Zahlungskrisen und Schuldenregelungen peripherer Länder im Weltsystem von 1820 bis 1986*. Frankfurt am Main: Anton Hain.

———. 1992. *Debt Cycles in the World-Economy: Foreign Loans, Financial Crises, and Debt Settlements, 1820–1990*. Boulder, CO: Westview Press.

Swiss Bank Corporation. 1921. *Cours extrêmes et derniers prix, dividendes, etc. des valeurs cotées à la Bourse de Genève*. Geneva: Société de Banque Suisse.

Sylla, Richard, and John Joseph Wallis. 1998. "The Anatomy of Sovereign Debt Crises: Lessons from the American State Defaults of the 1840s." *Japan and the World Economy* 10, no. 3: 267–93.

Taylor, A. Wellington. 1924. *Investments*. Modern Business Texts, vol. 23. New York: Alexander Hamilton Institute.

Taylor, Alan. 2006. "Foreign Capital Flows." In *The Cambridge Economic History of Latin America*, vol. 2: *The Long Twentieth Century*, ed. Victor Bulmer-Thomas, John H. Coatsworth, and Roberto Cortés Conde, 57–100. Cambridge: Cambridge University Press.

Taylor, Bryan. 2001. *Global Financial Database*. Los Angeles: Global Financial Data.

Taylor, John. 2002. "Sovereign Debt Restructuring: A U.S. Perspective." Address to the conference "Sovereign Debt Workouts: Hopes and Hazards?" Institute for International Economics, Washington, DC, April 2.

Taylor, Michael. 1976. *Anarchy and Cooperation*. London: John Wiley and Sons.

Tetlock, Philip E. 1999. "Theory-Driven Reasoning about Plausible Pasts and Probable Futures in World Politics: Are We Prisoners of Our Preconceptions?" *American Journal of Political Science* 43, no. 2: 335–66.

———. 2005. *Expert Political Judgment: How Good Is It? How Can We Know?* Princeton, NJ: Princeton University Press.

Thacker, Strom C. 1999. "The High Politics of IMF Lending." *World Politics* 52, no. 1: 38–75.

Tirole, Jean. 2002. *Financial Crises, Liquidity, and the International Monetary System.* Princeton, NJ: Princeton University Press.

Tollison, Robert D., and Thomas D. Willett. 1979. "An Economic Theory of Mutually Advantageous Issue Linkages in International Negotiations." *International Organization* 33, no. 4: 425–49.

Tomz, Michael. 2005a. "Democratic Default: Domestic Audiences and Compliance with International Agreements." Working paper, Stanford University.

———. 2005b. "Interests, Information, and the Domestic Politics of International Agreements." Working paper, Stanford University.

Tomz, Michael, Jason Wittenberg, and Gary King. 2003. *Clarify: Software for Interpreting and Presenting Statistical Results.* Version 2.1. *Journal of Statistical Software* 8, no. 1. Available at http://www.stanford.edu/~tomz/.

Toutain, Jean-Claude. 1987. *Le produit intérieur brut de la France de 1789 à 1982.* Paris: I.S.M.E.A.

Turkey. State Institute of Statistics. 1996. *Istatistik göstergeler (Statistical indicators), 1923–1995.* Ankara: T.C. Basbakanlik Devlet Istatistik Enstitüsü.

Turlington, Edgar. 1930. *Mexico and Her Foreign Creditors.* New York: Columbia University Press.

*Twycross v. Dreyfus,* 5 Ch. D. 605 (C.A. 1877).

Unger, Friedrich E. 1924. "Frankfurt's Anteil am Deutschen Kapitalexport: Vom Ende des 18. Jahrhunderts bis nach dem Wiener Krach 1873." Ph.D. diss., Universität Giessen.

United Kingdom. Board of Trade. 1883. *Statistical Abstract for the Principal and Other Foreign Countries in Each Year from 1872 to 1881–82.* London: H. M. Stationery Office.

United Kingdom. Customs and Excise Department. 1930. *Annual Statement of the Trade of the United Kingdom with Foreign Countries and British Countries, 1929, Compared with the Years 1925–1928.* London: H.M. Stationery Office.

United Kingdom. Department of Overseas Trade. 1930. *Report of the British Economic Mission to Argentina, Brazil, and Uruguay.* London: H. M. Stationery Office.

United Kingdom. Foreign Office. Various issues. *British Foreign and State Papers.*

———. 1927. *British Documents on the Origins of the War, 1898–1914.* Vol. 1: *The End of British Isolation.* Ed. G. P. Gooch and Harold Temperley. London: H.M. Stationery Office.

United Kingdom. House of Commons. Select Committee on Loans to Foreign States. 1875. *Report from the Select Committee on Loans to Foreign States, Together with the Proceedings of the Committee, Minutes of Evidence, Appendix and Index.* House of Commons Paper 367.

United Kingdom. Parliament. 1847. *Correspondence between Great Britain and Foreign Powers, and Communications from the British Government to Claim-*

*ants, Relative to Loans Made by British Subjects, 1823–1847.* Command Paper No. 839.

———. 1854a. *Correspondence between Great Britain and Foreign Powers, and Communications from the British Government to Claimants, Relative to Loans Made by British Subjects, 1847–1853.* House of Commons Paper 0.2.

———. 1854b. *Correspondence Respecting the Relations between Greece and Turkey.* Command Paper No. 1781.

———. 1874. *Correspondence Respecting the Ottoman Loans of 1858 & 1862.* C. 1077.

———. 1896–1915. *Report of the Commissioners of Her (His) Majesty's Inland Revenue.* Command papers C. 8226 (1896), C. 8548 (1897), C. 9020 (1898), C. 9461 (1899), Cd. 347 (1900), Cd. 764 (1901), Cd. 1216 (1902), Cd. 1717 (1903), Cd. 2228 (1904), Cd. 2633 (1905), Cd. 3110 (1906), Cd. 3686 (1907), Cd. 4226 (1908), Cd. 4868 (1909), Cd. 5308 (1910), Cd. 5833 (1911), Cd. 6344 (1912), Cd. 7000 (1913), Cd. 7572 (1914), Cd. 8116 (1915).

———. 1902. *Correspondence Respecting the Affairs of Venezuela, No. 1 (1902).* Cd. 1372.

———. 1903. *Correspondence Respecting the Affairs of Venezuela, No. 1 (1903).* Cd. 1399.

United Kingdom. Various issues. *Parliamentary Debates.* Commons.

United Kingdom. War Office. Intelligence Division. 1882. *The Armed Strength of Belgium.* London: H.M. Stationery Office.

United Nations. 1948. *National Income Statistics of Various Countries, 1938–1947.* Lake Success, NY: Statistical Office of the United Nations.

———. 1949. *International Capital Movements during the Inter-War Period.* Lake Success, NY: Department of Economic Affairs of the United Nations.

———. 1950. *National Income Statistics of Various Countries, 1938–1948.* Lake Success, NY: Statistical Office of the United Nations.

———. 1952. *Statistical Yearbook 1952.* Lake Success, NY: Statistical Office of the United Nations.

Uppal, Raman, and Cynthia Van Hulle. 1997. "Sovereign Debt and the London Club: A Precommitment Device for Limiting Punishment for Default." *Journal of Banking and Finance* 21, no. 5: 741–56.

U.S. Congress. 1825. *American State Papers, 24, Naval Affairs 2.* "Annual Report of the Secretary of the Navy."

U.S. Congress. House. Committee on Banking, Finance, and Urban Affairs. 1983. *International Bank Lending.* Hearings, 98th Cong., 1st sess. Washington, DC: U.S. Government Printing Office.

U.S. Congress. House. Committee on Ways and Means. 1985. *Comprehensive Tax Reform.* Hearings, 99th Cong., 1st sess. Washington, DC: U.S. Government Printing Office.

U.S. Congress. Joint Committee on Taxation. 1984. *Study of 1983 Effective Tax Rates of Selected Large U.S. Corporations.* Washington, DC: U.S. Government Printing Office.

U.S. Congress. Senate. Committee on Banking, Housing, and Urban Affairs. 1983. *Proposed Solutions to International Debt Problems.* Hearings, 98th Cong., 1st sess. Washington, DC: U.S. Government Printing Office.

———. 1986a. *Implications of H.R. 3838, The Tax Reform Act.* Hearings, 99th Cong., 2nd sess. Washington, DC: U.S. Government Printing Office.

———. 1986b. *Review of the International Lending Supervision Act of 1983.* Hearings, 99th Cong., 2nd sess. Washington, DC: U.S. Government Printing Office.

U.S. Congress. Senate. Committee on Finance. 1931–32. *The Sale of Foreign Bonds or Securities in the United States.* Hearings, 72nd Cong., 1st sess. Washington, DC: U.S. Government Printing Office.

U.S. Department of Commerce. 1931. *Statistical Abstract of the United States, 1930.* Washington, DC: U.S. Government Printing Office.

U.S. Department of Commerce. Bureau of Economic Analysis. 2006. *Gross Domestic Product: Implicit Price Deflator.* Series GDPDEF. http://research.stlouisfed.org/fred2/data/GDPDEF.txt.

U.S. Department of State. Various issues. *Foreign Relations of the United States.*

———. 1967. *Armed Actions Taken by the United States without a Declaration of War, 1789–1967.* Washington, DC: Historical Studies Division, Historical Office, Bureau of Public Affairs, Department of State.

U.S. Department of the Treasury. 1947. *Census of American-Owned Assets in Foreign Countries.* Washington, DC: U.S. Government Printing Office.

U.S. Securities and Exchange Commission. 1937. *Report on the Study and Investigation of the Work, Activities, Personnel and Functions of Protective and Reorganization Committees. Part 5: Protective Committees for Holders of Defaulted Foreign Government Bonds.* Washington, DC: U.S. Government Printing Office.

U.S. Securities and Exchange Commission Library. 1937. *Bibliography: List of References on Securities Which Are of General Interest to S.E.C., Compiled under the Direction of Lucile Donovan.* Washington, DC: Securities and Exchange Commission.

Valenzuela, J. Samuel, and Arturo Valenzuela. 1978. "Modernization and Dependency." *Comparative Politics* 10, no. 4: 535–57.

Vandenbosch, Amry. 1959. *Dutch Foreign Policy since 1815: A Study in Small Power Politics.* The Hague: M. Nijhoff.

Vanderauwera, Ch. 1855. *Fluctuations de la Bourse pendant une période de vingt ans, de 1835 à 1855 ou statistique des fonds publics.* Brussels: Vanderauwera.

Vázquez-Presedo, Vicente. 1978. *Crisis y retraso: Argentina y la economía internacional entre las dos guerras.* Buenos Aires: Editorial Universitaria de Buenos Aires.

Verdier, Daniel. 2003. *Moving Money: Banking and Finance in the Industrialized World.* Cambridge: Cambridge University Press.

Vernassa, Maurizio. 1980. *Emigrazione, diplomazia e eannoniere: L'intervento italiano in Venezuela, 1902–1903.* Livorno: Editrice Stella.

Villegas Revueltas, Silvestre. 2005. *Deuda y diplomacia: La relación México-Gran Bretaña, 1824–1884.* Mexico City: Universidad Nacional Autónoma de México.

Vreeland, James Raymond. 2007. *The International Monetary Fund: Politics of Conditional Lending.* New York: Routledge.

Wallis, John Joseph, Richard E. Sylla, and Arthur Grinath III. 2004. "Sovereign Debt and Repudiation: The Emerging-Market Debt Crisis in the U.S. States, 1839–1843." NBER Working Paper No. 10753. Cambridge, MA: National Bureau of Economic Research.

Walter, Barbara F. 2006. "Building Reputation: Why Governments Fight Some Separatists but Not Others." *American Journal of Political Science* 50, no. 2: 313–30.

Weidenmier, Marc D. 2005. "Gunboats, Reputation, and Sovereign Repayment: Lessons from the Southern Confederacy." *Journal of International Economics* 66, no. 2: 407–22.

Weingast, Barry R. 1997. "The Political Foundations of Limited Government: Parliament and Sovereign Debt in 17th- and 18th-Century England." In *The Frontiers of the New Institutional Economics*, ed. John N. Drobak and John V. C. Nye, 213–46. San Diego: Academic Press.

Welles, Sumner. 1928. *Naboth's Vineyard: The Dominican Republic, 1844–1924*. New York: Payson and Clarke.

Wellons, Philip A. 1987. *Passing the Buck: Banks, Governments and Third World Debt*. Boston: Harvard Business School Press.

Wendt, Alexander. 2001. "Driving with the Rearview Mirror: On the Rational Science of Institutional Design." *International Organization* 55, no. 4: 1019–49.

Whitaker, John Thompson. 1940. *Americas to the South*. New York: Macmillian.

Whitehead, Laurence. 1989. "Latin American Debt: An International Bargaining Perspective." *Review of International Studies* 15, no. 3: 231–49.

Winkler, Max. 1933. *Foreign Bonds: An Autopsy*. Philadelphia: Ronald Swain.

Winter, Pieter J. van. 1977. *American Finance and Dutch Investment, 1780–1805, with an Epilogue to 1840*. Trans. James C. Riley. Vol. 1. New York: Arno Press.

Withers, Hartley. 1926. *Hints about Investments*. London: Eveleigh Nash and Grayson.

———. 1930. *The Quicksands of the City and a Way Through for Investors*. New York: Jonathan Cape and Harrison Smith.

Woodhouse, C. M. 1968. *A Short History of Modern Greece*. New York: Praeger.

World Bank. 2003. *Global Development Finance 2003: Striving for Stability in Development Finance*. Washington, DC: World Bank.

———. 2006. *Global Development Finance: The Development Potential of Surging Capital Flows*. Washington, DC: World Bank.

Wright, Mark L. J. 2002. "Reputations and Sovereign Debt." Working paper, MIT.

———. 2004a. "Creditor Coordination and Sovereign Risk." Working paper, Stanford University.

———. 2004b. "New Empirical Results on Default: A Discussion of 'A Gravity Model of Sovereign Lending: Trade, Default and Credit.'" *IMF Staff Papers* 51, special issue: 64–74.

———. 2005. "Coordinating Creditors." *American Economic Review* 95, no. 2: 388–92.

Wynne, William H. 1951. *State Insolvency and Foreign Bondholders*. Vol. 2: *Selected Case Histories of Governmental Foreign Bond Defaults and Debt Readjustments*. New Haven, CT: Yale University Press.

Yuru, Wang. 1992. "Economic Development in China between the Two World Wars (1920–1936)." In *The Chinese Economy in the Early Twentieth Century*, ed. Tim Wright, 58–77. New York: St. Martin's.

Zouari, Abdel-Jawed. 1998. "European Capitalist Penetration of Tunisia, 1860–1881: A Case Study of the Regency's Debt Crisis and the Establishment of the International Financial Commission." Ph.D. diss., University of Washington.

# Index